D0049489

THOMAS JEFFERSON

AND

SALLY HEMINGS

❦

An American Controversy

THOMAS JEFFERSON
AND
SALLY HEMINGS

An American Controversy

Annette Gordon-Reed

University Press of Virginia

Charlottesville and London

The University Press of Virginia
©1997 by the Rector and Visitors of the University of Virginia
All rights reserved
Printed in the United States of America

First published 1997
Second printing 1997

⊗ The paper used in this publication meets the minimum
requirements of the American National Standard for
Information Sciences—Permanence of Paper for
Printed Library Materials, ANSI Z39.48-1984.

Library of Congress Cataloging-in-Publication Data
Gordon-Reed, Annette.
   Thomas Jefferson and Sally Hemings: an American controversy /
Annette Gordon-Reed.
      p. cm.
   Includes bibliographical references and index.
   ISBN 0-8139-1698-4 (cloth: acid-free paper)
   1. Jefferson, Thomas, 1743–1826—Relations with women.
2. Jefferson, Thomas, 1743–1826—Relations with slaves. 3. Hemings,
Sally.   I. Title.
E332.2.G67   1997
973.4'6'092
[B]—DC20   96-34550
                                                                      CIP

To the memory

of my mother,

Bettye Jean Gordon,

and to my father,

Alfred Gordon, Sr.

Contents

Preface
xi

Genealogical Tables
xxi

Introduction
1

1
Madison Hemings
7

2
James Callender
59

3
The Randolphs and the Carrs
78

4
Thomas Jefferson
105

5
Sally Hemings
158

6
Summary of the Evidence
210

7
Conclusion
224

Appendixes

A. Key to Important Names
239

B. The Memoirs of Madison Hemings
245

C. The Memoirs of Israel Jefferson
249

D. Henry S. Randall to James Parton, June 1, 1868
254

E. Ellen Randolph Coolidge to
Joseph Coolidge, October 24, 1858
258

Notes
261

Bibliography
273

Index
281

I write then in a field devastated by passion and belief. Naturally, as a Negro, I cannot do this writing without believing in the essential humanity of Negroes, in their ability to be educated, to do the work of the modern world, to take their place as equal citizens with others. I cannot for a moment subscribe to that bizarre doctrine of race that makes most men inferior to the few. But, too, as a student of science, I want to be fair, objective and judicial; to let no searing of the memory by intolerable insult and cruelty make me fail to sympathize with human frailties and contradiction, in the eternal paradox of good and evil. But armed and warned by all this, and fortified by long study of the facts, I stand at the end of this writing, literally aghast at what American historians have done to this field.

—W. E. B. Du Bois, "The Propaganda of History"

Preface

M<small>Y INTRODUCTION</small> to the life of Thomas Jefferson came in the third grade when I read one of a series of biographies designed to teach schoolchildren about some of the leading figures in American history. The books purported to recount the childhood exploits of these individuals that gave clues as to the great men and women they would eventually become. This was at the tail end of the 1960s in a small town in East Texas, neither the time nor the place for the more skeptical take on American history to which even the youngest children are exposed today. In keeping with that reality, these biographies were, in terms of sophistication, something on the order of the "George-Washington-chopping-down-the-cherry-tree-I-cannot-tell-a-lie" story. Though I read the biographies of Washington, Lincoln, and Madison (both James and Dolley), I was interested the most by Jefferson.

This was despite the fact that I had to wade through some fairly awful material to find out about him. The book I read must have been written in the 1940s or 1950s, if not earlier. I remember feeling a mix of exhilaration at reading history—which held even then a great attraction for me—and at the same time a deep sense of hurt and confusion about the racism on open parade as that history was being told.

The literary device used in the Jefferson biography was to have his story recounted by a fictional slave boy (whose name escapes me, probably due to deliberate repression). I suppose the character was modeled to some extent after Jupiter, a real-life slave who became Thomas Jefferson's personal servant when both were young teenagers, although in the biography the boys were younger.

In the beginning of the story, Jefferson and the slave are fast friends. As things progress, Jefferson's intellectual promise blossoms. His interest in books and science leads him further and further away from his slave companion, who is forever running around lamenting the fact that "Marse Tom [I was puzzled by the "Marse"; I thought it was supposed to have been "Massa"] always hab his nose in a book. He don't wanna go huntin' and fishin' no mo." Time and again, Jefferson's excellence was neatly played off against the

xi

backwardness of his young friend, who remained forever a boy while "Marse Tom" went on to what we know he went on to.

I was dismayed by the way the slave boy was presented, both because I felt a connection to him and because I knew that my white classmates might read the story. I assumed that the book's message probably would confirm what whites seemed to think of most blacks: that we are some lesser form of human being. That my classmates might think me an exception was not enough. My fear was that the boy in the book, as a representative of the first blacks in the country, i.e., slaves, would seem a more accurate representation of the essence of black people than I could ever be. They would read a certain subtext: In the beginning, blacks were something less than human, and then over the years, some of them changed. On the other hand, my white classmates could look to Thomas Jefferson and see that there was never a time when whites were not bright, curious, and attractive human beings. The contrast in the book told them this. As young Tom rose, the young slave boy fell lower and lower.

This book did tell part of the truth about the social customs of the Old South. Young whites and blacks did play together until it was time for young whites to get on with the serious business of being white and for young blacks to get on with the even more serious business of being black. The existence of customs, however, says nothing about the true feelings of the individuals who are forced to live under them, as customs exist, in large measure, to suppress the expression of people's true thoughts and feelings.

It is just as likely that a young slave in the position described in the Jefferson biography would not have resented Jefferson's interest in books and science but might have wished that he could have joined Jefferson in these endeavors. There were young slaves who were intellectually curious, who had an interest in science, who did not remain infantile all their lives. But that view could not be represented. For a third grader to think of a young slave as having an equal measure of humanity with young Tom Jefferson would force a consideration of the unfairness inherent in the story of one young boy who was free to pursue his happiness and another who was not. This certainly would do damage to the idyll of the coming of age of our philosopher-president.

My interest in Jefferson and the institution of slavery continued, and when I got to college I was determined to make a thorough study of both. I discovered how eccentric my interests were when I found myself the lone black person in class after class in southern history. I thought perhaps this was just a function of the college I had chosen to attend. Maybe the particular blacks at that school had no interest in the South. However, when I got to law school and talked my way into an undergraduate course on the Reconstruction era, I found the same thing: there I was sitting around a table with about seventeen or eighteen white students talking about the way blacks and whites had lived one hundred years before.

By then I had come to understand why some young blacks might feel reluctant to take these courses. By some fluke of nature, I suppose, I have always been more interested in people who lived in the past than in people who live in the present. Just as this trait enabled me to push through my third-grade reader on Jefferson, it helped me through some of the material that I read for my southern history classes. The subject of slavery is painful enough. Reading the writings of historians and the primary sources written by individuals whose attitudes toward blacks all too often ran the gamut from the condescending to the contemptuous did not make my examination of the subject any easier. I suspect that many of my black classmates found the prospect of going through this material just too depressing. One of my friends recently revealed to me that she had never liked to read American history for precisely that reason. Many of my readings in southern history—particularly the works of some historians writing before the 1950s and 1960s—presented a picture of black people that was not based on any reality other than the particular historian's or commentator's need to portray black people in a certain way. To see my ancestors presented through the prism of others' prejudices was not easy, and it has gotten no easier as the years have passed.

As an adult, I see this same process at work in discussions of perhaps the most controversial aspect of Thomas Jefferson's life: the allegation that he had a thirty-eight-year liaison with a slave woman named Sally Hemings. What has fascinated me over the years about this subject is the way the story has been discussed, particularly by those who deny it. That there are denials is neither surprising, nor interesting, nor—in the scheme of things—important. It is, rather, the vehemence and the substance of those denials that interest me, because historians, journalists, and other Jefferson enthusiasts have in the past (and continue to do so today) shamelessly employed every stereotype of black people and distortion of life in the Old South to support their positions.

This is so despite the fact that the historiography of the South has undergone a major revolution, with more historians seeking to bring the perspectives of all the participants in the southern "drama" into closer and more considered view. Some examples that come immediately to mind are John Blassingame's and Eugene Genovese's use of slave narratives to reconstruct the experiences of blacks during slavery. Even the scholarship about Thomas Jefferson has evolved as his views on slavery and his relationships with his slaves have been subjected to more intense scrutiny. Yet the consideration of the Sally Hemings story has remained in a curious time warp. When confronting this issue, scholars fall back upon notions and make arguments that seem to reverse the steady progress away from the too romantic or "through-the-eyes-of-white-southerners" view of southern history.

The underlying theme of most historians' denial of the truth of a liaison between Thomas Jefferson and Sally Hemings is that the whole story is too impossible to believe. This line of argument is troubling. For in order to sustain the claim of impossibility, or even to discuss the matter in those terms, one has to make Thomas Jefferson so high as to have been something more than human and one has to make Sally Hemings so low as to have been something less than human. It is the latter part of the equation that has prompted me to write this book.

What is also troubling is that arguments based upon the impossibility of the truth of this story have required the systematic dismissal of the words of the black people who spoke on this matter—Madison Hemings, the son of Sally Hemings, and Israel Jefferson, a former slave who also resided at Monticello—as though their testimony was worth some fraction of that of whites. This process has worked over the years because historians have been able to rely upon widely held prejudices about the people who were slaves in this country.

That people discuss and disagree about a subject is less important than the manner in which they discuss and disagree. Just as it was possible to tell a truthful story of young Tom Jefferson without denying the humanity of a young slave boy, it must be possible for people to present what they take to be the truth of Jefferson the man without denigrating the humanity of black people in the process. Many of the so-called defenders of Jefferson have been unable to do this, and their failure has implications that go far beyond the particular controversy at hand. After all, the Republic will neither rise higher nor fall lower if it is proved that this story is true or if it is proved false. Importantly, I think the same can be said for Thomas Jefferson's place in history. My chief concern is that the way scholars and commentators have dealt with this issue has been harmful to the extremely difficult but crucial task of writing the history of this country.

This book is a critique of the defense that has been mounted to counter the notion of a Jefferson-Hemings liaison. It is not my goal to prove that the story is true or that it is false. I suspect that if that is ever done, it will be the result of the miracles of modern science and all the wonders of DNA research, and not because of any interpretation of documents and statements. I, nevertheless, attempt in this book to present and analyze in as clear and strong a fashion as I am able the evidence that exists to support the story. This is necessary both for general interest and to show that my concerns about the nature of the response to the allegation are valid. It is important to keep in mind that the historical battleground in the dispute over the alleged Jefferson-Hemings relationship has not been over what amounts to absolute proof. The battle has been over controlling public impressions of the amount and the nature of the evidence. It is this effort, particularly on the part of Jefferson defenders, that has created the problem.

I approach this task as a law professor and lawyer looking at how professionals in other disciplines—historians and, to a lesser extent, journalists—analyze and use items of evidence and the concept of proof. My look at the writing on this subject suggests that some scholars and commentators, when confronting the Jefferson-Hemings controversy, often use terms or phrases typically associated with the law, such as *evidence, proof,* and *burden of proof,* as a way of demonstrating the serious nature of the enterprise in which they are engaged. However, there seems to be some confusion about what those terms and phrases actually mean and how they are most effectively and fairly used.

Consider the difference between the nature of evidence and the nature of proof. Evidence goes toward establishing proof. By way of analogy, evidence can be described as the bricks that go into making up a wall of proof. Some scholars and commentators, who almost invariably approach the subject of Thomas Jefferson and Sally Hemings in a defensive posture, have demanded that every brick of evidence that the two might have had a relationship amount to its own individual wall of proof. If the item of evidence offered does not itself add up to proof, they deem it to be "no evidence," or alternatively, never mention it at all. Demanding that individual items of evidence amount to proof sets a standard that can only be met in the rarest of circumstances, either in history or in the law. There are, no doubt, many things that have been designated historical truths on the basis of far less evidence than exists on this matter.

Significantly, biographies and articles that purport to debunk the Jefferson-Hemings liaison do not even tell readers the essential facts of the lives of Sally Hemings and her children that give rise to evidence that the story might be true. In some instances, when the writers do try to recount the facts, they make major errors. Thus, the normal and necessary process of accumulating and weighing evidence largely has been circumvented. The evidence must be considered as a whole before a realistic and fair assessment of the possible truth of this story can be made.

The writings in this area also show confusion about the relationship between the concept of a burden of proof and the standard for assessing evidence. To deal with the concern that accusations are easily made (whether in a legal or nonlegal context), the burden of proof is normally allocated to the accuser. The accuser can meet the burden by offering a certain quantum of evidence, which varies depending upon the nature of the accusation, for example—in the context of legal disputes—proof beyond a reasonable doubt for criminal charges or, for civil charges, proof that makes the truth of an accusation more probable than not. That is one thing.

The standard for assessing evidence, though related, is distinct. The establishment of a standard with regard to the acceptance and analysis of evidence ensures that only trustworthy evidence is considered and that both the accuser and the accused are treated with fairness. This standard must remain constant. It does not shift according to whether the accuser or the accused is offering the evidence. This is not just a legal point. It is at the heart of any concept of procedural fairness, whether one is speaking of a trial, a hearing, a playground dispute, or a historical controversy. This must be so, or else biased assessors of evidence, whether they are judges, hearing officers, playground monitors, or historians, can, on their whim, change the standard for assessing evidence in order to fit their own prejudices. This manipulation could result in the accuser never being able to meet the designated quantum of evidence, not because there is an insufficient quantity, but because the person who determines the merits of the evidence and whether it will be considered is constantly recalibrating the scales. The only way to ensure fairness is to assess each party's items of evidence according to a consistent standard.

It is fair to say that proponents of a Jefferson-Hemings liaison have the burden of proof. Even as they do, they are still entitled to have the basic standard for assessing evidence in the controversy remain constant. Procedural fairness demands this. To that end, if oral history cannot be taken as fact for one party, it cannot be so taken for another party. Though oral history, if accepted, ultimately may affect the quantum of evidence needed to meet a burden of proof, it must first be considered according to some set standard of determining its worth as evidence. The problems with oral history, which any historian's standard of judging evidence would take into account, do not disappear when it is offered by the supporters of the accused. It remains problematic and must be viewed with the same degree of skepticism whichever side presents it.

Jefferson defenders, as well as neutral commentators, seem to think that the way to deal with the problem of the "easy accusation" is to allow the assessors of evidence to manipulate the standard for considering evidence. For some, this approach is fueled by their anger at the accuser and their sympathy for the accused. It is directed at punishing the accuser for coming forward, rather than at ascertaining the truth of the accusations. It would be as if a supposedly objective judge were to say that a defendant in a case should be allowed to use hearsay, but the plaintiff—because the judge is angered by the substance of the plaintiff's "easy accusation"—should not be allowed to do so. That is not the way it does, or should, work. It is through the allocation of the burden of proof and the demand that a certain quantum of evidence be presented to meet the burden that our concerns about the ease with which a person can make an accusation are addressed.

Consistency with respect to assessing evidence is one of the hallmarks of a fair consideration of any dispute because, in the long run, it is the most effective way to ensure that the truth of the matter will out. The term *kangaroo court* calls to mind a situation where inconsistency and caprice reign. Such situations, whether in court proceedings or other contexts, disturb us because we instinctively understand that they tend to promote unfairness. Of course, at this time, whether Thomas Jefferson and Sally Hemings had a sexual liaison is, not a legal, but a historical question. The principles that demand a consistent standard for assessing evidence should apply, nevertheless. That consistency has been utterly lacking in the scholarly writing on this question, and that is cause for concern. It is possible, by examining the reactions to this story, to see the ways in which black people have been treated as lumps of clay to be fashioned and molded into whatever image the given historian feels is necessary in order to make his point. This, in my view, is the real scandal of this whole story.

It is not my intention in examining this question to attack Thomas Jefferson. He has been, since I was nine years old, a continuing item of fascination to me—magnificent and horrifying. Even as I recoil at some of his ideas and practices, I admire his intellect, his industry, and the legacy that has been important to all Americans. My goal is to consider the manner in which scholars and other commentators have dealt with one particular area of Jefferson's life story that seems to have given them great problems. Although I will refer to other scholars and commentators, I focus mainly on the writings and comments of Dumas Malone, Virginius Dabney, John C. Miller, and Douglass Adair because their writings and—in the cases of Malone and Dabney—the actions of these men have had a profound effect upon the way this controversy has been presented in contemporary times.

The ultimate truth or falsity of the Jefferson-Hemings story would not change my view of the way some scholars and commentators have mishandled their consideration of it and mistreated black people in the process. I cannot say that I definitely believe the story is true, but I can say that I believe that it is not the open-and-shut case that those bent on "defending" Thomas Jefferson at all cost would have the public think. I hope both to demonstrate this and, even more importantly, to reveal the corrosive nature of the enterprise of defense.

I am fortunate to have a great many people to thank for their support and their numerous acts of kindness as I completed this project. From New England, through New York, down to Virginia, individuals whom I'd never met—some whom I've yet to meet—gave me the enormous benefit of their insights.

The first thanks go to my colleague at New York Law School, Edward Purcell, for unwittingly giving me the idea to write this book. He was the first reader of my earliest draft and made dead-on suggestions and observations that improved its quality and helped me to clarify my purpose in pursuing this subject. He also spoiled me by taking the manuscript on a Thursday afternoon and giving me back a marked-up copy by the following Monday. I benefited both psychologically and intellectually from his attention and advice. I can't thank him enough.

Continuing the process of bringing forth the good, Ed put me in touch with the next reader of the manuscript, Charles Dew of Williams College, whom I thank for his thoughtful insights and comments, his encouragement and efforts to get this book published, and his sweetness in the face of my too frequent transmittals of revised versions of the manuscript.

As one who is not a professional historian, I have been astounded by the generosity and helpfulness shown to me by members of that profession after I contacted them out of the blue to read my work. Joseph Ellis, of Mount Holyoke College, was one from whom I received many helpful and provocative comments. Although we disagreed about some things, for example, the basic nature of Thomas Jefferson, we did find some areas of common ground. The process of getting to that point was enormously enriching.

Jan Lewis of Rutgers University was kind enough to talk with me at length about my work, to read it, and to write an extensive critique that was impressive for its detail and incisiveness. I thank Barnard College's Herbert Sloan for his comments on my chapter about Thomas Jefferson and his suggestions about Jefferson's handling of his financial affairs. I have tried to make revisions according to Herb's very correct criticisms and hope that I have succeeded to some satisfactory degree.

There are numerous individuals from Jefferson's home state Virginia who deserve my gratitude. Chief among them is Cinder Stanton, who was the Director of Research at Monticello when I began work and is now the Senior

Research Historian there. I had seen Cinder's name in newspaper articles about the Jefferson-Hemings controversy and had read her essay on Jefferson and his slaves. From the moment I started to write the book, I knew that if I wanted to do a serious treatment of this subject, she would be the first person to talk to. Cinder deserves my heartfelt thanks for providing valuable insights, expressing skepticism when needed, and helping me find material. One of the best outcomes of all of this is that I can now call her a friend.

In fact, I now consider Virginia as something of a second home because of all of the people there who have helped to completely obliterate any distinction between work on this project and having fun. A primary culprit in this has been Peter S. Onuf. In October 1995 I called the office of the Thomas Jefferson Memorial Foundation Professor of History at the University of Virginia, assuming that I could get his address from the secretary and then send a letter asking if he would read and comment upon what I had done. Instead, Peter himself answered and immediately agreed to read my manuscript. Since then he has been a great supporter of my work, giving me invaluable comments, bolstering my confidence by making me feel at home in his own home and in the community of historians. I look forward to continued associations with Peter, as well as more opportunities to spend evenings with him and his wife Kristin and their very handsome cats.

Peter is directly responsible for leading me to the University Press of Virginia, Dick Holway, and Nancy Essig. I thank them, as well as the Press Board, for their expression of confidence in this work and for the attention that they have shown to it. Dick's Saharan sense of humor and highly developed appreciation for the ironic have been useful in helping to bring me down to earth whenever the occasion warranted.

Other Virginians are owed my thanks. Scot French, a graduate student at Virginia who, with Edward Ayers, wrote an essay that explored historians' handling of the Jefferson-Hemings controversy, spent an afternoon with me giving me more thoughts about the subject. My coparticipants in the Central Virginia History Project (another Onuf-inspired creation) read an abridged version of a chapter from my book and made suggestions for changes and offered other insights. One of them, Peter's colleague Reginald Butler at Virginia, put some very probing questions to me that forced me to bring to the surface thoughts that I had too conveniently buried. I gave two talks before the group, which met at Kenwood, the home of the International Center for Jefferson Studies, headed by Douglas Wilson. I thank Doug for hosting those events and for allowing me to stay at Kenwood during my visits. I also thank his assistant, Erika Gentry, for so graciously making the necessary arrangements.

I must also thank the people at Monticello for the hospitality shown to me upon my visits there and their interest in this project. Elizabeth Taylor made a dream of mine—to see all of Monticello—come true by taking me on a personal tour of the house and, in the process, giving me a much better perspective of the place about which I write.

To return home, I offer my thanks to other colleagues at New York Law School who have been instrumental in helping me get this work done. Kate MacLeod, my library liaison, and Joelle Lemmons, who was responsible for interlibrary loans, turned my office into the Thomas Jefferson Memorial Library with books gathered from all over the country, and both deserve much credit. No book was too far away, no journal too obscure to escape their grasp. I also acknowledge the efforts of other members of the library's staff who filled in when Kate was not available.

I thank Arthur Leonard for his enthusiasm about the book and for introducing me to Bob Weil, who made it clear to me that a sense of art and the practical go hand in hand. Bill LaPiana acted as a sounding board for ideas and encouraged me to continue writing in the area of history. I thank Jim Simon and our dean, Harry Wellington, for their support, advice about publishing, and encouragement when I was unreasonably discouraged. Randolph Jonakait helped immeasurably by playing the role of opposing attorney as he read the manuscript and alerted me to soft spots in my reasoning and evidence. I thank Don Ziegler, Rudy Peritz, and Aleta Estreicher for their support, as well.

My husband, Robert, and my children, Susan and Gordon, deserve special thanks for bearing the burden of my obsession with great aplomb. For over a year they had, at most, one-third of a wife and one-half of a mother, respectively. I hope I can make up for being gone from them physically and/or mentally for so long a period, but I sincerely felt that I had no choice.

Finally, the great happiness that I feel at having completed this project is diminished in nearly equal measure by my sadness that my mother—the person most responsible for my being able to accomplish it and the one who would have relished this more than I—is not here to see this. I know that she would want me to banish such thoughts and give myself over to complete joy, but I cannot. Instead, I dedicate this book both to her memory and to my father as a way of thanking them for having had enough faith to come together and for their support of me over the years.

Genealogical Tables

The Jeffersons and Randolphs
(Relevant Connections Only)

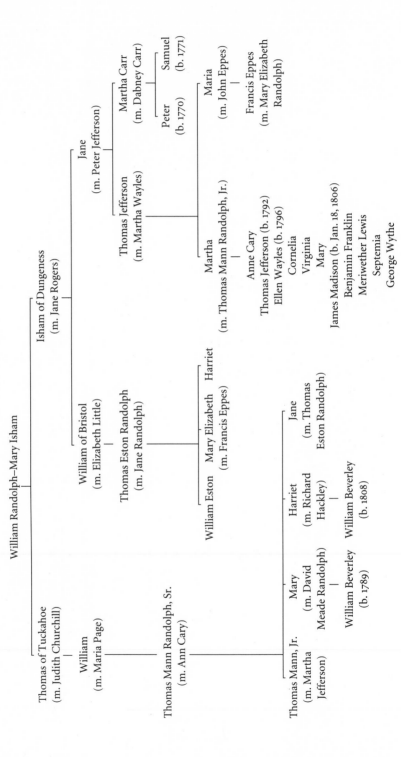

The Hemingses and Wayleses
(Relevant Connections Only)

John Wayles–Elizabeth Hemings

Robert   James   Thenia   Critta   Sally   Peter
                              |
                             James

Harriet I   Unnamed daughter   James Madison   Thomas Eston
(1795–97)   (1799)   Harriet II   (b. Jan. 19, 1805–78) (1808–185?)
William Beverley   (1801–?)   (m. Mary McCoy)   (m. Julia Ann Isaacs)
(1798–?)   (m. ?)
(m. ?)
| |
one daughter   several children

Sarah Unnamed son Julia Harriet Mary Ann Catharine Jane William Beverley James Madison Ellen Wayles Thomas Eston

John Wayles Beverley Anne

THOMAS JEFFERSON

AND

SALLY HEMINGS

❦

An American Controversy

Introduction

The Story

IN 1784 Thomas Jefferson went to Paris to serve as a minister to France. His oldest daughter, Martha, and a slave named James Hemings accompanied him. His younger daughters, Mary (Maria) and Lucy, remained in Virginia with Jefferson's in-laws, as his wife had died two years earlier. Three years later, after the death of Lucy, Mary Jefferson arrived in Paris accompanied by a young slave named Sally Hemings. Sally Hemings was the sister of James, whom Jefferson had brought to Paris to be trained as a chef.

Members of the Hemings family were especially favored by Jefferson. They had come to Monticello after the death of Jefferson's father-in-law, John Wayles. The matriarch of the Hemings clan, Elizabeth, had been Wayles's mistress and had borne him six children, two of whom were James and Sally Hemings. With few exceptions the Hemingses remained at Monticello until Jefferson's estate was sold after his death.

The three Jeffersons and the two Hemingses stayed in Paris for twenty-six months after Mary and Sally arrived, returning to Virginia at the end of 1789. This story begins in Paris because it was there, some have alleged, that Thomas Jefferson and Sally Hemings began a relationship that lasted for thirty-eight years. Naturally, this story has created a great amount of controversy over the years, beginning as early as the 1790s.

There had been rumors among the Virginia gentry that Jefferson and Hemings were lovers. The rumors exploded onto the national scene during the early part of Jefferson's first term as president. James Callender, a muck-raking journalist, published a series of attacks on Jefferson that accused him of being Sally Hemings's lover and of fathering the children she had borne after her return to the United States. Callender claimed that Jefferson and Hemings had a son named Tom who was approximately twelve years old. He referred to the boy as "President Tom" and made him the special focus of attention. The allegation started one of the most malicious political fights in American history. Jefferson's surrogates responded to the charges, as well as to others that had arisen at the same time. Jefferson himself never wrote specifically about the charges concerning Sally Hemings, although most scholars contend that he denied the allegation indirectly.

Sally Hemings had either six or seven children. There has been a dispute over whether she conceived a child while in France who was born after her return to America. It is known for certain that she had at least four children who lived to adulthood, three boys and one girl. Two of her children, Beverley and Harriet, left Monticello as runaways. Jefferson freed the remaining two, Madison and Eston, by his will executed in 1826. Sally Hemings was freed soon after Jefferson's death and went to live with these two younger sons. All three were listed on the census of 1830 as white. After her death in 1835, these sons left Virginia and moved west.

In 1858 one of Jefferson's granddaughters, Ellen Randolph Coolidge, wrote her husband that her oldest brother, Thomas Jefferson Randolph, had given her information that led her to believe that Samuel Carr, a nephew of Thomas Jefferson, was the father of Sally Hemings's children. In 1868 Henry Randall, a Jefferson biographer, wrote to James Parton, who was preparing his own biography of Jefferson, about the Hemings allegations. Randall reported that Thomas Jefferson Randolph had told him that Peter Carr, Samuel's brother, was the father of Sally Hemings's children.

In 1873 Madison Hemings gave a statement to an Ohio newspaperman in which he claimed to be the son of Thomas Jefferson and Sally Hemings. He recounted the history of the Hemings family and the origins of what he said was the relationship between Jefferson and his mother. Hemings said that while in Paris, his mother, who became pregnant near the end of her stay, had claimed the protection of French law and refused to return to the United States. Jefferson promised her that he would free all of their children when they reached age twenty-one if she would agree to return to the United States with him. Hemings's statement, long forgotten, was rediscovered in the 1950s.

The Historians

Henry Stephens Randall, in his biography of Jefferson written in 1858, set the tone for the discussion of this matter. Randall's treatment of the controversy was skeletal, and as have some modern historians, he expressed exasperation at having to address it at all. He felt, however, that circumstances compelled him to do so. The story, he said (again sounding a theme that one hears today), was on the verge of passing into pseudohistory and therefore required some response. He declared that the idea of a liaison between Jefferson and a slave woman was an invention of the Federalists, Jefferson's notorious enemies.

James Parton, with the help of Randall, took his turn with the issue in his biography of Jefferson that appeared in 1873. Parton's response was written after Madison Hemings's statement was published. He was the first historian to make use of information offered by Jefferson's family to refute the charge.

The issue was given new life in the 1950s with the rediscovery of Madison Hemings's memoirs. Merrill Peterson, in his seminal work *The Jefferson Image in the American Mind*, was the first modern historian to discuss Hemings's recollections in print. While acknowledging that many of the details in the statement were correct, he, too, saw the not-so-invisible hand of politics behind its publication. For Peterson, it was not only the Federalists who were responsible; the abolitionists had a role to play as well. Their desire to tell stories that discredited the institution of slavery made the substance of Hemings's claim suspect.

At about this same time, the noted historian Douglass Adair, after reading Hemings's memoirs, wrote an essay entitled "The Jefferson Scandals." Adair did not focus upon any outside forces who may have sought to use the story for their own political purposes. Adair's focus was more personal. It was Sally Hemings, not the often cited politically motivated cliques, who was responsible for Madison Hemings's flawed recollections. She had lied to her son. Adair's essay was not published during his lifetime, although he shared it with various Jefferson scholars. It was included in a collection of his writings that appeared posthumously in 1974, the year that Fawn Brodie's biography of Jefferson was published.

Peterson's and Adair's writings on this subject have had considerable influence upon historians, including Dumas Malone, generally regarded as the preeminent Jefferson scholar. He explicitly relied upon both men's work in his writings on the subject. Malone's rejection of the story has been pivotal to maintaining the consensus—among historians who write about Jefferson and those who do not—that Jefferson and Hemings did not have a sexual relationship. Having labored forty years to produce his six-volume masterpiece *Jefferson and His Time*, Malone earned the right to be listened to on the subject.

Winthrop Jordan's 1968 treatment of the controversy in *White over Black: American Attitudes toward the Negro, 1550–1812*, represented something of a departure from the attitude that had been taken until that point. Jordan wrote as an agnostic on the subject, considering the matter as part of his general analysis of Jefferson's personality and attitudes toward race. His generally balanced appraisal of what he considered to be the evidence paved the way for Fawn Brodie's more ambitious study of the issue.

Fawn Brodie's biography of Jefferson, *Thomas Jefferson: An Intimate His-*

tory, published in 1974, was the first extensive investigation of the Sally Hemings story. Brodie brought together disparate pieces of information that she believed to support the conclusion that Thomas Jefferson and Sally Hemings had a thirty-eight-year relationship that produced six children. Although there is no doubt that Brodie seriously overstated her case in a number of instances, on balance she presented it well, providing details and raising issues that had never been considered fully.

Unfortunately, Brodie also handed her detractors a club with which to beat her about the head and shoulders by also employing Freudian symbolism to support her claims. This allowed the focus to shift from the specifics of the evidence she offered to more generalized arguments against the genre of psychobiography, in which, as the name implies, biographers attempt to discern the underlying meaning of a subject's actions by employing the principles of psychology. The psychobiographer puts his or her subject on the couch, so to speak. Still, despite all the storms of protest and hoots at the idea of a plow as a sexual metaphor, a great deal of what Brodie cited as evidence has been neither refuted nor effectively analyzed.

This has not been due to want of effort. Three years after Brodie's book appeared, John Chester Miller included a chapter debunking the Hemings story in *The Wolf by the Ears: Thomas Jefferson and Slavery.* Later, Virginius Dabney devoted an entire book to the project without revealing that he was a direct descendant of Jefferson's sister Martha and her husband Dabney Carr and therefore a relative of the Hemingses as well. *The Jefferson Scandals: A Rebuttal* was designed to take on not only Brodie's biography but a fictionalized treatment of the story presented in Barbara Chase-Riboud's novel *Sally Hemings.* That book, which became a runaway best-seller during the latter part of the 1970s and early 1980s, probably has been the single greatest influence shaping the public's attitude about the Jefferson-Hemings story.

For whatever reason, the American public seems willing—almost anxious—to believe that Jefferson and Hemings did have a relationship. In their essay "The Strange Career of Thomas Jefferson," historians Scot A. French and Edward L. Ayers, Jr., analyzed how the image of Jefferson has gotten away from the scholars who had guarded it with such care, taking on a life of its own among the public at large. There is no question that the Hemings story has played a role in that process. As a result, historians and researchers working at and near Jefferson's Monticello are now taking a more balanced approach to the issue. They have even opened up the inquiry by doing extensive research into the lives of all the slaves who called Monticello home.

Still, the defensive posture of old has not gone away. In fact, that method of response seems to be resurging as a backlash against multiculturalism and "reinterpretation" of history moves across the nation. One sees a new boldness and aggressiveness in the tone of those who adamantly reject the story. Journalists and historians who do not specialize in writing about Jefferson have played an important role in this regard. In the late 1980s and the 1990s, several Jefferson biographers dismissed the allegation out of hand with no evidence of having attempted to investigate the facts themselves. Reliance upon the consensus of the older guard of Jeffersonians substituted for original research and/or thought. None of these new works make any use of the information that has been gathered about the Hemings family since the older generation of Jefferson scholars first wrote on the issue.

That is where we are now, and it seems a good time to revisit the issue in a way that takes into account the fact that some stories of these people's lives have never really been told. These stories tell us a great deal about our history and possible destiny as Americans. It is important to examine them with clear heads and open minds.

Five main stories must be examined carefully to arrive at a better understanding of the controversy that has smoldered for so many years. They are of Madison Hemings, James Callender, the Randolphs and the Carrs, Thomas Jefferson, and Sally Hemings. The chapters in this book discuss each with the goal of providing a critique of the scholarly (and not so scholarly) response to the interaction between them. Because he would have been an integral part of the story of Thomas Jefferson and Sally Hemings, whatever it was, Madison Hemings comes first.

1

Madison Hemings

In any debate between mind and conscience the omission of
evidence is unforgivable. This remains partly true when the evidence is not immediately at hand and must be sought, but the
sin is compounded after it is found and treated with disdain.
　　　　　—Arna Bontemps, *Great Slave Narratives*

Fari quae sentiat, "To speak what he thinks"
　　　　　—Motto of the Randolph family

IT HAS BECOME a cliché to refer to the "invisibility" of black people in the
United States as a way of suggesting that blacks are neither really seen nor
heard by their white countrymen. The term, which conveys the sense of powerlessness that many blacks feel, is a useful but not totally accurate metaphor.
It would be more correct to say that most white Americans do see and hear
blacks but only when and how they want to see and hear them.

The application of this principle can be seen quite clearly in the treatment
of the short memoirs of Madison Hemings, who claimed, among other
things, to be the son of Thomas Jefferson by his slave Sally Hemings (see
Appendix B). Although his statement is the only known recitation of the details of this controversial story by any of the parties involved, it has been either
ignored by historians or dismissed out of hand with no attempt to address
what Hemings actually said. In addition, he has been attacked through the
use of stereotypes about ex-slaves and the circumstances under which they
lived that should have been laid to rest long ago. Because it would be impossible to exaggerate the level of hostility that the story of Thomas Jefferson's
alleged slave mistress has engendered over the years, it is not surprising that
Hemings's recollections have not been studied with anything that could be
called objectivity. The time for doing that is long overdue. But before begin-

ning an analysis of his statement, it is useful to consider the methods most commonly used to discredit it.

The Attacks

Motive: S. F. Wetmore's and Madison Hemings's

There have been two chief means of attacking the statement that Madison Hemings gave to the *Pike County (Ohio) Republican* in 1873. The first and the most often used method has been to question the motivations of its publisher.[1] The statement is problematic, in this view, because it was taken as part of an effort to create sympathy for the blacks who resided in the area where Madison Hemings lived. Individuals who had been involved in the abolitionist movement shifted their focus after emancipation and embarked upon a campaign to win better treatment for the freedmen. Just as abolitionists reprinted anecdotes about the lives of slaves as a way of showing why slavery had to be ended, these former abolitionists (I suppose in the late twentieth century they would be called liberals) used the same kind of anecdotes to remind whites that blacks had suffered and should be helped or, at least, left in peace.

Stories of the misuse of black women were staples of abolitionist literature, and Hemings's statement can be seen as part of that genre. It has been suggested that S. F. Wetmore, the editor of the *Pike County (Ohio) Republican*, was sympathetic to the freedmen and, not coincidentally, was interested in increasing the fortunes of the Republican party in a county that was heavily Democratic.[2] Historian Julian Boyd surmised that Wetmore "must surely have been a fanatical abolitionist."[3] The great biographer of Jefferson, Dumas Malone, with his assistant and coauthor Stephen A. Hochman, pursued this same theme in "A Note on Evidence" in the *Journal of Southern History* in 1975. The article was intended to set forth the context in which Madison Hemings's memoirs appeared, giving some information about S. F. Wetmore and a few details about Madison Hemings himself.

Malone and Hochman stated that in 1870 S. F. Wetmore began to collect a series of short biographies of elderly residents of Pike County, having them tell him their life stories, which he then wrote down in his own words. By 1873 Wetmore had chosen to narrow the focus of his inquiries. During that year, in furtherance of his goal of drawing attention to the plight of the freedman, Wetmore "decided to begin a series on old colored residents of the area" and traveled around the county collecting their reminiscences.[4]

Earlier in the piece Malone and Hochman referred to Wetmore's con-

nections to and work on behalf of the Republican party. They noted that
Wetmore had been "rewarded with federal patronage by the Republican
administration" but did not state the nature of the reward.[5] Amid some controversy the Grant administration had appointed Wetmore postmaster of Pike
County in 1873.[6] Malone and Hochman seem not to have known that
S. F. Wetmore had occupied another position before his appointment as postmaster that is of great relevance to the Jefferson-Hemings controversy. In addition to being the editor of the *Pike County (Ohio) Republican*, Wetmore was
also a federal district marshal. In that capacity he had taken the census for
Pike County in 1870, which probably explains how he came to be interested
in gathering people's life stories and why he would have been a good choice
for the job as postmaster. He had traveled Pike County, and he knew where
people lived. As Wetmore went through the area conducting the census in
1870, he was, most likely, killing two birds with one stone.[7]

At that time Madison Hemings was living in Ross County, which borders
Pike County. The marshal who took the census in that area was a man named
William Weaver. When Weaver recorded the census data relating to Madison
Hemings's household, he wrote in the line next to Hemings's name, "This
man is the son of Thomas Jefferson!"[8] This notation, in Weaver's hand, looks
to have been made at the same time that he wrote in the census data, in 1870—
three years before Madison Hemings's memoirs appeared in Wetmore's newspaper.

Because parentage was not a category on the census form, there is no
obvious reason why the subject would have been raised. Did Madison Hemings spontaneously start talking about Thomas Jefferson during the course of
Weaver's questioning? Or did Weaver bring Jefferson's name into the conversation? A possible answer to both questions is that Jefferson may have been
on the minds of both of them, for Weaver took Hemings's census information
on July 7, 1870. The census report required a listing of the citizen's place of
birth, and Hemings told Weaver that he had been born in Virginia.[9] The subject may have come up after Weaver realized that he was talking to a Virginian
just three days after a celebration occasioned by the effort of one of the most
famous Virginians.

One of the many questions never addressed in the scholarly writing on
this matter is just how Madison Hemings and S. F. Wetmore came to know
one another. Those who believe that Wetmore made up the story see no element of coincidence to the fact that a man scouring the countryside to find
stories told by black people that would reflect badly upon white southerners
should have happened upon a black man who said he was the illegitimate and
somewhat neglected son of Thomas Jefferson. Of course, if Wetmore invented

the story or put someone up to telling it, there would be no element of chance, for Wetmore himself would have decided who was the best candidate to play the role. But if Wetmore had just wanted to find something negative to say about slavery, there would have been a great degree of luck in his happening upon Madison Hemings—and having Hemings volunteer this information—during the course of his survey.

When one considers that S. F. Wetmore was not just an editor of a newspaper but a census taker and that one of his colleagues had spoken to Hemings and made the notation about his parentage, the likely origin of Wetmore's interest in Hemings becomes clearer. Sometime between 1870 and 1873, William Weaver could have mentioned Madison Hemings and his alleged parentage to Wetmore, his fellow marshal and colleague in census taking. Or, with or without such prompting, Wetmore could have reviewed all the local census reports to locate elderly blacks appropriate for his series. Thus, Weaver's notation may have led him to Hemings.

After speaking with Madison Hemings, Wetmore interviewed Israel Jefferson, another former slave from Monticello who lived in the area. As likely as not, Hemings directed Wetmore to Jefferson as a corroborating witness. In an interview published nine months after the Hemings piece, Israel Jefferson confirmed, as far as he could, the substance of Madison Hemings's story. He said that Sally Hemings had been Thomas Jefferson's "chambermaid" and that from his relationships with both people he knew them to have been on "intimate terms" (see Appendix C). Malone and Hochman, as well as other commentators, saw the motivation of the newspaper's editor as seriously tainting these statements because they were "solicited and published for a propagandist purpose."[10]

There are at least two problems with focusing on Wetmore's motivation. First, this mode of attack does not deal with the substance of what Madison Hemings said. Malone and Hochman understood this problem, but others writing about the document have not. Even as one points to a motive for telling a story, those who are genuinely interested in discovering the truth have a responsibility to consider the specifics of what has been said. Unless one assumes, and one could hardly do this with good conscience or good sense, that every story recounted for the purpose of creating sympathy for blacks before or after slavery was a lie, the duty to look seriously at what Madison Hemings said remains. Establishing a motive for the appearance of the story in the *Pike County (Ohio) Republican* does not destroy the statement's worth as evidence.

The second critical problem with this mode of attack is the use of a stereotype to cast doubt upon the document's validity. This is not just a banal moral point that stereotypes are bad. It is a judgment about the effect that the reliance on stereotypes has on the finished product of historians. Stereotypes are a problem for the writing of history because they allow for the use of shortcuts. Whenever shortcuts are taken, essential and important parts of the story can be missed, and historians may end up not considering all possible paths to whatever can be called the truth.

The stereotype employed here is the feebleminded black person as pawn to a white man. Without knowing much about Hemings except that he was a former slave, an assumption is made about his strength of character that does not have to be subjected to any level of proof. Hemings does not stand by himself as a person whose identity has to be known and treated with any degree of care. One of the striking features of the writing about the Jefferson-Hemings controversy is the easy manner with which historians make the black people in the story whatever they want or need them to be, on the basis of no stated evidence. In considering Madison Hemings's statement, historians seem to be saying, "Oh, everyone knows what former slaves were like, so we do not have to consider this individual man and his capabilities when we make the suggestion that he was a pawn in this game of white people."

That there were blacks who were weak and who were used by whites is certain. Some of the slave narratives could be cited as evidence of this. Yet assuming that this held true across the board could lead one to miss the value of the information communicated in these documents. We might also question whether Madison Hemings was typical of those slaves who gave narratives. By the time this postslavery interview was conducted, he had been a free man for forty-seven years, his entire adult life. No one can simply assume that he would have allowed himself to be a pawn in Wetmore's game.

Malone and Hochman made the entirely legitimate point that "any document must be viewed by the historian in its actual setting of time and place."[11] Proceeding from this view, they used the historical context to ferret out Wetmore's possible motive in producing this document. They pointed to specific things about Wetmore that they believed supported the notion of an ulterior motive on his part. However, Wetmore was but one of the parties involved. Because Malone and Hochman presented their view of the world in which Madison Hemings lived, one would expect that they would have considered how setting, time, and place may have affected Hemings.

Madison Hemings was a skilled carpenter who had moved to Ohio after leaving Charlottesville. As Malone and Hochman pointed out, blacks in that state lived a precarious existence because the white residents of some counties resented blacks' attempts to settle there. Some towns for a period had barred blacks from living within the city limits.[12] So, from the time he moved to

Ohio, Hemings had been a black man with a family to raise in an environment that was hostile to blacks' very existence. This is the historical context in which he operated, not the world of Republican versus Democrat newspapers, not the world of white northern carpetbaggers and southerners. Malone and Hochman should have asked whether and why Hemings would have been inclined to make up, or participate in fabricating, a story about race mixing that would more likely inflame his neighbors than endear him to them.

If the story of Thomas Jefferson's alleged relationship with Sally Hemings has generated such heat and anger in modern times, what might the likely reaction have been in 1873? What about Israel Jefferson? He, like Madison Hemings, probably would have been aware that his statement could just as likely provoke anger on the part of some whites as feelings of affection. S. F. Wetmore may have been naive enough to think otherwise, but not Madison Hemings and Israel Jefferson.

In the historical context as laid out by Malone and Hochman, telling this story would have been extremely risky, and one cannot assume that the two men would have spoken to a newspaper without due consideration. People sometimes risk suffering in order to tell the truth. Lying is another matter, since it is more often done to avoid pain and suffering or to achieve some fairly certain gain. Because neither Hemings nor Israel Jefferson could have been sure that by telling this story they would realize either of these goals, one cannot so easily assume that they would be willing to risk telling a lie. In addition, if Wetmore had added items in his published version of Hemings's statement that were mischaracterizations or gross inaccuracies, there would have been ample time (perhaps as much as nine months) for Madison Hemings to have alerted Israel Jefferson as to the nature of Wetmore's game. Under the circumstances, Israel Jefferson would not have agreed to talk to Wetmore knowing that the editor was prone to writing whatever he wanted, regardless of what Jefferson might actually have said.

If Madison Hemings did lie, what could have been his motivation to do so? Malone and Hochman did not raise this question directly, instead describing Madison Hemings, somewhat condescendingly, as "an estimable character" whose "sincerity" they did not doubt.[13] However, at the end of the article they reproduced Wetmore's introduction to the Hemings piece and then gave the editor of the *Waverly Watchman*, a rival newspaper, the last word on Madison Hemings. The editorial fairly bristles with contempt for Hemings and for black people in general.

The editor of the *Waverly Watchman,* John A. Jones, said that it was "a well known peculiarity of the colored race" to "lay claim to illustrious parentage." He went on to say:

It sounds much better for the mother to tell her offspring that "master" is their father than to acknowledge to them that some field hand, without a name, had raised her to the dignity of mother. They [black women] want the world to think that they are particular in their liaisons with the sterner sex, whether the truth will bear them out or not.

A perusal of Hemings' autobiography reminds us of the pedigree printed on the numerous stud-horse bills that can be seen posted during the Spring season. No matter how scrubby the stock or whether the horse has any known pedigree, the "Horse Owner" furnishes a free and complete pedigree of every celebrated horse in the country. One of these is copied, and the scrawniest "plug" rejoices in a descent that would put Sir Archy to shame. The horse is not expected to know what is claimed for him. But we have often thought if one of them could read and would happen to come across his pedigree tacked conspicuously at a prominent crossroad, he would blush to the tips of his ears at the mendacity of his owner.[14]

It is not surprising that in 1873 the editor of a newspaper would speak so openly and hatefully of black people. What is surprising is that in 1975 his editorial would be reproduced as the last word on this subject without any comment about the tenor of Jones's remarks. Malone and Hochman did state that Wetmore and Jones "spoke for their political constituents as well as for themselves." This may have been the authors' indirect attempt to distance themselves from Jones's words. Their statement is still problematic because it creates a false equivalency between the writings of Wetmore and of Jones.[15]

Wetmore's piece introduced his series "Life among the Lowly" and then went on to talk about Madison Hemings. After criticizing the institution of slavery in general, he made a strong attack on Thomas Jefferson. Commenting on Madison Hemings's intelligence and speculating on what his life could have been like had he not been a slave, he then declared that Madison Hemings was "kept under, by his own father, an ex-President of the United States, and a man who penned the immortal Declaration of Independence which fully acknowledges the rights and equality of the human race!"[16]

One can understand why admirers of Thomas Jefferson would be dismayed by this harsh statement. Still, Wetmore was criticizing an individual man for what Wetmore thought that individual had done. Jones, on the other hand, attacked Madison Hemings by referencing the alleged negative characteristics of an entire race. The difference between "Wetmore v. Jefferson" and "Jones v. Hemings" is the difference between a legitimate dispute with an individual—which is always allowable—and an expression of racial prejudice, which is never. That Jones disbelieved Madison Hemings and chose to attack him is not the problem. The problem is in the way he chose to express his disbelief. Wetmore's piece on Hemings could appear in print today with little problem. Jones's piece on Hemings would allow people to recognize him for what he most assuredly was.

Virginius Dabney reproduced the Jones editorial in *The Jefferson Scandals*, his 1981 rebuttal to Fawn Brodie's biography of Jefferson and Barbara Chase-Riboud's novel *Sally Hemings*.[17] Neither Malone and Hochman nor Dabney saw a problem with offering Jones's over-the-top response to Hemings in order to cast doubt upon the validity of his statement. They seem not to have considered that an individual who would write that way about black people might not be the best person to consult—or to associate oneself with—on the issue of race and sex. Even a brief glance through the *Waverly Watchman* reveals that John A. Jones had negative feelings toward blacks that verged on the pathological.[18] The authors' failure to discern the nature of the problem with Jones and his editorial is instructive, as it suggests the level of care with which they weighed and evaluated the claims involved in this dispute. Jefferson scholars have a recurring tendency to highlight parts of a statement denying the existence of a Jefferson-Hemings liaison and to ignore other parts of the statement that are contradictory, perhaps dissembling, or even irrational.

Malone and Hochman and Dabney took the trouble to reproduce Jones's editorial even though Jones, as a source, did not add much of substance to the controversy. As Jones knew nothing of Madison Hemings specifically (and apparently did not try to learn anything), his only recourse was to appeal to his readership through the use of negative stereotypes about blacks in general, to "nigger-bait." Jones presented nothing in the way of reasoning that Malone and Hochman or Dabney could not have expressed in a less inflammatory and contemptuous fashion.

Not surprisingly, the truth of Madison Hemings's life is more complex than has been presented. Historians interested only in presenting their view that Hemings's allegations were false felt so comfortable in relying on the charge that his memoirs were prompted or invented by a northern carpetbagger (and felt so sure that their readers would accept this uncritically) that they, like John A. Jones, apparently did not bother to try to find out any more about Madison Hemings. Had they done so, they would have known that as early as the 1840s, thirty years before Wetmore arrived in Ohio, it was rumored in the area where Madison Hemings and his brother Eston lived that they were the sons of Thomas Jefferson and Sally Hemings. What is more, this notion apparently was accepted by some whites in their community.

Both Madison Hemings and his younger brother, Eston, were well known in Chillicothe, Ohio. Madison Hemings did an extensive amount of carpentry work in the area, working on some of the most important buildings in the town. Eston Hemings, like Madison and their older brother, Beverley, played the violin. Eston, who also played the pianoforte, was the most musically talented (or the most dedicated) of the brothers, for he was able to make a living as a musician. In the early 1900s the *Daily Scioto Gazette* recalled his professional life in Chillicothe during the 1840s and discussed the community's talk during that period about his alleged relationship to Thomas Jefferson. Eston Hemings was a highly regarded leader of a band that played at society functions in the area. Described as a "master of the violin, and an accomplished 'caller' of dances," he was said to have "always officiated at the 'swell' entertainments of Chillicothe." [19]

Eston Hemings's fame increased after five white residents of Chillicothe visited Washington and saw a statue of Thomas Jefferson. One turned to his companions and asked who the statue looked like. "Instantly came the unanimous answer, 'Why, Eston Hemings.'" When they returned to Chillicothe, one of the men, "happening to have some business with Hemings," told him what had happened in Washington and asked about his connection to Jefferson. "'Well,' answered Hemings quietly, 'my mother, whose name I bear belonged to Mr. Jefferson,' and after a slight pause, added, 'and she never was married.'" He did not elaborate. Hemings's inquisitor saw this as confirming the rumor. [20]

Although the *Scioto Gazette* article spoke only about Eston Hemings, the residents of the small town of Chillicothe no doubt also knew of his brother Madison. In addition to being a much-sought-after carpenter, Madison Hemings had bought and sold property numerous times. [21] The buying and selling of land by a black man, with some transactions involving what would have been a good deal of money in those days, would have attracted the attention of citizens in the area. William Weaver may have heard the rumors about the Hemingses before he came to Madison's home to take the census. Thus, his notation could have been based upon the rumors rather than anything Hemings said during the census interview.

Of course, the earlier talk about Eston Hemings and Weaver's notation about Madison Hemings do not prove that they were Jefferson's sons. Still, as the talk preceded by decades Wetmore's conversation with Hemings, and Weaver's notation was made three years before the publication of Hemings's memoirs in the *Pike County (Ohio) Republican,* it is clear that Madison Hemings should not be seen as a mere tool of S. F. Wetmore and that the idea that a black son of Thomas Jefferson resided in Ohio did not come from the mind of the district marshal and newspaper editor. Scholars wrote about Wetmore's alleged bad motive to suggest that this motive gave rise to the basic substance of the story and made the story false. But if the basic substance of the story was set years before Wetmore decided to write his series, his motive for writing it could not have given rise to the substance.

The additional information about Madison and Eston Hemings, S. F. Wetmore, and William Weaver, not sought or analyzed by any of the Jefferson scholars and defenders who first wrote on this subject, helps to explain why Madison Hemings would have felt safe in speaking to a newspaper about this matter. It would not have been clear to a black man telling this story for the first time for publication—as historians have assumed—what effect his words might have had upon his neighbors. As it turns out, Madison Hemings probably knew from the reaction that he and his brother had gotten up until that point that it would be safe for him to talk about his life story because others had heard it, in varying degrees of detail, before.

It has been common throughout American history for blacks who provide some form of entertainment to whites to be treated with favor, and so Eston Hemings's celebrity status in the area may have shielded the brothers from negative reactions to the rumor. Eston Hemings was very well liked in his community, and his musical talent evidently made the story that he was Thomas Jefferson's son believable to some. The personal manners of both brothers also seem to have helped in this regard. Both men were viewed as exceptional and impressive individuals. S. F. Wetmore noted Madison Hemings's appearance and high degree of intelligence. The author of the *Scioto Gazette* article described Eston Hemings as "quiet, unobtrusive, polite and decidedly intelligent" and noted that after coming to Chillicothe "he was soon very well and favorably known to all classes of our citizens, for his personal appearance and gentlemanly manners attracted everybody's attention to him."[22]

It seems, then, that Jefferson defenders, in their reliance on stereotypes about carpetbaggers, former slaves, and slave narratives, took a shortcut and as a result created what can only be called bad history. That history has been given to generations of college students and other members of the public, helping them to form their opinions about this specific matter and about the minds and characters of former slaves in general. An entire course of dishonorable conduct was attributed to three men on the basis of no evidence save one man's political affiliation and northern origins and the status of two other men as former slaves. All of the ink that has been spilled purveying the notion that S. F. Wetmore invented the idea, or put Madison Hemings up to saying, that he was the son of Thomas Jefferson, turns out to have been just that: spilled ink.

Madison Hemings's Motive: The Views of John C. Miller
and Andrew Burstein

Unlike Malone and Hochman, other historians have speculated more openly
about Hemings's motivation for speaking with the *Pike County (Ohio) Republican.* Writing in 1977, the historian John Chester Miller, who also believed the
memoirs to be a Wetmore invention, explained:

> If Madison Hemings actually told this story to the editor of the Pike County
> *Republican,* doubtless he hoped to achieve instant fame as the unacknowl-
> edged natural son of Thomas Jefferson. Madison was now an old man and,
> like most blacks and mulattoes in nineteenth century America, he probably
> felt cheated by life. In the community in which he lived, he was classed as
> "colored" and no doubt was treated as such by his white neighbors—which
> meant that they had nothing to do with him. But if he could prove that he
> were a natural son of a president of the United States, his position would
> change dramatically overnight; he would appear not only as good as a white
> man but as the white man's superior and, as such, entitled to the respect and
> consideration that had hitherto been denied him.[23]

Miller's analysis is curious: "blacks and mulattoes" in the nineteenth century "probably felt cheated in life," he said, as if it were a close question as to
whether people who had just escaped chattel slavery could have harbored
such a sentiment. There is also monumental arrogance in Miller's presumption that Madison Hemings would have cared so much about what his white
neighbors thought of him that he would take so drastic a step to change their
attitude. Why should it be assumed that Madison Hemings would have
yearned for the love of Chillicothe's white residents? If he ever did, why would
he have sought their affection so late in his life? In the absence of any evidence, how was Miller qualified to describe with such particularity Hemings's
state of mind on this question?

The last part of Miller's statement is incomprehensible: that a sixty-eight-
year-old black man could think that by announcing in a newspaper that his
black mother had his white father begging her to return to the United States
with him, he could make what Miller presumed to be his hostile white neighbors want to be his friend. What could possibly have happened in Madison
Hemings's life that would make him believe such a thing? If anything, his
experiences would have taught him the opposite lesson. One detects a note of
bitterness in Hemings's statement when he indicated that Jefferson favored
his white grandchildren over him and his siblings. If Madison Hemings felt
that the white man whom he said was his father did not treat him as his true
son, why would he have believed his white neighbors would do so? Miller's

perspective on the likely thought processes of a black man are so far wrong, so colored by his certainty that all blacks want to ingratiate themselves to whites, that he cannot be credited on the question of the likely motivations of Madison Hemings.

Andrew Burstein, in his 1995 book *The Inner Jefferson: Portrait of a Grieving Optimist,* echoed Miller's sentiment in his brief examination of the Hemings memoirs. Burstein wrote:

> Madison told an Ohio newspaper in 1873 that his mother informed him that Thomas Jefferson was his father, and that Sally first carried a child of Jefferson when she returned from France in 1789. Presumably, Madison believed these statements to be true. But it is also possible that his claim was contrived—by his mother or himself—to provide an otherwise undistinguished biracial carpenter a measure of social respect. Would not his life have been made more charmed by being known as the son of Thomas Jefferson than the more obscure Peter or Samuel Carr?[24]

The answer is most probably no. If one takes the time to consider the circumstances of Hemings's life, one could see that Hemings most likely would have known this. By 1873 all of his siblings had left the world of blacks to become a part of the white world. They did so for a reason. Living as a black person during that era, even as one favored by whites, meant suffering debilitating attacks upon one's humanity. Evidently, for Beverley, Harriet, and eventually Eston Hemings, the favor of whites was insufficient balm to heal the inevitable wounds that they and their progeny would have sustained if they had remained black. Eston's experiences, in particular, would have demonstrated to Madison Hemings the folly of thinking that a filial connection to Thomas Jefferson would be enough to render his life "charmed." Eston Hemings had achieved a measure of success living as a black man whom some thought to be the son of Thomas Jefferson. Yet that link to Jefferson did not ensure that he and his family would be treated as full human beings, which for the former slaves would have been the very definition of living a "charmed" life.

The man who wrote of Eston Hemings in the *Scioto Gazette* in 1901 was able to recognize a fundamental feature of America's racial landscape that later historians writing near the end of the century, after all that has been written and said about the problem of the color line, seem unable to discern. He wrote, "But notwithstanding all his accomplishments and deserts the fact remained that he had a visible admixture of negro blood in his veins and in Chillicothe before the war, between those who had, and the whites—even the lowest of them—there was a great gulf, an impassable gulf; and Eston

Hemings quietly moved away from Chillicothe, and I believe, told no one whither."[25]

Miller's and Burstein's conjectures that Madison Hemings thought that he could improve his lot in life by pretending to be the son of Thomas Jefferson seem to have been based on a notion that anyone would like and respect one of Thomas Jefferson's children, whether black or white. Their assumption, however, does not comport with the actual experiences of black people. To Miller and Burstein, it would be normal for a black man to want to gain the approval of whites and to think that he could do so by making up such a story. For the average black person, it most likely would be taken as a sign of Hemings's madness.

Most telling of all, neither Miller nor Burstein made any use of what is known about Hemings and his family. Both historians' accounts could have been written in the exact same manner if Wetmore's piece had never used Hemings's name and had, instead, referred to him as "an otherwise undistinguished biracial carpenter." Madison Hemings, the flesh-and-blood individual with a story of his own, who existed within a particular cultural context that could have been known and made use of, does not live in the writings of either Miller or Burstein.

It Just Does Not Sound Right

The second method employed to discredit Madison Hemings's memoirs is even weaker as a refutation. In this view the memoirs, in standard English, are not to be trusted because Madison Hemings may not have written them himself.[26] Notice that this argument employs a non sequitur: if one dictates memoirs to another, one is presumptively lying. This may come as a surprise to the many people who have prepared their memoirs with the aid of ghost writers or editors. It is no more true that one who dictates memoirs is lying than it is true that one who writes them out himself or herself is telling the truth.

Part of the difficulty that some have with the wording of the Hemings memoirs, and the reason people assume that it was all made up by the white reporter, stems to some degree from the notion that we know what every ex-slave in America sounded like. How do we know what all ex-slaves sounded like? Why, because Margaret Mitchell and David O. Selznick told us what all slaves and ex-slaves sounded like. As a result, any presentation of the statement of an ex-slave that is not in exaggerated dialect—"Who dat? Lawd Amighty, I don't know nuthin' 'bout birthin' babies"—is suspect to many. Even if it were true that all slaves sounded alike, and sounded like that, the rendering of such phrases as "Who is that? Lord Almighty, I don't know any-thing about delivering babies" would not indicate that the ex-slave had not, in fact, wondered who someone was, made an exclamation to the Lord, or said that he or she did not know how to deliver a child.

The demand that the words of black people appear "black" in print is, in some quarters, a requirement that exists today. It is not uncommon for jour-nalists to use dialect when reproducing the statements of black people but not to use it when reproducing the words of whites who have equally idiosyncratic pronunciations. If such a requirement exists even today, it is easy to under-stand how Hemings's statement might, for some, present a conceptual hurdle to believing that he could have been telling the truth.

Virginius Dabney cited one specific passage in Madison Hemings's state-ment as proof of the charge that it must have come from the mind of a "news-paper editor or some other college educated individual." At one point during the narrative, Hemings referred to his mother as having been "*enciente*" when she returned from France with Jefferson. Dabney, picking up on Hemings's reference to his limited formal education, asked, "If all he learned was to read and write, where did that word *enceinte* come from?"[27] Well, perhaps from his mother who had spent over two years in France during her teenage years and who may have received tutoring in the language while there.

John C. Miller expressed similar skepticism about Hemings's use of the word *enceinte,* saying, "Madison Hemings had only a rudimentary education, and he could not possibly have used the stilted overblown 'literary' language in which the 'interview' is couched: among other things, he is made to say that Sally Hemings was 'enciente' (sic) by Thomas Jefferson when they returned to Monticello." Jonathan Daniels noted that Hemings's "attainment in life was that of a small town carpenter" and went on to say that it was "doubtful that such a man would have used such a word as *enciente.*"[28]

It is possible that the use by newspapers of the word *enceinte* instead of *pregnant* was a Victorian convention. Even so, what is the picture of black people painted by Dabney's question and Miller's and Daniels's statements? Why would it be so implausible that a man whose mother had spent some of her formative years in France would know a French word? Wouldn't one ex-pect a mother to talk to her children about this time of her life? Edmund Bacon, Jefferson's overseer at Monticello, said that he had "often heard her" tell about her trip to France.[29] Isn't it common for people who learn a lan-guage to use that language to impress others or just to remind themselves that they know it? Why would it be inconceivable that Sally Hemings would have done this both in and out of the presence of her son?

The answer is that these historians' words betray no conception of slaves as human beings: the normal human processes of communication and love between mother and child did not exist for this group. Sally Hemings lived in France for over two years, yet nothing impressed her, no experience expanded her outlook on life, she brought back not one word of French. Slaves had no secret prides, ambitions, daydreams, or regrets to share with their families. Nothing, no matter how out of the ordinary, could touch them. They existed only in relation to their servitude, as mere props in the real story of slave masters and their lives. To use common human points of reference when considering the capabilities, knowledge, and feelings of a slave would be as ridiculous as considering the capabilities, knowledge, and feelings of a rocking chair. Dabney, Miller, and Daniels knew that Sally Hemings had lived in France, yet not one of them made the connection between that fact and her son's possible use of a French word. Plainly, they were not thinking of the Hemingses as a set of people but as a set of slaves, with all the negative connotations and stereotypes that they associated with that label.

Compare these historians' assumption about Hemings with their assumption that the editor of the *Pike County (Ohio) Republican* would be more likely to know the French word for pregnancy than would Madison Hemings. Here again they lumped Hemings into some nameless, faceless category of individuals without taking any account of the circumstances of his life. He had a connection to the French language that could be demonstrated. The same was not said for the editor of the *Pike County (Ohio) Republican*. Dabney even pointed out that the word was misspelled in the newspaper, a circumstance that would not have been Madison Hemings's fault, since he did not write the story down or set the newspaper's type.[30] It is more reasonable to believe that Madison Hemings would know how to say the word from hearing his mother say it and yet not know how to spell it because of the poor quality of his education, than it is to believe that a "college educated" editor of a newspaper, whom Dabney, Miller, and Daniels presumed to have studied French, would know the word and not be able to spell it.

Virginius Dabney's conception of the Hemingses can be seen in another aspect of his critique of Madison Hemings's statement. Dabney noted that Hemings's memoirs contained factual inaccuracies and contended that this made his statement about his parentage all the more unreliable. He fixed upon Hemings's statement that Thomas Jefferson had no real interest in agriculture and that "he always had mechanics at work for him, such as carpenters, blacksmiths, shoemakers, coopers, &c. It was his mechanics he seemed mostly to direct, and in their operations he took great interest." Dabney found this assertion particularly incredible and pointed out that Jefferson's meticulous notations in his Farm Book and Garden Book, as well as some of his letters, countered Hemings's observation.[31] Certainly, when one thinks of Thomas Jefferson, one thinks of a farmer.

When confronting a statement that goes so contrary to one's understanding of a person or a situation, there is a duty—if one wants to get at the truth—to consider how the individual making the statement might have arrived at so startling a conclusion. In the case of Madison Hemings, this would require an attempt to see Thomas Jefferson as Madison Hemings would have seen him. To do this, one must think of him as a person and draw upon what we know about people to help us figure out what Hemings could have been thinking when he said that Thomas Jefferson was more interested in being with his mechanics than he was in agriculture.

Madison Hemings was born in 1805. He was apprenticed to his uncle John Hemings at age fourteen. This was close to the age at which Jefferson thought that young slaves became more like adults and should settle into whatever role they would play at Monticello. We can say then that Madison Hemings came of age in 1819. What was Thomas Jefferson doing during the intervening years? He was supervising the building of the University of Virginia, which Dabney, who had written a history of the university, knew well. Jefferson was riding to the site on a regular basis. He was poring over plans with architects and builders. Notice that "carpenters" are included in Hemings's definition of "mechanics." So at the precise moment that Madison Hemings would have been old enough to pay serious attention to him, Jefferson was obsessed, not with his farm, but with building his university.[32]

Madison Hemings's vision of Jefferson is not a historian's static sketch of the man that takes no account of how his interests may have waxed and waned. It is, rather, a snapshot of a particular time from an eyewitness. At the very least, Dabney should have allowed that Hemings may have been accurate for the time when he knew Thomas Jefferson. In fact, a strong case can be made that Hemings's opinion about Jefferson's favoring mechanical interests over agriculture is an accurate assessment of Jefferson's preferences at all stages of his life. Jefferson himself stated that he liked nothing so much as putting things up and tearing them down. Both his contemporaries and other historians have echoed the same sentiment.[33]

The Statement

What we see in some historians' responses to Madison Hemings's statement is a tendency to rely upon stereotypes in the place of research and a refusal to engage the material in any but the most superficial manner. There is an alternative way of looking at the document. Rather than starting with the proposition that what Madison Hemings said was wrong and then reading his statement in a way designed to confirm that belief, it is possible to go through the statement and see if this human being—not this ex-slave, not this darky with delusions of grandeur—tells his story in a way that is believable. Let us see what happens when one attempts to assess the veracity of this statement by the same means one would use when evaluating other written or oral statements. This involves considering the way the story is told, the degree of calculation that seems to have gone into constructing it, and whether what Madison Hemings says can be corroborated by any extrinsic evidence.

The Way He Tells the Story

Madison Hemings began his family saga with the story of his African great-grandmother, who was the mistress of a white sea captain named Hemings. She was the property of John Wayles, who refused to sell her and her child, Elizabeth, to Captain Hemings. Wayles kept both slaves, and eventually Elizabeth became his mistress after the death of his third wife. John Wayles and Elizabeth Hemings had six children together, one of whom was Madison's mother, Sally. John Wayles was also the father of Thomas Jefferson's wife, Martha. When her father died, Martha brought Elizabeth Hemings and her children to Monticello.

According to Madison Hemings, his mother's relationship with Jefferson began in Paris while Jefferson was serving as a minister to France between 1784 and 1789. Sally Hemings had come to France in 1787, when she was between fourteen and fifteen years old. She was sent along as the companion to Jefferson's daughter Mary, or Maria, who was nine years old. Consider this bit of information and ask, What is the significance of France to Madison Hemings, or for that matter to S. F. Wetmore, for anyone who believed that he made up the story? Why does Hemings begin the story there when it makes what he says no more or less believable?

We know that France means something to modern-day believers in the Jefferson-Hemings liaison. The assertion that Sally Hemings was pregnant when she returned from France has been offered to counter the notion that one of Jefferson's nephews, Samuel Carr or Peter Carr, or in some versions both of them, was the father of Sally Hemings's children, as neither of them was in France with Hemings. In addition, her pregnancy in 1789 would have produced a child the right age to have been the "President Tom" that James Callender referred to in his 1802 newspaper articles about the alleged affair.

But neither of these considerations could have been in Madison Hemings's mind. First, there is no reason to assume that he even knew that the

Carr brothers had been designated to have been his father or the father of his siblings. This story, told by Jefferson's grandchildren after the deaths of Jefferson, Sally Hemings, and the Carr brothers, was first made public in 1874, a year after Madison Hemings's statement. In fact, had Hemings known that there was a competing theory about his parentage—or if the theory were true—he might have taken the opportunity during the course of speaking with Wetmore either to refute the idea head-on or to tell his story in a way that undercut the idea without specifically mentioning it. In addition, one cannot say that Wetmore was using the conception of the child in France to refute the idea that another man was Hemings's father, for there is no evidence that Wetmore knew about the Carr brothers either.

As for the pregnancy in France leading to the birth of Callender's "President Tom," Madison Hemings said that the child his mother conceived in France died shortly after it was born. The existence of this child was unimportant to Madison Hemings's story. He was not attempting to draw a line from Callender's story to his own version of events. If S. F. Wetmore used Callender's treatment as a guide, one wonders why he departed from Callender's story line on this point. In the Callender articles "President Tom" is almost as prominent as "Dusky Sally." Yet Hemings's statement does not employ this character.

Again, why France? Certainly the overwhelming majority of liaisons between American slave masters and slaves did not start in that country. Hemings would be believed no more had he said that the whole thing began at Monticello. If Hemings's statement is a concoction, starting the story in France was unnecessary. Its lack of importance to the person telling the story suggests that it was more an assertion made without guile than a concerted calculation.

Madison Hemings next stated that his mother and her brother James at some point declined to return to the United States. It was then, Madison Hemings said, that Jefferson promised Sally Hemings that her children would become free at age twenty-one if she agreed to return with him.

Now we ask, What is the significance of the citing of a specific age, twenty-one, and how does Hemings use this claim during the course of telling the story? As Hemings continued, he made no use of the specifics of this promise. That is to say, when he told how his older brother, Beverley, and his sister, Harriet, left Monticello, he did not say, "And when they got to be of age . . . they left." Here too, there does not seem to be any calculation in the way Hemings presented these facts. They do not fold into one another in the manner of a design.

Let us step away from the narrative for a moment and analyze Jefferson's alleged promise to free Sally Hemings's children by way of analogy. In law, claims that an individual has made an oral agreement to do something are looked upon with great suspicion. A written and signed document serves as the best evidence that a promise has been made. As with every rule, there are exceptions, and the exception that is relevant here involves the concept of partial performance. If there is a claim that a promise has been made, that one of the alleged parties to the agreement rendered some level of performance (from partial to complete) can be offered as evidence that a prior agreement existed. This makes sense, for why would the party perform, and perform in the manner that they were supposed to, in the absence of an agreement?

With this analogy in mind, consider Madison Hemings's statement about the alleged agreement between his mother and Thomas Jefferson that he would grant freedom to her children. One does not have to speculate at this point about why the agreement was made but just whether there was an agreement. The first question that should come to mind is, of course, If Madison Hemings said that Thomas Jefferson promised Sally Hemings that her children would be allowed to go free at twenty-one, what actually happened to Sally Hemings's children?

Beverley Hemings

Besides Callender's "Tom" Hemings, Beverley Hemings is the most mysterious of Sally Hemings's offspring. Most Jefferson biographies do not mention Beverley, even when they discuss the Sally Hemings story. As Madison Hemings noted, Beverley Hemings ran away from Monticello. For our purposes, what is interesting about Beverley's departure is that he left around the age of twenty-three. How do we know this? Not from Madison Hemings. We know when Beverley left Monticello because Thomas Jefferson wrote in his Farm Book, "Beverly, ran away 22," meaning in 1822.[34] Beverley Hemings did not leave Monticello exactly at age twenty-one, as Madison Hemings said was promised, but he did not leave before the designated time. Jefferson was not in the habit of freeing slaves. When slaves ran away, he sent after them; he even sent slaves to get other slaves.[35] There is no evidence that Jefferson made any attempt to bring Beverley back.

At least one other slave left Monticello and was not forced to return. That happened in 1804, when Jamey Hemings, the son of Sally's sister Critta, left Monticello. Jamey Hemings's case can be distinguished from Beverley's on two grounds, although Jefferson historians do not make these distinctions. First, there is a record of a precipitating event. Jamey Hemings, who had worked in the nail shop that Jefferson maintained, had been subjected to extremely brutal treatment by the man who directed operations at the shop, Gabriel Lilly. Lilly had beaten Hemings so badly that he was sick for several days and at some point was so weak that he could not ward off Lilly's blows. The young man ran away after this treatment. What Jefferson did when Jamey Hemings was found is the second distinction between his and Beverley's departures. Jefferson directed that he be sent back to Monticello. When Jamey refused, Jefferson tried to get Jamey's cooperation by promising that he would remove him from the nail shop and place him under the direction of John Hemings. After additional attempts at negotiation, Jamey still declined to return, and Jefferson eventually took his name off the slave rolls.[36]

Jefferson, who had always treated the Hemingses with great solicitude, may well have felt that Jamey was justified in leaving after the level of abuse he had suffered. That Jefferson thought this way is supported by the indications that Jamey Hemings returned to Monticello in later years to visit his family.[37] Certainly, Jefferson did not want or expect Jamey to run away. He seems to have acquiesced because he decided that the game was not worth the candle. Jamey would have to be physically recaptured and brought back to Monticello; then Jefferson would have had to deal with the aftereffects of what had happened between Lilly and Hemings. Jefferson apparently thought it easier just to let Jamey go.

Beverley Hemings's situation was different. There is no record of an event that led to his departure, and no evidence that Jefferson tried to bring him back. Jefferson's intent regarding Beverley's departure is harder to gauge because it was expressed through an act of omission rather than commission. Other reasons besides a desire to see Beverley Hemings go free may have led Jefferson to take no action when the young man left Monticello. However, Jefferson's intent with respect to Beverley's freedom can be reasonably inferred by looking at his actions toward Beverley's three younger siblings.

Harriet Hemings

The next child of Sally Hemings to leave Monticello was Harriet Hemings. Madison noted her departure without mentioning her age or tying it to the specifics of the alleged promise. When did Harriet Hemings leave Monticello? She left at age twenty-one. We know this not from Madison Hemings but from Jefferson's Farm Book. Jefferson noted her departure, "Harriet. Sally's run, 22.," the same year as Beverley Hemings.[38]

This gives us extrinsic evidence from the person who was supposed to have rendered performance of the alleged agreement that the terms of the alleged agreement had been fulfilled in a timely fashion. The question is why did the party (Jefferson) perform? We have no explanation from him of why he took these actions, but we do know that no one else on the plantation was ever given freedom upon reaching adulthood.

One could argue that Madison Hemings knew when his brother and sister left and therefore tailored his statement to fit that knowledge. But when Hemings told of Beverley's and Harriet's departure from Monticello, he did not point out they had, in fact, left around the time he said that they were to leave; he did not tell the story as if he were making a case. Rather, he presented the story simply as a story. The only way we know when they left is by consulting Thomas Jefferson's Farm Book. Even so, regardless of Hemings's intention in telling the story, one still is left with the question, Why were these young people allowed to go free, either directly after they reached adulthood or upon reaching adulthood, when no one else in the history of Monticello was similarly favored?

In considering the likely states of mind of Beverley and Harriet Hemings during this time, one should also ask, at the least, the following questions. How likely is it that these siblings, both slaves—one male and one female—would decide to leave a plantation at around the same age if they attached no significance to their ages? Why not leave before reaching twenty-one? It is likely that both young people had thought of being free and that they had talked about it at least between themselves. They would have considered, in advance of their departure, the manner in which their freedom could be achieved. They would also have known that the decision to run away would be a decision to leave their family behind in a very particular way. Madison Hemings revealed that Harriet and Beverley also had decided to pass for white, which meant that they would never again have easy or extensive contact with their black relatives. We cannot assume, without engaging in stereotype, that the actions of this young man and woman were totally spontaneous and taken without some degree of forethought. If these two young people intended to run away, they would have considered the appropriate timing of their departures.

Edmund Bacon, Thomas Jefferson, and Harriet Hemings

The circumstances of Harriet's departure from Monticello are, in fact, more suggestive than Beverley's. Edmund Bacon, who was Jefferson's overseer for nearly twenty years, recounted a version of her leaving.

> He freed one girl some years before he died, and there was a great deal of talk about it. She was nearly as white as anybody, and very beautiful. People

said he freed her because she was his own daughter. She was not his daughter; she was ". . . .'s" daughter. I know that. I have seen him come out of her mother's room many a morning, when I went up to Monticello very early. When she was nearly grown, by Mr. Jefferson's direction I paid her stage fare to Philadelphia and gave her fifty dollars. I have never seen her since, and don't know what became of her. From the time she was large enough, she always worked in the cotton factory. She never did any hard work.[39]

Bacon's claim to have known the identity of the true father of Sally Hemings's children stands as one of the two pillars supporting the defense of Jefferson against the charge of miscegenation. The second pillar is a statement by Jefferson's grandson T. J. Randolph. Bacon's account contains three assertions that should concern us. First, there is the declaration that Harriet was not Jefferson's daughter. The second is that Bacon had often seen someone other than Jefferson coming from Sally Hemings's room in the morning. The third is that Jefferson arranged for this young woman to leave Monticello, with money, bound for a safe destination. These assertions can be considered in order of their relative strength as evidence.

The statement that Jefferson told Bacon to put Harriet on a stagecoach to Philadelphia and to give her fifty dollars can be described as a fact that Bacon could have known with great authority, because he was personally involved. He was either lying, and thus admitting to the world that he had stolen Thomas Jefferson's property and sent her to Philadelphia, which seems unlikely, or he was telling the truth.

What of the statement that he had seen someone coming from Sally Hemings's room "many a morning." This, again, can be characterized as a fact that could have been in the possession of Edmund Bacon. This statement is important because if Bacon was telling the truth in his memoirs, he was establishing that someone else may have been romantically involved with Sally Hemings.

But there are other problems with this assertion. Bacon may well have seen a person coming from Sally Hemings's room. The question that should immediately leap to mind is, When did he see the person? Were the many mornings in 1806 through 1824, Bacon's tenure as Jefferson's overseer at Monticello?[40] Were they in 1812 or 1815? The lack of a time frame for Bacon's observation makes this statement not useless but deficient as evidence that Jefferson was not Harriet's father or the father of Sally Hemings's other children. It may well be that even if there had been a relationship between them, at some point Thomas Jefferson and Sally Hemings were done with one another sexually, and someone else could have been coming from her room. Without a time period for Bacon's sightings of this other individual, this part of his statement is not as helpful as some would like to think. Note that those who cite Bacon's recollections as proof that someone other than Jefferson was the father of Sally Hemings's children are employing a double standard in assessing evidence. Bacon's statements, with no independent extrinsic evidence to back them up, are accepted uncritically while Madison Hemings's statements are treated as mere "oral tradition" that is not fact.[41]

The last statement of Bacon's to be considered is his flat-out assertion that the person he saw coming out of Sally Hemings's room, the person who was not Jefferson, was the father of Harriet Hemings. This is the weakest of all the statements. Yet it has been given the most prominence by Jefferson's defenders. Harriet Hemings was born in 1801, and Edmund Bacon did not come to Monticello until 1806.[42] The identity of Harriet's father could not possibly have been within Bacon's certain knowledge, especially when one considers how he says he knew the identity. Bacon did not claim that Sally Hemings had told him who had fathered Harriet. He was, at best, stating his opinion on this matter, an opinion rendered dubious by the date of Harriet's birth and the date of Bacon's arrival at Monticello. In their eagerness to establish a defense of Thomas Jefferson, historians too quickly raised a generally weak item of evidence to the status of proof.

So, in sum, we have (1) a statement of a fact about an action taken by Thomas Jefferson that could have been within Bacon's knowledge, (2) a statement of fact about an observation that Bacon could have made, but with no time frame for that observation, when timing is critical, and (3) a statement that could only be an opinion. The strongest by far is the first statement, which has Thomas Jefferson acting in a way that suggests that Harriet Hemings was not just another slave to him. The question is, Does the strength of that first statement support the veracity of Madison Hemings's account more than the two weaker statements hurt it?

The Context

As always, when one views an action that Thomas Jefferson took with respect to Sally Hemings's children, it is worth considering the context in which the action was taken. Until Harriet Hemings left in 1822, Jefferson had never freed a female slave. There may have been several reasons for this, but we know at least one that was probably the most important to him. Two years before Harriet Hemings left Monticello, Jefferson wrote a letter to his former son-in-law John Eppes in which he said that he considered female slaves to be far more valuable than male slaves. Why? Because female slaves had children and, thus, added to capital.[43]

At the time of Harriet's departure, Jefferson was in dire financial circumstances. Bad economic times in Virginia, along with Jefferson's expensive way of life, had set him on the road to financial collapse. In 1818 Jefferson had co-signed a loan for the benefit of his grandson's father-in-law, Wilson Cary Nicholas. When Nicholas died without repaying the debt, Jefferson became liable for the whole amount. Upon his death four years after Harriet's departure, Jefferson was over $100,000 in debt.[44] It is reasonable to ask why, under these circumstances, Jefferson would have felt compelled to direct his overseer to put an item of his capital, a potential source of more capital, on a stagecoach to Philadelphia with fifty dollars, about three months' wages for a common laborer in Philadelphia during that period.[45] Harriet Hemings was valuable. She was a twenty-one-year-old woman who might bear children who could also be valuable, if not to Jefferson himself, to his beloved daughter Martha who he hoped would inherit whatever wealth he was able to salvage before his death.

Most defenses of Thomas Jefferson on the Hemings question are based upon a view of Jefferson's character and the belief that he could not act out of that character. In freeing Harriet Hemings, Jefferson was so far out of character as to have been almost another person. This episode is one of the most extraordinary events in Thomas Jefferson's personal life. One would think that historians would be greatly interested in discussing this action, as it implicates Jefferson's attitude toward slavery and, to some extent, toward women. John C. Miller in his book *The Wolf by the Ears* took Bacon's description of Jefferson's emancipation of Harriet Hemings as fact but sped right over it to get to one of his main points: that Thomas Jefferson could not have been the father of Sally Hemings's children because there is no evidence that he ever took any action that showed that he looked upon them with special favor.[46]

At the end of his book, Miller described Jefferson's final descent into poverty and the effect that it had upon his attitude toward slavery. Miller declared that "in his old age Jefferson was faced with the alternative of giving up Monticello or running his estates more efficiently with slave labor and cherishing each slave child born on his estates for its cash-surrender value."[47] Yet this was the same period that Jefferson put a young slave and potential bearer of more slave children on a stagecoach to Philadelphia, an act contrary to Jefferson's expressed sentiments and detrimental to his financial and social wellbeing.

Given the extremely small number of people Thomas Jefferson freed during his life and the extraordinary circumstances under which Harriet Hemings was freed, who could fail to see the importance of this event? How could an author writing a book about Jefferson's attitude toward slaves and slavery think this emancipation unworthy of analysis? Perhaps Miller would have discussed the method and timing of Jefferson's sending Harriet away from Monticello had the story not come loaded with implications that were anathema to him.

Why Jefferson Freed Harriet Hemings: The Defenders Explain

Why did Jefferson free Harriet Hemings? Dumas Malone, who also accepted Bacon's account, said that Jefferson's action "seems to have been designed to protect her virtue."[48] Aside from the fact that Malone cited no evidence to indicate that Harriet Hemings's virtue was imperiled, this response does nothing but bring us back to the original question. Why was her virtue more important to Jefferson than the virtue of any other slave woman who had lived at Monticello? Surely, Harriet Hemings was not the only slave girl in Jefferson's history as a slave owner whose virtue had been in jeopardy. Why didn't any other young women receive similar treatment, particularly in the years when Jefferson could have better afforded it?

It simply must be conceded that Harriet Hemings was, for some reason, special to Thomas Jefferson. He treated her differently in the most important way that a slave could be treated differently by a master: he allowed her to go free. The more one thinks about what would have been involved in arriving at the decision to free Harriet Hemings and then freeing her in the manner chosen, the more the extraordinary nature of Jefferson's action becomes clear.

First, the idea for doing it had to originate from someone. From whom? Jefferson, Harriet Hemings, her mother, Sally? One might think of circumstances under which Jefferson might have decided on his own that it was best for Harriet to leave Monticello. There is no record of a precipitating event—a rape or attempted rape of Harriet Hemings, for example—that might have increased the sense of urgency to have her leave Monticello. There is no indication that there was a persistent but unwanted suitor with whom Harriet had to contend. If such a person did exist, Thomas Jefferson could have dealt with that circumstance without adopting so drastic a remedy. In the absence of any stated reason, one wonders why Jefferson would have involved himself in this fashion.

If the idea came from Harriet or Sally Hemings, what would make either woman think that she could approach Jefferson about so delicate a matter? Sally Hemings had lived at Monticello for almost a half a century. During that time she must have noticed that Jefferson had never freed a female slave. Why

would she think he would act differently with respect to Harriet? Why would
Harriet think that Jefferson would respond to a request that she be freed?

Whoever raised the idea of freeing Harriet, after the decision was made
to do so, there would have to have been some consideration of how it would
be accomplished. Jefferson must have talked to Harriet about this, and one
would think he would have talked to her mother. The means chosen for getting her to freedom required forethought and planning: a stagecoach to a
particular destination with which Jefferson, more than Harriet, would be familiar. If he was concerned about getting her through Virginia to a safe place,
might not he also have a concern for her safety once she got there?

Both Dumas Malone and Douglass Adair attempted to address this underlying concern. In Malone's version, "Harriet was given $50 and put on the
stage for Philadelphia, where she may be presumed to have joined her brother
James." Malone was probably referring to Sally Hemings's brother James Hemings, the chef whom Jefferson had freed in 1796 and who had taken up residence in Philadelphia; Harriet Hemings had no brother named James. Adair
fleshed things out a bit, writing, "If James was established in that city, he
would have been in a position to give Harriet a home and to offer her protection that the words 'home' and 'family' imply."[49]

We may not "presume" that Harriet Hemings was sent to join James
Hemings, and there is a good chance that Harriet would not have been particularly comfortable in any "home" that James Hemings could have provided
for her in 1822, since James Hemings had committed suicide in 1801.[50] That
neither Malone nor Adair knew this, or had forgotten it, shows the degree of
attention they gave to this important aspect of the story. It seems a mistake
borne of the habit of seeing the details of the lives of slaves as unimportant,
in the same fashion that they saw the details of Madison Hemings's life unworthy of careful consideration and with a similarly unfortunate result for
their scholarship on this particular controversy.

Both Malone and Adair knew that there is virtually no chance that
Thomas Jefferson would have sent a twenty-one-year-old woman (who was,
most likely, *some* farmer's daughter) to a big city without knowing that she
would be helped once she got there. This would not have been the way to
protect the virtue of a beautiful young woman. Because his actions indicate
that he cared something for Harriet, making sure that she had help once she
got to her destination would likely have figured into any plan he made for
freeing her.

Jefferson defenders often attempt to justify Jefferson's freeing of so few
slaves by saying that he had a policy of freeing only those who had a skill
because he thought it cruel to send a man out into a hostile environment with

no way to care for himself.[51] If this was his attitude toward men, what standard would he have employed when he decided to take the unprecedented step of freeing a woman? Jefferson's concerns along these lines would have been particularly warranted if the young woman in question was one whose work history consisted of spending a few years learning how to weave. As did most men of his era, Jefferson took a paternalistic attitude toward women, thinking that they should be under the protection of men. If any harm came to Harriet Hemings because he had not taken adequate steps for her protection, it would have been Jefferson's fault for having sent her away under those circumstances. This would have been in the calculations of a man as paternalistic as Jefferson.

Jefferson's Farm Book and Madison Hemings's memoirs suggest how Jefferson planned to have Harriet protected in her freedom. Although one page from the Farm Book indicates that both Beverley and Harriet Hemings left Monticello in 1822, the last reference to Beverley in that record was made during 1821, making it likely that he left Monticello in the waning months of that year. Harriet Hemings is listed during the early part of 1822 as being a part of a household with her mother and her brothers Madison and Eston, with no mention of Beverley.[52] It seems, then, that Beverley Hemings left Monticello before Harriet and went to Washington. He departed two years after the time his brother Madison said the Hemings children were to be emancipated, around the time that Harriet Hemings turned twenty-one. The timing of the two siblings' departures may have been coordinated.

Think of their mother's likely desires. Her family had not been fractured by the slave system. They had lived together as one unit from her first son's birth and no doubt had formed the normal bonds that exist in most families. Why would there not be an expectation that an older brother would provide protection to a younger sister when she reached the age of majority and was to be allowed to leave Monticello?

What about the seeming discrepancy between Bacon's account of Harriet Hemings's destination after she left Monticello and that of Madison Hemings. Bacon said he bought Harriet a ticket to Philadelphia. Hemings said that both Beverley and Harriet had gone to Washington. Apparently, Bacon was instructed to buy a ticket to Philadelphia, but Washington (as Madison Hemings said) was actually Harriet's final destination. Although Bacon would have been useful to Jefferson and the Hemingses for preliminary matters (to purchase a ticket in Charlottesville without drawing attention), they may not have wanted him to know exactly where Harriet Hemings was going. When the stagecoach arrived in Philadelphia, Harriet could then go on to Washington to meet the waiting Beverley.

Bacon's recounting of Harriet Hemings's emancipation reveals that there was a great deal of gossip about her departure.[53] A man as astute as Jefferson would have known that this would happen; he could not keep slaves from talking about Harriet's leaving and the way she left, nor could he be sure that Bacon would not say anything. We can see from Bacon's memoirs and from other sources that some of Jefferson's neighbors were watching the goings-on at Monticello. This was a small rural area where local gossip by whites and blacks would, and evidently did, spread the word. It would also most likely be noted that Harriet's older brother, Beverley, had simply walked away from Monticello.

Despite this, Jefferson took this action knowing that it might result in discomfort to his daughter and grandchildren because it raised the issue of Sally Hemings once again. The question remains, why? Madison Hemings gave an explanation that historians writing on this subject do not want to accept. Yet either they do not venture their own explanation, or they posit one that puts us right back where we started. Why Harriet, and no other woman?

The Double Standard with Respect to Evidence

The final point to be made about Bacon's memoirs is that the treatment of his recollections represents a clear example of historians' double standard regarding the analysis and acceptance of evidence in this controversy. Recall the discussion of S. F. Wetmore and his alleged abolitionist sympathies as creating a motive for publishing Madison Hemings's memoirs, a motive which made the contents suspect. The man who recorded Edmund Bacon's memories, the Reverend Hamilton W. Pierson, seems to have had a purpose in presenting Bacon's memoirs as well. While it is true that Bacon did have a fascinating story to tell, it is also clear that Pierson used Bacon's memoirs, which appeared during the Civil War, as a vehicle for capturing the legacy of Thomas Jefferson for the Union cause.

In the last chapter of the book, omitted in James Bear's edition of Bacon's memoirs, Pierson summed up:

> While the author has been engaged in the preparation of this volume, linger-
> ing in spirit amid the sacred shades of Monticello, and dwelling upon its
> hallowed associations, an utterly causeless and wicked rebellion has culmi-
> nated in the establishment of the so-called Confederate States.
>
> 　　The facts presented in this volume, while they increase our reverence
> for those master-builders who laid the foundations of our glorious Union,
> give intensity to our abhorrence of their traitorous successors, who are en-
> deavoring to tear down the magnificent structure. There could be no more

sad and striking illustration of the folly and madness of this rebellion, than the fact that the home of Jefferson has been confiscated, because its owner is loyal to the Stars and Stripes. The banner of treason—the Confederate flag—now waves over the bones of the author of the Declaration of Independence.[54]

The omission of this material prevents readers from knowing the depth of Pierson's feelings about Jefferson and hides the important purpose for writing the book. Despite its absence, Pierson's sentiments come through at other points. Earlier in the book, during Bacon's discussion of Jefferson's view on slavery, Pierson included a footnote describing Bacon as a "stanch Union man, utterly opposed to the whole secession movement." Bacon sounded this theme himself with a touch of humor. At one point in the narrative, describing his love for his wife, Bacon said, "We have now lived together nearly forty years, and I believe neither of us is tired of the union, or anxious to secede."[55]

Both Pierson and Bacon had the desire and motive to present Thomas Jefferson in as good a light as possible, not only because they admired him but because the appropriation of his image would have been useful to the side they favored in the Civil War. Whether Bacon also supported freeing the slaves is unknown; however, a great part of his remembrances involves showing just how much Jefferson did not like the institution of slavery and how well he treated his slaves. Bacon also indicated that the only reason Jefferson did not free his slaves was because his desperate financial situation made that action impossible.[56]

Under the circumstances, would either Pierson or Bacon have wanted Thomas Jefferson, whose legacy they were attempting to claim for their own, to be associated with miscegenation? Pierson announced at the beginning of the book that Bacon's memoirs would deal with Jefferson's personal life. Therefore, a reader would expect some comment about the most controversial aspect of Jefferson's private life. Bacon may have wanted to tell the story of Harriet Hemings as an extraordinary example of Jefferson's kindness to a slave, but he understood that this action might be taken as proof of the old allegation against his boss. At one point in the narrative, Bacon remembered, with evident pride, that another man had said that Bacon would "go into the fire if Thomas Jefferson asked him to."[57]

A man who felt this way about Jefferson might have thought it his duty to tell of Jefferson's good act, but to do so in a way that protected him. Despite the confidence of the tone with which Bacon disputed the notion that Jefferson could have been the father of one of Sally Hemings's children, he may have, in fact, harbored at least some suspicions about Jefferson's relationship to Hemings, for he had seen firsthand Jefferson's actions toward her family.

Bacon as overseer at Monticello knew that Jefferson had let Beverley Hemings run away without taking any steps to retrieve him. Bacon also knew that Beverley was Harriet's brother. Yet in recounting the story of Harriet's departure as part of his way of showing Jefferson's benevolence, Bacon did not mention that Jefferson had let her older brother, Beverley, leave the same year. One could understand why Bacon might not have mentioned the example of Jamey Hemings, the young man who ran away after being beaten. Jefferson tried to have Jamey returned to Monticello and seems to have backed down only in the face of Jamey's defiance. To show Jefferson benevolently allowing slaves to run away would be one thing; to show him as having retreated in the face of a recalcitrant slave would be quite another. But Beverley Hemings's situation was different. Why wouldn't Bacon, intimately familiar with the departures of both Beverley and Harriet, mention Jefferson's freeing of Beverley?

There are at least three possible answers. The first is that Bacon was an elderly man, and he simply forgot about it. This seems unlikely given the detail with which he remembered many other events in the personal life of Jefferson. Perhaps Bacon did not think it important. However, at that point in Bacon's narrative—when he discusses Jefferson's ambivalent attitude toward slavery—Jefferson's reaction to the flight of Beverley Hemings would have fit in very neatly with the idea that Bacon was trying to convey. The problem for Bacon, however, was that Jefferson's freeing of this pair of siblings might contradict his assertion about Harriet's paternity, suggesting as it did that Jefferson was making decisions about Beverley and Harriet on the basis of some common attribute they shared.

This point is supported further by the fact that during the course of his discussion of Jefferson and slavery, Bacon mentioned every slave that Jefferson freed in his will except Madison and Eston Hemings, Beverley and Harriet's two younger brothers.[58] Why would he leave them out? The list was not extensive. Jefferson freed only five slaves through the terms of his will. If John Hemings, Burwell Colbert, and Joe Fossett came to Bacon's mind during the course of this discussion, why not Madison and Eston Hemings? Bacon may well have understood that mentioning that Thomas Jefferson had, in one way or another, freed all four of Sally Hemings's children might make the idea that he was their father more credible. There is no reason to suppose that Bacon was an ignorant man. He most likely understood that his words could, as they actually have, become a part of the historical record of Thomas Jefferson. That is, after all, why Pierson wanted to talk to Bacon. The selectiveness of Bacon's memory raises the possibility that he may have been self-editing his reminiscences to avoid incriminating Jefferson on this point. Alternatively, Pierson, acting in the manner often attributed (with no particular evidence) to editors of slave narratives, may have edited Bacon's statements himself, not wanting his book to be the source of information about Jefferson's actions toward Sally Hemings's children.

Consider the atmosphere in which Pierson and Bacon were engaged in their project. It was wartime. Everyone had chosen sides, and Americans were at each other's throats. Can we fairly say that the strength of convictions that existed during this time would have been weaker than the zeal and fervor of abolitionists who had won their struggle by the time Madison Hemings was interviewed in 1873?

No historians have used the possible motivations of Bacon and Pierson to cast doubt upon the glowing picture of Jefferson contained in the memoirs. Nor has anyone considered the possibility that both men may have had a motive to dispute the charge that Jefferson had a slave mistress. Merrill Peterson, in his seminal work *The Jefferson Image in the American Mind,* cited Bacon's rejection of the notion that Jefferson was the father of Hemings's children without mentioning the context in which Bacon's statement appeared. In contrast, Peterson described at great length the role that abolitionists played in disseminating the Jefferson-Hemings story and suggested that Madison Hemings's memoirs were part of that process.[59] He thus accepted without question the account promoted by the two white men while expressing skepticism about the black man's narrative.

Virginius Dabney wrote of Bacon's account as though motivations to lie arise only out of fear of reprisal. In his view, "since Jefferson had been dead for more than a third of a century when Bacon gave his interview, and Bacon was living in Kentucky, the latter was under no obligation or pressure to misrepresent what he had seen with his own eyes long before."[60] The question does not turn solely on whether Bacon may have felt compelled by an outside source to fabricate; the question is also whether he may have had his own personal reasons for having done so. Bacon's and Pierson's discussion make it clear that there were personal reasons that may have led Bacon to shade the truth.

Unlike Madison Hemings, Bacon and Pierson have been given the benefit of being seen as individuals rather than as stereotypes. We do know more about these two men than we know about Madison Hemings. But some things we know about them—that Bacon was Jefferson's loyal and trusted overseer for many years and was against secession; that Pierson was a Jefferson admirer and a fervent antisecessionist who took the opportunity in producing Bacon's memoirs to further this cause—should strengthen rather than allay the concern that they might have tailored their story about Harriet Hemings to present a vision of Jefferson more palatable to the readers of that era and to posterity.

Madison Hemings and Eston Hemings

After Beverley and Harriet left Monticello, Sally Hemings's youngest children, Madison and Eston, remained. Both of these young men were freed by Thomas Jefferson's will of March 1826, the only public example of Jefferson's preferential treatment of any of the Hemings children. The question of why a slave master freed some slaves and not others invites inquiries into motivation. This is even more true when the slave master was the author of the Declaration of Independence and was not in the habit of freeing slaves. The first reason that comes to mind when one thinks of why a master freed a slave is that the action was taken for reasons of sentiment. The slave freed had performed some service for the master, and his or her freedom at the master's deathbed was recognition of that fact.

Jefferson's will provided for the freeing of five slaves. In *The Sage of Monticello,* the final volume in his six-volume biography of Jefferson, Dumas Malone listed their names.[61] If sentiment was Jefferson's reason for this provision, there is a problem with the list of slaves he chose to free.

First on the list was a man named Burwell Colbert, a relative of Sally Hemings. Colbert, whom Malone described as a factotum, had been Jefferson's personal valet for a number of years, and Jefferson had promised him that he would free him. Edmund Bacon said that Jefferson had "perfect confidence" in Burwell. It is understandable why a master would free his personal valet since this individual would have rendered important and intimate services to him, particularly during Jefferson's illnesses during the last years of his life. Sentiment in this case would seem especially appropriate. Edmund Bacon, after describing Burwell's services, said, "Mr. Jefferson gave him his freedom in his will, and it was right that he should do it."[62]

The next slaves freed were John Hemings and Joe Fossett. John Hemings, Sally Hemings's younger brother, was the master carpenter at Monticello. Hemings had contributed to the look of the home that Jefferson loved, and Jefferson wanted him to work at the University of Virginia. These two men, over many years, had discussed the planning and the execution of various projects at Monticello. Jefferson owed John Hemings a great deal, and again, one could understand why Jefferson would free him. Joe Fossett, another relative of Sally Hemings, was a master ironworker at Monticello. In charge of Jefferson's metal shop, Fossett also had fairly substantial interaction with

Jefferson over the course of his life about things that mattered to Jefferson, and therefore his emancipation makes sense as well.[63]

If sentiment was an important consideration in the decision to free these individuals, there is no question as to why these people deserved their freedom. The problem comes with the last two names that appear on the list, those of Madison and Eston Hemings. In Jefferson's will they are listed as apprentices to John Hemings, and Jefferson described himself as giving John Hemings their services until they reached twenty-one.[64] Malone identified them the same way. He did not mention that they were the sons of Sally Hemings, even though Madison and Eston Hemings have not been topics of discussion because they were John Hemings's apprentices.

If sentiment played a role in Jefferson's choice of these five people, then what were Madison, who was twenty-one, and eighteen-year-old Eston doing on the list? Their contributions to Monticello and to Thomas Jefferson could in no way have matched those of Burwell Colbert, John Hemings, or Joe Fossett. If sentiment played a role in the freeing of these slaves, in the cases of Madison and Eston Hemings there had to be some alternative reason for its origin.

Malone's explanation of why these five were chosen rejects sentiment as a primary motivation and suggests that the choice was a practical one. Jefferson freed these 5 slaves because they were the only ones of his almost 140 slaves who had a skill. Malone gave no specific citation for this justification, but he noted that the two other male slaves Jefferson freed in earlier years had possessed a skill. According to Malone, Jefferson was concerned that slaves who had no trade would not be able to make it in the outside world, so he made the decision to free only those who were skilled laborers.[65]

There was at least one other slave at Monticello who had a skill. What of Peter Hemings, another of Sally's brothers, who had been trained by James Hemings to be a cook?[66] Surely, Peter Hemings can be said to have had a skill. While it is true that James Hemings eventually committed suicide and may not have been the best role model, it would be hard to blame his depression on his cooking skills. It would have been a relatively simple matter for Jefferson to have given Peter Hemings, of whom he had spoken highly, a letter of introduction mentioning that he had been his cook for a number of years and that he had been trained by a man who had apprenticed in Paris while Jefferson served as minister there. Why Madison and Eston, and not Peter?

Perhaps Jefferson was so grateful to John Hemings that he decided to let him keep his apprentices for some reasonable period of time. His desire to have John Hemings do carpentry work at the University of Virginia may also have entered into the calculus. Jefferson may have wanted the three men freed to be sure that they could work there together. This still does not defeat a charge that sentiment could have played a role in Jefferson's decision to free Madison and Eston Hemings. As master of the plantation, Jefferson would have made the decision that these two young men, and not others, would be put in the position of gaining a trade. One could just as easily say that Jefferson had put Madison and Eston on this course and prepared them for freedom. He had done the same for their older brother, Beverley.

The decision to free these two brothers could not have been reached without weighing some important considerations. As he faced death, Jefferson knew that there was a chance that he could lose all of his property. He was conscious of the effect that this calamity was having on his family, and he was especially worried about his daughter Martha. He confided his concerns to his grandson Thomas Jefferson Randolph, saying that "she was sinking every day under the sufferings she was enduring and was literally dying before his eyes." He exacted a promise from Randolph never to leave Martha.[67]

In the midst of all of this, why would Thomas Jefferson as part of his last official act on earth free the two remaining children of the woman who had been the source of such turmoil. Jefferson not only freed these slaves, he petitioned the Virginia legislature to allow them to remain in the state.[68] Scandals are not easily forgotten, particularly those involving sex. It is unlikely that Jefferson would think that Virginians, black and white, had forgotten about Sally Hemings. Although Edmund Bacon does not mention the Hemings controversy specifically, at the end of his memoirs he says of Jefferson, "He may have had the faults that he has been charged with, but if he had, I could never find it out."[69] Bacon probably was not referring to the "fault" of being a Jacobin or the other epithets that were hurled at the public Jefferson. He was more likely referring to allegations about Jefferson's private life, since that was what the book was specifically designed to address. As late as the 1860s, Bacon felt compelled to refute old charges that were seen as a cloud over Jefferson's reputation.

In 1826 even those who did not believe the story of Sally Hemings's relationship to Jefferson would still remember the tales. The names and number of slaves that this great man of Virginia had decided to free would be of interest to everyone. That two of them were the children of Sally Hemings could not reasonably have been kept a secret in Jefferson's home territory. Just as people talked about the fact that he had informally freed their sister four years before, his freeing of Madison and Eston started the gossip about Sally Hemings anew.[70] It is almost certain that slaves in the community would have talked about who had been freed and who they were. His gossiping neighbors talked about it, and members of the legislature could easily know who they were.

Jefferson must have considered that freeing Madison and Eston Hemings would be taken by some as confirmation of what they had long suspected, that he did indeed have children by Sally Hemings, and that it might, at least, raise doubts among those who did not believe the story. In view of Jefferson's often-cited great love for his daughter and grandchildren, why would he raise the issue of Sally Hemings again, even momentarily, when his daughter and grandchildren were facing the loss of him and everything they had known up until that point.

In fact, the language in Jefferson's will suggests that he may have been cognizant of the impression that his freeing of Madison and Eston would create. "I give also to John Hemings the services of his two apprentices, Madison and Eston Hemings until their respective ages of twenty-one years, at which period, I give them their freedom: and I humbly and earnestly request of the Legislature of Virginia a confirmation of the bequest of freedom of these servants, with permission to remain in this State, where their families and connections are."[71]

Why did Jefferson write his will in a way that tied the freedom of Madison and Eston to their uncle John Hemings? When he prepared this document, a codicil to a will written the previous day, Jefferson knew that the will did not really give John Hemings the services of Madison Hemings because Madison was already twenty-one years old when the document was drafted. Whatever their relationship, Jefferson had reason to know Madison Hemings's age because he had noted his birth in his Farm Book and would have had occasion to come upon the listing numerous times over the years. If the young man's age was not a part of his everyday knowledge, Jefferson would have taken care to determine it because Madison's age was crucial to the operation of a section of his will. Under the circumstances, why not simply state, "I give Madison Hemings his freedom," and continue with the plan for Eston? Eston, three years younger than Madison, would have been required to work with John Hemings for two years. During that time, Eston could have learned more about his craft, and it may have been Jefferson's intent that he do so.

Jefferson was a lawyer. He knew that there were ways to draft this document that would free Madison and Eston and bind both men to working with their uncle without using the words, "I give to John Hemings the services of . . ." He could have granted both young men their freedom conditioned upon their continuing to work with their uncle. He could have directed the executors of his estate or his heirs to see to this. Jefferson was always meticulous when it came to details, and paid a great amount of attention to the contents of his will. He worked very carefully in drafting it to ensure that the creditors of his son-in-law Thomas Mann Randolph, Jr., would not be able to take the property that he left to his daughter.[72] We can assume that everything in the will was put there after serious thought about the language to be employed and the goals to be achieved. Every word was there for a purpose.

In this regard, consider the difference in the perception created by freeing these young men in the manner Jefferson chose and the perception that would have been created had he made a simple declaration that he was freeing Madison immediately and Eston upon his twenty-first birthday, or both young men upon his death. The first creates the superficial impression that John Hemings was the impetus for the action; he was receiving the benefit of someone's services. One Jefferson biographer, probably confused by Jefferson's creative drafting of this part of the document, assumed that Madison and Eston must have been John Hemings's sons.[73]

The strangeness of this part of the language in Jefferson's will is further illustrated by the fact that Eston Hemings was "given his time" shortly after Jefferson's death.[74] When all was said and done, the will gave John Hemings the services of Madison Hemings until Madison turned twenty-one, even though Madison was already twenty-one when the will was drafted. It also gave John Hemings the services of Eston Hemings until Eston turned twenty-one, and Jefferson's heirs then freed Eston right after Jefferson died. John Hemings can hardly be said to have received a benefit from Jefferson.

While this part of the will did not bestow a significant gift upon John Hemings, it did accomplish something else. It established an identity for Madison and Eston and hinted at a reason for their grant of freedom upon reaching twenty-one: they were apprentices to Jefferson's valued servant John Hemings. Jefferson's regard for John Hemings had rubbed off on them. Freeing Madison and Eston without reference to John Hemings would have created the clear impression that they as individuals or as a pair meant something to Thomas Jefferson.

Jefferson may well have been attempting to undercut, as much as he could, the inevitable speculation about why he freed Sally Hemings's last two sons. This could be so whether they were his sons or not. To free them without some explanation as to why they were in the company of skilled men who had rendered services to him for many years would have been too suggestive. One Petersburg newspaper reported that "Mr. Jefferson has also left free, by his will, three faithful and respectable servants, and entreats the Legislature, the favor of permitting them to remain within the Commonwealth," evidently omitting the two young men from the tally.[75]

Linking Madison and Eston to a less problematic member of the Hemings family offered an alternative to the conclusion that Jefferson must have known many would draw. In the end, if this was his reason for drafting that part of his will in this fashion, it was to no avail because Jefferson's neighbors still gossiped about the emancipation of Madison and Eston Hemings. Whether they were his sons or not, Jefferson seems to have been trying to do the best that he could in a difficult situation.

Is it likely that Madison and Eston Hemings's identities as apprentices to John Hemings would have been enough for Jefferson to take the risk of hurting his family and reputation, or is it more likely that the other part of their identities, as explained by Madison Hemings, would make him do this? There must have been a strong force countering what would have been the normal impulse to save his family and himself from negative reactions. Even if one does not accept that Sally Hemings could have been that force, that there was some compelling reason for his action is evident. It cannot have been an unconsidered judgment on his part. Jefferson took an extreme risk in this situation, and he knew that any potential fallout from that risk would be borne by Martha and her children because he would be gone. The man who could write, in another context, that the earth belongs to the living would have considered that maxim as he pondered his final legacy to his family.

It may well be that if, for whatever reason, Jefferson had given his word that Sally Hemings's children would go free at twenty-one, he would not have gone back on so monumental a promise. The notion that Jefferson's decision to free these two young men was a hardheaded practical judgment about their skills compared to those of his other slaves seems unlikely when one considers that both the emotional well-being of his family and, possibly, his reputation were at stake.

Madison Hemings on Thomas Jefferson

In addition to detailing the family history of the Hemingses, Madison Hemings presented a brief description of the domestic life of Thomas Jefferson. His statements about Jefferson's habits and personality—that he was generally of even temper and did not dwell on the disappointments of life—comport with the observations of Jefferson's relatives and acquaintances. John A. Jones, the *Waverly Watchman* editor who skewered Hemings's claims, said that Wetmore could have gained this knowledge from extant biographies of Jefferson.[76] This is not correct; the information about the Hemings family and other items about the personal lives of slaves at Monticello most likely would not have been in any biography of Jefferson at the time. In addition, Madison

Hemings made statements about Jefferson that seem to have been his own personal observations. For example, Hemings's view that Jefferson was more interested in being with his mechanics than in agricultural pursuits was not a staple of writings on Jefferson at that time. Wetmore would have gained nothing by making this point.

More importantly, Madison Hemings focused on specific things when talking about Jefferson and did so in a way that S. F. Wetmore probably would not have. When discussing his relationship with Jefferson, Hemings sounds like a man recalling disquieting memories from his childhood. From the tone of his remarks, it seems clear that he was bitter. If Hemings was telling the truth about his life, or thought that he was telling the truth, one could understand why he would be. Hemings pointedly noted that Jefferson was "not in the habit of showing partiality or fatherly affection" to him and his siblings. He contrasted this with Jefferson's "affectionate" attitude toward his grandchildren.

There are two interesting things about this part of Hemings's statement. First, Madison Hemings did not say that Jefferson never showed him or his siblings any partiality or affection. He characterized Jefferson as not being in the habit of doing so, which suggests ambivalence on Jefferson's part. If there were times when Jefferson did show some level of fatherly affection to the Hemings siblings, such acts would have raised Madison Hemings's expectations and may account for his apparent resentment.

Second, Hemings did not compare Jefferson's attitude toward him and his siblings with his attitude toward Martha Jefferson Randolph, who would have been their half sister. Instead, Hemings used as a yardstick Jefferson's attitude toward his grandchildren, who were of the same generation as the Hemings children. Martha Jefferson Randolph and her family became permanent residents of Monticello when Madison Hemings was five years old. Hemings probably knew that Thomas Jefferson loved his daughter Martha, but his displays of affection for her would not have been the likely measure of comparison for a young boy. Jefferson's demonstrations of affection for the other young children in his life—playing games with them, bragging about them, or telling them stories—would have been the measure. This is the kind of attention that a young child needs and would, most likely, never forget that he had not received enough of.

When Madison Hemings spoke of Jefferson as not being in the habit of showing him "partiality" or "fatherly affection" and then immediately brought up Jefferson's grandchildren, he was probably defining what those terms meant to him. He did not seem to be complaining that Jefferson had not given him material goods. He was saying that his father did not pay him the right kind of attention. Hemings's drawing of the contrast between himself and Jefferson's grandchildren—and not between Jefferson and his other child—reveals a preoccupation on Hemings's part. A third party inventing this story would not think to skip over Martha Randolph and be so interested in Jefferson's twelve grandchildren, whose names Hemings painstakingly listed. Madison Hemings focused on Jefferson's grandchildren for a serious reason.

Madison Hemings on Harriet Hemings

Madison Hemings's statement about his sister Harriet is the most sustained negative portrayal in the memoirs. It strongly suggests Hemings's anger toward her. He described Harriet as having "thought it in her interest, on going to Washington, to assume the role of a white woman," implying that she selfishly thought only of herself in making the decision. Hemings also said that as far as he knew, no one ever suspected that Harriet's children were "tainted with African blood." John C. Miller posited that these were the words of S. F. Wetmore because Hemings would not have thought of African blood as tainting white blood.[77] It is more likely that Hemings was being sarcastic. One can see a difference in Hemings's description of this aspect of Harriet's life and that of their brother Beverley's. Of Beverley's daughter, Madison Hemings simply stated that no one knew she had "any colored blood coursing in her veins." There was no talk of that blood "tainting" anything.

A possible reason for the undercurrent of hostility running through Hemings's remarks about Harriet appears near the end of his descriptions of her life. Hemings mentioned that "I have not heard from her for ten years, and do not know whether she is dead or alive." He made no similar statement about Beverley and spoke as though he knew what was going on in his brother's life. Madison lived in the same area as his brother Eston for some years. That the four Hemings siblings felt close to one another is suggested by the fact that Eston, who was ten years younger than Beverley and was only twelve when Beverley ran away from Monticello, named his youngest son after Beverley. Madison Hemings named one of his sons Thomas Eston and another William Beverley; he also named one of his daughters after Harriet.[78] The four seem to have kept in touch with one another for a long time after they left Monticello, but apparently Harriet at some point decided to discontinue their association. If Hemings felt it more likely that he had not heard from Harriet because she had chosen not to communicate, one could understand his resentment and his dismissive recounting of her family situation.

Why would historians ever have thought that any of this would have been of concern to S. F. Wetmore? Why would he have created an elaborate story about the whereabouts of Beverley and Harriet Hemings and have shown resentment at Harriet's failure to keep in touch? These sound more like the words of a sixty-eight-year-old black man who had lost the family of his childhood to either death or whiteness. One senses in these statements the experiences of a real person confronting true-to-life circumstances and conflicts.

Historians Consider Madison Hemings's Account

Dumas Malone Weighs the Evidence

Most commentators who have considered the main idea contained in Madison Hemings's statement seem determined to treat it as something to be defeated rather than an idea that can be objectively considered. Having decided at the outset that they did not want it to be true, they have proceeded to handle the investigation of the facts in a different manner than they do the more acceptable issues in Jefferson's life. When Jefferson took an action in another context and did not explain exactly why he acted as he did, historians have filled in the blanks based upon their supposed knowledge of him. But they have been hesitant to discuss his actions with respect to Sally Hemings and her children, lest they reveal that their knowledge of Jefferson was not so complete as they believed.

Of the scholars who have considered this question, Dumas Malone made the most reasonable attempt to explain why Jefferson showed special concern toward Sally Hemings and her children. Malone's writings on the subject leave the impression of a man who was afraid to let himself think about this issue too freely because doing so might lead him places that he was determined not to go. One has no sense that he approached this material with the same degree of curiosity or insight that characterized most of his other writing about Jefferson.

Malone's basic approach to the evidence of a liaison was to avoid the subject as much as possible. In the fourth volume of his biography, *Jefferson the President: The First Term, 1801–1805,* he included an appendix that dealt with what he called "The Miscegenation Legend." There Malone gave an account of the origins of the story and set forth his reasons why he did not believe that it could have been true. He acknowledged that there were circumstances in Jefferson's life and actions toward the Hemings family that might have fueled the charge, namely, his preferential treatment of Hemings family members. However, he posited that the catalyst for this preferential treatment was Elizabeth Hemings, not Sally Hemings. Because Elizabeth had been the mistress of John Wayles and the mother of some of his children, Jefferson associated her with his dead wife, Martha. He felt a responsibility toward the family because Martha evidently did. It was, therefore, out of respect and love for his wife's memory that Jefferson treated the Hemingses with such favor.[79]

This is a plausible explanation as far as it goes. The fact is that Sally Hemings's membership in a family that Jefferson trusted and dealt with so well in general may have made it easier for him to have been involved with her. If he was going to be involved with a slave woman, it would most likely have been a member of the Hemings family. Elizabeth Hemings may have been the reason the special relationship began; she may not have been the reason that it continued.

What Malone never did was reveal the extent to which Sally Hemings's children and she herself fared exceptionally well even compared to Elizabeth Hemings and her other children. As much as Jefferson may have liked Elizabeth Hemings, he did not free all of the children she had with Wayles. It is true that three of these children were female, and this may have prevented Jefferson from emancipating them. However, Jefferson did not free Elizabeth's youngest son by John Wayles, Peter, and he did allow Sally Hemings's daughter to go free when she came of age.

Malone dealt specifically with Madison Hemings's statement but did not mention the alleged promise to free Sally Hemings's children at twenty-one. He did not discuss Beverley Hemings at all, so readers could not judge whether Beverley's departure from Monticello supported the substance of "the legend." He noted Harriet Hemings's departure but did not say that she left at age twenty-one. He accepted the "oral tradition that is not established fact" of Edmund Bacon that Harriet was not Jefferson's daughter.

To dispel the notion that Sally Hemings's children received preferential treatment, Malone mentioned that Jefferson freed other Hemingses, Robert and James, and noted that no one had commented upon that. He did not tell readers that Robert had to buy his freedom from Jefferson, and he did not address the possibility that Jefferson may have had to promise freedom to James Hemings in order to get him to return from France to the United States.[80] There is no evidence that Sally Hemings's children obtained their freedom under similar circumstances. In Harriet's case, we know that Jefferson gave her money rather than making her pay to leave.

A central tenet of the defense of Thomas Jefferson rests on the notion that there is no evidence that Sally Hemings herself received any special or preferential treatment from him.[81] This is so despite the fact that the evidence of preferential treatment was always immediately obvious. What could a woman who was a slave and a mother want most in the world?

Considering the normal thoughts and feelings of human beings would make it clear that the grant of freedom to a slave woman's children would have been the highest and most profound form of special treatment that a mother could receive, more important to her than her own freedom. Thomas Jefferson gave this to Sally Hemings four times. All of her children—even her daughter—went free. He did this for no other slave woman. The failure to see this as an example of her preferential treatment can only be counted as willful. If a white woman had children, and there were rumors of an affair between her and a particular man, and that man had done a similarly important turn for that woman's children (say, sending them all to college, although that in no way compares to a grant of freedom), it is hard to imagine that historians would not perceive the man as having done something for the mother and would not wonder about the man's relationship to her.

Popular Biographies and Madison Hemings in the 1990s

Though flawed, Malone's discussion of some of the circumstances in Jefferson's life that might have encouraged people to believe that Madison Hemings was his son remains one of the more thoughtful treatments of the issue. His efforts did not settle the matter, and the combination of Fawn Brodie's book and an extremely popular fictional treatment of the alleged Jefferson-Hemings affair gave the story added credibility among the public. In the face of this, some Jefferson biographers decided to depart from Malone's more genteel approach. The most aggressive of all was Willard Sterne Randall, whose book *Thomas Jefferson: A Life* appeared in 1993. Although Randall did not write extensively about the Sally Hemings story, what he wrote deserves comment, for his work is a telling example of what can happen when the desire to control the public's thinking about this controversy outstrips the desire to render a fair assessment and recounting of the facts.

   Willard Sterne Randall wrote about Madison Hemings's statement, and Hemings himself, contemptuously. He described Fawn Brodie as having

> dusted off a highly inaccurate and uncorroborated memoir by a man who described himself as Madison Jefferson, son of Jefferson and Sally Hemings. The account published by an abolitionist journalist only in the *Pike County (Ohio) Republican* in 1873, where the aged former slave was homesteading, resembles many uncorroborated slave narratives and cannot be credited. It is full of hearsay about events that the would-be former house slave could not have seen or known firsthand, if only because of his age, and must be put down as mere gossip about a great man published in the absence of journalistic standards much less historical ones.[82]

The first thing to note is that Madison Hemings's memoirs are not highly inaccurate. Historians have used Hemings's statement as a source of information about Thomas Jefferson and Monticello.[83] If Randall had evidence that the memoirs were highly inaccurate, he would have done his readers a service and made his case stronger by detailing the inaccuracies. Criticizing the accuracy of Hemings's memoirs is a common technique among some Jefferson defenders. They usually do not go on to say what those errors are. If they list any inaccuracies, it is never more than one or two, and the ones they cite are not material errors or are just differences of opinion. Even Merrill Peterson, who emphatically discounted the main thrust of Hemings's statement, wrote, "The recollection checks remarkably well with the data accumulated by scholars on Jefferson's domestic life and the Monticello slaves."[84]

As to the point of the statement being uncorroborated, Randall was in error. Israel Jefferson corroborated Hemings's statement nine months after Hemings had spoken with the *Pike County (Ohio) Republican*. The recollections of both men are conveniently placed one right after another in Fawn Brodie's biography of Jefferson. Even if one does not believe the substance of Israel Jefferson's statements, it is not correct to tell readers that no one corroborated Madison Hemings's account of his parentage. This is an example of a historian rendering nonexistent some available evidence that hurt his position.

Madison Hemings never referred to himself as "Madison Jefferson" in his memoirs, and there is no evidence that he ever did so in any other context. Randall somehow conflated the two names Madison Hemings and Israel Jefferson into "Madison Jefferson." After doing this, he was left with one person named Madison who told a story, and no second person named Jefferson who corroborated it.

One wonders just what is a "would-be former house slave"? When the phrase "would-be" is used as an adjective, it refers to an individual's desire to be something. Did Madison Hemings want to be a "former house slave"? How did Randall know that he did? What is it about a "former house slave" that would make that person a presumptive liar?

Randall also wrote, with no citation, that Sally Hemings was "probably the daughter of Nelson Jones, a white carpenter at Monticello." Earlier scholars generally have accepted Madison Hemings's statement that John Wayles was the father of Sally Hemings.[85] Because Wayles was also the father of Jefferson's wife, Martha, some have theorized that Sally Hemings and Martha Jefferson resembled one another, making it understandable how Jefferson might have developed affection for Hemings. If she were the daughter of Nelson Jones, however, that possibility would be obviated. Given the degree of the scholarly concordance on this point, even among those most hostile to the Hemings story, Randall should have explained how he came to this conclusion.

Randall was evidently speaking of Joseph Neilson. The difficulty with the idea that Sally Hemings was the daughter of Joseph Neilson, or Nelson, is that Hemings was two years old when her mother came to live at Monticello, where Joseph Neilson was employed as a carpenter. There is no evidence that Elizabeth Hemings and Joseph Neilson knew each other before that time. It was John Hemings, Jefferson's master carpenter, who was the child of Joseph Neilson and Elizabeth Hemings, conceived and born after Elizabeth and her family came to Monticello.[86]

Randall ignored one of the most important pieces of evidence supporting the existence of a Jefferson-Hemings liaison, Jefferson's freeing of Hemings's children. Nor did he mention the departures of Beverley Hemings or Harriet Hemings. His account of the terms of Jefferson's will states that Madison and Eston Hemings were the sons of John Hemings, rather than his nephews. In fact, Randall's index lists both "Madison Jefferson" and Madison Hemings, indicating that these were two separate people. It is hard to understand how he might think this. Madison Hemings's statement makes it clear that he was named in Jefferson's will. He said that Eston was his brother, that Sally Hemings was his mother, and that John Hemings was "the youngest son of my grandmother." Madison Hemings's identity should have been clear to Randall. That it was not is both frightening and ironic considering his dismissal of "Madison Jefferson's" memoirs as "gossip about a great man published in the absence of journalistic standards, much less historical ones." Randall purported to dispute a story whose essential details he seems not to have discovered.[87]

Randall also challenged other details that touch upon the life of Madison Hemings. He noted that "Brodie and other writers since her book was published in 1974" used as evidence "descriptions of a host of mulattoes at Monticello who resembled Jefferson, and a declaration that one could even play the fiddle!"[88] But Brodie never claimed that there was a host of mulattoes at Monticello who looked like Thomas Jefferson. She merely repeated what Jefferson's grandson had said about Sally Hemings's children: that they all looked like Jefferson, one of them so closely that if he was seen at twilight, one might mistake him for Jefferson. As to the fiddle-playing slave who had Randall aping Dr. Johnson on women preachers, it was Isaac Jefferson, a Monticello slave whose memoirs were taken down in 1842, who stated that Madison Hemings became a "fine fiddle player." His recollections have been accepted and used for a number of years for many enlightening details about the personal habits and characteristics of Thomas Jefferson. Even Randall cited Isaac Jefferson for a number of propositions, though he erroneously described him as part of the Hemings family.[89] It is from Isaac that we know that Thomas Jefferson rode around Monticello singing most of time, talked with his arms folded, and bowed to people upon meeting them. Yet Randall characterized another of Isaac Jefferson's statements as an invention of "Brodie and other writers." Why? Because the substance of the statement—that one of the alleged children of Jefferson shared his interest in and ability to play the violin—invites the question whether Jefferson had anything to do with that child's possessing and learning to play the instrument.

The truth is that all of Sally Hemings's sons, Beverley, Madison, and Eston, played the violin, with Eston becoming a professional violinist. No one who was seriously and objectively thinking about whether Thomas Jefferson might have been these young men's father could fail to wonder whether this was a mere coincidence. Even if only one of Hemings's sons played the violin, it might suggest that Jefferson took an inordinate interest in her offspring, for he most likely would have provided the instrument that the young man played. The level of suggestiveness is substantially raised by the fact that all three of Hemings's sons played the violin. There is a distinct possibility (if not probability given other items of evidence) that their access to violins and ability to play the instrument might have come as the result of actions taken by the best-known violinist at Monticello.

After considering Willard Sterne Randall's comments on the alleged Jefferson-Hemings liaison, it is hard to escape the conclusion that his hostility to the idea prevented him from thoroughly reviewing and considering it. Because of his prejudices, his readers were deprived of a fair opportunity to both know and weigh the information that has been offered as evidence to support the existence of the relationship. His lack of knowledge of the most basic facts about the Hemings family seriously undermines his energetic attempt to dispute the substance of this story.

From Jefferson to the Hemingses

If one changes the perspective a little and moves from the Jefferson-centered approach to focus on Madison Hemings and his family, it is possible to view the evidence in a different light. While it is true that Thomas Jefferson means more to American history than the Hemings family, it is important to try to learn as much as we can about the lives of the people who were held in slavery in this country. In this regard we can ask, How common was it, at that point in history, for a slave woman who was not the mistress of the slave master to see all of her children go free? The answer, almost certainly, is that it was not common.

Not only did all of Sally Hemings's children go free, they all went free in what could be considered the prime of their lives, as young adults with long futures ahead of them. Their coming of age was the signal for Jefferson to let them go. This happened to no other person or group of slaves he owned. The three young men had all learned a trade and a skill that would help them support themselves. The daughter was sent away from Monticello with some financial support. Even scholars who dismissed the notion of a Jefferson-Hemings relationship did not believe that Jefferson would have done this without making sure that the young woman would be safe and supported once she arrived at her destination. Think of what an enormous victory this was for a slave mother, to see all her children freed. Think of this good fortune and remember that when one does something for the children of a mother, one is doing something for the mother herself.

It is necessary for those who maintain that there is no strong evidence to support the idea of a relationship between Jefferson and Sally Hemings to separate out the destinies of Hemings and each of her children. Even though they were separate individuals, they had a relationship that linked them together. They were a family, and we should consider their remarkable destiny as a family. In the 1940s the loss of seven brothers on a warship was viewed differently than the loss of seven unrelated individuals. The tragedy was especially poignant because it happened to people who were part of a unit, and Americans mourned that unit's terrible misfortune. Similarly, the fact that four siblings born into slavery went free just as they reached adulthood should be viewed differently than if they were four unconnected individuals who went free. We should ask not just, Why should those four people as individuals have been so lucky? We should also ask, How could that family have been so fortunate?

That Thomas Jefferson, by both omission and commission, had a hand in their good fortune is important, and it is both reasonable and necessary to ask why. Jefferson knew who these young people were as individuals, and he knew that he was taking actions with respect to individuals who were part of an extremely specialized unit: the children of Sally Hemings. To be sure, they belonged to other units, the larger unit of slaves at Monticello and the subunit of Hemings family slaves. The question is which membership, for the purposes of what happened to them, was the most important? Was it that they were slaves on the plantation? There were many other slaves on the plantation who were not freed, so membership in that group could not have been important. Could it have been because they were Hemings family members?

While it is true that the Hemings family was treated specially by Jefferson, no other unit of Hemingses was treated as well. Was their membership in the unit of Sally Hemings's children the chief reason for their good fortune, and if so, why was that membership significant to Thomas Jefferson?

An Alternative Explanation

Historians have been so intent upon ignoring the obvious fact that Sally Hemings's four children were treated specially by Thomas Jefferson that they failed to discern that there might have been another possible reason for their singularity. Perhaps Jefferson freed Sally Hemings's children because, regardless of the exact identity of their father, they were, according to his calculations and interpretation of the laws of Virginia, white.

In 1815, in a letter correcting an erroneous statement of law that he had made to a man who had asked when a black person could be considered a white person under the laws of Virginia, Jefferson wrote out an algebraic equation demonstrating that after "three crossings" with whites, the black person was legally white. By this definition, Sally Hemings's children were, in fact, Caucasian. Their father, whoever he was, was white, their grandfathers were white, and their great-grandfathers were white. Jefferson went on to say that if such a person were to be emancipated, that person would become a "citizen of the United States for all intents and purposes."[90]

It is understandable that Thomas Jefferson may have been concerned about keeping white people in bondage. This would be particularly so if the "white slaves" were the children of his nephews—the sons of Jefferson's sister Martha and Dabney Carr, Jefferson's closest friend when they were young men.[91] He may have felt that the best he could do was to keep the Hemings-Carr children at Monticello until they reached adulthood and then let them go once they became adults. Although no family member mentioned the children's family connection as a possible reason for their freedom, Jefferson's granddaughter Ellen did say that Jefferson let four slaves who were "sufficiently white to pass for white men" leave Monticello, characterizing his acts as being in furtherance of a Jeffersonian "principle" (see Appendix E).[92]

Coolidge's explanation of why Jefferson allowed those slaves to run away is particularly interesting because of its improbability. Not only is there no evidence that Jefferson, as a principle, allowed slaves who were white enough to pass for white go free, there is, in fact, abundant evidence to contradict this notion. One of the remarkable features of Monticello noted by visitors as early as the 1790s and continuing through Jefferson's retirement was the great prevalence of white slaves at the plantation. Visitors to the mountain before

Sally Hemings's children were even born reported seeing many slaves who had no visible trace of African ancestry in them and were whiter than many whites.[93] Eston Hemings was described as being "light bronze colored" with a "visible admixture" of African blood. His wife, also of mixed parentage, was described as being much whiter than he, and their children as completely white in appearance.[94] Thus, there is some evidence that some slaves at Monticello looked whiter than at least one of the Hemings siblings, yet those slaves were not freed. Moreover, one wonders why Jefferson would have chosen the period in his life when he was in financial extremis to free these slaves. There were many better years between the 1790s and the early 1820s when he could have exercised that option. That Jefferson did not do so when he was in a sounder financial position—and when his opposition to slavery seemed more vigorous—must be considered.

The most important reason for doubting a link between Coolidge's explanation and Jefferson's interpretation of the state's laws is that there is a big difference between being white enough to pass for white and being white, which is what, according to Virginia law, Sally Hemings's children were. A lawyer and former legislator would have recognized and responded to the different issues raised by these two circumstances. A major purpose of having a numerical standard for determining racial classifications was to prevent someone who was only white enough to pass for white from being eligible to be considered a white person. Evidence shows that Jefferson knew the law about such matters. But there is no evidence that he would have been inclined to follow a policy of freeing a person who was seven-eights white. It might be a reasonable inference that he would be, but there is no evidence that he was.

The lack of evidence from any contemporary source that Jefferson freed the Hemings children because they were white militates against the idea. Because it would have been a justifiable reason for treating them differently and for freeing them—one that would not have provided any cause for personal embarrassment on Jefferson's part—one wonders why any motivations he may have had along these lines would have remained secret. If the children's legal whiteness was the issue, why did no one else in the Jefferson-Randolph family know of Jefferson's concern and his decision to resolve the problem through emancipation?

For example, it seems unlikely that Jefferson would not have mentioned to at least one of the executors of his estate, his grandson T. J. Randolph, that he was freeing Madison and Eston Hemings in his will because they were white by law. What of Beverley and Harriet Hemings? The living area at Monticello is fairly compact. Surely T. J. Randolph, who grew up with Beverley and Harriet Hemings, would have noticed their absence and asked about their departure. Why wouldn't Jefferson have mentioned the law to his grandson at that point? If questioned by T. J. Randolph (or Ellen Coolidge), Jefferson most likely would not have explained, "I let them go because they are white enough to pass for white." Actions based upon such an explanation would have undermined the structure of Virginia law on racial classifications and slavery, issues about which Jefferson would not have been careless. Ellen Coolidge's white enough to pass for white statement does not begin to approach the mathematical definition of legal whiteness, to which Jefferson would have been greatly attuned and which he could have explained to his family without a moment's hesitation.

T. J. Randolph was in his early thirties when the Hemings children began to leave Monticello. He was his grandfather's confidant. He would have been mature enough to be told that the Hemings children were white by Virginia law, and yet there is not one hint of this reason in any statement or writing that he ever made about this issue. Randolph later said that he had found out, at least twelve years before Jefferson's death, that one (or both) of Jefferson's nephews was the father of the Hemings children. Randolph said that the nephews' activities with Sally Hemings were well known at Monticello, and one can assume that Jefferson had heard the stories too. If Jefferson had said that he knew that the father of the Hemings children was white, and therefore her children could be considered white, there would be no reason for T. J. Randolph—or any other member of the Randolph family—to think that Jefferson was the white man in question.

Had Jefferson told T. J. Randolph about the Hemings children's legal status, Randolph probably would have mentioned this to other members of his family, particularly his sister Ellen Randolph Coolidge, with whom he discussed the issue of the paternity of the Hemings children. Members of the Jefferson-Randolph family were willing to speak about their Carr relatives' involvement in miscegenation among themselves and to others but did not make the connection between those circumstances and the Hemings children's racial status. In correspondence with her husband about this issue, Ellen Coolidge described the emancipation of Hemings's children. After noting that two of them were freed upon Jefferson's death, she described the other two has having been "suffered to absent themselves permanently" from Monticello. She gave no indication for any legal basis for their departure.[95]

If there were such a rational explanation for his freeing of Sally Hemings's children upon their reaching majority, it seems likely that over the years, even before Beverley, Harriet, Madison, and Eston were freed, Jefferson would have discussed this with someone. One could even suppose that Jefferson had determined the children were white, told Sally Hemings this, and that is why she knew and could tell her children that they would be free at twenty-one. Were this the case, there should be some correspondence or statement from members of his family—who talked in some depth to one another and others about the parentage of Hemings's children—citing their legal whiteness as a reason.

One must also ask, if it was the whiteness of Sally Hemings's children that motivated Jefferson to free them, why did he not use the law to free Beverley and Harriet formally, rather than allowing them to run away? By emancipating them, Jefferson would have recognized their correct status under the law and would have given them what they, as white people, would have been entitled to have: their citizenship. Thomas Jefferson, of all people, would have understood the importance of this as he had helped define what that term was supposed to mean for Americans. Letting Beverley and Harriet run away without formal emancipation deprived them of the chief benefit of whiteness and made them fugitives.

Why take this tack, and not the one provided for by what Jefferson believed to be the laws of Virginia? To emancipate Beverley and Harriet formally would have required the creation of a document that would become part of the public record.[96] Whether he was their father or not, one could understand why Jefferson would not want to draw attention to his serial manumission of his alleged slave mistress's children. By allowing (and helping) them run away, Jefferson avoided a public declaration of his desires with regard to their status. Because Beverley and Harriet Hemings left Virginia, Jefferson also avoided having to petition the state to allow them to remain within its boundaries.

This raises an important issue concerning Jefferson's character. If Jefferson was truly concerned about the issue of keeping white people as slaves, and if Beverley and Harriet Hemings were not his children, choosing to allow them to run away over formally freeing them seems a staggering example of cowardice on Jefferson's part. Jefferson, in effect, would have deprived these two young white people of the chance to enjoy the benefits of citizenship in order to protect himself from the resurgence of gossip about an allegation that he knew to be false.

If Beverley and Harriet were his children, his choice, though troubling, is more understandable. One can even sympathize with the fear and inner turmoil that might have led Jefferson to adopt a strategy designed to hide real-life circumstances that could have given him and his family significant problems. Aside from the issue of reputation, miscegenation was against the law in Virginia. Freeing Beverley and Harriet in a way that avoided the scrutiny that could lead to the discovery of evidence of miscegenation would make sense, even if it meant that Beverley and Harriet would live with insecurity.

One could argue that it was best for Beverley and Harriet Hemings to disappear into the white world without being formally freed. A person who was technically white and a citizen due to emancipation would still have a record of having been a slave and having once been considered black. Madison Hemings said that both his sister and brother married into white families that were in good circumstances. It is unlikely that they would have been able to do this if it were known that their freedom was based upon emancipation papers given them by Thomas Jefferson. With no papers, they could rely on their appearance and whatever training they had at Monticello in order just to be white. However, there was no reason to suppose that anyone had to find out about their past. Beverley and Harriet Hemings could have had their emancipation papers recorded in Virginia, moved to another state, hidden their past by assuming a new name (as they indeed did), and been free in every sense of the word. Instead, as runaways, they were technically white but retained the status of slaves.

Why did Jefferson not just allow Madison and Eston to run away? We do not know about Madison, but Eston was white enough to pass for white in at least one community. If both young men were white enough to pass for white, why not just let them go as their siblings had gone? If Madison Hemings's memoirs are correct, the answer seems to be that Jefferson ran out of time. If he had made a promise to Madison's mother that he would free all of her children when they reached twenty-one, by the time her last two children were approaching this age, Jefferson knew that he was at the end of his life. Malone noted that although Jefferson suffered periodic health problems during his final years, his health did not really break until 1825.[97] Madison was twenty at this point, and Eston was eighteen. Jefferson knew that there was a chance that his creditors would attempt to take his property—which included his slaves—in order to satisfy his debts. Had Madison and Eston run away during this period of turmoil, his creditors might have made a more concerted attempt to retrieve them, and they, unlike their older siblings, might have missed their chance at freedom. Because slaves could be attached to satisfy a decedent's debts, Jefferson must have appealed to his creditors to allow him to free a few slaves, Madison and Eston included. In this way he could be assured that they would not be sold.

Perhaps formal freedom was not the real issue for Jefferson and the Hemingses. Jefferson's formal request in his will that the legislature allow the two men to remain in the state could not have been granted without their legal emancipation. This may have been important, not so much to Madison and Eston, but to their mother, for whom they were responsible. When Eston was freed soon after Jefferson's death, the two brothers took their mother to live with them. There is some indication that it was she who was keeping at least Madison in Virginia, because he left the state almost immediately after she died.

While Beverley and Harriet Hemings could still have been vulnerable to Jefferson's creditors, by the time Jefferson made his final will they had been gone from Monticello for four years. It would have been less likely that creditors would pursue them, or be successful in that pursuit, because the two probably had established identities and lives that could give them a measure of protection. If Madison Hemings is to be believed, with death closing in on him, Jefferson had no choice but to make the formal and public declaration of his decision to free the last remaining Hemings siblings and to arrange to have them remain in the place that their mother seems to have wanted to be.

Conclusion

Was Madison Hemings telling the truth when he said that Thomas Jefferson and Sally Hemings were lovers and that Jefferson promised his mother that their children would be free at twenty-one? Some might say definitely yes, others would say definitely no, and depending upon the time of day, I might agree with either position. What I would not waver on is my belief that no fair-minded person could decide that the circumstances I have recounted amount to "no evidence" that the story could be true or that it would be "irresponsible" to believe that Madison Hemings was telling the truth.

Hemings's memoirs cannot be dismissed as the concoction of a northern carpetbagger out to make southerners look bad. Nor can it fairly be portrayed as the outlandish tale that Jefferson defenders and other commentators would have the American public believe. Hemings's statement, along with other circumstances described in later chapters, makes it clear that rather than discussing the issue of a Jefferson-Hemings liaison in terms of its possibility, one should, instead, consider its relative degree of probability.

2

James Callender

What we have got to know, so far as possible, is what
actually happened in the world.

—W. E. B. Du Bois, "The Propaganda of History"

Iᴎ 1802, during Thomas Jefferson's first term as president of the United
States, James Callender made the first public allegation that Jefferson had
been involved in a sexual relationship with Sally Hemings. The response to
Callender's account has always been an important part of the defense of
Jefferson against the charge of miscegenation because it is possible that without Callender, the public might never have known the name Sally Hemings.[1]
S. F. Wetmore might not have been so inclined to believe that Madison Hemings was the son of the president or to print his story had Callender's charges
never appeared in print. Over the years the basic strategy employed in dealing
with Callender and his exposé has been to use the outrageousness and absur-
dity of Callender himself to make the notion of a Jefferson-Hemings liaison
equally outrageous and absurd; in effect, to make the evil Callender personify
the nature of the charge of race mixing on the part of Thomas Jefferson.[2]

Callender's character has made the use of this tactic extremely easy. He
was a despicable individual ruled by venom and racism. Ironically, Callender
started out as an admirer of Jefferson, and Jefferson was impressed with
Callender, thinking that his journalistic talents would be of use to the Republican party. As time passed and Callender became more intemperate in his
descriptions of their Federalist foes, Jefferson became wary of him and turned
aside Callender's attempts to get closer. Jefferson continued, however, to give
Callender small sums of money, describing them as "charity."[3]

Eventually Callender's vituperative style landed him in jail in Richmond
on a charge of violating the Federalists' Sedition Act. Jefferson considered the

act a violation of the Constitution and promised to pardon all those who had been convicted under it once he took office. He kept the promise, but Callender had already served his sentence by that time. Jefferson's attorney general directed Callender's jailer, federal marshal David Meade Randolph, to reimburse Callender for the $200 fine that he had paid. Fawn Brodie posited that it was during his time in jail that Callender began to hear gossip about Jefferson's private life and decided to look into the matter himself.[4]

After his release Callender went to Charlottesville to make inquiries into the stories about Jefferson and Hemings. Meanwhile, David Meade Randolph refused to follow the attorney general's order to repay Callender. When Callender complained, Jefferson made arrangements with James Monroe to give the impoverished journalist fifty dollars. Callender then went to Washington and met with Jefferson's secretary of state, James Madison. During that meeting, in addition to discussing reimbursement of his fine, Callender demanded that he be made postmaster in Richmond. Madison later indicated to Jefferson that Callender was seeking to impress a lady friend by obtaining a prestigious job. He also apparently believed that he deserved an appointment because of his journalistic services in support of Jefferson's successful candidacy for president. He had gone to jail for attacking Jefferson's political enemies.[5]

Upon hearing that Callender was in Washington and seemed intent on causing trouble, Jefferson directed his secretary Meriwether Lewis to give Callender another fifty dollars. After Lewis reported that Callender was threatening some form of blackmail, Jefferson withdrew the draft. In a letter to James Monroe describing the situation, Jefferson declared that "he knows nothing of me that I am not willing to declare to the world myself."[6]

By this time Callender, stung by Jefferson's refusal to give him the job at Richmond, had moved squarely into the role of enemy of Jefferson, and he began a steady barrage of attacks on the new president. After a Republican newspaper alleged that Callender had mistreated his late wife, he decided to retaliate by reproducing the stories about Sally Hemings that he had learned from members of the Virginia gentry.[7]

That Callender was angered by Jefferson's distancing himself from him and refusal to give him a position is clear. Other evidence suggests that these were not the only reasons for Callender's ire: he seems to have been genuinely upset at the notion of Jefferson's involvement in miscegenation. Callender was greatly offended by the extent of the easy contact between white men and black women in the South. He found Richmond's "black dances" particularly repellent because they were often attended by white males of the local gentry. Upon his arrival in that town, Callender led a campaign to shut down the dances because married white men were using these occasions to meet and consort with black women. He also exposed local white men who went to theaters and other outings with black women.[8] There is no wonder that he seized upon the charge against Jefferson and the fact that some of Jefferson's neighbors were willing to confirm the story. Dumas Malone took note of Callender's statement that the "aristocracy of his . . . neighborhood" during a stay in Loudoun County was "one of the vilest in America" but did not explore why Callender might have described rural Virginia with this tone of moral censure.[9]

Callender brought the full force of his hatred for black people to bear in his descriptions of the Jefferson-Hemings relationship. His first statement on the subject, though overheated, was mild compared to what came later.

> It is well known that the man, whom it delighteth the people to honor, keeps and for many years has kept, as his concubine, one of his slaves. Her name is SALLY. The name of her eldest son is Tom. His features are said to bear a striking though sable resemblance to those of the president himself. The boy is ten or twelve years of age. His mother went to France in the same vessel with Mr. Jefferson and his two daughters. The delicacy of this arrangement must strike every portion of common sensibility. What a sublime pattern for an American ambassador to place before the eyes of two young ladies! . . .
>
> Some years ago the story had once or twice been hinted at in Rind's Federalist. At that time, we believed the surmise to be an absolute calumny. . . .
>
> By this wench Sally, our president has had several children. There is not an individual in the neighbourhood of Charlottesville who does not believe the story, and not a few who know it. . . . Mute! Mute! Mute! Yes very Mute! will all those republican printers of biographical information be upon this point.

Callender later corrected his error about the circumstances of Sally Hemings's trip to Paris. Apparently his sources let him know that she had not gone to France with Jefferson but had traveled at a later date with his daughter Maria.[10]

It was not enough for Callender to state that Jefferson kept a slave mistress. As damaging as such an allegation would have been to a man of Jefferson's position and reputation, this was not an unheard-of arrangement in the South. The situation called for more. In later articles Callender went out of his way to attack Sally Hemings personally, referring to her as a "slut as common as the pavement" and to her children as "a litter." He christened the son who was said to have resembled Jefferson "President Tom" and referred to him as "our little mulatto president." At one point he referred to Jefferson as sending to "the kitchen or perhaps the pigstye" for Hemings. This was not simply an attempt to reveal a breach of etiquette on the president's part. With each missive Callender was reminding white southerners (race mixers and non–race mixers alike) of their professed belief that blacks were subhuman. He was accusing Thomas Jefferson of something on the order of bestiality.[11]

This is not a pretty story. Still, while one might hesitate to believe such a man even if he said that the sun rises in the East and sets in the West, the fact that he was a loathsome character does not mean that he always lied. Callender was a blackmailer, but blackmailers who lie are not particularly successful because it is the possession of at least some truth that makes the blackmail effective. As Michael Durey has pointed out in his biography of Callender, the journalist had a good record in reporting the basic truth of matters. Exaggeration, rather than fabrication, was Callender's chief journalistic flaw. He had been right about his charge that the married Alexander Hamilton had been involved in an affair with a married woman. He had been right about his other allegation against Jefferson, that as a young man Jefferson had attempted to seduce the wife of a friend.[12]

Callender anticipated the arguments that Jefferson's defenders of that era and today would make against him and in favor of the president. Three weeks after his initial story on the alleged Jefferson-Hemings liaison, Callender, putting himself in the role of Jefferson defender, wrote: "It cannot possibly be true. A thing so brutal, so disgraceful. A thing so foreign to Mr. Jefferson's character. The scoundrel has been disappointed and affronted, you know and he seeks revenge."[13]

That he was out to exact revenge for Jefferson's refusal to bring him into his inner circle and that he had a deep and abiding hatred of blacks are both relevant considerations when assessing the merits of what Callender wrote about Thomas Jefferson. Certainly, questioning the motives of an individual who had shown himself to have been a snake seems more legitimate than doubting those of people like Madison Hemings and S. F. Wetmore. The question remains, Does having a motive for telling a story mean that the story is false? No, people who are looking for the truth in this matter are not absolved from the need to subject the substance of the statement to scrutiny.

This is particularly so when one considers that the story had been told by others before Callender. To the extent that Americans know anything about James Callender, they probably have the impression that he originated the claim that Thomas Jefferson kept a slave mistress. Commentators, historians, and journalists alike regularly promote the notion that James Callender's anger at Jefferson for not giving him a job led him to invent a story about the president having a slave mistress. At the same time the impression has been created that no one else believed the story at the time.

Neither of these impressions is true. At least one other newspaper editor considered publishing the story as early as 1799, a full three years before Callender's piece appeared. In addition, while taking note of Callender's charge, an editor of a Federalist newspaper indicated that he had heard members of the Virginia gentry talk about Jefferson having a slave mistress for some period before Callender's writings. The editor went on to say—rather disingenuously since he had raised the issue at the heart of Callender's writing—that as there was no proof of it, the paper would not reprint Callender's entire piece. Merrill Peterson acknowledged that the rumors were circulating before Callender's story was published. But he presented the rumors as having arisen solely out of partisan concerns. He wrote: "The beginnings of the tale are obscure. Federalists whispered it in the bitter campaign of 1800; but it did not become public knowledge until 1802 when James T. Callender included it among his libels of the President." [14]

One early biographer of Jefferson, Henry Randall, stated that Jefferson's neighbors had given information to Callender. [15] Because those who lived in the neighborhood of Monticello probably were not all members of the Federalist party, it is likely that some of the talk arose out of the human need to gossip, and not as part of a master Federalist plot to destroy Thomas Jefferson. Most importantly, the story does not seem to have sprung forth full blown from James Callender.

Other Federalist newspaper editors of the day, while waiting for Jefferson to deny the story, claimed to have done investigations themselves and found the basic substance of the story to be true. [16] Of course, these people were Federalists, and the allegations against Jefferson the Republican arose in the midst of an extremely bitter political battle. As one would expect, the Republican newspapers defended Jefferson against Callender's charge, and the Federalist newspapers were happy to have a weapon to use against him. Thus, the Federalist editors would have had a motive to claim that they had found proof of the story themselves. Yet, while it is appropriate to be skeptical of their claims, one cannot take the position that because they were Federalists, the newspaper editors were lying when they said they had confirmed the story. The editors who spoke on the subject did not parrot Callender's line about Jefferson's alleged relationship with Hemings. It is a long way from Callender's base accusations about "pig-stye[s]" and "slut[s]"—which he never really rose above—to the words of the editor of the *Frederick-Town Herald,* who wrote:

Other information assures us that Mr. Jefferson's Sally and their children are real persons, and that the woman herself has a room to herself at Monticello in the character of a seamstress to the family, if not as a house-keeper; that she is an industrious and orderly creature in her behavior, but that her intimacy with her master is well known, and that on this account she is treated by the rest of his house as one much above the level of the other servants. Her son, whom Callender calls president Tom, we also are assured, bears a strong likeness to Mr. Jefferson. We make bold to mention these circumstances of confirmation, because although the subject is a delicate one, we cannot see why we are to affect any great squeamishness against speaking plainly of what we consider as an undoubted fact interesting to the public.[17]

This tone is completely different from Callender's. Some of the details in the passage suggest that the newspaper did some independent checking on the Hemings story. For example, the assertion that Sally Hemings was a seamstress is supported by Madison Hemings, who described his mother as being responsible for doing "light sewing." Callender did not speak of this, and it is not something that journalists could have guessed.

The description of Sally Hemings as "industrious and orderly" cannot be confirmed by existing descriptions of her. But Sally Hemings was a mother, and we can perhaps know something of her by knowing things about the children she raised. We know that she had three sons who became talented artisans and musicians, who were very hardworking, responsible individuals. Three of her children passed for white, two of them marrying into white families "in good circumstances," which suggest that someone had seen to it that they received a level of training above what one would expect. All of her children married and raised children of their own, some of whom went on to become prominent businessmen and citizens.[18] As in most families, the origins of these circumstances can be found in a mother's handiwork. Therefore, it is fair to feel justified in trusting the assertion that Sally Hemings was "industrious and orderly," a contradiction of Callender's characterization of her.

That other Federalist editors did not speak with one voice about the allegations also can be seen in Callender's appraisal of the editor of the *Gazette of the United States,* who declined to publish the full text of his story about Jefferson and Hemings, saying that it was old gossip that had not been substantiated. That editor went on to say that the story was so foul that if it was not true, Callender should be prosecuted for libel. Callender responded: "Mr. Bronson hardly knows what he speaks about when he conceits that, if this mulatto charge is *untrue* the author could be prosecuted for *libel.* . . . The latter part of his paragraph amounts to nothing but a silly attempt at looker

wiser than his neighbours. There is no question but what Bronson is very willing to tell the very world which he knows of Jefferson, and if he had been
master of SALLY's affair, the world would *long been made acquainted with it*." [19]
To Callender, the other editors were upset merely because he had been the
first to dare to put the story in print.

Does the fact that others had been saying for some years before
Callender came onto the scene that Jefferson had a slave mistress mean that
the story was true? No. Do the claims of others to have checked into and
confirmed the basic thrust of the story make the story true? No. But these
facts can alter the way one views the information that Callender published.
If a person whom you know to be contemptible says that a thing is true, you
may be inclined to disbelieve it, even without full consideration. But if you
later discover that other people had said the same thing years before, you
would have a different reaction to the statement. You might not believe it,
but you would be more inclined to think that it was possibly true. There is
a difference between an individual's making up a story out of whole cloth
and maliciously repeating a story that has been told by others. In the former
case, of course, the story cannot be true; in the later case, it could well be.
If other individuals checked on the story and said that as far as they could
see, the story was true, it would also make you view the story in a different
light. Even though the other individuals might be mistaken in their view,
their independent verification would make you more willing to believe the
story might have merit.

This is important because the battleground in the dispute over the
Jefferson-Hemings allegation is not over what amounts to absolute truth or
definitive proof. The battleground is over public impressions of the nature of
the evidence. Therefore, to discredit a Jefferson-Hemings liaison, it is necessary to discuss James Callender as though he invented the story and as though
none of Callender's contemporaries looked into the matter and, in their view,
substantiated the charges. This characterization makes it easier to present the
story as something so fantastic and without foundation that it is unworthy of
a second thought. Callender is the story, the story is Callender. That can be
the only reason that most commentary on this subject begins, not with the
information that Jefferson's neighbors had been gossiping about the alleged
affair for some years before Callender knew about it and that another editor
had considered using the story several years before Callender's reports, but
with the assertion that the story had its origins in the imagination and writings of one man.

One must also keep in mind that the story did not end when Callender ceased to write about it. Twenty years after Callender's last published piece on the alleged liaison, Thomas Jefferson himself began to take actions that added support to the main point of Callender's charge: he began to free the children of the woman with whom he was said to have had a relationship. Jefferson scholars who have labeled this allegation an invention by Callender (or the Federalist party) that died and was revived by the abolitionists have ignored what occurred at Monticello between 1822 and 1826. All of Sally Hemings's children, and she herself, left Monticello as free persons, the only nuclear family on the plantation who achieved this feat.

Imagine that a person lives in Albemarle County from the end of the 1790s until 1803. He hears gossip about Thomas Jefferson's alleged liaison with a slave woman named Sally Hemings and then reads about the allegation in a newspaper. The charge is vigorously denied by other newspapers, as well as his neighbors, who are sure there is nothing to the story. The controversy dies down. The person leaves the state. Twenty-five years later he returns to Virginia shortly after Thomas Jefferson's death. His old neighbors tell him that Jefferson, by his will, had freed the two youngest children of Sally Hemings. He then hears that her two oldest children had been allowed to leave the plantation several years before Jefferson's death and that one of them, the female, had been given money and placed on a stagecoach at Jefferson's direction. In addition, the person learns that Sally Hemings has been allowed to leave Monticello with her youngest sons. Wouldn't the person see a possible relationship between the controversy in 1802 and what had happened between 1822 and 1826? Wouldn't he be likely to think that these activities made the original charges more than just a Federalist story, because the Federalists had nothing to do with what happened to Hemings and her children during the 1820s? Even further, might not knowledge of these later events make the person think that there was more support for the substance of the earlier charge than existed at the time he left Virginia?

Just as it was necessary to separate the destinies of Hemings and her four children as a way of preventing the full picture (and possible meaning) of their lives from emerging, it has also been necessary to proceed as though the actions of Jefferson and his family in the 1820s did not cast a different light upon what was written in 1802. Most Jefferson scholars think Callender's charges are to be discussed as one phenomenon. The emancipations of Hemings and her children, when mentioned at all, are discussed as another. Madison Hemings's statement is still another. These three items are treated as though they are unrelated, when they should be considered in light of one another.

Was There a Tom Hemings?

What of the substance of Callender's writings? In order to cast doubt on the veracity of his allegations, critics point to an alleged major inaccuracy in his presentation. That Sally Hemings existed, that she was a house servant at Monticello, and that she had children by a white man cannot, and has not, been denied. The principal method of showing that Callender was lying rests on the assertion that there was no Tom Hemings who could have been the "President Tom" referred to so contemptuously by Callender.[20]

The nonexistence of Tom serves two functions for opponents of the Jefferson-Hemings story. First, it suggests that Callender lied about an essential item of his story. If he was lying about that, he was lying about the Jefferson-Hemings liaison.[21] This line of argument does not resolve matters. The invention of a fictitious boy would not automatically disprove the existence of a Jefferson-Hemings relationship. Callender could have invented the child Tom, and Jefferson could still have been the father of Hemings's other children, just as Sally Hemings was still the mother of other children even though Callender may have invented a son named Tom for her. In addition, the argument that Callender's lie about Tom would undermine his whole story does not address the fact that the alleged relationship was old gossip among Jefferson's neighbors. That gossip does not make the allegation true, but it does show that Callender did not invent the most important aspect of the story, that Jefferson may have had a slave mistress.

The second reason it is important for Tom not to exist is that it would suggest that Sally Hemings was not pregnant when she came back from France. Douglass Adair's essay on the Sally Hemings controversy discussed this point at length. Adair noted that Jefferson did not list the birth or death of any child named Tom in his Farm Book, a fact which for Adair provided "neutral" evidence that Sally did not have a child when she came back from France. The lack of any record of a Tom Hemings in the Farm Book meant to Adair that Tom had not existed.[22]

Jefferson was not diligently keeping his Farm Book from 1790 through 1794, the years he was often away from Monticello serving as secretary of state. Even if he had been making regular entries, he would have had a reason not to list the birth of the child. Had he done so, anyone who looked at the Farm Book could count back and know that the child was most likely conceived in France. This might have raised suspicions of his possible parenthood or that Jefferson had allowed someone else to take advantage of Hemings. The notion that Sally Hemings was not pregnant when she came back from France is crucial to Jefferson's defenders because it makes it much easier to argue that someone other than Jefferson fathered all of Hemings's children.

The existence of Tom is important to present-day supporters of the story because it tends to prove that the Jefferson and Hemings relationship began in France, and that he was the more likely father of all of her children. Fawn Brodie accepted that Tom existed and posited that he may have been sent away from Monticello after the Callender story appeared. She went on to suggest that Tom may have returned to Monticello periodically, noting the listings over the years of a Tom who does not appear along with the other slaves and whose identity cannot be verified. She also noted that Jefferson listed a Tom in the Farm Book during 1810 and 1811 and offered that this may have been a deliberate attempt to make sure that his existence was recorded during the time he would have turned twenty-one had he been born the year Sally Hemings and Jefferson returned from Paris.[23]

In further support of her belief that Tom existed, Brodie cited a letter from Martha Jefferson Randolph to Jefferson in 1797. Reporting on a wave of illness that had struck Monticello, Martha wrote, "Our intercourse with Monticello has been allmost daily. They have been generally well there except Tom and Goliah who are both about again and poor little Harriot who died a few days after you left us."[24] There was a slave child named Goliah who was six and an old man named Goliah. There was also an older slave named Tom Shackelford. If Tom Hemings existed, he would have been seven years old. Was Randolph giving Jefferson a report on the condition of children who had recovered from some childhood disease that killed Sally Hemings's first daughter, or was she reporting on the recovery of two older slaves and the death of Harriet Hemings?

Brodie thought that there was a good chance that the Tom in this story was the child that Hemings was said to have borne after she came back from France. Martha Randolph referred to the problem as being "pleurisies, rheumatism and every disorder proceeding from cold"; this, Brodie speculated, may have been the childhood disease diphtheria. If so, it would be unlikely that the older slaves would have been sick from it because they probably would have had it as children and recovered with complete immunity or else died, like Harriet.[25]

Finally, Brodie cited the statement of Jefferson's granddaughter Ellen Randolph Coolidge that she knew of four slaves who were white enough to pass for white who ran away from Monticello. Jefferson's Farm Book only lists three runaways, Jamey Hemings, Beverley Hemings, and Harriet Hemings. Brodie argued that the fourth runaway could have been Tom Hemings. Because Jefferson had never placed his birth in the Farm Book, he could not note Tom's departure next to his date of birth as he had done with the other runaways.[26]

Additional confirmation that Tom may have existed comes from a family that claims descent from this individual. According to the oral history of the Woodson family, which has been accepted by the Thomas Jefferson Memorial Foundation as accurate—except for the part about Jefferson being Tom's dad—Tom was sent to live with a family called the Woodsons after the scandal broke. He dropped the name Hemings in favor of Woodson. A Woodson descendant noted that Jefferson was connected to the Woodson family through his mother's sister Dorothy (Dorothea) Randolph, who was married to John Woodson.[27]

Thomas Woodson went on to become a very prosperous individual who believed that blacks and whites should live apart. In keeping with that notion, he started a black community. By chance, two of his modern-day descendants met each other. After talking they realized that they had relatives in common. One of the descendants began to recount the story of Tom Woodson who had left Monticello as a young boy. The descendant then stopped the recitation, the other relative picked up the thread of the story and finished it. This encounter prompted them to seek out other family members. They discovered that others, from both within the country and outside it, knew the story as well. The family has since created a network across the country of Woodson descendants who meet regularly in family reunions. The family has been interested principally in establishing that Tom Woodson existed rather than proving that he was the son of Thomas Jefferson.[28]

After the publication of her biography of Jefferson, Brodie did additional research based upon the oral history of the Woodson family and found that a number of the details the family has passed down about Tom Woodson could be verified. She discovered that in addition to John Woodson, there was a Tarleton Woodson who owned a plantation in Albemarle County; notations in Jefferson's Farm Book indicate that he knew both men. Brodie speculated that Tom was sent to live with either John or Tarleton. The John Woodson who was married to Jefferson's aunt died in 1790, and his wife died in 1794, well before the Callender story broke. They had two sons, John and Josiah, who inherited the family home. The census records to which Brodie referred seem to have concerned the younger John Woodson, Jefferson's first cousin. Tarleton, the other Woodson whom Brodie found, died in 1818. Brodie tracked Tom Woodson through census records that initially did not give his precise age. During the course of further research Brodie discovered a reference to his age in a later census document, and from that she was able to determine that he had been born in 1790, the year that the mysterious Tom Hemings would have been born.[29]

Tom Hemings Existed: An Argument

Although the existence of a Tom who was the son of Thomas Jefferson is the weakest link in the Hemings saga, some issues need to be considered before one accepts the assertion that he did not exist. The first issue centers on Callender and his technique, if one can call slash and burn a technique. While James Callender was a vile man, there is no evidence that he was a stupid one. He understood that in attacking Thomas Jefferson he was taking on a very powerful man and all the people who had an interest in seeing that man remain powerful. One would think that he would not gratuitously deliver to Jefferson's defenders a way to show that he was lying. In discovering Sally Hemings's existence, Callender also discovered that she had children, a son and a daughter. Why make up a son for Thomas Jefferson and Sally Hemings when Sally Hemings already had a son, Beverley?

One of Jefferson's grandsons admitted that all of Sally Hemings's children looked very much like Thomas Jefferson. Beverley could just as easily have been the boy who bore a "striking though sable resemblance" to the president. Beverley would have been four years old at the time of Callender's writings, and there is no reason to suppose that white America would have been more upset if the president's son by a slave woman was twelve instead of four. The point for Callender's story was that the existence of children who looked like Jefferson would tend to prove that he was having sex with Sally Hemings. A boy old enough to compare closely to Jefferson and one named after him, too, would strengthen Callender's case; "President Tom" was an effective device. But was it so effective that Callender would have employed it knowing that Jefferson's supporters could easily point out there was no such boy?

The defenders of Jefferson never offered this rebuttal to Callender's claim. It has been left to Jefferson scholars in the modern era to try to make this argument. Jefferson's most vociferous defender at the time of the scandal, Meriwether Jones, publisher of the *Richmond Examiner,* conceded that Hemings had children but simply said that they were not Jefferson's. According to Jones, "That this servant women has a child is very true. But that it is Mr. Jefferson's, or that the connection exists which Callender mentions is false."[30] Jefferson might well have preferred not to mention—even in order to deny— the more salacious aspects of the story, but the fact that there was no twelve-year-old child at Monticello named Tom would have been an innocuous enough bit of information to pass along to those who were defending him. This alleged child appeared as a prominent and regular feature of Callender's articles. What if there had been no Sally Hemings at Monticello? Would the supporters of Jefferson have mounted a defense against the allegation of an affair with her without mentioning that she did not exist?

Other newspapers were investigating this story. If Tom did not exist, it seems likely that someone among Jefferson's supporters or anyone who could be described as neutral would have stumbled upon the fact that Tom did not exist, if he did not. Why would this be something knowable only by twentieth-century authors and not by parties who were present at Monticello and its environs during the time of the crisis? If they knew it, why would not one of them have had the wit to point it out?

Tom Hemings Did Not Exist: An Argument

It may well be that Madison Hemings's version of the story is true; that Sally Hemings was pregnant when she returned from France and the child she bore upon her return to the United States died shortly after it was born. This conclusion satisfies neither those who believe the Hemings story to be false nor those who believe it is true, although it takes more away from the believers. Tom as a living being can be cited as the physical embodiment of evidence that something happened between Jefferson and Hemings in France. A child who died shortly after their return leaving no independent record does not provide as compelling evidence of the existence or the possible beginnings of the relationship.

But the issue should not be looked at solely in terms of its potential as evidence one way or the other. There are, in truth, some reasons to doubt that Tom existed, or that a Tom who was the son of Thomas Jefferson and Sally Hemings existed, that go beyond Callender's reputation. The doubts stem not from the fact that Jefferson did not list Tom's birth in his Farm Book. Again, if the boy was his son, one could easily understand why Jefferson would not have listed the child's birth.

The doubt springs from Madison Hemings's failure to mention Tom. Brodie offered, as an explanation for this omission, the theory that Tom was sent off to pass as a white child and that Sally Hemings may have been following the convention of blacks in refusing to speak of such a relative as a way of protecting his new identity. But then, why did she mention having a child at all? She did not have to invent a pregnancy in France to prove to her son that she and Jefferson had been lovers, as Douglass Adair claimed.[31] There is no reason to suppose that Madison Hemings would not have believed his mother if she had stated that she became Jefferson's mistress in France and that Jefferson promised her special privileges if she would return and remain his mistress. The pregnancy in France is a litmus test for modern-day historians, but it would not have been so for her own son.

The matter can be considered most effectively by asking questions. First, why would Tom be sent to live with another family for good when Callender's reign of terror lasted only a year and did no damage to Jefferson's political career? Jefferson was soundly reelected to office despite Callender's charges and was an extremely popular man. With his second inauguration, he reached the pinnacle of his political career and could neither have expected nor wanted anything more in the way of a public life. Why would Tom's permanent absence from Monticello have been necessary at this point? It is one thing to send an adult Beverley or Harriet off into the world; it is quite another to send a twelve-year-old away from his home forever when the reason for doing so was transitory.

Brodie's suggestion that Tom may have returned to Monticello periodically over the years was probably her attempt to soften the implications of Tom's alleged banishment. Why let him visit and not stay after Callender was dead and buried and Jefferson was safely ensconced in his second term? Perhaps he did not want to stay, but that would not have been a fourteen- or fifteen-year-old boy's decision. The notion seems even stranger in light of the fact that Sally Hemings had more children after the Callender story appeared. One might argue that Tom was different because he had been the subject of intense publicity. But his presence at Monticello would not have been more potentially damaging to Jefferson than that of Sally Hemings's other four children.

There are other questions. If Tom was close enough to return to Monticello for visits, he would also have been within the sight of Jefferson's prying neighbors who had fed Callender information about the Hemings family. Wouldn't they know about the Woodson connection? How could his identity and whereabouts be kept secret? Just as people talked about the circumstances of Harriet Hemings's departure from Monticello, the banishment and whereabouts of "President Tom," and his occasional returns to Monticello, would have been remarked upon as well. One would expect other sources for the story that young Tom had been sent to live with a family in the area.

There are other more concrete suggestions that Tom Hemings did not exist. In 1805 a Virginian named Thomas Turner raised the Hemings allegation in a private letter to a friend that found its way into a Boston newspaper. Turner's main topic was the accusation that Jefferson had attempted to seduce John Walker's wife when they were all in their twenties, and he recounted in great detail what he knew of that matter, then fodder for a Federalist attack on Jefferson. On the subject of Jefferson and Hemings, he wrote:

> The affair of black (or rather mulatto) Sally is unquestionably true. They have cohabited for many years, and the fruit of the connexion abundantly exists in proof of the fact—To crown this affair, an opinion has existed to which Mr. Jefferson, it is supposed, cannot be a stranger, that this very Sally is the natural daughter of Mr. Wales, who was the father of the actual Mrs. Jefferson—The eldest son (called Beverly) is well known to many.[32]

At the time of Turner's writing, Beverley Hemings was seven years old, Harriet was four, and Madison was four months old. Whatever Turner's motives were for writing the letter, he knew enough about the situation at Monticello to know that Sally Hemings had several children and to know the name of the one whom he described as "the eldest."

One could take the position that Turner, like Callender, was lying about his overall point—the truth of the Hemings allegation—and therefore that nothing in his statement could be true. One still must consider Turner's words closely. Though he was familiar with Callender's articles, he did not follow Callender's lead on his point. Turner did not mention a Tom or that such a child had been sent away from Monticello as a result of the Callender exposé. Turner would have had no reason to safeguard the identity of Tom Hemings by speaking of Beverley as the oldest child.

Turner's contradiction of Callender on the question of Tom Hemings brings us back to Madison Hemings's statement. It further illustrates why all the stories told by the parties must be checked carefully against one another. James Callender wrote that Sally Hemings had five children, of whom he thought Tom was the oldest.[33] At the time of his writing, we know for certain only that she had two children, Beverley and Harriet. Is there any reasonable explanation for Callender's statement?

The answer is yes. Sally Hemings would have had five children if all the children she is reported to have given birth to had lived. The first is the child that Madison Hemings said she bore after returning from France, the one he said died in infancy. The second is her first daughter Harriet, who lived for two years. The third is Beverley Hemings. The fourth is a daughter whose existence was rediscovered only in 1993. That child, born in early December 1799, died as an infant.[34] The fifth is Hemings's second Harriet. This list suggests that Callender may not have been talking off the top of his head. He had been given information about her children, but the information was stale. His source, or sources, knew that Sally Hemings had borne several children but did not know that any of them had died.

What does Callender's error say about the likely source of his information? While minimizing the gossip of Jefferson's neighbors about a Jefferson-Hemings liaison, historians have assumed that David Meade Randolph, a cousin and enemy of Jefferson, was the main source of Callender's information. Jefferson had arranged for Randolph to become a marshal in the 1790s, and Randolph had arrested and jailed James Callender on the charge of sedition. Jefferson and Randolph had enjoyed cordial relations during the early 1790s, with Jefferson's youngest daughter spending time at Randolph's home and Randolph visiting Monticello. David Randolph was married to the sister of Jefferson's son-in-law Thomas Mann Randolph. Randolph was an ardent Federalist, and the relationship between the two men began to deteriorate as Jefferson's star in the Republican party rose toward the end of the 1790s.[35]

There was also a more personal reason for animus between the two men that has not been noted when scholars suggest Randolph's motive for hurting Jefferson. During the latter half of the 1790s, Jefferson and Randolph had been involved in a complex legal dispute involving the fallout from a failed joint venture between Jefferson's father-in-law, John Wayles, and Randolph's father Richard. Jefferson, as one of the executors of the Wayles estate, sued David Randolph and his brothers for the return of property transferred to them by their father to avoid his obligations to creditors. Jefferson's other cousin and enemy John Marshall represented the Randolph brothers. The final break between Jefferson and David Randolph came when Jefferson was elected president and removed Randolph from his post as marshal because of accusations that Randolph had been involved in packing juries, including the jury that had heard James Callender's case. When Randolph and Callender came into contact with one another, Randolph may have said some unkind things about Jefferson.[36]

However, James Callender had been arrested for writing scathing material about the Federalists. We should be at least a little wary of the notion that David Meade Randolph, the Federalist, and James Callender, the scourge of the Federalists, could have so quickly come to see one another as allies during Callender's incarceration. The suspicions that Randolph had tampered with the jury that decided to send him to jail for many months would not have gone unnoticed (and been forgiven) by Callender. After Callender's release, Randolph deliberately held off on the repayment of Callender's fine. When Randolph could not longer avoid remitting the money, he suggested that Callender come to a designated place for repayment. Callender declined, fearing that he was being led into a trap and would be beaten. Shortly after Callender left jail, when he learned that Randolph had been removed from his post as marshal, he wrote to Jefferson, "David Meade Randolph in Virginia has gone, ha, ha!"[37]

Another problem with the idea that Randolph was the main source of Callender's information about Sally Hemings's children is that Randolph would have known how many Hemings children were alive. His wife, Mary Randolph, despite her husband's falling-out with Jefferson and her own dislike of Jefferson, remained a visitor to Monticello. She gossiped about Jefferson's private life to others, which suggests that she had enough interest in the matter at least to have kept tabs on the Hemings offspring, particularly since her own son shared the name Beverley with Sally Hemings's son and her sister Harriet shared her name with Sally Hemings's daughter.[38]

David Randolph may have put Callender onto the story, but Callender's mistake about the number of Hemings's living children supports the suggestion that his information came primarily from Jefferson's neighbors. They may have heard rumors about Hemings giving birth after she returned from France and about the births of her other children, events that would have been preceded by her obvious pregnancies and would have been of intense interest. They may not have been close enough to the situation to have known that any of the children had died, their absence unnoticed to casual observers in the press of other light-skinned slave children or even Jefferson's white grandchildren.

On the other hand, Randolph's name came up in connection with Turner's letter to the *Boston Repertory* in 1805. The publisher of Turner's letter had apparently shared the contents of the letter with David Randolph, who told the publisher that Turner could "unfold tales which would cause Mr. Jefferson to tremble."[39] The Randolph-Turner connection thus was explicit. Turner's omission of Tom Hemings is of great importance because Randolph would have known if there was a Tom Hemings who had been sent away in the wake of the Callender scandal. The hiding of "President Tom" would have been too delicious an item for him to have kept secret. It is also a further indication that Randolph was not Callender's main or only source.

Bad Person Equals Bad Story

What historians have done when confronting the contemporary writings about Jefferson and Hemings is to shift the focus from the content of these primary sources to the personalities of the individuals who produced them.

Instead of accurately recounting and analyzing what the writings say, they declare over and over that those who claimed Jefferson and Hemings were involved in a sexual relationship were bad people. When one reads Thomas Turner's letter, it is clear that he knew a great deal about some aspects of Thomas Jefferson's private life. One can challenge some of Turner's interpretations of the facts, but he was certainly in possession of them.

The focus on personality over the content of writings is especially evident with respect to James Callender. Adjectives—"loathsome," "drunken," "vile"—substitute for analysis. Historians refuse to acknowledge that there was always a basic truth to the allegations for which Callender is most famous. He had been right about Alexander Hamilton's affair with Mrs. Reynolds. When he claimed that Jefferson had been his patron, and Republicans denied the charge, Callender produced Jefferson's letters showing that Jefferson had encouraged his literary efforts against members of the Federalist party. The relationship was less of a partnership than Callender claimed, but Jefferson can be said to have supported him. Callender was also correct about Jefferson's attempted seduction of the wife of his friend John Walker, even though he overstated his case against Jefferson.

James Callender's modus operandi was to take the basic kernel of truth that existed in a given situation and use his white-hot prose style to exaggerate matters to make a better story. Knowing that this was his habit, what is the best approach when assessing his Jefferson-Hemings story? Does one state or imply, as most historians have done, that Callender had a record of lying about everything, when that claim is not correct? Or does one consider his track record and face the unpleasant truth that even a despicable man can be right about some things?

The better, and more honest, method is too try to separate the wheat from the chaff. It may be possible to do this by looking closely at what Madison Hemings, Thomas Turner, and James Callender said and comparing those statements to what we know from Thomas Jefferson's records about Sally Hemings's childbearing. The version of the story that emerges is completely reasonable in light of other information about the lives of Hemings and her children. Callender took outdated information from Jefferson's neighbors about the births of Sally Hemings's children and the basic truth of a boy who may have been known to be favored by Jefferson, Beverley (whom Turner described as being "known to many"), and created "President Tom."

This scenario might explain why Meriwether Jones and other Jefferson supporters did not point out that there was no Tom Hemings. Callender's mistake would have alerted Jefferson and his supporters about the state of his information and the knowledge of his likely informants. It would have been apparent that Callender's sources knew some things about Sally Hemings's children but were not close enough to the situation to know other important details. Under the circumstances, the smartest course of action was to let James Callender go as far as he could go with his flawed story and let the phantom "President Tom" run interference for the real Beverley. Explaining that there was no Tom would have sent Callender and his sources back to making more inquiries.

Conclusion

The existence or nonexistence of Tom Hemings has taken on a significance beyond its actual importance as a way of proving or disproving a Jefferson-Hemings liaison. To Jefferson defenders nonexistent Tom is a weapon to kill off James Callender and the Sally Hemings story. To supporters of the story, existent Tom is proof of where the story began and evidence against "the Carr brothers did it" theory. We do not know with a degree of certainty that Tom Hemings existed. We do know that Beverley, Harriet, Madison, and Eston Hemings existed. Therefore, it seems reasonable to focus upon the circumstances of their births and their life stories as a way of considering whether a Jefferson-Hemings liaison existed.

Whether James Callender was lying about "President Tom" is still an open question, and proof that he was lying about this one child would not defeat Jefferson's possible paternity of Sally Hemings's other children. What is clear is that most modern commentary on this subject, particularly the summaries in the popular press, does not give a full picture of the circumstances under which Callender's exposé arose and how it played itself out. James Callender was not the first person to have said that Thomas Jefferson had a slave mistress. He was only the first to put the specific allegation on paper.

Finally, the portrayal of Callender as a journalist who always made things up out of thin air distorts historical reality and has prevented focusing on what Callender wrote. In the zeal to render Callender meaningless, a detail of critical importance given in one of Callender's articles has been largely ignored. Callender's statement that Sally Hemings had given birth to five children by the year 1802 can be supported by extrinsic evidence. It provides an additional reason to believe Madison Hemings's assertion that his mother gave birth to a child upon her return from France, even if one does not believe that child grew up to be the "President Tom" of James Callender's articles.

3

The Randolphs and the Carrs

> If history is going to be scientific, if the record of human action
> is going to be set down with that accuracy and faithfulness of
> detail which will allow its use as a measuring rod and guidepost
> for the future of nations, there must be set some standards of
> ethics in research and interpretation.
>
> —W. E. B. Du Bois, "The Propaganda of History"

NO WHERE can historians' double standard for assessing evidence in the
Jefferson-Hemings controversy be plainer than in the promotion of the
idea that one of Thomas Jefferson's nephews, Samuel Carr or Peter Carr, was
the father of Sally Hemings's children. The chief qualifications that the Carr
brothers have for this designation are (1) neither one of them was Thomas
Jefferson, (2) neither seems to have been a very good guy, so that they can be
cast as having engaged in miscegenation, and (3) neither man means anything
to the American public. Because the Carrs possess these characteristics, broad
and categorical statements have been made about them that are without adequate foundation.

Just as the depiction of James Callender as the originator and sole contemporary believer of the story of Sally Hemings's relationship with Thomas
Jefferson has been put into the popular consciousness without due examination, the stories about the Carr brothers have been accepted with insufficient
skepticism by historians and journalists who have followed their lead. Statements such as "Most historians believe that Samuel Carr was the father," "The
best available evidence indicates that Jefferson's nephews were the fathers," or
"The father of Sally Hemings's children was most likely Peter Carr" appear
with the predictability of seconds on a chronometer in every piece written
about this topic.[1]

Yet what exactly is the nature of that evidence? Remember that Madison
Hemings's reminiscences have been rejected as the self-serving statements of

a man who either was lying or had been misled into lying by someone else with a personal interest in having the public believe his story. Dumas Malone, while musing about whether historians could accept the "oral tradition" handed down by slaves at Monticello, said, "Oral tradition is not established fact."[2] So what is the source of the idea that Samuel Carr and Peter Carr were the fathers of Sally Hemings's children? The oral tradition of the Jefferson-Randolph family.

How the Carr Brothers Came into the Picture

Thomas Jefferson Randolph, Thomas Jefferson's oldest and favorite grandson, was the primary source of this story. The historian Henry Randall, who was writing a life of Jefferson, spoke to T. J. Randolph about the Jefferson-Hemings allegation. Writing ten years after his biography came out to James Parton, who was himself to publish a biography of Jefferson in 1874, Randall reported that T. J. Randolph had told him that "Sally Henings was the mistress of Peter [Carr], and her sister Betsey the mistress of Samuel [Carr]." Randolph had gone on to describe these relationships as "perfectly notorious at Monticello, and scarcely disguised by the latter—never disavowed by them," and he also told Randall that "Samuel's proceedings were particularly open" (see Appendix D).

Randolph claimed to have obtained direct evidence of Peter Carr's connection to Sally Hemings under dramatic circumstances. He said that he had come upon an article that referred to Jefferson's mulatto children in a newspaper that a guest had left at Monticello. Greatly upset about the story, Randolph confronted Peter and Samuel Carr about the matter as they lay under a shade tree. According to Randolph, the two men broke down and cried and expressed shame that they had brought "this disgrace on poor old uncle who has always fed us!" (see Appendix D).

In 1858 Randolph's sister Ellen Randolph Coolidge sent a letter to her husband discussing the issue. Coolidge reported that she and her brother had recently had a conversation about the Hemings children. She reported that T. J. Randolph had told her that he had overheard Peter Carr say that Jefferson was being blamed for things for which he and his brother Samuel were responsible. Because she had the "general impression" that Samuel Carr was intimately involved with Sally Hemings, Coolidge took her brother's statement as confirming that Samuel Carr was the father. She described her uncle as "the most notorious good-natured Turk that ever was master of a black seraglio kept at other men's expense," a colorful description but hardly dispositive of the paternity of Hemings's children.[3]

Dumas Malone wrote of Madison Hemings's statement that "at all events, it must be weighed against the testimony of Jefferson's grandchildren, his [Jefferson's] categorical denial of the alleged liaison, and his own character."[4] It seems that Jefferson scholars have not done much actual weighing of the testimony of Jefferson's grandchildren about the Carr brothers.

Henry Randall

Henry Randall's role in perpetuating the Carr brothers story must be examined. In his letter to Parton, Randall recounted another anecdote told to him by T. J. Randolph. According to Randolph, his mother Martha had discussed the Sally Hemings affair with him and his youngest brother, George Wythe Randolph. She reminded them of the birth date of one of the Hemings children—the one who looked the most like Thomas Jefferson. Randall's letter does not reveal the identity of that child. T. J. Randolph said that he got the book containing the list of slaves, most probably Jefferson's Farm Book, and verified the birth date. At that point Martha told her sons that Jefferson could not have been the father of this child because "Mr. Jefferson and Sally Henings could not have met—were far distant from each other—for fifteen months prior to such birth. She bade her sons to remember this fact, and always to defend the character of their grandfather."

Because of Malone's thorough chronologies of Jefferson's life, we know now that Martha Randolph was most likely wrong. Jefferson was at Monticello at least nine months before the birth of each of Sally Hemings's children.[5] Martha was an elderly woman at this point, and perhaps her memory of specific events so far in the past was unclear; she either made a mistake or lied. T. J. Randolph was a child himself during the years that Sally Hemings was giving birth to her children, so that he may not have known firsthand whether his grandfather was at Monticello during the relevant time period. He would have no reason not to believe his mother when she said that Jefferson was away from Monticello when the Hemings child in question was conceived.

At this point Randall's statements on the matter become problematic. Randall claimed in his letter to Parton that while "examining an old account book of the Jeffersons," he came "*pop* upon the original entry of this slave's birth: and I was then able from well known circumstances to prove the fifteen month separation—but those circumstances have faded from my memory." He went on to say, "I have no doubt I could recover them however did Mr. Jefferson's vindication in the least depend upon them." However, whatever the circumstances were that Randall forgot, he must have used Randolph's date for the child's birth, and we from know other sources that Jefferson was not gone from Monticello for a full fifteen months before the birth of any of Sally Hemings's children. Therefore, we must consider the following possibilities:

1. Randall was mistaken. He saw the birth date of the slave but erred in his arithmetic or misread a document. Or,

2. Randall was lying because he thought doing so might protect Thomas Jefferson. Neither Randall nor Martha Randolph could have anticipated that there would one day be a scholar who would map out, month by month, the whereabouts of Thomas Jefferson from 1784 until his death in 1826. Both of them may have felt that they were saying something that could never be disputed.

Whether Randall was merely mistaken in his observation or whether he was lying, it seems that he made a major error with respect to one critical aspect of this story. It is Randall's account of his conversation with Jefferson's grandson that has formed the strongest pillar supporting the defense of Jefferson against the change of miscegenation. Edmund Bacon's statement is important but secondary. From Merrill Peterson to Andrew Burstein, Randall's letter has been a staple of Jefferson scholars' treatment of the Hemings controversy. In view of Randall's error, it seems appropriate to be wary of his account of the substance of his conversation with T. J. Randolph. Yet even after Malone's chronology of Jefferson's life showed that Randall (and Martha Randolph) were mistaken or lied about the whereabouts of Jefferson at the time of the conception of this unnamed child, historians have continued to cite Randall's letter as though there is no reason to doubt the veracity or accuracy of its content.[6]

Apparently, James Parton did not take Randall up on his offer to attempt to remember the facts that led him to believe that he had verified Martha Randolph's assertion. Had Parton done so, he probably would have included them in his account. Parton, no doubt, thought of himself, Henry Randall, and T. J. Randolph as gentlemen and of Martha Randolph as a lady. He may have been reluctant to cast any doubt on the word of these individuals. But ladies and gentlemen do on occasion make mistakes or even lie, and not challenging a puzzling account can allow falsehood to masquerade as unbiased truth. We should at least consider the possibility that something on that order happened in this situation.

Merrill Peterson and Henry Randall

Some historians have recognized that Henry Randall approached his project with a distinct bias. Merrill Peterson discussed Randall's biography of Jefferson at length, noting that Randall had been concerned that previous writings about the life of Jefferson did not do justice to the greatness of the man. Peterson described Randall as having "approached the biographer's charge in the spirit of a knight who if he could not rout the entrenched foe, was nerved for the martyr's faggot and stake in the cause of his hero."[7] Could not the "knight" have desired to do his best to absolve "his hero" of the charge of miscegenation?

There is no acknowledgment of Randall's bias in Peterson's discussion of Randall's letter to Parton on the Sally Hemings story. Compare this to Peterson's discussion of Madison Hemings's statement. Describing the historical context in which that statement arose, Peterson wrote:

> Three factors were chiefly responsible for the rise and progress of the miscegenation legend. The first was political: the hatred of the Federalists, the hope of his enemies inspired by Callender that the African harem revelations would destroy him, and later the campaign of British critics to lower the prestige of American democracy by toppling its hero from his pedestal. The second was the institution of slavery: the Negroes' pathetic wish for a little pride and their subtle ways of confounding the white folks, the cunning of the slave trader and the auctioneer who might expect a better price for a Jefferson than for a Jones, the social fact of miscegenation and its fascination as a moral theme, and, above all, the logic of abolitionism by which Jefferson alone of the Founding Fathers was a worthy exhibit of the crime. The third revolves around the personal history of Jefferson himself: his wife's early death, his brief affair with Mrs. Walker (an Albemarle neighbor), his great interest in Negroes generally along with his particular kindness to some of his slaves, and items of a similar nature, with which some imaginations could piece together the intriguing "Black Sal" relationship.[8]

Peterson also said that the story persisted, sustained by abolitionists, British commentators, and "the memories of a few Negroes," "although the overwhelming evidence of Jefferson's domestic life refuted the legend."[9] He could not have been speaking of dispositive evidence, such as evidence that Jefferson was away from Hemings when she likely conceived her children or that facts existed to prove that another man had fathered them, because this type of evidence does not exist. What he probably was referring to as overwhelming evidence was the fact that Jefferson had great affection and regard for his daughters and grandchildren. In other words, it was Peterson's view of Jefferson's character that constituted the "overwhelming evidence" that the story was not true.

Madison Hemings's statement most likely would fall under Peterson's second reason for the propagation of "the miscegenation legend." To Peterson, Hemings would have been one of those "Negroes" with the "pathetic wish to gain a little pride." Consider for a moment Peterson's phrase, which appeared in 1960. How could the wish to gain pride ever be thought "pathetic"? One could only think the wish pathetic if one thought the fulfillment of it unlikely or impossible. One might say that a particular mechanism for gaining pride is pathetic, but the wish itself? Substitute the name of any other ethnic group in Peterson's formulation, and it is clear that no other people but blacks could be written of in so careless a manner. Some comment would be made about it, and the writer would not be considered an objective source on a question that involved that ethnic group.

Peterson believed that Hemings's statement could not be considered without examining the role of surviving abolitionists in the resurrection of the Sally Hemings story in the middle part of the nineteenth century. The point of this linkage, of course, was to suggest that Hemings should not be credited. Yet Randall's bias toward Jefferson and the effect it may have had upon him did not receive similar scrutiny. In fact, Peterson's characterization of Randall's statements is cast in a way that reinforces Randall's power as a source.

Peterson noted that Parton

> made inquiry of Henry S. Randall, who recalled in a personal letter, first, the determination he had reached after investigation of pertinent records on the Monticello slaves, that the father of the Hemings children was a near relative of Jefferson's; and second, T. J. Randolph's report of an investigation made at the request of his mother, not long before her death, on the birth of one of the Hemings who claimed Jefferson's paternity. Randolph concluded from his investigation that the slave's mother, Sally, and Jefferson could not possibly have seen each other for a period of fifteen months prior to the birth. Randall appreciated the feelings and fully accepted the position of Jefferson's grandchildren on this subject. He made no reference to the miscegenation legend in his *Life*.[10]

One gets the impression from reading this passage that Randall looked at documents that proved that one of Thomas Jefferson's relatives was the father of Sally Hemings's children. Randall's letter suggests that his conclusion about the identity of the likely father was based, not upon any "pertinent records," but upon the statements of T. J. Randolph. The only item in a record that Randall or T. J. Randolph made reference to was Jefferson's listing of the birth date of the child. There are no documents implicating a relative of Jefferson besides Ellen Randolph Coolidge's letter to her husband, citing the same source as Randall did, her oldest brother. Randall said only that his independent verification had confirmed that Jefferson was away from Hemings for fifteen months before the birth of the child in question, not that a relative of

Jefferson was the children's father. Peterson spliced two separate ideas into one and characterized them both as being based upon "pertinent records."

To describe what passed between Martha Randolph and her son as an "investigation" also seems questionable. All that happened was that Martha Randolph called her sons' attention to the birth date of one of Sally Hemings's children, had one of them verify that date by looking at Jefferson's Farm Book, and then herself provided the most important part of the information exonerating Jefferson: that he was away from Sally Hemings for fifteen months before the birth of that child. Martha Randolph simply raised a question and then answered it, wrongly, herself. Instead of considering whether Randall's bias made his statements on this matter suspect, Peterson gave Randall extra strength by making his efforts to get at the truth seem more extensive and reliable than they were.

Assessing the Errors

Compare the treatment of Henry Randall and Martha Randolph with the treatment of Madison Hemings and S. F. Wetmore. Critics cite Hemings's mistakes: saying that his mother was in France for eighteen months when she was there for twenty-six months and saying that Jefferson's will provided for the freedom of his older brother and sister as crippling his account of his life story. Hemings was wrong about the length of his mother's stay in France. He was also wrong about the terms of Jefferson's will.

Hemings made other minor errors, but none went to the direct issue at hand. The most serious of his errors was his statement about Jefferson's will. As there is no evidence that Madison Hemings saw Thomas Jefferson's will, he may have just assumed that provision for Beverley and Harriet Hemings's freedom at twenty-one had been included in the document and that their departure from Monticello before Jefferson died was in furtherance of his plan for Sally Hemings's children. This can certainly be cited as carelessness on Hemings's part, but it does not presumptively indicate bad faith. If Hemings had said that Jefferson had made provision for the freedom of his older siblings and they had, in fact, remained at Monticello as slaves, this would pose a serious problem with respect to his account. Hemings, however, was not wrong in saying that the thing he and his siblings thought would be allowed to happen when they turned twenty-one had taken place. They had all gone free at Jefferson's decision. Even if Hemings was mistaken about Jefferson's mechanism for doing this, his error does not contradict Hemings's main point and can be considered *de minimis*.

On the other hand, both Martha Randolph's and Henry Randall's assertions on this matter are material misstatements about the substance of the issue. Martha Randolph's age and her love for and devotion to her family may explain her actions. Randall is another matter. He was a historian claiming that during the course of his research, he claimed to have established a fact that he most likely could not have established. Moreover, Randall claimed to have forgotten "well known circumstances" that had helped him establish that fact. He could remember that the circumstances were well known, but he could not remember what they were.

Randall made another material mistake in his letter when he wrote that "at the periods when these Carr children were born, he, Col. Randolph, had charge of Monticello. He gave all the general directions, gave out their clothes to the slaves, etc., etc." Sally Hemings's children were born in the 1790s through 1808, and the dates were available to Randall in the Farm Book. Thomas Jefferson Randolph was born in 1792, and he was sixteen years old when Sally Hemings's last child, Eston, was born.[11] If Randolph told Henry Randall that he was in charge of Monticello during this period, he lied. If Randall believed him, he was grossly negligent in not realizing the obvious impossibility of this claim.

Randall's acceptance of this proposition, and transmittal of it to Parton, is all the more curious since Randall wrote in his biography of Jefferson that T. J. Randolph began to "take the management of his [Jefferson's] estate in 1814," five years after the last of Sally Hemings's children was born.[12] It was actually Martha Randolph who performed the functions described in Randall's letter, but she would not have performed them on a regular basis until she moved to Monticello in 1810, after all of Hemings's children were born.[13] Perhaps T. J. Randolph had given Randall the impression that his mother was doing this all the years that Hemings was having children. This would not have been true. If the discussion came up, Randall may have confused "Col. Randolph" with Martha Randolph when he wrote to Parton ten years later describing his conversation. This seems doubtful. While Randall may have forgotten some details, one wonders how likely it is that he would have confused T. J. Randolph with his mother Martha, particularly given the context in which this anecdote was offered. Martha Randolph was dead by the time Randall spoke with T. J. Randolph, so Randall had no memories of her statements to get mixed up with those of her son.

Randall included the assertion about the management of Monticello to bolster the notion that T. J. Randolph would have been in a good position to see whether there was any special relationship between Jefferson and Hemings. This seems to be a case of a historian offering an untruth to make the claims of his witness more credible. This is the height of calculation and should have alarmed those who relied upon Randall's statements on this matter. Anyone remotely familiar with Thomas Jefferson's family, including anyone who claims to be a biographer of Jefferson, should immediately spot the problem with the contention that T. J. Randolph was running Monticello from the 1790s through 1808. One would expect that historians, after finding this error, would alert their readers to it and then proceed with caution when offering any of the claims within Randall's letter as evidence for anything.

Andrew Burstein's use of the Randall letter further illustrates the problem. He noted T. J. Randolph's claim that Sally Hemings received no special consideration, quoting Randolph's statement that Hemings "'was treated and dressed like the rest' of the Monticello servants."[14] Burstein did not mention that this excerpt was part of a discussion in which Randolph was quoted as having said something that could not have been true: that he knew Hemings received no favored treatment because during her childbearing years he was in charge of giving out clothing and supplies to slaves. Randolph's statement on this point should not have been used without apprising readers of the glaring problem with it. Readers trying to decide whether to rely upon Randolph need to know this kind of information in order to make an informed judgment.

Burstein then described Martha Randolph's so-called investigation of the Hemings allegation: "She wished for her sons to be able to refute the rumors for the sake of history, and, before her death gathered two of them in order to make some calculations concerning her father's whereabouts at the time Sally Hemings had conceived the male child who most resembled Jefferson."[15] However, he did not go on to explain that Martha's calculations were wrong or that the sole source describing their effort, Henry Randall, tried to lend support to the flawed calculations by proclaiming that he had reproduced them and had gotten the same result. Again, salient facts needed by a reader attempting to judge the level of the declarant's credibility were not reported.

Randolph and Randall have been allowed to be wrong in serious ways without losing their credibility because historians have wanted to believe the substance of what they had to say. It is also likely that they are believed because of who they were: Martha Randolph, daughter of an icon, and Henry Randall, noted historian. The credibility of Madison Hemings, a former slave, who said something that historians do not want to believe, has been summarily dismissed with far fewer grounds to do so.

Jefferson's Grandchildren versus Madison Hemings

The biases of historians and commentators can be further demonstrated by comparing their reactions to Madison Hemings's statement and those of Jefferson's grandchildren. On one hand, we have a memoir of a black man taken down by the editor of a newspaper who seems to have been motivated by his sympathy for black people. The substance of some of the most important parts of the statement can be supported by extrinsic evidence, that is, documents that were created for purposes other than for supporting the notions being put forth by Madison Hemings. Remember the alleged promise that Sally Hemings's children would be freed at twenty-one. The extrinsic evidence that tends to support the idea that such a promise was made was created by Thomas Jefferson for a reason wholly unrelated to supporting the story Madison Hemings told. Similarly, the most reliable part of Edmund Bacon's statements, about the circumstances under which Jefferson freed Harriet Hemings, tends to support Madison Hemings's statement. Bacon certainly was not offering this recollection to support the notion that Jefferson fathered Sally Hemings's children.

On the other hand, consider the statements of Jefferson's grandchildren, neither of which can be supported by any truly extrinsic document or circumstance that would make what they say more believable. First, Thomas Jefferson Randolph, through his conversation with Randall, is the source of the allegation that Peter Carr was the father of Hemings's children. In that same conversation he allegedly recounted a story that had both Carr brothers crying when confronted under the shade tree about the article concerning Jefferson's mulatto children. The description of this melodramatic moment, does not sound particularly credible, not because men do not cry, but because of the timing of this alleged event.

By 1813, the worst of the Callender crisis had long since passed. Comments about Jefferson's slave mistress cropped up occasionally, but it was old news that was well past the power to hurt him. Jefferson had served two terms as president, had retired to his beloved Monticello as a well-respected national figure, and was not yet caught in the nightmare of his slide into poverty. That Samuel and Peter would have been so upset, as if their uncle was in some immediate crisis, seems unlikely, for the time for tears had long passed. Ellen Randolph Coolidge's very different version of how her brother came to know of the Carr-Hemings connection renders the story of a confession even more suspect.

Coolidge said that T. J. Randolph told her "in confidence" that he had learned of her uncle's relationship to Sally Hemings when he and a friend overheard Peter Carr "say with a laugh, that 'the old gentleman had to bear the blame of his and Sam's (Col. Carr) misdeeds.'" One wonders why Randolph did not tell his sister of Peter Carr's dramatic under-the-shade-tree confession, which was supposed to have taken place around 1813 or 1814?[16]

There is a big difference between "I, along with a companion, overheard a person laugh and admit something" and "I alone confronted two people, they began to cry, and then confessed their guilt to me." If Randolph decided to tell his sister who fathered Sally Hemings's children, why not give her the best evidence of that, that is, the Carr brothers' confession to him? Why would Randolph tell Henry Randall that Peter Carr had confessed, and not tell his sister, with whom he discussed the matter.

If that confession had actually taken place, there is no rational explanation for why Randolph would seek to prove to his sister that one of the Carr brothers was the father of the Hemings children without telling her about Peter Carr's confession. Randolph might have thought it more effective to tell Randall about a confession, as it established more forcefully the proposition that Randolph had put forth: that Thomas Jefferson was not the father of Sally Hemings's children. Randolph may have failed in 1858 to tell his sister about the confession because there was no confession.

Alternatively, the problem may have been with Henry Randall's or Ellen Coolidge's transmission of Randolph's statements. T. J. Randolph's version of events comes to us through Randall and Coolidge. No direct statement from Randolph on the Carr brothers has ever been discovered. One might be tempted, given some of the other errors in his letter, to suggest that Randall may have taken Randolph's statement about overhearing Carr's remark and turned it into a more direct admission of guilt. However, in the draft of a letter written in response to Israel Jefferson's statement to the *Pike County (Ohio) Republican*, T. J. Randolph said that unnamed others had admitted their guilt to him long ago.[17] The letter was never published, but the draft remains in Randolph's papers. It seems, then, that the notion of a confession actually did come from Randolph.

If Randolph did tell his sister of the confession, why would she not mention it to her husband? There is no indication that Coolidge was under the influence of the well-known modesty of that era. She was, in fact, speaking of these matters in a somewhat crude fashion, describing her uncle as the master of a seraglio and noting that it was at another man's expense—as if things would have been any better if he had paid for it himself. Moreover, her story of her uncle's mirth while admitting his activities in the slave quarters and his disregard for his uncle's suffering is actually more shocking and salacious than

Randolph's story of Carr's tearful admission of wrongdoing and contrition. If she knew both versions, why would she choose to tell the former?

When viewed objectively, it seems as though this trio—Randolph, Randall, and Coolidge—were saying things to build a case, rather than just recounting a story. There are enough problems with the evidence they offered to support the Carr brothers' connection to Sally Hemings to do serious damage to the theory as whole. There are even more problems.

Coolidge gave her opinion that the true father was Samuel Carr. Malone indicated that Coolidge may have picked Samuel Carr because she did not think him as good a person as Peter Carr, not because she had any specific information about Samuel's dealings with Sally Hemings. Coolidge's opinion of Samuel Carr may have been justified, but a source's admitted overall prejudice against an individual should make one wary of that source's statements about that person.

Malone blamed Randall for the apparent conflict in the Randolph siblings' view as to whether Peter or Samuel was the father of the Hemings children. He noted that Randall was recalling from memory a conversation that had taken place a number of years earlier, so that he may have inadvertently switched the two brothers' names in assigning one to Sally Hemings and the other to her sister Betsey Hemings. Coolidge's statement was more contemporaneous and, in Malone's view, probably more accurate.[18] This is certainly possible. But of all the things for Randall to confuse! The main purpose of his inquiry was to learn the name of the man who had caused his hero such trouble. Given the vague nature of the alleged overheard conversation, and of the siblings' comments in general, it is just as likely that their reports did indeed differ.

It could be argued that because Samuel Carr may have had sex with black women, he would have been willing to have sex with Sally Hemings. It is, however, a very long way from that general assertion about Samuel Carr's propensities to the specific claim that he fathered Hemings's children. Coolidge would not be believed if she had attempted to prove that a man in her neighborhood was the father of a blonde white woman's children simply by citing that man's philandering nature and his attraction to blondes. She would have to have given more information about her knowledge of the interactions between the two parties before she would be given any credence on the issue.

When read in its entirety, Coolidge's letter has the sound of a statement for posterity rather than a true effort to impart information to an intimate contemporary correspondent. It seems to have been written with an extreme amount of self-consciousness to be used exactly as it has been used: to provide a defense of Jefferson from a member of his own family. The letter is more interesting for what it does not say that for what it says. For example, Coolidge speaks about Samuel Carr's reputation and the "impressions" that he was the father of Hemings's children. Her letter does not offer any discrete facts to support those notions. Instead, Coolidge spends a good part of the letter making an argument to her husband, who knew Thomas Jefferson, about the nature of Jefferson's character.

If one does not want to accuse Coolidge of lying, one could say that her statements about the specific question reveal a lack of real knowledge about the matter, and indeed, Ellen Coolidge was a child when Sally Hemings was having her children. Ellen and her siblings visited Monticello in the summers and during Jefferson's vacations from Philadelphia and Washington. Her family moved there permanently only after Hemings had given birth to all of her children. One would not expect Coolidge to have known intimate details about any affair that Hemings and Samuel Carr may have been carrying on. But she should have been able to offer at least one item from her personal knowledge of Sally Hemings and Samuel Carr that would indicate these two people did, in fact, know each other. This she did not do.

Coolidge's contribution to this inquiry was based upon her brother's ambiguous statement and her alleged knowledge of Samuel Carr's reputation for sleeping with black women. She seems to have had no specific facts in her possession—or chose not to share them—that would tie Samuel Carr to Sally Hemings. Israel Jefferson, who corroborated Madison Hemings's story, at least indicated how he might have been able to know that Jefferson and Hemings were on "intimate terms": he said that he sometimes came in and out of Jefferson's rooms to run errands and that Sally Hemings was Jefferson's chambermaid. He may have actually seen these two people in one place at the same time. There is no indication that Coolidge ever saw Hemings and Carr in a similar circumstance. Had Coolidge been talking about the life history of any woman besides an American slave, the hollowness of her claim would have been quickly discerned and duly noted.

Nevertheless, Virginius Dabney found Coolidge's account particularly persuasive. Although he acknowledged that Coolidge and T. J. Randolph would have wanted to protect their grandfather, he thought Coolidge would not have implicated another relative in order to do so. He wrote: "Again, it seems reasonable to ask whether the granddaughter of Thomas Jefferson would have quoted one of her close relatives as accepting blame for the mulattos at Monticello, and accused that man's brother of fathering Sally's children, if she had not been confident that she was speaking the truth. Like her brother, Thomas J. Randolph, she was naturally anxious to clear her grandfather's name, but did not have to implicate her cousins in the process."[19]

Coolidge did not think well of Samuel Carr. Between his reputation and that of her beloved grandfather, there could not have been much of a choice. Because her brother's statement to her about the Carr brothers was unclear, she probably thought it more likely that the father was Samuel, and not Peter. Yet her supposition, in the absence of any extrinsic evidence, is meaningless. Madison Hemings may have been just as confident about the validity of his story as Ellen Coolidge was about hers. But in the absence of any outside reason to believe their statements, confidence gets neither person anywhere.

As to why Coolidge and T. J. Randolph would have implicated one of their relatives, the answer is obvious. Randolph told Henry Randall that all of Sally Hemings's children "resembled Mr. Jefferson so closely that it was plain that they had his blood in their veins." There had to be some explanation for this resemblance. If it was not through the activities of Thomas Jefferson, it had to be through those of someone who was related to him. Neither Randolph nor Coolidge could speak credibly about Jefferson's lack of involvement without offering up a person who could have produced Thomas Jefferson look-alikes, that is, a blood relative.

Randall also recalled T. J. Randolph saying that Sally Hemings had a sister named Betsey, the alleged mistress of Samuel Carr, and that no one had ever accused Jefferson of having had an affair with her even though she also had children who resembled Jefferson. Randolph offered the allegation about Betsey Hemings to support his statement that the Carr brothers were the reason the Hemings children resembled Thomas Jefferson. If another woman associated with one of the Carr brothers had produced children who looked like Jefferson, the other woman associated with a Carr brother could do the same.

This aspect of the Carr brothers theory should be considered in light of the Randolph's and Randall's other statements on this matter. Both men offered material items of evidence to support their claims about the theory that are demonstrably false or not altogether credible. Ellen Coolidge did not mention that there were two women at Monticello with children who looked like Thomas Jefferson. Why wouldn't this explanation have occurred to Martha Randolph? When she sought to give her sons evidence that Jefferson could not have fathered the Hemings child who looked most like him, she did not cite Betsey Hemings's children as evidence that Sally Hemings's children did not have to be Jefferson's. If the Carr brothers' activities were so notorious that even Martha's children claimed to have known about them, certainly Martha, as the mistress of Monticello, would have known.

One must consider whether the assertion that Betsey Hemings's children looked like Jefferson was truthful or whether it was in line with the other incorrect statements that Randolph and Randall made. If true, it would show that one of the Carr brothers could produce children who looked like Jefferson; if one brother could, maybe the other could, as well. However, the Carr brothers were not the only ones who could have produced children who looked like Thomas Jefferson. Jefferson himself had already done it once in the person of Martha Randolph. Perhaps one of the Carr brothers was the father of Betsey Hemings's children, and Thomas Jefferson was the father of Sally Hemings's children. If Randolph's assertion about Betsey Hemings's children was not true, then it can take its place alongside the other false or dubious propositions offered to support the Carr brothers theory.

Coolidge's vague statements about the Hemings-Carr connection are not the only cause for concern about her letter. Coolidge claimed that Jefferson had a policy of allowing those of his slaves who were white enough to pass for white to go free. She offered this assertion to refute the idea that Jefferson freed Hemings's children because they were also his. The problem is that there is no evidence whatsoever that Jefferson had such a policy. The facts of life at Monticello, of which Coolidge would have been aware, completely contradict this idea. Hundreds of slaves went in and out of Jefferson's life as a slave master. A good number of them, by visitors' accounts, were white in appearance. Such a policy, if it existed, was applied to only four people. Moreover, Jefferson's Farm Book lists only three runaways. One of them was Jamey Hemings, who did not leave Monticello with Jefferson's initial approval. The other two were Beverley and Harriet Hemings. One understands why Coolidge might have attempted this defense. What is less comprehensible is why a notion so contrary to fact would ever have been treated as having any merit.

Edmund Bacon and the Grandchildren's Claim

We might cite Edmund Bacon's statements about Sally Hemings as support for the grandchildren's claim. Douglass Adair was adamant about doing just that. Adair declared that Bacon's statement naming ". . . ." as the father of Sally Hemings's children, when added to Thomas Jefferson Randolph's recollections, "established grounds for declaring Thomas Jefferson innocent of the charge that he fathered a mulatto family by his slave Sally Hemings." Adair attempted to fill in the missing name by saying that there was "presumptive" evidence that the person was Peter Carr. Dumas Malone said that when Adair wrote those words he had not seen Ellen Randolph Coolidge's letter naming Samuel Carr as the father of Hemings's children. That letter was made public by Malone in the 1970s.[20] This may account for the certainty of Adair's tone as he filled in Edmund Bacon's blank with the name of Peter Carr.

Although Bacon's statement supports the idea that someone else may have fathered Sally Hemings's children, it does not provide as strong corroboration for the Jefferson grandchildren's accounts as has been suggested. Bacon cannot be presumed to have been a neutral source, not only because of the circumstances under which his memoirs were produced, but because he had been a part of the Jefferson household for nearly twenty years. Although he did not think much of T. J. Randolph, it was plain that he adored Jefferson and Martha Randolph.[21] He would not have wanted to do damage to the memories of either of them.

More importantly, Bacon's statement is problematic as an item of evidence because he came to Monticello after Sally Hemings had given birth to all but one of her children and he did not specify whether he saw someone coming from her room before or after that last child was born. Pierson, the man who took down his memoirs, did not print the name of the individual whom Bacon named, and the original manuscript has been lost. So no one knows for certain who ". . . ." was, and unless the manuscript makes a miraculous re-appearance, we never will. Even if we knew that Bacon did name one of the Carrs, these evidentiary problems would still undercut the statement's power. Bacon was not in the position to have known with any degree of certainty who fathered Sally Hemings's children.

When one considers the weakness of Bacon's statements along with the Randolphs' unreliable attempts to promote the Carr brothers story, one comes away with the idea that perhaps Peter Carr, who died in 1815, and Samuel Carr, who was not as close to the Randolph family as Peter had been, may have become convenient scapegoats. Their names would have been very useful during the years that the Hemings children were coming of age and their resemblance to Jefferson would have been even more noticeable.

Motivations All Around

The truth is that all of these people—T. J. Randolph, Ellen Coolidge, and Edmund Bacon—had reasons for putting forth their version of the story that are as great, if not greater, than those of Madison Hemings or S. F. Wetmore. Bacon revered Jefferson. The grandchildren did, too, and they had other motivations as well.

It is probably safe to say that most people do not want to think about their grandparents' sexuality. This would particularly be true if it took a form that would likely cause embarrassment, such as a partner of the wrong class, race, or sex. T. J. Randolph had been exhorted by his mother to defend his grandfather's reputation, and one would assume that he would follow her instructions. The fact that both of their uncles had gone on to their reward made things easier.

Jefferson's grandchildren had much to lose if the stories about a Jefferson-Hemings liaison were thought to be true. There is no doubt that Randolph and Coolidge loved their grandfather. They were his favorites. Although Jefferson had not left them much in the way of worldly goods, his reputation was a substantial legacy to them. To the extent that the stories might tarnish that reputation, one can understand why they might have been willing to do or say whatever they thought necessary to prevent that outcome.

An interesting feature of the Randolph family defense of Jefferson is that each member of the family who spoke about the Hemings allegation had a different reason for why it could not be true. Consider the ambiguities that their different answers, particularly the grandchildren's, raise. In one of their versions, Peter Carr is the father of the Hemings children. In another, Samuel Carr is the father. In one recounting, Samuel and Peter Carr break down and cry when considering this subject. In another version Peter Carr laughs about the situation. To one person Randolph said that he was alone when he confronted the brothers and they confessed. To another person, Randolph said that he and a companion overheard one of the brothers admit responsibility. Even if we do not choose to think the Randolphs would lie, we still must be concerned about the contradictory nature of their statements. At a minimum, we can say that neither T. J. Randolph nor Ellen Coolidge knew who fathered Sally Hemings's children. If they did not know whether it was Samuel or Peter Carr, they may not have known whether it was Samuel Carr, Peter Carr, or Thomas Jefferson.

Slave Narratives and Slave Masters

Why should the words of T. J. Randolph and Ellen Coolidge, despite their motivations to tell the stories they told and despite the serious flaws and ambiguities in their accounts, be given such credence and Madison Hemings's statement be dismissed out of hand? The answer brings us back to the problem of stereotypes in historical writings. Madison Hemings's statement appears to the world in a form that comes with a degree of baggage. When a document is characterized as a slave narrative, or as being reminiscent of a slave narrative, the idea conveyed is that one must be on guard because the information within the document is inherently suspect. This is alleged to be so because of the characteristics of the person giving the statement—the person is old, uneducated, and has a motive to stretch the truth—and because the interviewer or editor may be biased—the abolitionists or former abolitionists want to promote a viewpoint. For some, the unspoken reason for skepticism is, of course, that the speaker is black and he may be saying things that reflect badly upon white people.

Madison Hemings's race and previous condition of servitude put him at a distinct disadvantage in a contest between his word and those of Jefferson's grandchildren. His status gave historians license to attribute base motivations and bad character to him. Randolph and Coolidge were not slaves but slave masters. There is no such thing as a "slave master narrative" that triggers a response of automatic skepticism, although it is a strange turn of events when individuals who held other human beings in bondage are given presumptive moral superiority over their captives. Moreover, that the Randolph siblings could speak in so detached and dismissive a fashion about people with whom they shared a set of great-grandparents—Peter and Jane Jefferson—gave historians no insight into their capacity (and need) for self-deception and denial. Randolph's and Coolidge's comments appear in forms that are more acceptable to historians who regularly rely upon such material for their work. Randolph was talking to a historian and biographer of his grandfather, a late president of the United States. Ellen Coolidge, an aristocratic southern gentlewoman, was writing a letter to her husband. Apparently these circumstances do not raise the same concerns that exist about slave narratives. Thus, the appearance of their statements in these contexts do not encumber Randolph and Coolidge in the way that the presentation of Hemings's statement encumbers him. In fact, their status gives them the presumption of believability.

This is true despite the fact that during the course of vindicating Jefferson, both Randolph and Coolidge make insupportable claims. Significantly, their mistakes are never to their detriment or neutral; each advances their overall point. Normally, when a person offers an untruth to support a proposition or seems to err strategically, that person's credibility suffers. If the untruths and self-serving mistakes are very large or become too numerous, one begins to doubt the truth of the proposition itself. This phenomenon does not apply to the Randolphs. No matter how many material, and seemingly calculated, errors they made, they have received no demerits. Historians prefer to focus only on the bottom line of their statements—Jefferson was not the father of Hemings's children—and to ignore the serious problems with the way they make this point.

Madison Hemings is twice-handicapped because his memoirs not only have received increased scrutiny as a slave narrative but have been denigrated because he was essentially reciting his family's oral history. Even if there is no genre of slave-master narrative, one might think that Randolph's and Coolidge's statements would be subjected to similarly strict scrutiny because they, too, are oral history. If slave narratives are problematic because they offer the opportunity for error, family histories are equally problematic. It is not unheard-of for members of a family to conceal information or to lie in order to protect other family members—for their own sake and for the sake of the family's image. Of course, this applies to Hemings's memoirs as well. The difference is that substantially more extrinsic evidence exists to support Madison Hemings's oral history than exists to support the oral history presented by Randolph and Coolidge.

James Parton

It is important to understand the result of reliance on T. J. Randolph's oral history. Randolph claimed to have established that Jefferson could not have been the father of one of Sally Hemings's children, and Randall said he had confirmed that claim. According to Merrill Peterson, while James Parton was working on his biography of Jefferson, he received advance warning that Madison Hemings's story would be printed in a newspaper.[22] This intelligence led him to contact Henry Randall to try to get some information on the subject—most likely, something that would refute Hemings's claim. Parton responded to Madison Hemings's memoirs in his biography by noting: "There is even a respectable Madison Henings, now living in Ohio, who supposes that Thomas Jefferson was his father. Mr. Henings has been misinformed. The record of Mr. Jefferson's every day and hour, contained in his pocket memorandum books, compared with the record of his slave's birth, proves the impossibility of his having been the father of Madison Henings."[23]

Parton then reproduced part of Randall's letter, excising the section on the Carr brothers. Unless there was other correspondence between Parton and Randall on this matter, the identity of the slave who was the subject of Martha Randolph's discussion with her son is unknown. The letter from which Parton quoted does not name the child who looked exactly like Jefferson and whose birth date T. J. Randolph was supposed to have verified.[24] Parton knew that Sally Hemings had more than one child and that the Randolph anecdote did not, on its face, refute Madison Hemings's particular claim because it did not name the child whose birth Martha Randolph and her son investigated. Parton nevertheless presented this information to the public as though it was as clear as day that the "memorandum books" and "record of [the] slave's birth" applied to Madison Hemings.

Parton the historian was out neither to discover the truth nor to disseminate it. He was out to refute the substance of Madison Hemings's claim, no matter what. There is every chance that if Beverley, Harriet, or Eston Hemings had spoken to the *Pike County (Ohio) Republican,* Parton would have claimed the indisputable records applied to one of them. It is perhaps because of Parton that it has been said that the subject of T. J. Randolph's "investigation" was Madison Hemings.[25] We do not know who it was. There is one indication as to the possible identity, however. It was, after all, the bronze statue of Thomas Jefferson in Washington that in the 1840s left the visitors from Ohio dumbstruck because they thought it looked exactly like Eston Hemings.

One should take note of whom the historians have been willing to believe, the quantum of evidence that they required in order to justify their beliefs, and the lengths to which some historians were willing to go in order to support their contentions. James Parton was willing to believe Henry Randall's account of his conversation with T. J. Randolph and the underlying assertions of Martha Randolph and T. J. Randolph contained within that conversation. He was also willing to believe, without further question, what Randall said he had done to confirm the Randolphs' statements. Parton himself then compounded his error by engaging in his own textual sleight of hand to accomplish the goal of defeating Madison Hemings's claim.

Readers are still invited to believe all of these individuals' pronouncements on this controversial issue without reservation. Some modern historians seem to have felt no discomfort in offering this patently flawed material as proof—not mere evidence—that one or both of the Carr brothers fathered Sally Hemings's children. They have done this even as they deemed Madison Hemings's statements, and those of Israel Jefferson who supported him, unworthy of serious attention because the historians did not like what the men were saying and because their status made them easy to dismiss.

Two Kinds of Oral History

We have two examples of oral history, and the question must be raised squarely, Why should the demonstrably flawed oral history of a white family be taken as truth and the oral history of a black family that can be supported by a fairly large amount of extrinsic evidence be presumed a lie? What are black people, or any people for that matter, to make of this: that the words of whites carry more weight than the words of blacks and do not have to be subjected to rigorous scrutiny, or that the words of formerly wealthy aristocrats carry more weight than those of former slaves?

Jefferson's grandchildren are cited for two propositions: that Jefferson was not the father of Hemings's children and that one or both of the Carr brothers were. One could be sympathetic to their opinion that Jefferson was not the father and still see that they must be held to some standard when they so specifically accuse the Carrs. Instead, there are no standards for them at all. The problem is that someone was the father, and it is better for those who want Jefferson out of the picture to have a named culprit as a substitute. Because members of Jefferson's family readily acknowledged that Sally Hemings's children closely resembled Jefferson, the father of her children had to be within the Jefferson family. The Carr brothers are the men who could most easily fit this requirement, if it was not Jefferson himself, and for most historians it does not matter which brother it was. Scholars believe what Randolph and Coolidge said about the Carrs, not because their assertions have any demonstrable validity, but because they want to believe them. With this mindset in place, attention to detail can play no useful role.

In truth, this is not just a simple matter of black versus white. It is, rather, a complex matter of black and white, for the Carr brothers have been treated almost as unfairly as Madison and Sally Hemings. Both men have now gone down in history as adulterers and, by some accounts, participants in a ménage à trois with Sally Hemings, solely on the basis of the conflicting and uncorroborated accounts of two people who had no strong extrinsic evidence to back up their contentions. All the normal standards for judging evidence have been abrogated, with the result that Peter Carr and Samuel Carr have served as human shields to protect the man who personified America. Their shabby treatment is instructive, for it proves that even whites whom some see as being of no particular consequence can be sacrificed to maintain certain white people's image of themselves and America.

The Evidence That Is Needed

What kind of evidence might support the idea that either Peter Carr or Samuel Carr, or both, fathered Sally Hemings's children? Martha Jefferson Randolph gave us a clue when she called two of her sons to her and tried to tell them that Jefferson could not have fathered one of the Hemings children because he was not there when the child was conceived. Though Martha Randolph was wrong on this point, she at least understood the importance of showing a putative father's access to a woman as a means of supporting or destroying the charge of paternity.

None of the most vigorous promoters of the Carr brothers' involvement with Sally Hemings have offered any credible evidence of their whereabouts during the time Hemings conceived her children. One scholar, Andrew Burstein, claimed to have done so. After noting the conflict between the Randolph siblings over whether Peter or Samuel Carr was the father, Burstein wrote, "Either explanation is plausible, insofar as Jefferson's Account Books show that both nephews were present at Monticello or having transactions with Jefferson during the specific periods that correspond to Sally's conceptions." That the Carr brothers may have had "transactions with Jefferson" during the relevant time periods does not establish that they were present to conceive children with Hemings, as those transactions could have taken place by mail. In addition, Burstein cited Jefferson's account books for a series of five years without listing any months. It is not significant that one or both of the Carr brothers was at Monticello at some point during the years that Hemings gave birth. The question is whether they were there during the months that she likely conceived.

The most serious problem with Burstein's claim is that his source material does not support it. The years he cited in which Jefferson's account books show that the Carr brothers were at Monticello, and Hemings conceived, do not correspond to the number or birth dates of Hemings's children. Hemings had six known children. Yet Burstein cited only five years—1795, 1798, 1800, 1802, and 1803—for her conceptions. Hemings bore a child in the first weeks of December 1799 who also would have been conceived in that year. Although the years 1795 and 1800 are years when Hemings likely conceived, the other three years are not. Hemings gave birth to Beverley Hemings in April 1798. He was, therefore, conceived in 1797. After her daughter Harriet was born in 1801, Hemings did not give birth again until 1805. Her last child was born in 1808. The years 1802 and 1803 are, thus, irrelevant to their conceptions.[26]

Journalists consulting Jefferson scholars seem unaware of or indifferent to the flimsiness of the evidence with regard to the Carr brothers and repeat these scholars' claims as though they were established fact. What Jefferson's grandchildren could not have known at the time that this story was first promulgated—and what supporters of the notion do not seem to understand now—is how the idea of the Carr brothers as fathers is undercut by information about Jefferson's whereabouts during the months when Sally Hemings conceived her children.

It is often said with regard to this controversy that one cannot prove a negative. In other words, that because it would be impossible to prove that Thomas Jefferson was not the father of Hemings's children, proponents of the idea that he was the father are operating with an unfair advantage. This is not correct. It is possible to prove that a man is not the father of a woman's children. One of the main ways of doing this, before the advent of blood and DNA tests, was to show that the man had no access to the woman during the time when she could have conceived the child. In that situation a negative could be proved by the introduction of a type of evidence—evidence that the man had no access to the woman during the relevant period. As it turns out, it is possible that the process can be applied to at least one of the men in this story, Samuel Carr. Family correspondence suggests that he was away from the environs of Monticello when Sally Heming's second daughter was likely conceived.[27]

The notion that Jefferson defenders are being held to an unfair standard because they cannot prove a negative in the Jefferson-Hemings controversy exists only because defenders are unable to offer "no access" as a defense. Proponents of the liaison have met what always has been the first test of establishing paternity: access to a woman during the time she would have conceived the child. Their ability to do this does not amount to having an unfair advantage. It merely means that they have met a threshold test. They do not have proof of paternity at this point, but they are legitimately on the road to building a quantum of evidence that with other items may amount to proof.

Sally Hemings had a childbearing history that spanned about fifteen years, if we leave out "Tom Hemings." During that time she had six children. Four of them survived to adulthood. The period of Hemings's childbearing roughly spans Jefferson's years as a public servant in the national government as secretary of state, vice president, and president. During that time he went back and forth from Philadelphia, and then Washington, to Monticello. We know from Malone's chronology of the events in Jefferson's life that he was present at Monticello at least nine months before the birth of each one of Sally Hemings's children, even the one that was most recently discovered.[28]

Had Thomas Jefferson never had the occasion to serve in high office and had he spent every one of those fifteen years at Monticello, it would not be particularly significant that he was there when Sally Hemings conceived. He would be just like any other white male who lived at Monticello, in terms of the possibility that he could have been the father of her children. Or rather, one must specify any male Jefferson relative who lived at Monticello, to take into account the striking resemblance that Hemings's children bore to Jefferson. It is the very fact that he was coming and going from the place that lifts the possibility that he fathered Hemings's children to some level of probability, for his leaving and coming home can be directly related to the timing of their conceptions.

The relationship was so strong that it can be described as creating a pattern. The pattern went like this: Jefferson comes home for six months and leaves. Hemings bears a child four months after he is gone. Jefferson comes home for six weeks. Hemings bears a child eight months after he is gone.

Jefferson comes for two months and leaves. Hemings bears a child eight months after he is gone. This went on for fifteen years through six children. He was there when she conceived, and she never conceived when he was not there.[29]

It is the last point that creates the greatest problem for the Carr brothers theory. Those who state as a fact, or claim that there is strong evidence, that one or both of the Carrs fathered Hemings's children must explain why one man's fertility—or, even more improbably, two men's fertility—should be so unerringly tied to another man's presence. Why could not Peter Carr or Samuel Carr get Sally Hemings pregnant when Thomas Jefferson was not at Monticello—not once in fifteen years? T. J. Randolph and Ellen Randolph Coolidge present a picture of easy access on the part of the Carrs to the slave women at Monticello. The more expansive the claim of access, the harder it is to understand how the sexual unions undertaken as a result of that access would never once result in a conception during a time when Thomas Jefferson was away.

Douglass Adair, not understanding the conceptual hole that he was digging for himself, noted that Sally Hemings's last child was born the year before the end of Jefferson's last term. He posited that once Jefferson came home permanently, Peter Carr lost the free access he had to Sally Hemings, and this is why she had no more children.[30] But Jefferson was at Monticello every time Hemings conceived. If Peter Carr fathered Hemings's children, he would have had to be there too, so that one cannot say that he was inhibited by Jefferson's presence. Jefferson's grandchildren also moved to Monticello after Jefferson's retirement. Was it they who inhibited Carr? Some of Hemings's children were conceived during summers when Jefferson's grandchildren were in residence at Monticello, as well. If the presence of Jefferson and other members of his family had not stopped Carr before, why would it have done so after they were at Monticello permanently?

Even more importantly, Adair was claiming that Peter Carr, who lived a few miles from Monticello, was taking advantage of Jefferson's absences to pursue his affair with Hemings. If this were the case, one would think that there should have been at least one time when Thomas Jefferson came home and found Sally Hemings pregnant even though he had not been there when the child she was carrying was conceived. It never happened, not even during the many years when Jefferson was away from Monticello for as many as six to eight consecutive months at a time. After some of those long absences, Jefferson would return home and Hemings would conceive a child within a few weeks after his arrival.[31] The evidence of access at the relevant time period—which Martha Jefferson Randolph understood was critical—is 100 percent with respect to Jefferson. He was there when the event (conception) occurred, and when he was not there, the event did not occur.

What of the Carr brothers? Although Peter Carr lived closer to Monticello than his brother Samuel, it is very likely that they both visited Jefferson when he returned for his vacations, especially if he "had always fed them." However, one can safely doubt that Samuel and Peter Carr, having come to see their beloved uncle, presumably with wives and children in tow, would run off to have sex with their slave mistress to whom they had access when Jefferson was gone and when they did not have to bring their families along.

Even if Peter or Samuel were at Monticello during the crucial time periods, it would not solve the problem of the flip side of the equation. One would have to show that Peter Carr or Samuel Carr, whom Virginius Dabney named as the most likely father, did not visit Monticello when Thomas Jefferson was away.[32] If they visited when their uncle was away, how probable is it that over a fifteen-year period, through the conceptions of six children, one or both of the Carrs would be infertile during the many consecutive months that Jefferson was away and fertile when he was at Monticello, sometimes for as short a period as six weeks?[33] Or, how probable is it that Peter or Samuel Carr, allegedly involved in a fifteen-year affair with Sally Hemings and most of the time living within five miles of Monticello, would choose to visit her only when Jefferson came home? That the Carr brothers acted as shadows to Jefferson has never been the claim of those who have stated with certainty that one, or both, of them fathered the Hemings children. They have indicated that the Carrs were at Monticello at will.

But what of Adair's point that Sally Hemings bore no more children after Jefferson retired? Would this not tend to prove that he was not the father of her children? There could have been physiological and psychological reasons that Sally Hemings had no children during Jefferson's retirement. She was thirty-six years old when he returned home for good and had given birth the year before. Fertility in women drops off after their mid-thirties. It was an era of poor hygiene, and Hemings had borne six, maybe seven, children. Infections or difficulties encountered during childbirth could easily have impaired her capacity to conceive or carry another child to term. The nature of their relationship could have changed as the thirty-year age difference loomed much larger when Jefferson approached his seventies and Hemings her forties.

There is no absolute proof to be had in any of these suggestions, but there is much more and stronger evidence linking Sally Hemings to Thomas

Jefferson than to either of the Carr brothers. More substantial evidence about Peter or Samuel Carr may come in the future, but it is not here now.

Conclusion

What we are left with is a situation where the oral history of one family is pitted against the oral history of another family. It is black against white, under circumstances where whites for the most part have controlled the assemblage and dissemination of information. While there is a need to be careful in approaching the question of who is more correct, one must consider seriously what being careful means. One cannot be careless in the analysis and assessment of evidence offered by one side and extra careful when assessing the evidence from the other. This way of proceeding is not designed to help reach a better understanding of the truth; it is, instead, designed to protect a particular image of the truth.

The standard for judging the evidence must be equally applied. If oral history is not fact, it cannot be discarded for the Hemingses but accepted as fact for the Randolphs of the world. If it is going to be accepted, then it must be assessed and examined according to common ground rules. It should be what the declarants say, how they say it, and the amount of extrinsic evidence that exists to support their statements that counts, not their status, family background, or race.

On this score what Madison Hemings said and the way he said it establishes him as a more credible declarant than either T. J. Randolph or Ellen Randolph Coolidge. By any measure the extrinsic evidence supporting Madison Hemings's statement, which should be the prime focus of the inquiry, is of greater weight than the extrinsic evidence supporting the Jefferson-Randolph oral history, if one can even say that such extrinsic evidence exists. Therefore, it is incorrect to treat the latter statements as being of more value than the former, or to even treat the two histories as being of equivalent value. That they have been so treated can be attributed to the fact that the weaknesses of the Jefferson-Randolph oral history have been shored up with the advantages of their status and historians' desire to believe them. As no evidence has been offered to prove otherwise, there is no reason to presume that T. J. Randolph or Ellen Coolidge were any more decent or honorable than Madison Hemings or Israel Jefferson. We should not allow phrases such as "would-be former house slave" or "ex-slave" to substitute for reasoned analysis in this inquiry. Epithets will not do. That some historians have felt they could proceed on this basis with impunity suggests how little the considerations and sensibilities of blacks figured in either their deliberations or their writings on this subject and how useful the employment of stereotypes can be when historians lack the basic facts to support their claims.

4

Thomas Jefferson

> We shall never have a science of history until we have in our
> colleges men who regard the truth as more important than the
> defense of the white race, and who will not deliberately encour-
> age students to gather thesis material in order to support preju-
> dice or buttress a lie.
>
> —W. E. B. Du Bois, "The Propaganda of History"

IN OCTOBER 1994 the Association of the Bar of the City of New York spon-
sored a mock trial of Thomas Jefferson. The issue to be decided by the trial
was whether examples of hypocrisy in Jefferson's life significantly diminished
his contributions to American society. Charles Ogletree of the Harvard Law
School served as a prosecutor of the case, and Drew Days, the solicitor general
of the United States and a former professor at the Yale Law School, was the
attorney for the defense. William Rehnquist, chief justice of the United States
Supreme Court, presided as trial judge. The jury consisted of audience members, including myself and my husband; we arrived early to get a seat in what
we knew would be a packed house. The irony was exquisite. Two distinguished
black attorneys stood in front of a predominately white audience and presented the cases for and against Thomas Jefferson, a man who had owned
blacks and disparaged their mental abilities. That this event was made possible because of some of the other loftier ideals Jefferson expounded is clear.
What is less clear is whether he would have been delighted or horrified at
that thought.

After presenting their opening arguments, the lawyers called historians
as expert witnesses to make their respective cases. Each talked about Jefferson,
the author of the Declaration of Independence, with his plantations worked
by black slaves; Jefferson the republican, with his royal tastes in food, wine,
and property; Jefferson, proponent of the rights of man and opponent of
the rights of women. When it came to a vote, my husband and I, along with

the overwhelming majority of other members of the audience, voted in favor of Jefferson.

Note that the trial was not about whether Thomas Jefferson was prone to hypocrisy, which seems to have been taken as a given. The question for the evening was whether we were willing to forgive him for it. That the answer would be yes was never in doubt; even the "prosecutor" expressed relief at the decision. The decisiveness of Jefferson's victory was not surprising either, because of all those who figured prominently in the American Revolution, Jefferson stands apart in the minds of many Americans. George Washington may have been the "Father of Our Country," but he exists for most Americans as a face on a bill, a man with bad dentures and a strange wig who stood in a boat while crossing a river.

Jefferson's authorship of the Declaration of Independence lifted him above the rest of the Founding Fathers. His vision of life, liberty, and the pursuit of happiness has been taken to heart by Americans, many of whom seem to think this triumvirate of rights is guaranteed by the Constitution. Thus, it is often said that Jefferson is the personification of America. His strengths are the strengths of the country, and the same can be said for his weaknesses. For this reason, the knowledge that Jefferson himself did not live up to the vision he set before us has troubled some Americans from his time until today.

While many Americans may be unaware of some of the examples of hypocrisy cited during the mock trial, everyone knows that even as he wrote passionately about the rights of human beings and, on occasion, the evils of slavery, Jefferson owned slaves. Because we live in a country in which Jefferson's way of life was repudiated with force of arms, in considering him (and wanting to have affection for him) we are constantly reminded that there was something terribly wrong about the way he lived. It has been suggested that it took Abraham Lincoln to rescue the ideals of Jefferson and bring them forward to modern America. Having used those ideals to preserve the Union and to end slavery, Lincoln made it easier to forgive Jefferson for not having been true to his own remarkable vision.

Actually, one should say that it has been easier for *some* Americans to forgive. Black Americans have long been ambivalent about Thomas Jefferson. While most whites may admire Jefferson's elegant identification of George III as a tyrant, most blacks might say that it took one to know one. If whites tend to focus on the ways in which Jefferson reflected the ideals of America, blacks and their sympathizers, while admiring the ideal, tend to focus upon the reality that lay underneath. This constant friction created the circumstance under which hundreds of people would come out on a weeknight in 1994 to decide whether a man who died 168 years before should be forgiven for something.

The allegation that Thomas Jefferson had a long-term liaison with his slave Sally Hemings presents a particular challenge to the grant of forgiveness that Jefferson is almost ritually given. Some historians are willing to accept certain contradictions in Jefferson's attitude toward blacks and slavery but seem unable to accept the possibility that there may have been others. It is, in fact, hard to escape the conclusion that there is a correlation between a given historian's willingness to believe the story might be true and whether that person would be able to forgive Jefferson if it was. In this view Jefferson was capable of doing only those things for which he can be forgiven. This way of viewing the matter is an understandable and maybe unavoidable consequence of the process of writing biographies. It is important to recognize, however, that it has no basis in the possible reality of what was, after all, another person's life. It derives from one's personal values and the need to believe that Jefferson lived in accord with those values.

That personal values offered as fact have become an integral part of the commentary about Thomas Jefferson can be seen most clearly in the "defenses" offered against the charge of miscegenation, both in explaining why the story could not be true and in responding to the evidence indicating that it could be true. It fell to Dumas Malone, the greatest and most famous of Jefferson scholars, to set the tone for this strategy. Others have picked up on Malone's themes, most notably Virginius Dabney, John C. Miller, and, more recently, Andrew Burstein, one of a new generation of Jefferson scholars.

The arguments advanced as to why the allegation could not be so rely primarily upon a particular view of Thomas Jefferson's character that would make such a relationship impossible. Malone wrote of the charges, "They are distinctly out of character, being virtually unthinkable in a man of Jefferson's moral standards and habitual conduct."[1] In using the term *character* and speaking of "moral standards" and "habitual conduct," Malone and others who offer Jefferson's character in answer to the charge that he was involved with Sally Hemings seem to be referring to attributes that can be summed up as: (1) Jefferson was a gentlemen who would have recoiled at the thought of such a liaison because it would have amounted to taking unfair advantage of another person. (2) Jefferson was a man whose intellect ruled over his emotions, so much so that he was indeed, as one early newspaper put it, a man whose blood was "very snow-broth." (3) Jefferson was a family man who would not have carried on such a liaison because of his affection for his daughters and grandchildren. (4) Jefferson was a racist, and this condition would have prevented him from developing either an emotional or even a purely sexual relationship with a black woman.

Some assumptions lie beneath these defenses of Jefferson, and each should be examined closely. It is important to do so, not simply because of how the arguments affect the particular controversy at hand, but because of the view of southern history, the nature of family life, and the nature of race relations in this country, past and present, that they promote.

Jefferson the Gentleman and the Problem of Miscegenation

Consider first the argument that Jefferson's status as a gentleman would have precluded a liaison of this nature. This contention is most often framed in terms of disbelief at the idea that Thomas Jefferson would have "overreached" himself in this fashion. Engaging in a sexual relationship with a slave was an abuse of power by the master (a curious concept, that), and Jefferson was not known as an "abusive" individual.[2]

This line of argument promotes at least two questionable theses. The first is that the type of overreaching involved in a sexual liaison with a slave actually was, and was thought at the time to be, vastly different—and worse— than the other types of overreaching that were also part and parcel of the slave system. The claim that southern gentlemen saw and were able to maintain a clear demarcation between the types of exploitation involved in starting a sexual relationship with a slave and, say, making that slave work from sunrise to sundown for nothing or selling that slave's children must be viewed with some skepticism given the extent of violations of this item in the code of honor. It may have been necessary to the maintenance of order in society— to avoid giving offense to white women and to make sure that white women would not take a sauce for the goose approach to miscegenation—for southern gentlemen to say that this demarcation was clear and rigid. There is much evidence, however, that the many components of the slave system, which included miscegenation, could not be so easily compartmentalized.[3]

In Jefferson's case it is by no means obvious that a man who owned people, bought and sold them, gave them away as wedding presents, and impressed them into the armed services to risk their lives fighting in a war for other people's freedom would believe that having sex with one of the people so used would amount to overreaching so great as to be beyond his contemplation. His contradictory statements about the nature of freedom and slavery and of black people suggest that his ability to draw absolute lines on these matters was not as refined as some would allege.

On one hand, Jefferson wrote that slavery was an abomination. On the other hand, he seldom freed slaves. On the one hand, he argued that slaves could not be freed because they were like children. On the other hand, he saw to it that many slaves on his plantation became skilled craftsmen. This was done to suit Jefferson's purposes, but the end result was the creation of adults who could have worked to support themselves. On one hand, Jefferson seems to have been revolted by the notion of amalgamation and social relations with blacks. On the other hand, he took products of amalgamation and made them favored members of his household. He also maintained cordial relations with some blacks and encouraged one black family to send their children to the local white school in Charlottesville. The truth is that Thomas Jefferson can be cited to support almost any position on slavery and the race question that could exist.[4]

This part of the character defense also posits that what Jefferson was accused of doing amounts to an act so heinous that it could only have been carried out by a depraved individual.[5] In keeping with this idea, the picture painted of what any Jefferson-Hemings relationship necessarily would have been like is almost invariably something along the lines of forcible rape or, by some commentators, child molestation. "What you're saying then is that Thomas Jefferson was a rapist." "What you're saying then is that Thomas Jefferson had sex with an eight-year-old girl."

This immediately brings to mind a picture of Thomas Jefferson knocking down a woman's door and dragging her by her hair to his bedroom, precisely the image that defenders want to project because they know that most people who have ever read anything about Jefferson would discount that scenario. The goal is to make any conception of Jefferson's actions so bad that no one would, or would want to, believe that it could be true.

Actually, characterizing a Jefferson-Hemings relationship as thirty-eight years' worth of nights of "Come here gal!" is a sophisticated technique. It presents the proponent of the idea as enlightened and forward thinking with regard to the nature of slavery, even as that individual promotes a cardboard version of the system. It is all the more seductive because the idea is not without merit. The slave system was inherently coercive. Therefore, one could argue, every act of sex between a master and slave was the equivalent of nonconsensual sex, in other words, rape.

We may know this is true in the theoretical sense, but something should tell us that it cannot have been true in every situation, under every circumstance, that existed from the early 1600s until emancipation. Do we really believe that over the entire course of slavery in the United States, no master and slave woman ever experienced a mutual sexual or emotional attachment to one another? Can we really believe that a slave woman confronted with a master whom she knew, or reasonably believed, would desist if she refused his advances was in the same position as a woman whose master would knock down the door and drag her off to his bedroom? Both women would have existed in a state of relative powerlessness. But we instinctively feel that there is a difference. In the former situation the woman would have had a small but important individualized bit of power even as she existed in a state of general powerlessness. The power was, of course, to say yes or no. In the latter situation her powerlessness would have been total.

The idea of total powerlessness on the part of all slaves is attractive to both whites and blacks for different reasons. For some whites, even as they denounce the barbarity of slavery, the fantasy of white omnipotence may remain secretly appealing. Their presentation of slaves as having been totally helpless evinces sympathy for blacks, but it also imagines a time when whites allegedly had the power to rule blacks, mind, body, and soul. To admit that there might have been some instances when blacks exercised a degree of free will interrupts the dream of omnipotence and forces consideration of the ways in which that will may have been exercised and what effect it may have had upon whites.

It is especially hard (and unpleasant) for some to think that a black woman might have exercised her will, circumscribed as it was, by saying yes to Thomas Jefferson and, in doing so, have been able to exercise some influence over him. Scholars have scoffed at the notion that Sally Hemings, no matter how beautiful or appealing, could have had enough power to extract a promise from Jefferson to free her children and then over the years hold him to that promise.[6] Jefferson, the personification of America, simply cannot be put in that position. The actions he took with respect to Hemings's children, for example, must be seen as a product of Jefferson's will alone. It should not be considered for a moment that he may have been acting under the influence of so insignificant a person as a black female slave.

The notion of total powerlessness has appeal to some blacks because it seems to make the slave system worse, as if that were possible. Saying that there were instances where blacks had room to maneuver can be taken as an attempt to minimize the horror of the slave system. This is not the case. The idea brings forth the truth that there were two sets of human beings involved in that sorry state of affairs, not one race of all powerful gods and another race of totally dominated submortals. While it is true that the balance of power dramatically favored whites, it is not true that blacks were unable to influence the lives of whites on an individual and societywide basis. No matter what amount of short-term gain may be achieved by focusing on black powerlessness (to trigger white guilt), it can never be in the long-term interests of blacks to accept so limited and distorted a version of history.

The Character Defense at All Costs

It has not been enough to evoke the vision of the totally powerless slave for use as a weapon in the arsenal of Jefferson defenders; the vulnerability of children has been deployed as well. In considering this campaign in the battle of perceptions, the saying "All's fair in love and war" seems especially appropriate. The writings of historians Alf E. Mapp, Jr., and Willard Sterne Randall come the most quickly to mind in this regard. Both historians' defenses of Jefferson depend, in part, upon telling readers that to believe in the truth of the Hemings story is to believe that Thomas Jefferson had designs upon a prepubescent girl.

Mapp wrote of the Hemings allegation:

> Some with imaginations less restrained than Mrs. Brodie's have suggested that Jefferson had Sally accompany his daughter to Europe so that he might consummate his passion for the slave girl. Since Sally was fourteen or fifteen when she arrived in France in 1787 and Jefferson had not seen her for more than three years, one is asked to believe that even amid the caresses of the cultivated belles of Paris he pined for an ignorant serving girl whose eleven or twelve year old charms were indelibly burnt into his brain.[7]

Mapp did not identify who had made such suggestions. One would think that the name or names of anyone who made so outrageous a charge—and the context in which they made it—should have been exposed. If any historian had said this, Mapp's readers should have been alerted so that they would know in the future to view that scholar's other claims with suspicion.

Willard Sterne Randall created his own variation on Mapp's theme, reducing Hemings's age at the time of her alleged seduction and thus raising the stakes for belief in the Hemings story. He discussed Fawn Brodie's attempt to draw a relationship between what she thought was Jefferson's excessive use of the term *mulatto* in his descriptions of the terrain of certain European countries and his interest in Sally Hemings. Randall seized upon this admittedly problematic contention and said that because Hemings was not yet in France at the time Jefferson took this trip, he would have to be remembering Hemings from the last time he had spent much time around her, which was when she was eight years old. Several reviewers of Randall's book picked up on this aspect of his analysis, and trumpeted the claim that Brodie had accused Jefferson of starting his affair with Hemings when she was eight years old.[8]

However, Jefferson took two trips through the European countryside, one before Hemings arrived and one after. Brodie made it explicit—indeed it was the whole point of the passage—that she was contrasting the number of times he used the term in the descriptions of the terrain before Hemings got to Paris and the number of times he used it afterward. She was clear that she believed the liaison began sometime after Sally Hemings accompanied Jefferson's daughter to Paris.[9] Hemings, who was born in 1773, would have been between fourteen and fifteen at the time she arrived there and between sixteen and seventeen when she left. Yet, even for those who did not further distort Randall's reading of Brodie, Hemings's youth relative to Jefferson's age has been invoked to suggest that Brodie's thesis amounted to a charge of child molestation on the part of Jefferson.[10]

But did Thomas Jefferson, and other men and women of the eighteenth century, think of teenaged girls in the same way that we think of them today? One particular circumstance from the life of one of Jefferson's closest friends, and his direct involvement in the situation, suggests that they did not. The great love of James Madison's life (before he met and married Dolley) was a fifteen-year-old girl named Catherine Floyd. Madison was thirty-one years old at the time. Jefferson, who was awaiting instructions for his trip to France, actively encouraged the relationship. He went so far as to speak with the young girl about Madison, becoming in the words of Madison's biographer Irving Brant, "an energetic matchmaker." When he was certain of her affection for his friend, Jefferson wrote to Madison assuring him that a marriage between the two would "render you happier than you can possibly be in a single state." Madison and Floyd got to the point of setting a date for their marriage, but Kitty eventually broke Madison's heart by casting him aside for another teenager. Jefferson wrote a sympathetic letter counseling Madison that if reconciliation proved impossible, he would eventually find other "resources of happiness."[11]

If Brodie was correct, Jefferson was in his mid-forties and Hemings was either fifteen or sixteen when their alleged relationship began. He was older than Madison. But child molestation is not judged by the age of the adult who is said to engage in it, it is judged by the age of the child. If the forty-four-year-old Thomas Jefferson could be characterized as something on the order of a child molester for having allegedly started a relationship with a female who was either fifteen or sixteen, then one must also question the activities of his friend the adult James Madison who courted a female of the same age.

Ultimately, this argument against the notion of a Jefferson-Hemings liaison is problematic, not only because it distorts Jefferson's views about the appropriateness of sexual relations with fifteen-year-olds (we can presume he thought that Madison and Floyd would consummate their martial relationship), but because it gives readers an incorrect impression of eighteenth-century standards and practices. Females of Hemings's age at the time of her stay in France were thought eligible for relationships with men.

Historians and the Problem of Miscegenation

What are black Americans to make of all this? Do the people who frame their responses to this allegation in these desperate ways know or even care how they might sound? Why should the thought that a white president may have had a long-term relationship with a black person be the source of such a venomous reaction? When I have discussed this issue with blacks, they almost instantly and invariably see the reaction to the story in the same way. They say that the belief that having sex with a slave was the most base activity in which whites could engage has its origins in the discomfort and fear that some whites felt and still feel at the thought of miscegenation—whatever has been the actual practice. It is that fear, rather than any concern about the abuse of the power held over blacks, that is the driving force behind the response. For what other reason would modern commentators forgive Jefferson for all the other things he is known to have done to blacks but view this particular story as something so awful that they recoil in horror at the very thought that it might be true? The horror is not at the thought of the defilement of Sally Hemings but at the thought of Thomas Jefferson defiling himself by lying with Sally Hemings. By doing so, Jefferson would have hurt himself and, by extension, other whites. That particular sin would be unforgivable.

That is the most reasonable conclusion that can be drawn when one considers the posture in which this issue resurfaced with the appearance of Fawn Brodie's biography of Jefferson. The Jefferson-Hemings story and the alleged details of the relationship have had two major public airings. The first was given by James Callender and the second by Brodie. The two writers had completely different takes on the matter. Callender was offended by the charge that Jefferson had slept with a slave woman because he was revolted by miscegenation and what he saw as the too casual acceptance of the practice in the South. He was appalled that the vehemence of white southerners' rhetoric against miscegenation did not seem to match their actual practices. Callender's charges against Jefferson were designed to play into that society's purported equation of miscegenation with bestiality. He drew a picture of

Sally Hemings as being so low a creature that only an equally low individual would have had anything to do with her. His hysteria on this point stemmed from his own racism.

Fawn Brodie's depiction of the nature of the Jefferson-Hemings relationship was markedly different than Callender's. She saw Jefferson's actions with regard to Sally Hemings and her children from a vantage point that Callender did not, and would not have wanted to, view it. Brodie was not the enemy of Jefferson. Her view led her to conclude that Jefferson had done the following things. He had engaged in a thirty-eight-year liaison with a woman who was a slave. The length of the relationship suggested to her that both parties derived some satisfaction from it, because it would have taken a monster to have forced his attentions on a woman for so long a period. Because she did not think Jefferson a monster, it was likely to her that this was a case of mutual affection. Brodie accepted the claim in Madison Hemings's statement that Jefferson promised to free Sally Hemings's children when they attained majority. The fact that all of those children went free at that time suggested that Jefferson cared enough about Hemings to keep his promise, even though he knew that his actions could cause problems. She then said that Jefferson arranged to have Sally Hemings freed a discrete length of time after his death, to protect both his white family and his slave family.

One wonders why people writing in the twentieth century should view this scenario with such disgust. After all, if this is what happened, it is not the depiction of deviance and depravity that James Callender was making it out to be. If Brodie was correct, this was, rather, a tragic story of people trapped by the circumstances of their times into doing the best that they could do, a scenario that played itself out in other households across the Old South. For no matter how strenuously some may resist believing it, there were slave masters who had long liaisons with slave mistresses and who freed the children from these unions and the women as well.

A Fantasy of the 1970s

It has been suggested that in constructing her theory about the nature of the Jefferson-Hemings relationship, Fawn Brodie was imposing twentieth-century notions onto the eighteenth century or, in other words, engaging in presentism. Douglas Wilson made this point in an essay on Thomas Jefferson's character. Wilson defined *presentism* as "applying contemporary or otherwise inappropriate standards to the past." Wilson said that Brodie was compelled to present a vision of the Jefferson-Hemings relationship that

would be palatable to Americans, who wanted to view the liaison in a romantic light.[12]

Wilson's reading of Brodie ignores the fact that she reached her conclusion about the likely nature of the Jefferson-Hemings relationship by looking
at facts and drawing inferences from those facts. The pattern of Sally Hemings's conceptions and the freeing of all of her children by Jefferson are facts
that belong to the time in which they occurred. The inferences Brodie drew
from those facts must be the focus of any inquiry into the charge of presentism. One must ask whether Brodie's inferences would be unique to the
time in which they were drawn, the early 1970s.

They would not be. The fact that Jefferson freed Hemings's children and
the ways in which he did it might lead in any age to an inference that he cared
something for her. It may be an incorrect inference (not to be confused with
an unreasonable inference, the mistake to which presentism is addressed), but
it is, in fact, an inference that draws upon sensibilities that would exist in any
era. The length of time that had elapsed between the alleged promise of freedom and the fulfillment of the promise; the fact that an important event
(Callender's exposé) occurred in the intervening years that made fulfillment
of the alleged promise substantially more difficult; the fact that it was nevertheless carried out and done so under circumstances that could cause great
distress to people whom Jefferson loved, all might lead at any point in history
to an inference that the man in question cared about the feelings of the
woman to whom he had made the promise.

A historian in any era who believed a subject to have been extremely
sensitive, disinclined to engage in open conflict, inclined to make deep and
lasting attachments, and fearful of rejection might infer that such a man
would not have been in a thirty-eight-year relationship with a woman unless
she welcomed him. A man with those characteristics would not be able to
ignore the woman's suffering, which would be readily apparent at so close a
range. He would also be too thin-skinned to take the humiliation of continually presenting himself for body-to-body contact when he knew he was not
wanted. This would be particularly true if the liaison was one to which other
loved ones might be hostile, since their disapproval would have given him an
additional excuse to exit the relationship.

That Sally Hemings conceived no children during Jefferson's long absences from Monticello suggests monogamy on her part and also might suggest in any era that she felt something for him. It is not as though she had no
other option. Sally Hemings was, by accounts of her, a remarkably attractive
woman. During the years that Jefferson was often away from Monticello, she

was between seventeen and thirty-six years old. She could have attracted, and been attracted to, other men. Drawing from these facts the inference that the two probably had affection for one another does not amount to engaging in presentism. Brodie's inferences may not have been correct, but they were inferences that could be reasonably drawn in any age.

Presentism to a Different End

Just as it is possible to use presentism to idealize a Jefferson-Hemings liaison, it is also possible to use presentism to demonize it. It seems that Wilson in his brief analysis of the situation did the latter. He wrote:

> If he [Jefferson] did take advantage of Hemings and father her children over a period of twenty years, he was acting completely out of character and violating his own standards of honor and decency. For a man who took questions of morality and honor seriously, such a hypocritical liaison would have been a constant source of shame and guilt. For his close-knit family, who worshipped him and lived too near him to be ignorant of such an arrangement it would have been a moral tragedy of no small dimensions.[13]

Well, what was "slavery time" (as southern blacks sometimes refer to it) but a series of "moral traged[ies] of no small dimensions"? Why should Jefferson's family have not known some of the "moral tragedies" that grew out of the system of which they were so intimately a part? Why would we assume for a moment that the Jeffersons and Randolphs could live in the midst of the slave system and not be touched by some of the more common circumstances that it spawned?

Families all over the South had fathers, brothers, grandfathers who had relationships and children with black women, just as southern families, including Jefferson's, had emotionally disturbed relatives, wastrel nephews, granddaughters who were physically abused, and ne'er-do-well relatives. These things were part of life. To write of this alleged circumstance as though it would have amounted to some special horror unknown in the annals of southern history misleads as to the extent of the contradictions and complexities of antebellum southern life. It also seems an attempt to rescue the Jeffersons and Randolphs from their immersion in a way of life that now embarrasses us—to suggest that they were somehow in that slave system but not really of it, when it is clear that they were both.

As to Jefferson and his personal code of honor and the turmoil that a relationship with Sally Hemings would have caused within him, an answer may be found by examining closely Jefferson's attitudes about slaves and slavery. Historians tend to divorce Jefferson's ownership of slaves from his personal needs. His attitudes about this subject are most often analyzed in terms of what he thought it meant for society as a whole. In this view Jefferson remained a slave owner, not for himself, but just because he could not see society's way out of the system. He was afraid of what would happen to the slaves if they were freed, because they were like children. At the same time he was afraid of what free blacks would mean for American civilization. As a result, he adopted a posture of saying something on the order of, "It's a tough job, but somebody has got to do it."

Thomas Jefferson kept slaves primarily because he needed them to help him live the way he wanted to live. He knew very well the moral issues at stake with respect to slavery. As a lifetime participant in that system, he had to make rationalizations every day of his life about how he could be a part of it and remain honorable, decent, and moral. If he could do this for all the other aspects of the slave system, why would he have been incapable of making similar rationalizations about another inevitable part of the system: sexual contacts between masters and slaves?

It is difficult for us at this remove to understand how people could cope with such situations, even though we know that many southerners did. But we are seeing this through the eyes of a society solidly rooted in modern bourgeois value and sensibilities, where our more equalized vision of relationships between men and women and parents and children would militate against such behavior. This is presentism of the highest order. There are so many things about a society built upon slavery that are difficult for us to reconcile or imagine. The accommodations that had to be made—the mode of thinking that people had to adopt in order to keep the system going—often pass all understanding: Blacks are dirty and subhuman, but I will put my infant child to the breast of a black woman. Black men are infantile, but they are sexual predators who must be kept away from our women. Black women are animals, but I will have sex with them.

The world of the antebellum southern planter was not the world of the late twentieth-century bourgeoisie. There is no way to assess the capabilities, beliefs, and professed moral standards of the individuals who lived in that society without keeping that fact in mind. Jefferson, for all his understanding of and stated appreciation for democratic institutions, was a despot in his own realm. He may have been a benign despot, but he was a despot nevertheless. Women and children were cherished and indulged, friends were deeply appreciated, but in the final analysis they did not rule; he did.

The evidence indicates that other than the times when forces beyond his control had the upper hand, death and disease for example, Thomas Jefferson did pretty much what he wanted to do and had things pretty much as he wanted them. Two of his most often cited characteristics were his ability to speak only of those things of which he wanted to speak and his capacity to will his vision of how matters would proceed upon even those whom he loved. To say that it would have been impossible for Jefferson to have carried on a liaison with Sally Hemings would be to assume that he voluntarily allowed himself to be ruled by others in a matter as intensely personal as his sexual life. It is by no means clear that he would have allowed this.

At one point, when Jefferson realized that he was in terrible financial straits, he sat down to draw up a long-term financial plan for ridding himself of his debts. He projected that his farm would operate in the black for each successive year until all debts were retired, even though his operations had never operated in the black.[14] This is only one example of many that reveal the extent to which Jefferson could see the world in exactly the way he chose to see it despite all evidence to the contrary. Indeed, this ability is a useful, if not essential, trait for a visionary to possess.

Why could he not bring this trait to bear on the alleged relationship with Sally Hemings? Jefferson had been widowed at a young age, and there is evidence that he felt himself bound to a promise to his dying wife not to remarry. Almost nine months to the day after he married Martha Wayles Skelton, his first child was born.[15] Thereafter, Martha, who was sick during much of their marriage, was pregnant every two years until her death. Jefferson must have known that he had no problems with fertility. With what type of white woman could he have developed a long-term relationship and not fear that a circumstance might develop that would require him to marry? If he needed companionship, and his dalliance with Maria Cosway is evidence that Martha Jefferson's death had not killed his desire for the company of women, where could he turn to find it? Why could Thomas Jefferson not—as he did in so many other contexts—turn to a slave from Monticello for an answer to his predicament?

It is illustrative of the depth of passion that this topic excites, that some scholars—with an almost audible sigh of relief—have suggested that Jefferson solved his dilemma by seeking attachments to women who were already married.[16] To them, the thought of Jefferson perhaps cuckolding one of his neighbors and running the great risk of having small Jeffersons living under the roof of an unsuspecting husband is more comforting than the notion that the widowed Thomas Jefferson would have bound himself to the unmarried but inconveniently one-quarter black Sally Hemings. The former transgression would be understandable (and forgivable), the latter not so.

There is evidence from a man whom Malone described as Jefferson's friend that he did turn to a slave woman to satisfy his desire for companionship. John Hartwell Cocke, who worked closely with Jefferson as a founder of the University of Virginia and who served as one of the original members of its Board of Visitors, spoke of this matter in two entries of his diary. Writing in 1853 Cocke bemoaned the fact that many slave owners had children by slave women on their plantations. He went on to say that there was no wonder that this should be so when "Mr. Jefferson's notorious example is considered." In an 1859 entry Cocke complained about what he said was the common practice of unmarried slave owners keeping a slave woman "as a substitute for a wife." "In Virginia," he wrote, "this damnable practice prevails as much as anywhere— probably more—as Mr. Jefferson's example can be pleaded for its defense."[17]

Although Cocke expressed his disdain for what he said was this particular feature of Jefferson's life, there is ample evidence of his overall high regard for his colleague on the board. Edmund Bacon remembered that Cocke was often at Monticello during Jefferson's retirement. Against significant opposition Cocke was one of the key figures in helping Jefferson persuade the legislature to let him sell some of his land by lottery to avoid losing all of his estates. Even though Cocke, under the influence of religion, had become a fervent opponent of slavery by the time he wrote of Jefferson's liaison with a slave woman, to assume that having become an abolitionist, he also became a liar would be unfair. There were many other ways for Cocke to express his displeasure at Jefferson's involvement with slavery than making passing references in his private diary to Jefferson's having had a slave mistress.[18]

It seems that most Jefferson defenders have chosen to respond to the presentation of the Jefferson-Hemings liaison that was made in 1802, and not to the presentation made of it in the 1970s. By taking this tack they are falsely equating Fawn Brodie with James Callender, and they are also implicitly accepting as true Callender's depiction of the basic nature of this alleged relationship. In their view none of the events that happened in the years between 1802 and 1873 that shed additional light on this matter should be considered. Only James Callender's framing of the issue counts. Commentaries on this subject carry a tone of outrage that implies that the commentators themselves believe that Thomas Jefferson is being charged with something on the order of bestiality. This view of the allegation has affected their judgment and, consequently, their ability to present and assess the evidence in a fair or even a coherent fashion.

Jefferson and His "Very Snow-Broth" Blood

A variation on the theme that Thomas Jefferson's character would not have allowed a liaison with Sally Hemings centers, not on how the code of the southern gentleman would have shaped Jefferson's attitudes regarding such a liaison, but on how Jefferson's personal eccentricities would have made a relationship (especially one with a component of affection), if not impossible, at least improbable. This view is premised on the belief that while Jefferson had a great capacity for platonic love, he had no strong interest in expressing love in a romantic or sexual way.

Before looking at the substance of the argument, it is important to consider why it has been necessary to make it. In most historical writings the boundaries of Thomas Jefferson's sexual life have been firmly set as starting with his marriage to Martha Wayles and ending upon her death. As sexuality is, for most people, thought to be a normal part of human life, the question naturally arises about what Jefferson may or may not have been doing with respect to that issue over the forty-five years he lived after Martha Wayles died. There are no serious allegations of his sexual involvement with any woman over the course of that period but Sally Hemings. Because most scholars have been unwilling even to consider the possible truth of that story, they have had to put forth an explanation for the apparent absence of sexual activity on Jefferson's part.

The idea that Thomas Jefferson was a man lacking in sexual passion has been the most often cited explanation, and it is one of long standing. At the time the Sally Hemings story broke, one writer in a Federalist newspaper took extreme delight in expressing his surprise that the "solemn, the grave, and the didactic Mr. Jefferson" would have had a mistress. The writer was indicating that Jefferson's demeanor and his reputation for having a philosophical bent implied that his blood was "very snow-broth."[19] Of course, this enemy of Jefferson was having a bit of sport at the president's expense, and one would not expect much depth of insight from that quarter. To equate being solemn, grave, and didactic with being without sexual passion is, at best, a simplistic formulation. It is a caricature of the human personality which fits nicely with the goal of ridiculing Thomas Jefferson. The writer of those words was presenting a literary cartoon.

Surprisingly, this way of viewing Jefferson has leached into the scholarly writing about him as well. For some scholars Jefferson's fastidiousness, his attachment to reason and rationality, his zeal for exactitude, his obsession with orderliness, all signal that he was without a real capacity for romantic involvement or sexual passion.[20] What one makes of the fact that an individual possesses some or all of these characteristics is a function of one's own values and experiences and, of course, one's personal view of what it takes to be sexual or romantic. People who are compulsive about making lists have no interests in sex or romance. People who hold their emotions severely in check have no interest in sex or romance. People who are extremely clean have no interest in sex or romance. None of this follows. It is not even remotely a fact that a person who possesses all of these traits—even in abundance—is without sexual passion or romantic yearnings.

One could just as easily look to other aspects of Jefferson's activities and tastes to come to an opposite conclusion. He was a physical man, riding horses some great number of miles a day, laboring with his slave artisans to make furniture and metal tools, pitting himself against much younger men in competitions designed to test strength and winning. Jefferson was also a man oriented to the senses. He had a stated appreciation for beauty in women, music, and art. He loved good food and good wine. Even if individual character traits were reliable indicators of a person's level of sexual passion (a claim that requires the employment of stereotypes and extremely subjective judgments), it would be wrong to seize upon some aspects of Jefferson's character to draw inferences about the likely state of his sexual drive to the exclusion of other aspects. Malone described Jefferson as "a half dozen men rolled into one."[21] While one of those men may have been Jefferson the cerebral engineer (a specimen who hardly qualifies for presumptive asexuality), another of them was most certainly Jefferson the sybarite.

Even Jefferson's youthful romantic misadventure with Rebecca Burwell, in which he pined somewhat pathetically for a young woman who decided to marry another, has been employed to suggest that Jefferson's emotional development was abnormal. Certainly, some variation of Jefferson's experience with Burwell while he was a student in Williamsburg has happened to almost everyone, particularly in their youth. Jefferson's crush, which came when he was in his early twenties, has been treated as an event of singular importance that shaped his sexual profile over the sixty years that followed. It was long thought that the youthful and disappointed Jefferson placed misogynistic clippings in his Literary Commonplace Book in reaction to the Burwell affair, as though the event so traumatized him that he shunned women until he met Martha Wayles. But Douglas Wilson, the most recent editor of the Literary Commonplace Book, has demonstrated that the quotations were gathered well before Jefferson even met Burwell.[22] Jefferson's attraction to Burwell and, later, to Martha Wayles suggests that whatever negative feelings he may have had about women as group, he remained susceptible to the attractions of individual women.

Jefferson's written response to being thrown over by Rebecca Burwell has only rarely been considered. Jack McLaughlin noted it as one of Jefferson's few references to his attitude about sex. After he discovered that Burwell was lost to him, Jefferson wrote to friend: "Many and great are the comforts of a single state, and neither of the reasons you urge can have any influence with an inhabitant and a young inhabitant too of Wmsburgh. For St. Paul only says that it is better to be married than to burn. Now I presume that if that apostle had known that providence would at an after day be so kind to any particular set of people as to furnish them with other means of extinguishing the fire than those of matrimony, he would have earnestly recommended them to their practice."[23]

Jefferson was saying, in this extremely convoluted fashion, that he was glad that one does not have to be married in order to have sex. To paraphrase Jack McLaughlin's very perceptive question about this quote, who were the "particular set of people" whom "providence" had given the "means of extinguishing the fire" that St. Paul suggested should be extinguished through the marital bed? Loose women in Williamsburg? Prostitutes? One could argue that these words were the idle boast of a young man attempting to hide his pain. On the other hand, Jefferson may not only have been hurt, he may also have been serious about what he wrote. If so, this would indicate that Jefferson considered sex with females to be a natural part of life, his life in particular.

Scholars also have employed the Rebecca Burwell episode along with Jefferson's clumsy attempt as a young bachelor to seduce Mrs. Walker, his friend's wife, as evidence that he was awkward and shy with women, once again using incidents that occurred in his youth to define him at all stages of his extremely long life. Even if Jefferson continued to be awkward and shy with women all of his life, does that state necessarily indicate that he was without sexual passion or sexual partners? For all his alleged awkwardness, at least some of the women of Jefferson's era adored him. The correspondence of Eliza House Trist and the memoirs of Margaret Bayard Smith demonstrate that both were smitten with Jefferson. These two women's very warm responses were registered at two different periods in Jefferson's life, when he was in his forties and in his sixties. He spent his thirties as a married man. This all suggests that Jefferson knew very well how to make himself attractive to women and that the desire to do so was a basic feature of his personality.[24]

Jefferson's Head and Heart

Jefferson himself contributed to the view that he lacked the capacity for erotic passion by giving historians a handy phrase to use as a guidebook to his psyche. The title of Jefferson's love letter to the artist Maria Cosway, "My Head and Heart," has served as an all-purpose way of explaining him. Put simply, the argument goes, Thomas Jefferson's head always ruled over his heart.[25] This view of Jefferson has been useful to his worshipers and detractors alike. It allows worshipers of Jefferson to portray him as a man of supreme intellect, which can, of course, be seen as a good thing. Jefferson detractors can take that same belief and portray him as having been emotionally unbalanced; after all, what healthy person always does what his head tells him to do?

Certainly, "My Head and My Heart" was effective as a literary device, and it was self-revelatory. Jefferson was telling Cosway of the conflict that existed within him about their relationship. The problem arises when one lifts that phrase out of its very specific context and attempts to use it to explain or analyze other situations. Scholars who see Jefferson through the prism (and, it turns out, prison) of his literary device fail to understand its inherent limitations as a means for conducting a serious analysis of an individual's personality.

What matters are of "the head," and what matters are of "the heart"? Who decides? The historian? Jefferson? Are the head and heart always in opposition to one another? Don't they, in fact, usually work together in some combination? It is common for people whose hearts are deeply committed to something to see the matter as one of the head and, on other occasions, to take calculated (headlike) actions and then convince themselves that those acts arose from their sincere feelings (their hearts). Given that reality, historians who insist upon taking the "head and heart" vehicle seriously must negotiate some difficult mental terrain. That is not an impossible task; it does, however, require the historian to try to know and consider with great care what Jefferson knew and considered at the time he took a particular action. The scholarly writing on the Hemings story gives no hint that such an attempt has been made.

Historians have taken it for granted that if Jefferson was involved with Sally Hemings, it would have been an instance in which the head failed to do its duty, because Jefferson would have made himself vulnerable politically were it widely known that he had a slave mistress. Jefferson might have seen matters differently than historians writing in the twentieth century. He existed in a society where a slave master taking a slave as a mistress, though frowned upon, was not unheard of. All that was required was discretion on the part of those involved and those who knew of it. James Callender's injection of this issue into the public domain undoubtedly was taken by southerners as further proof of that journalist's low status. Even if Jefferson's fellow countrymen believed the charge, they may have felt more anger at the one who exposed

Jefferson than at Jefferson himself. Northerners seemed to view the matter as just another example of the strange things that went on in the South.

Of course, Jefferson's political enemies used the Hemings story as they would have used any other tool they thought would hurt him. It was to no avail, either because a critical mass of voters did not believe the charge— which seems unlikely given the story's persistence over the years—or it didn't matter. Jefferson's greatness outstripped whatever meaning could be derived from the Hemings allegation. Why couldn't Jefferson, one of the most astute politicians the country has produced, have used some combination of his head and heart to realize that he could weather whatever storm might arise by keeping his mouth shut, staying above the fray, and letting his enemies reveal themselves for the small men they were?

While Andrew Burstein's portrait of Jefferson moves beyond the simple head and heart formula, he fell back on the device when discussing Sally Hemings. Burstein's employment of the formula as a way of debunking the Hemings story is illustrative. He argued, based upon the prevailing view of scholars, that Jefferson "would have been uncharacteristically imprudent to be responsible for giving Sally the two children she bore after [Callender's] charges surfaced, while he remained president."[26] Burstein's analysis is a product of his virtual certainty that the Jefferson-Hemings relationship was not real. It is not very useful to think of the Hemings allegation only in terms of its being false. One must also consider the state of affairs that would have obtained if it was true.

Think of Burstein's argument and ask, If the story was true, how would Jefferson have responded to the Callender crisis? Before he was a lawyer, politician, president, or any of the other roles he played, Thomas Jefferson was a slave owner. It was the one role that he was born to. Is it so clear that Jefferson would not reasonably see Callender's attacks as touching, not only upon his political life, but upon his life as the master of Monticello as well? If so, would the master of Monticello alter his living arrangements because of a scandal created from the outside? That would mean, in Jefferson's eyes and those of everyone else at Monticello, that a group of newspaper columnists, not he, ran the plantation. Jefferson would not have been inclined to let this happen.

What would have been the state of affairs between Jefferson and Hemings in 1802 if Madison Hemings's account is accurate? The relationship would have begun fourteen years before Callender's articles appeared. By that time Hemings would have borne him five children, three who died as infants. How would Jefferson have extricated himself from the relationship? Would Thomas Jefferson, portrayed in Burstein's book as an extremely sensitive man who made deep connections to others and held fast to those connections, have summarily abandoned a young woman who had placed her faith in him by giving up her chance for freedom and who had suffered for him in childbirth and in lost children? If so, this would be more than just a case of a man who used his head more than his heart; it would be Thomas Jefferson, a man with little heart and not a shred of honor or decency.

Perhaps the strangest thing of all about the view of Jefferson as a man ill-equipped for women and romance is that there is such obvious evidence against the proposition. Jefferson successfully courted and married a woman. Did his heart tell him to do this or his head? To be sure, Martha Wayles's father was a very wealthy man, but Jefferson's actions and others' accounts of their relationship show that he truly loved Martha. He loved one woman; why couldn't he have loved another? If reason always reigned supreme for Jefferson, how could he have put his beloved wife through the rigors of frequent childbearing when reason should have told him that she was unsuited to that particular task?

No matter what Jefferson's youthful statement to his friend suggests about the importance of female companionship, no matter what his courtship and marriage say about his ability to be touched by and to touch women, no matter what the Cosway-Jefferson affair demonstrates about his continuing interest in doing that, and no matter what evidence exists to support the notion that Jefferson's sexuality was expressed through a relationship with a woman on his plantation, those who believe that Jefferson had no great interest in sex rely on their already formulated and entrenched opinion and refuse to consider anything that suggests otherwise. Jefferson can never be let out of whatever box the given historian has chosen to place him in.

Ironically, historians who fasten upon the Burwell and Walker encounters and the phrase "head and heart" to make definitive statements about Jefferson's personality are engaging in psychological analyses every bit as tenuous as any of Fawn Brodie's Freudian speculations. Brodie's mistake was to be open about the fact that she was, at points, analyzing Thomas Jefferson according to the dictates of a particular school of psychology. The more traditional scholars who use the above-cited tools to make pronouncements about Jefferson's sexuality, or lack thereof, are doing the same thing but obscuring it by presenting their assertions in matter-of-fact declarative statements. They are using the tenets of their own method of psychoanalysis to construct their version of Thomas Jefferson.

The better approach would be to have some humility about one's capacity to know an individual with whom one has never interacted. Caution is certainly required when making judgments about an aspect of human life—sexuality—that is so personal and likely to be influenced by a myriad of hidden subtleties and nuances. Even when one knows another personally, making a judgment about that individual's level of sexual drive, or when or how it can be triggered, is risky.

For Thomas Jefferson historians must rely upon documents or circumstances to give guidance. That is all that is left to us, and those sources of information have limitations. Despite the existence of a voluminous body of Jefferson's personal letters, very little is known about his private life that could tell us about his sexuality. In his own writings Jefferson managed, as very private people often do, to impart a great deal of personal information without being particularly informative.

The views of Jefferson's daughters and grandchildren are important but must be taken with a grain of salt. They loved him. It is to be expected that there might be some bias in their assessments and that they would have had no interest in discussing examples of his sexuality even if they knew any. The all too widespread practice of cannibalizing one's family members for public consumption is largely a late twentieth-century sport. Therefore, they would not have left for posterity any thoughts they might have had about his sexual nature. Even if the Jefferson grandchildren could have presented totally unbiased remembrances of him, the Jefferson they knew was in his sixties, seventies, and eighties. A man at those stages of life could present himself in a very different guise than a man in his forties, the age at which Jefferson allegedly became involved with Sally Hemings.

In any case, one should be wary of the notion that Thomas Jefferson can be known by devouring the large body of documents that he and his family left for our perusal. Jefferson knew that he would be considered by posterity to have been a great man. Being familiar with the classical tradition, he also knew some of the ways in which posterity handles the lives of great men. The writings of, and about, the great man are pored over, analyzed, and discussed with the aim of discovering the source of his greatness. The basic nature of the great man is always of interest.

When Thomas Jefferson destroyed the letters that had passed between himself and Martha Wayles Jefferson, he was most likely destroying the best source of insight into who he really was. He would have been with her as he was with no one else. When he took similar actions on other occasions, asking correspondents to return his letters or to destroy them, the end result was the same: some important aspect of his true self was hidden from the world. What is left when one considers the remaining body of Jeffersonian documents, then, is generally a road map for how Thomas Jefferson wanted people to think of him. This does not mean that Jefferson's correspondence contains no insight into his character. He was not omnipotent. He could not hide everything. It does suggest that whatever certainty about the nature of his character one forms from such a body of documents must be tempered by the knowledge that key documents are missing and they are missing because of Jefferson's deliberate action.

The day-to-day Thomas Jefferson may have been, not the opposite of, but perhaps very different than, the Jefferson who appears in his self-consciously constructed documentary legacy. If one gets the impression that Thomas Jefferson's blood was snow-broth from his extant letters and the actions and thoughts described in them, it may well be that for some reason Jefferson wanted to be thought of in that way, whether he was actually that way or not. When Jefferson destroyed, or asked others to destroy, letters, it may have been precisely because they showed him to have been in some material respects different than the image he wanted to project to posterity. If that is the case, and it seems a reasonable one to make, then it is unwise to think that a complete picture of his character or aspects of his character like his sexuality can be drawn from the extant documents. Those who feel that the character reconstructed from this incomplete file would have precluded a liaison with Sally Hemings must confront the possibility that aspects of the character that could have been gleaned from the deliberately discarded pieces (indeed, the very fact that certain pieces were discarded) indicate otherwise.

The Father and the Grandfather

The third prong of the character defense purports to debunk the Jefferson-Hemings liaison by citing Jefferson's love for his children and grandchildren as having been too great to have allowed for such involvement.[27] The first thing to observe about this assertion is that it is not a fact in the sense that Thomas Jefferson was the third president of the United States or that he was the founder of the University of Virginia could be considered facts. It is a value judgment. A person making this assertion is revealing his or her own values more than Thomas Jefferson's.

One need not have a detailed knowledge of the character of every master who ever owned a slave to know that there were slave masters who had slave mistresses and who at the same time loved their white children deeply. One could argue that Thomas Jefferson was not every slave master. But are we to consider Jefferson's capacity to love as greater than what we would expect from an average person just because he had the ability to express his love through his many elegantly written letters to his family? Thomas Jefferson was a genius, but there is no reason to believe that his genius made the character, depth, and nature of his love for his family any greater than those of a person of more modest capabilities. Nor can we assume that his family's love for him was so shallow that it could only have been sustained if he remained a picture of perfection in their eyes.

Aside from the deficiency of this argument as a fact that could effectively turn aside the claim of a Jefferson-Hemings relationship, there is another more pressing reason to examine it. The proffered contradiction between love of family and willingness to engage in miscegenation as a test of character is problematic in itself. It is even more troubling for the vision it presents of antebellum southern life, a vision that may comfort present-day sensibilities, but is contrary to the facts.

This proposition, even more than the argument about overreaching, seeks to carve miscegenation out of the normal scheme of slavery, which is most often thought of just as a system where people were bought and sold and made to work for no pay. In this view having sex with black slaves was not a natural part of the system but rather an extreme aberration engaged in by those few individuals (usually overseers and the ignominious relatives of slave masters) who had no regard for their family or were deviant. So while it is conceivable that Jefferson could engage in all the acceptable activities of a slave owner and still remain within the good graces of most Americans, it would be somehow strange or impossible for him to have engaged in the "aberrant" behavior of consorting with a slave. This sets a standard by which all interracial encounters during slavery are to be measured. If it is true that only masters who did not love their families engaged in sex with slaves, then sex with slaves must have been rare, since most people believe (or want to believe) that most men love their children and grandchildren.

In truth, miscegenation was a prevalent and inevitable part of slavery. Just as whites accommodated themselves to the other aspects of the slave system, they must have made accommodations for miscegenation as well.[28] One has only to recite the family history of Jefferson's in-laws to make the case that his engaging in miscegenation would not have produced the shock and angst in Jefferson's daughters and his grandchildren that historians would have us believe.

Historians concede that Jefferson's father-in-law, John Wayles, had taken a slave mistress and had six children with her, including Sally Hemings. Jefferson's wife, Martha, before she married her first husband at age eighteen, had spent the latter part of her teenage years at home when Elizabeth Hemings had at least two children by Wayles. Upon her father's death she brought Elizabeth Hemings and her children to Monticello, installing them as favored house servants. According to a Hemings family member, on her deathbed

Martha Jefferson gave the nine-year-old Sally Hemings a handbell to remember her by, not an act that one associates with fear and loathing.[29]

There has been a suggestion that Martha Wayles did not know that Elizabeth Hemings was Wayles's mistress, even though Thomas Jefferson did.[30] This seems more like wishful thinking than anything that approaches reality, an attempt to maintain the image of the delicate white southern belle who knew nothing of the rough ways of the world that white men and black people knew. Thomas Jefferson could know of the Wayles and Hemings connection. The slaves on the plantation could know. Thomas Turner, the Virginian who wrote of the Hemings matter in 1805, could know. But not Martha Wayles, the person who lived in a household with John Wayles and Elizabeth Hemings and would have had the most interest in the matter.

Women of that period were not so accomplished educationally as men, but there is no reason to believe that the demonstrated facility (and some studies say superiority, relative to men) that women show in judging the implications of unspoken communication would not have held sway in that period as well as today. That Martha Wayles could live with Elizabeth Hemings and John Wayles and not know that they were having children together seems, to use a favorite Jefferson defenders' word, preposterous. Martha may never have spoken of it, but it is hard to believe that on some meaningful level she would not have known.

Historians seem to have assumed that Martha Wayles Jefferson did not know that Elizabeth Hemings was her father's mistress because she did not act with hostility toward Hemings and her children. This, again, is not a fact; it is a value judgment, and a rather patronizing one at that. Martha Wayles Jefferson may well have been acting on the basis of the particular circumstances of her life, and not according to some notion of what the typical southern woman would (or should) have done in this situation.

Apparently, when John Wayles took Elizabeth Hemings as his mistress, he was a widower. Martha's mother, his first wife, was long dead, and Martha had had two stepmothers in the interim. Martha's dying request that Jefferson not remarry, rather than being an expression of her too extreme possessiveness of him, seems to have been prompted by concerns about the treatment of her children, for she indicated that she did not want another woman "over them."[31] Perhaps Martha had experienced some difficulties with one or both of her stepmothers and actually preferred Elizabeth Hemings. We cannot dismiss out of hand the possibility that Martha Wayles may have liked her father's mistress.

Why is it so important for Martha Wayles Jefferson to have been ignorant of her father's relationship with Elizabeth Hemings? Perhaps because Martha's fondness for Hemings and her children while possessing that knowledge would suggest that she accepted the relationship, and the children that resulted from it, without rancor. That possibility should have a bearing on any consideration of the circumstances in Thomas Jefferson's household. For if Martha Wayles Jefferson was able to function with the knowledge that her widowed father had taken a slave mistress, why could not her daughters, Martha and Maria?

Martha Jefferson's actions toward Elizabeth Hemings suggest that attitudes about miscegenation were more complicated than typically portrayed. While it is true that the Wayleses, Jeffersons, and Hemingses existed in a society obsessed by notions of racial purity, there was another important obsession at work of which some account must be taken: the obsession with notions of blood and family. What happened when one obsession collided with another? We know that the public posture was to pretend that such collisions never took place, and if they did, the need to maintain white superiority demanded that the allegiance to blood and family yield to the allegiance to blood and race. Can we be as sure about the private relations between individuals who were related by blood but divided by race? Can we assume that families in the privacy of their own homes (or on their own mountain) were always able—or felt inclined—to maintain the public face about such matters.

Elizabeth Hemings's children grew up with Jefferson's daughters. The children of Elizabeth Hemings's children, in turn, grew up with Jefferson's grandchildren. Two generations of Jeffersons and Randolphs had lived with slaves who were as white as they. They knew, maybe better than other households, that race mixing was a part of the slave system. Moreover, the favored treatment that the Hemings family received compared to other slaves on the plantation would have tended to soften the message that miscegenation was an evil beyond all comprehension. Martha, Maria, and their children most likely knew at some point that John Wayles, their grandfather and great-grandfather, respectively, had participated freely in this aspect of the slave system. Why assume that they would be unable (why would it not be expected) that they should accommodate themselves to the fact that their father and grandfather, respectively, might have done the same thing?

The accommodation that was made in such situations in the Old South was to build a wall of silence around the circumstance. People did not talk about it to outsiders.[32] One can understand that Jefferson's family would be horrified at the breach of that wall, but to think that they would have been baffled and wounded—other than perhaps by normal levels of embarrassment or jealousy—because of what was going on behind that wall seems unrealistic given what we know about the extensive evidence of the results of miscegenation at Monticello.

To illustrate the contention that deeming a Jefferson-Hemings relationship impossible because of Jefferson's regard for his family is primarily a value judgment, consider the reaction to another aspect of Jefferson's life that can be established as a fact: he died bankrupt, over $100,000 in debt. Jefferson's misfortune was primarily the result of some debts that he had inherited, bad luck in the business of farming, and Virginia's poor economy. But it was also the result of insufficient attention to business decisions and a way of life that was truly profligate. Jefferson's enormous salary as president was enough for him to have paid all of his debts and have started with a clean slate when he returned to Monticello. Instead, after eight years of lavish spending on guests and entertainment, Jefferson left office in greater debt than when he entered.[33] Even as his debts mounted, Jefferson continued to make costly and never-ending renovations of Monticello. He also entertained lavishly there, receiving, housing, and feeding dozens of guests at a time, particularly after he retired. Historians have written of how loath he was to be thought stingy or inhospitable, even if it meant that he drove himself to financial ruin to prove he was neither. Even his overseer said he could see that the manner and frequency of Jefferson's entertaining eventually would bankrupt him.[34]

This way of life proved an emotional strain as well. Both his daughter and his grandchildren considered the constant presence of visitors to Monticello a great burden.[35] Even the strongest of individuals would resent living in a perpetually unfinished home that was being run like a hotel. One can easily understand how Martha Randolph, a wife and mother with responsibility for raising numerous children, would feel additional pressure. It is also understandable that the grandchildren would not feel comfortable growing up in enforced intimacy with strangers.

This would be especially so in view of the condition of Martha Randolph's husband, Thomas Mann Randolph, Jr., who had periodic emotional problems during the course of their marriage and for substantial periods was unable to care for the family.[36] Jefferson was much closer to the end of his life than the beginning, and the precarious nature of Thomas Randolph's state of mind and finances made Jefferson's financial condition particularly important to the continued well-being of both Martha and his grandchildren.

Jefferson's knowledge of these circumstances did not stop him from taking actions that seriously undermined his financial position and made it more likely that he would have little or nothing to leave his daughter upon his death. As it turned out, Martha Randolph ended her life in such dire straits that the legislatures of South Carolina and Louisiana voted to give her money for her maintenance. Her response to one of these acts, reprinted in a Virginia newspaper, reveals the extent of her deprivation. She wrote, "I will do myself the injustice to attempt an expression of my deep feelings of gratitude to the generous hearts whose liberality has given support to my old age; to understand them, it is only necessary to know, it found me prostrate in health and spirits, in poverty, and with eight children unprovided for, five of them still of an age to go to school." [37]

Martha Randolph's financial condition was well known, and other admirers of her father attempted to see to her well-being. One group set up the Jefferson Fund in Philadelphia. The *Richmond Enquirer* of May 1, 1827, printed part of a communication from the fund to Thomas Jefferson Randolph, Alexander Garrett, and Nicholas Trist, the executors of Jefferson's estate, and to Martha Randolph granting $2,571.64 for the "sole and exclusive use of Mrs. Randolph." In her final years Thomas Jefferson's daughter became an object of pity. Her son-in-law Nicholas Trist was given jobs because he was known to be helping to support her. Trist even used his mother-in-law's situation to get a raise, telling his employer, President Andrew Jackson, that he needed it "as much for Mrs. Randolph as myself." [38]

Parents are expected to attend to the well-being of their children; it is, in fact, seen as their highest duty. Jefferson's handling, or, more accurately, not handling, of his finances in the final two decades of his life conflicted with that duty. Why wouldn't Jefferson's actions on this score count as examples of insufficient regard for his family? Why can we know that Jefferson's financial troubles were partly of his own making and not question the assumption that he lived for the sake of his daughter and grandchildren—because he wrote them effusively affectionate letters?

Although Herbert Sloan's illuminating *Principle and Interest: Thomas Jefferson and the Problem of Debt* takes a hard-nosed look at Jefferson's management of his finances, for the most part historians have given Jefferson a pass on this subject. His failures are seen, not as the result of any faults, but as a fallout of his exaggerated virtues. He was too much the aristocrat and the public servant; he was too kind and too hospitable to turn anyone away from his home. That other prominent Virginians, James Madison and James Monroe, acted in a similar fashion with similar results may help explain the choices Jefferson made, but not entirely. Madison had no children, and Monroe did not have to support his two.

Jefferson might not have saved his estate by changing his expensive way of life or taking a more realistic approach to his business dealings. Yet a more timely and concerted attempt to attend to these matters would have indicated he understood that failing to take action would be in derogation of his duties to his family. It is doubtful that any man other than Thomas Jefferson could avoid serious criticism on this point. If another man had amassed such a record, people might question the level of regard that he had for his family.

Why, on the other hand, does the idea that Jefferson, widowed at thirty-eight and sworn to a promise not to remarry, might have taken a slave mistress appear so awful that it denotes a lack of love for his family? Because we are dealing in the realm of value judgments, the response depends upon one's perspective. If one's horror at the thought of miscegenation and fornication outweighs one's horror at the thought of a person allowing his family to slide into financial ruin and onto public charity, then the answer is clear.

The strongest case to be made, however, is that neither Jefferson's handling of his finances nor his alleged liaison with Sally Hemings can be taken as a measure of his love for his family. Human beings are far too complex for such a simplistic calculus. The conflict between our personal needs and our sense of duty to others (as defined by us, our loved ones, or society) is a chief contributor to that complexity, and the manner in which we resolve the inevitable conflicts that arise often will be unpredictable and highly idiosyncratic. What is more, the people who truly love us understand this.

For whatever reason, Thomas Jefferson felt the need to spend a lifetime building and rebuilding his houses and interacting with people through letters by the thousands and as host to hundreds. That these needs contributed to his financial decline and sometimes caused his family great emotional distress was not enough to deter him from his course. The idea that he may have acted in a similar fashion in order to fulfill other needs cannot be so easily discounted.

Jefferson the Racist

The final prong of the character defense of Jefferson is somewhat ironic. The first three prongs rely on citing the positive aspects of Thomas Jefferson's character: his gentle breeding, his great intellect, and his love of family. This last prong points to what most people would concede was the negative part of Jefferson's nature: his racism. To blunt criticism of Jefferson on the matter of race, scholars have often presented him as a man ahead of his time on the question of slavery or have emphasized his kindness to his slaves. When dealing with the Sally Hemings charge, some of those same historians and commentators wave his racism about like a cross in front of a vampire. Thomas Jefferson, they say, was too racist to have touched a black woman, even one who by all accounts looked white. The pseudo-scientific racism in Jefferson's *Notes on the State of Virginia* and his statement that "amalgamation produces a degradation to which no one . . . can innocently consent" are said to settle the matter.[39] How could a man who wrote such things engage in a sexual liaison with a black person? One might answer, the same way that a man who wrote the Declaration of Independence and various ringing indictments of slavery and who was forever railing against tyrants could hold people in bondage and act as a tyrant himself.

There can be no question that Thomas Jefferson was deeply and profoundly racist. But where is the empirical evidence that racism invariably trumps sexuality? If it is true that when one talks about Thomas Jefferson one might as well be talking about the nation, historians' suggestion that Jefferson's racism would have inevitably overcome his sexuality presents a view of this country's history and the nature of racism that is seriously flawed.

The notion that a racist white man will not engage in a sexual relationship (even one of long duration) with a black woman is, to put it charitably, quaint. The evidence of miscegenation is far too extensive to support such a claim. It should be clear to all by this point in our history that what some slave masters said they felt about the idea of sexual relations with black women and what they did were often two different things. Being attracted to or having affection for one member of a race does not mean that one has to love or respect other members of that race. It just means that whatever it is that attracts one person to another (something that may be a matter of instinct) can sometimes operate independently of any social construct that tells us how to react to groups of people. As there is sufficient evidence that this happened to other slave masters and slave women, it could have happened to Thomas Jefferson and Sally Hemings.

Thomas Jefferson's racism was not extraordinary. It looms large for us only because he put his views about blacks—and practically every other matter under the sun, trivial and nontrivial—on paper. Those views were horrific. He pronounced whites more physically attractive than blacks, citing whites' ability to blush and "long flowing hair." Jefferson also disparaged blacks' ability to reason, saying that he had never heard a black person make a statement above "a simple narrative" and that he could not conceive of any among their number with the capacity to comprehend Euclid.[40] These sentiments represented the views of many whites then and even now. Moreover, Jefferson's attitudes were shared by white men who had relationships with black women and those who did not.

Jefferson's stated preference for Caucasian features over those of blacks is no answer to the Hemings allegation. Sally Hemings was fair-skinned enough to have blushed, and her hair was described as having been long and flowing. As to Jefferson's claim that he had never heard a black utter a statement above a simple narrative, one could take him at his word, but it would be unwise to do that given the improbability of the claim. When he wrote that comment, Jefferson was a grown man who had come into contact with many blacks. Some black person must have said something to him that was above the level of reciting a story. The comment may not have been enough to signal to Jefferson that the person could comprehend Euclid (a talent he knew that not all whites possessed), but blacks must have made statements to him that involved some form of reasoning.

It is impossible to make informed judgments about the extent of Jefferson's adherence to these notions without knowing something of what went on at Monticello. Jefferson told slaves on his plantation to do many things that required the ability to reason, and others with whom he dealt knew this. To take one example, Jefferson's overseer Gabriel Lilly was aghast that Jefferson would allow slaves with no supervision to use dynamite on his various construction projects.[41] The safe use of dynamite requires the use of judgment, that in turn requires an ability to reason, and reasoning requires more than the simple recitation of a narrative. If the illiterate Gabriel Lilly knew this, so did Thomas Jefferson. Lilly did not think slaves capable of exercising that particular function; Jefferson expected them to do so.

So, what do we make of Jefferson's comment about blacks, narratives, and Euclid? Though he wrote those words before Lilly made his observations, there is no evidence that he learned better over time. Is Jefferson to be taken literally on this point, or do we consider that while he believed blacks inferior, the extreme nature of his comments suggests that they were made in service of something else? As his great friend James Madison explained, Jefferson had a tendency to make extravagant statements during the course of making a larger point. Put in that context, Jefferson's extremist comments about blacks were part of his justification to those who might expect better from him (which now includes a good part of the world) for his involvement in a system that he knew to be wrong. The slave owner who had to build and run Monticello knew what blacks were capable of doing, and he made them do it as the situation required. The philosopher and scientist, having gone out on a limb on the subject of freedom and the rights of man, felt compelled to provide a strong public rationalization for private wrongs that he had no intention of righting.

In addition to highlighting his disparagements of blacks, historians also cite Jefferson's desire to have blacks emancipated and separated from the white population to prevent race mixture and racial conflict to show that he was too racist to have been involved with Sally Hemings.[42] But the world after slavery that Jefferson was addressing was markedly different from the world in which he lived. Racist whites such as Jefferson greatly feared the idea of living with blacks who were not directly under their control. The history of the South indicates that when whites exercised direct control over blacks, they were far less concerned about exchanging intimacies with them than they became after their system of direct control was shattered. After emancipation, whites who had used black women as wet nurses for their children, as cooks, housekeepers, and maids in the crowded living area of ordinary plantation houses, suddenly became unwilling to sit next to a black person on a park bench. Jefferson may have felt comfortable enough in his milieu where he was the master of himself and of all he surveyed to do things that he would not have thought possible in the less controlled setting that he so feared.

One must also consider that Jefferson, because of the circumstances of his own household, knew that slavery, as well as emancipation, provided opportunities for race mixing. He was able to live with the race mixing that went on during slavery. It was going on all around him, but it was race mixing of a particular sort. During the era of slavery, miscegenation was largely a white man–black woman phenomenon. Jefferson had seen the examples of his father-in-law, whom he liked and admired, and his venerated law teacher George Wythe, who was said to have had a son by a black mistress.[43] His revulsion at the notion of miscegenation did not lead him to turn his back on either of them. In fact, he named his youngest grandson after George Wythe.

Jefferson's personal actions with regard to one particular interracial relationship give some insight into his actual response to—as opposed to his rhetorical musings about—miscegenation. During the 1780s one of Jefferson's slaves, Mary Hemings, was leased to a local businessman named Thomas Bell. Mary Hemings, one of Sally Hemings's half sisters, and Thomas Bell became lovers and had two children, a circumstance of which Jefferson as her owner was almost certainly aware. After several years Mary Hemings asked Jefferson to sell her and the two children to Bell, a request that Jefferson granted. Even after these events, Jefferson spoke highly of Bell. Bell and Hemings, who adopted the last name of her master/lover, lived as husband and wife for the rest of Bell's life in a relationship whose continuance Thomas Jefferson made possible.[44] It is worthwhile to ask whether a man, who in some scholars' depictions is almost Hitlerian in his phobia of blacks and race mixing, would have facilitated such a liaison when he could have put an end to it.

One could also wonder what Jefferson's response would have been if the races of the respective parties had been different. What if Jefferson had hired out a black slave to a white woman and those two individuals had entered into a romantic relationship and had children together. If the black man had come to Jefferson to ask to be sold to the white woman so that they could go on living together and having children, Jefferson might not have been so accommodating to the couple.

If slavery ended and black men remained in the United States and, perhaps, enjoyed the benefits of equal citizenship, Jefferson evidently felt that the emergence of such relationships was an all-too-real possibility. White men would not have the same degree of control over black men if they could not restrict their mobility. The only solution to this problem was to separate blacks from whites. It is likely that the real horror of horrors that Thomas Jefferson saw if slavery was ended with no deportation was the possibility that white women and black men could do more easily what white men and black women had been doing up until that point. Even white men who had black slave mistresses would have reacted negatively, perhaps even violently, to relationships between white women and black men. The nightmare of such pairings would have had little to do with any liaison Thomas Jefferson may have had with Sally Hemings, as the maintenance of that relationship would have been in keeping with the double standard of the society in which Jefferson lived quite comfortably.

Racists versus Racists

Another important fact to consider when one contemplates the claim that Jefferson the racist would not have been involved with Sally Hemings is that there are racists, and there are racists. There are, in fact, white people who are racist and who are at the same time basically decent people. That is to say, they are people who are not naturally hateful but who have been captured by the customs, thinking, and mores of the society in which they live. Even though their racism can go to the very marrow, under the right circumstances the basic decency of such people allows them to see the humanity of an individual black person. When this happens, that black person is seen as an exception, not like all the others. This allows them to treat that one black, or a few blacks, in a way that they would never think other blacks could or should be treated.

Recognizing that such people are basically good is not to minimize the harm that they can do to blacks. In truth, they can cause a substantial amount of harm. Their inability to transfer their recognition of the humanity of an individual black person in a particular context to the black race in general allows racists of a different sort to press their agenda. The chief flaw of this type of person is that when push comes to shove, they are cowards. They can know something is wrong, but they can only rarely bring themselves to defy custom openly to fight against that wrong. Their acknowledgments of blacks' humanity remain particularized, private, and tightly controlled.

On the other hand, there are racist whites who cannot be reached at any level, and there is no point in trying. There are no, or too few, circumstances under which they can respond to the humanity of a black person. In their case the customs and mores of society combine with the basic meanness of their personality to form something stronger and more sinister than either racism or misanthropy alone could create. Their feelings about blacks border on the pathological, beyond reason or experience.

These are, of course, polar-opposite descriptions of what is a continuum of feelings. The question to ask about Thomas Jefferson is where on the continuum would he fall? Would he be closer to the first description of a racist or to the second? Jefferson scholars, when they want to refute the Sally Hemings charge, place him closer to the end of the continuum that includes those who have a pathological or phobic reaction to blacks. He would not have been able to respond to Sally Hemings in an emotional or sexual way. When they are trying to defend him against the notion of hypocrisy on the slave question or to show his benevolence to his slaves, they put him at the other end of the continuum.[45] He is to be forgiven for not using his presidency to make a more forceful stand against slavery because he was a hostage to his times and his way of life, and even if he was a slave master, he exercised that power in a fashion that reflected his basic sense of humanity.

The balance of the evidence suggests that Thomas Jefferson was probably more like the racist of the first sort. Jefferson's negative ideas about black people do not seem to have sprung from an evilness of spirit. He seems to have reached his conclusions about blacks, including the chance that blacks and whites could live together in the postslavery world, by a process of reasoning that, while deeply flawed, can be characterized as a form of reason.

Some episodes in Jefferson's life give hints about his personality and the type of racist he was. Jefferson, as is common among those who are racist, also had his exceptions among blacks. He knew well and liked the Scotts, a family of black musicians whom he hired to play at his daughter Martha's wedding and whose children he suggested should be sent to the local white school in Charlottesville. Jefferson had no desire to see the general integration of school systems across America. Had one of his plans for emancipation gone through, the Scotts presumably would have been on the boat as well. But in this part of Jefferson's world, not the Republic of Letters, but the world built upon face-to-face interaction and communication, the black Scotts were different. Because Jefferson liked the family personally and had something in common with them—the love of music and the violin—the Scott children were good enough to go to school with white children.[46]

The correspondence between Jefferson and Benjamin Banneker is also instructive. Banneker, the noted black mathematician, sent a copy of his almanac to Jefferson with the aim of correcting the then secretary of state's views as to blacks' mental inferiority, outlined in *Notes on the State of Virginia.* Jefferson wrote back to thank Banneker, stating that he was impressed by Banneker's work and that no one more than he wanted to find further examples to disprove the ideas he had advanced about blacks in his *Notes.* In truth, Jefferson was skeptical of Banneker's accomplishments. He hinted to others that Banneker may have received help in his mathematical work and said that even if this were not so, Banneker's letter showed him "to have had a mind of very common stature indeed." [47]

When his correspondence with Banneker was made public, Jefferson was excoriated by some. His detractors questioned what he was doing corresponding with a black person. Some felt that it was beneath Jefferson's dignity to take such an action because it put him (and because he was a representative of white men, put them) on the same level as a black person.[48]

Certainly Jefferson's privately expressed attitude toward Banneker was a product of his racism. He could not fully accept Banneker's talent because of the mathematician's race. Still, there is a difference between a white person who, upon receipt of a letter from a black person, sits down and responds (albeit insincerely) to his correspondent and a white person who would take the position that the black correspondent was unworthy of any response. In the context of the Banneker dispute, it turns out that both people were racists. But one person had a trait that could have an impact upon his personal relations with individual blacks: that person enjoyed the sensation of being well-thought-of. Any person who has a strong desire to be liked can be induced to act as a human being, at least on a one-on-one basis. All that is required is that he be given the opportunity to have his wish for approval fulfilled.

Jefferson's grandson T. J. Randolph told an anecdote about Jefferson that lends support to the theory that Jefferson was just such a person. While walking together, the two encountered a black man who, upon seeing them, raised his hat and bowed. Jefferson responded to the man by doing the same. T. J. Randolph remembered that when he did not respond to the man and kept walking, his grandfather asked "if I permitted a Negro to be more of a gentleman than myself." [49]

Jefferson's question was racist. He was attempting to teach Randolph a lesson by comparing him to a black man and finding his grandson to suffer in that comparison. If that could not shock Randolph into better manners, what could? Jefferson's automatic response to the black man offers some insight into his personality, as did his response to Banneker, and places him in a different category than his grandson. Jefferson and Randolph were no doubt equal in terms of the depth of their racism, but they did not share one important personality trait: the inability to allow a human gesture made in a one-on-one context to go without an equivalent response. This suggests that without knowing, or even attempting to understand, what human gestures or circumstances confronted Thomas Jefferson when he encountered Sally Hemings in France, one cannot say with any degree of certainty what his response to her would have been.

This is not an attempt to make Jefferson out to be something other than the thoroughgoing racist he was or to ignore the corrosive effect of his beliefs. People like Jefferson can be more dangerous and, in the long run, pose more difficulties for blacks than the sort of person who would express disgust at corresponding with a black person or would ignore a black person's salutation. Some blacks prefer dealing with the more openly hostile racist than with those who hide their contempt for blacks because they have an impulse to want to be liked—even for the time it takes to pass someone on the street. One can be clear about the aims and intentions of the more demonstrative racist; one can know when to expect nothing from that person—and that is always. With the less aggressive racist, a black person never knows, once he or she has developed a specialized relationship with such a white person, whether that white person will, as William Faulkner declared, "stand and fight for old Mississippi" or defend the black person's legitimately held interests when it really counts.

The final thing to consider about Jefferson's racism is that although he believed blacks to be inferior to whites, he thought that an infusion of white blood improved them. He saw a difference between blacks and mulattoes. When people wrote to Jefferson with examples of blacks who disproved his claim of blacks' mental inferiority, he sometimes would reply that the correspondent had not told him the degree of mixture with whites that the person possessed, thus suggesting that such a mixture might account for the black person's talent.[50]

Jefferson's response to the question of when a black person could be considered white is also pertinent to the Hemings story. Sally Hemings was nearly white. By Jefferson's calculations her children were white, for their father (whoever he was), their grandfathers, and their great-grandfathers were white. So any relationship between Jefferson and Hemings would have produced white children. An emancipated child of that union would, according to Jefferson, become a full-fledged American citizen.[51] How could such a person be a degradation? We know that Thomas Jefferson was capable of finding rationalizations for his sometimes contradictory beliefs and actions. A relationship with Sally Hemings would have been one of the easier ones for him to rationalize.

In sum, the idea that Jefferson's racism would have blocked any attraction to Sally Hemings is unconvincing. The dubious assertion that racism is invariably stronger than sexuality stems from a mistaken view of racism as an all-encompassing, one-dimensional phenomenon. The failure to consider the ways in which individual personality traits interact with one's racial attitudes and behavior has prevented a more realistic assessment of the likelihood of Jefferson's involvement with Hemings.

Jefferson's Response

What was Thomas Jefferson's reaction to the Sally Hemings allegations? Historians have presented several interpretations of letters that are relevant to the question. Malone, in his first extensive coverage of this issue, said that "there seems to be no record of his ever having referred specifically, even in private, to the story connecting him with his slave Sally Hemings." He stated later in the same discussion that "without referring to it explicitly, Jefferson did deny it in private . . . when it was included in a list of charges against his morals that was hotly debated in Massachusetts." At another point in the same volume, as he reiterated his disbelief in the Hemings allegation, Malone cited as one of the reasons for his skepticism the fact that Jefferson had made a "categorical" denial of the allegation in a letter to a friend.[52]

Malone's belief that Jefferson made a categorical, though not explicit, denial was based upon a letter that he wrote to his attorney general, Levi Lincoln, a copy of which was sent under separate cover to his secretary of the navy, Robert Smith. This correspondence was written during a period when John Walker, husband of the woman whom Jefferson attempted to seduce while he was a young unmarried man, had challenged Jefferson to a duel in order to obtain satisfaction. Jefferson and Walker, with Henry Lee acting as intermediary, entered into negotiations on the matter.[53]

Jefferson wrote the letter to Lincoln in the summer of 1805. The language in the cover letter that went to Smith suggests that in the letter to Lincoln, Jefferson addressed the issues involved in his dispute with Walker and admitted that he had made improper advances to Walker's wife. This cover letter is the only part of the correspondence that survives, and it is this document that Malone and other scholars take to be Jefferson's repudiation of the charge that he was sexually involved with Sally Hemings. In the cover letter Jefferson wrote:

The enclosed copy of a letter to Mr. Lincoln will so fully explain its own object, that I need say nothing further in that way. I communicate it to particular friends because I wish to stand with them on the ground of truth, neither better nor worse than that makes me. You will perceive that I plead guilty to one of their charges, that when young and single I offered love to a handsome lady. I acknolege its incorrectness. It is the only one founded in truth among all their allegations against me.[54]

The last three sentences have been cited as Jefferson's specific rebuttal of the Sally Hemings story. The supposition is that within the body of the main letter that has been lost, Jefferson referred to the charges about Sally Hemings. In singling out the charge about the attempted seduction of Mrs. Walker as the "only one founded in truth," Jefferson was denying that he had a slave mistress.

How did this letter come to be written? In the first volume of his biography of Jefferson, Malone included an appendix entitled "The Walker Affair" in which he set forth the details of this dispute. At one point Malone referred to Jefferson's statement to Smith that he wanted "to stand with them on the ground of truth," which suggests that this was the primary reason for writing the letter. Walker's charges had become a part of bitter fight in Massachusetts after legislators in that state attempted to punish two editors who had used them in their published attacks on Jefferson. One of the attacks accused him of being "a coward, a calumniator, a plagiarist, a tame, spiritless animal" and said that Jefferson had "taken to his bosom a sable damsel" and had "assaulted the happiness of Mrs. W——."[55]

During this same period the Virginian named Thomas Turner wrote a letter that was printed in the *Boston Repertory* outlining what he claimed to know about the Walker affair in some detail. In addition to discussing the attempted seduction of Mrs. Walker, Turner made other charges against Jefferson in regard to his dealings with the Walkers and included a paragraph about Jefferson's alleged relationship with Sally Hemings.[56] It would not be surprising that Jefferson's friends and supporters would be alarmed by this attack upon his character and that Jefferson would have wanted to reassure them.

Fawn Brodie presented these matters in a different light. Rather than seeing the letter to Lincoln and Smith as a spontaneous effort by Jefferson to calm the fears of his cabinet, Brodie suggested that it was written as a result of the negotiations between Jefferson and Walker. Although the attacks in Massachusetts were serious, the prospect of fighting a duel was a more immediate problem. She saw a connection between Jefferson's letter to Lincoln and a letter from John Walker to Henry Lee written a few months earlier in which Walker specified that it was "*indispensable*" that "some mode . . . be devised, whereby it might be made known to the world that satisfaction had been given me."[57] Brodie surmised that the "mode" was the letter Jefferson wrote admitting that he had tried to seduce Mrs. Walker.

Brodie believed that as a substitute for having a pistol fight, Walker and Jefferson had hit upon the mechanism of Jefferson admitting to third parties that he had attempted to seduce Mrs. Walker and declaring that she was completely blameless. The following year, when Walker apparently felt Jefferson had not stated Mrs. Walker's innocence strenuously enough and had tried to minimize his own fault by referring to his youth and unmarried state, Henry Lee informed Jefferson that Walker insisted upon "a written paper from you going only to his lady's entire exculpation without the mixture of any exculpation of yourself. This paper he desires should be acknowledged before any two of your friends in the world, to prevent at any future day the intimation of forgery." Jefferson apparently complied with this request, although no copy of that letter has been found.[58]

It was Brodie's position that because Jefferson wrote the letter to Lincoln and Smith to provide satisfaction to John Walker, he would have had no reason to bring up the Sally Hemings charge, for it had nothing to do with that dispute. In addition, because Walker and the other individuals who had taken up his cause had made multiple allegations of bad acts on the part of Jefferson in his dealings with the Walkers, Brodie believed that Jefferson's reference to "all their allegations against me" was not clearly a denial of a liaison with Hemings.[59] In her view Jefferson was speaking of the allegations about his conduct toward the Walkers, for they were the ones that could force him to face someone on the field of honor.

John C. Miller's interpretation of the origins and meaning of the Walker letter blended Malone's suggestions with Brodie's in a particularly disturbing way. After detailing the extent to which the Federalist press was using the Walker story to hurt Jefferson, Miller wrote:

> Finally the pressure generated by the press reached such a pitch of intensity that Walker demanded—and he threatened Jefferson with a duel unless the president met his terms—a public statement absolving Mrs. Walker and admitting his own culpability. In 1806, Jefferson admitted his transgression in a private letter sent to several of his friends (and attested to by two witnesses to forestall possible claims of forgery), fully acquitting Mrs. Walker. "I plead guilty to one of their [the Federalists'] charges" (the other charge related to Sally Hemings and the "Congo Harem").[60]

In support of his version, Miller cited Malone, Brodie, and Douglass Adair.[61] But Miller seems to have confused three separate letters that Jefferson wrote on this matter. Aside from the fact that the letter from which Miller quoted was written in 1805, not 1806, neither Malone, Brodie, nor Adair say that the letter Jefferson wrote to Lincoln was "sent to several of his friends (and attested to by two witnesses . . .)." The letter Miller referred to, and reproduced language from, went to Levi Lincoln and a copy went to Robert Smith. There is no record of it having gone anywhere else or having been attested to by any witnesses. The cover letter to that main letter is all that remains of the correspondence, and it is that document that historians have cited as Jefferson's denial of the Hemings story.

What letter written in 1806 could Miller have been talking about? Miller cited pages in Brodie's book where she discussed and quoted from a letter that Jefferson wrote to John Walker after a meeting they had in 1803. A copy of the letter was certified as authentic by Chief Justice John Marshall and Bishop James Madison in 1806. It contains no language about pleading guilty to anything and no references to Sally Hemings. In it Jefferson stated that he would try to rein in the Republican press if the Federalists would stop Callender and others from pursuing the Walker story.[62] This was not the cover letter to which Miller made reference.

As Malone said, Jefferson did write a letter to Walker in 1806 after his previous efforts failed to satisfy Walker. Irving Brant, Madison's biographer, described that letter as having been witnessed by James Madison and Henry Lee, and Lee made reference to it later. Perhaps this is the letter of which Miller wrote, but no copy of that letter exists, so Miller could not have known that it said, "I plead guilty . . ." or referred to the Congo Harem. This, then, was not the cover letter to which Miller referred.[63]

Miller mixed up several items of correspondence. He did so in a way that made Jefferson's "I plead guilty" cover letter, with its purported denial of Sally Hemings, seem to have been attested to by witnesses and seen by "several" of Jefferson's friends. This strengthens the notion of a Jefferson denial of the relationship, because the presence of witnesses calls to mind proceedings where a person makes an oath. It gives the impression that Thomas Jefferson was swearing to the truth of whatever statements he made in the letter Miller mistakenly cited. Two individuals certified the letters from Jefferson to Walker as being authentic. There is no evidence of any certification by outside individuals of the cover letter to Robert Smith to which Miller alluded and from which he produced the well-known sentence.

Miller also stated with too great a degree of certainty that Jefferson mentioned Sally Hemings in his letter to Levi Lincoln. He had never seen that letter. Under any other circumstance a scholar would speak of the possibility that Jefferson had said the words or the likelihood that he had done so. But Jefferson defenders have not felt that they were dealing with normal circumstances when confronting the issue of Sally Hemings. Their desire to show that Thomas Jefferson denied the allegations with respect to Hemings seems to have overridden the needed caution about the specific contents of the no-longer-extant main letter.

If Fawn Brodie was right about why Jefferson wrote the letter to Levi Lincoln, it seems less likely that he would have included the Hemings allegations. If Jefferson wrote the letter as a way of giving John Walker satisfaction, why would he take the opportunity to raise an issue beyond the scope of their dispute in a letter that already must have been galling for him to have to write? Why would a man who guarded his privacy so greatly raise this extraneous issue as he was attempting to deal with the Walker affair?

On the other hand, we can also ask whether Jefferson would have chosen a public official, his attorney general, to be the recipient of a letter written as a part of his negotiations with John Walker about a private matter. This particular private matter did have public implications. Lincoln was the chief legal officer for the United States, and the controversy involved a First Amendment issue, because journalists had been threatened with punishment for publishing attacks upon the president. It would have been appropriate to apprise the attorney general of the basic facts that gave rise to the dispute. There may have been another reason for the choice as well, one that would have been of interest to John Walker. Lincoln was from New England and was Jefferson's liaison to that region. Setting Lincoln straight would have been an effective way of spreading the truth of the matter throughout the region where the Walker story had been aired in some great detail.

If Malone was correct in implying that Jefferson wrote to Lincoln strictly on his own accord, Jefferson might have referred to the Hemings allegations as a way of setting the record straight on all matters of concern. But so many charges had been leveled against Jefferson during this period—including that he was a "tame, spiritless animal"—that one would not think he would have tried to list and deny each of them in his letter to Lincoln. This is especially so if Jefferson believed that to respond to the Hemings allegation was beneath his dignity. Why would Jefferson want to appear undignified in writing to members of his cabinet?

Perhaps Jefferson wanted to make a statement on the controversy in Massachusetts and satisfy Walker at the same time. He may have included in the letter a request that it be returned to him or destroyed, a course of action he requested on other occasions. Malone suggested that this was most likely the case. One must remember that Jefferson kept copies of his correspondence, so there were three opportunities (through Jefferson, Lincoln, and Smith) for the letter to Lincoln to have found its way into the historical record. That Jefferson may have requested the letter be destroyed may aid Fawn Brodie's supposition that this correspondence was intended to mollify John Walker. That all copies would disappear, leaving only the short cover letter to Smith for the historical record, seems strange. Note that Jefferson told Smith that his explanations in the main letter were so clear that there was no reason for him to give additional information, and then Jefferson proceeded to do exactly what he had just said was unnecessary: he gave Smith additional information in the form of a mea culpa on the Walker affair. If Jefferson's coverage of this issue in the main letter was as thorough as he suggested, why did he pull that particular issue out for the cover letter? The only person who derived any benefit from this action (and the extant cover letter itself) was John Walker. It is the only way that the world knows, from Thomas Jefferson's own hand, that he admitted responsibility for attempting to seduce Mrs. Walker.

All speculation aside, it is wrong for anyone to state unequivocally that Jefferson raised an issue in a document that is not extant and was not described by anyone else who saw it. One might wish that he had referred to the Hemings allegation, but that is quite different from possessing knowledge that Jefferson did so. The handling of this episode is another example of the lowering of the standard for assessing and offering evidence in order to defeat the idea of a Jefferson-Hemings relationship. No one can state with any degree of certainty that Sally Hemings was or was not repudiated by the cover letter to Smith. As is often the case with Thomas Jefferson, ambiguities occupy the field.

Would Thomas Jefferson Tell a Lie?

To some extent the notion that Jefferson would never lie about his alleged relationship with Sally Hemings sounds a little too much like my third-grade reader on Jefferson. It has become a part of the lore of this saga that has been accepted by both sides. Supporters of the story argue that Jefferson did not say anything directly about Sally Hemings because he would not tell a lie. Those who disbelieve the story argue that in his letter to Smith, Jefferson did say the story was false; and Jefferson must be believed because he would not tell a lie.[64] It is hard to know what to make of either of these arguments, because both sides share a view of Thomas Jefferson to which I cannot subscribe. Although I admire Jefferson greatly, I cannot say with complete assurance that he would never lie about this situation.

There are, of course, many ways to respond to a question without actually answering it. A lawyer and a diplomat, Jefferson would have known how to respond yet not really answer his critics, and still maintain a sense of his own honor and guard his privacy, particularly if the criticism concerned circumstances that he may have felt no one had the right to expect him to explain. It is likely that any answer Thomas Jefferson provided to his cabinet—whether it responded to the Hemings charge or not—would have been accepted without complaint. Would either Levi Lincoln or Robert Smith, even if they had been dissatisfied with his statement, have demanded that Jefferson be more specific? My own answer, if asked whether Thomas Jefferson would lie about this issue or obfuscate, would be the typical lawyer's response: it depends on the circumstances. There are too many unknown variables, of which we cannot take account, to know the answer.

The Character Problem

A Personal View

With all of this said, there is a character question that bothers me when I ponder this situation. It reflects to some degree the divide that exists between black and white sensibilities. Most white commentators focus on what a Jefferson-Hemings relationship would have meant to Jefferson's white family and purport to be concerned about the idea that Jefferson would take advantage of Sally Hemings, although the latter point is more likely a cover for anxiety about Jefferson's possible involvement with miscegenation. They do not want the story to be true because of what its truth might say about Jefferson's character. This is a function of their determination to follow James Callender's lead and see the relationship in as negative and degraded a light as possible.

I, on the other hand, immediately focus on what such a liaison would have meant to the children born of that relationship. At some level my hesitancy to believe this story stems from my own view of what its truth would say about Thomas Jefferson. This, of course, puts me in league with some of those whom I have criticized, indicating that a story is not true because I do not want it to be. As irrational as I know it is, I do not want this story to be true because I do not want to believe that Jefferson could treat his own flesh as slaves. Even as I think it, I know this sentiment makes no sense. Slave masters have done this in every slaveholding society that has existed on earth. Yet the idea of Thomas Jefferson acting in this manner is hard to accept.

One of the more poignant parts of Madison Hemings's memoirs is his statement that he learned to read, not by any efforts on the part of his alleged father, but by coaxing white children to teach him the alphabet. He speaks of Jefferson as not "being in the habit of showing partiality to" him and his siblings and as being "uniformly kind to all around him." This raises a more profound character issue than the one most often raised about the effect that a Jefferson-Hemings liaison would have had on his daughter Martha and his grandchildren. On that point Jefferson had promised Martha's mother, and the grandchildrens' grandmother, that he would not marry again. If he could not marry, all that was left to him was to find an alternative arrangement or to burn. No one—not Martha or her children—could think that he would have a duty (or be likely) to undertake the latter course on their behalf. Jefferson would, however, have had a duty, if Madison and his siblings were his children, to treat them—to the extent that he could—as if they were.

Perhaps I have fallen prey to the same tendency to present the situation in as bad a light as possible as a way of convincing myself that the story could not be true. This would not be to defend Thomas Jefferson but to avoid what may be the ultimate truth, that although he was an extremely talented and visionary man who has been of immense value to us, he was at heart just a typical southern slave owner.

It is also likely that I am being unfair in my vision of what Sally Hemings's children's lives were like and unrealistic in my view of what could have been the alternatives. There was undoubtedly more to Madison Hemings's view of his life than is immediately apparent in his statement. Hemings deserves to be considered as a person, with all the possible complexities and quirks that can exist within human beings.

Madison Hemings on Thomas Jefferson Reconsidered (Partially)

One of the many intriguing things about Madison Hemings is that he was the only one of the four Hemings children who did not finally choose to live as a white person. This may have been because he was too black in appearance to have done so or because the idea of passing was not attractive to him. In either case, his status as the only Hemings child who remained black opens a host of possible explanations for the manner in which he portrayed his life.

Many black families of Madison Hemings's era absorbed the dominant society's notions about the hierarchy of color. Being the darkest member of a family or the one with the kinkiest hair could be an ordeal. Families who were, as it is phrased, "color struck" could treat a darker person in the family differently than lighter members. Or the relatively darker individual himself or herself could be overly sensitive and perceive disparate treatment even when it did not exist. If Madison Hemings was the most black-looking of the Hemings children, he could have felt, rightly or wrongly, that he was devalued because of this.

Hemings seemed upset that Jefferson had neglected his formal education, so that he had to persuade the white children on the plantation to teach him his letters. Yet one would think that other members of the Hemings family, who had somehow learned to read, would have been able to tell him the alphabet. There are indications that his mother Sally received some formal instruction while in France. Her brother James Hemings wrote with some competence, and she spent over two years there with him. Madison Hemings's uncle John, to whom he was apprenticed for seven years, knew the alphabet, as he corresponded with Thomas Jefferson. Knowing these facts about some of the older members of Madison Hemings's family makes his assertions about his schooling seem strange. In addition, Hemings's account of the lives of his older brother and sister, as well as what we know of his younger brother from other sources, tends to suggest that he exaggerated the level of deprivation he suffered in this regard or that he was treated differently for some reason.

That Beverley and Harriet Hemings were able to pass for white and marry white people "in good circumstances" suggests that they must have had some level of education or training—or had considerable talent for faking it. Eston Hemings, after he left Ohio, changed his name to Eston H. Jefferson and passed for white as well. Think of the issues of language and culture that these three people confronted. They had to carry themselves like white people, speak like white people, and, in the cases of Beverley and Harriet, know the things that a white person who marries into a good family needs to know.

Historians have expressed considerable skepticism about the language employed in Madison Hemings's memoirs. They assumed that as a former slave he would have been too inarticulate to speak in standard English. Most of the language may have been S. F. Wetmore's because that was Wetmore's way of producing the memoirs of whites and blacks. Still, there is no reason to suppose that Hemings's speech would have been drastically different from Wetmore's. The descriptions of Eston Hemings contained in the *Scioto Gazette* retrospective on his time in Chillicothe suggest that he stood out precisely because of his gentlemanly bearing and manner of speech. Why would his brother Madison, with whom he grew up, have been so different? How can one square the assumption that Madison Hemings would speak in slave dialect with the notion that his three siblings (two of them married to white people) could pass unnoticed into the white world? Their success at doing this comports neither with Madison Hemings's implication that he and his siblings were neglected nor with the idea that Madison Hemings did not know how to speak standard English.

One cannot discount the possibility that Hemings's bitterness played a role in the way he described his life. He seems ambivalent about Jefferson, recounting with pride his alleged father's accomplishments and noting the good aspects of his personality. At the same time Hemings did not hide the fact that the man whom he said was his father had not done enough to further his education and had not shown him a sufficient amount of affection. Whether this means that Jefferson did nothing at all for the Hemings siblings, or whether he did some things and Madison Hemings didn't think it was enough, remains unclear given the circumstances of the other Hemings children's lives.

The Hemings Children and Work

Although Hemings says that Jefferson neglected his formal education, he put Madison and his brothers under the direction of his best slave artisan, their uncle John. This ensured that all three men would have a way to make a living. The typical arrangement at Monticello was for children to care for younger children or to run errands until age ten. The boys then went to work doing the repetitious and difficult tasks in Jefferson's nail factory, while the girls learned to weave and spin. At age sixteen the boys went either to the fields or to learn a trade.[65]

Jefferson's nailery was originally staffed with boys, but by the time Madison and Eston reached the age of ten, grown men had largely replaced young boys as workers in the factory. Only Beverley Hemings was born early enough to have worked at the nailery before the change. He is listed in Jefferson's Farm Book as being a tradesman when he was only twelve years old.[66] There is no record of what he was doing between the ages of ten and twelve, when he could have been at the nailery. Madison Hemings did not mention the nailery but noted that he and his brothers spent their time running errands until they were put under the direction of their uncle to learn carpentry. However, he said that this happened when they were fourteen, apparently not knowing, or having forgotten, that Beverley Hemings's apprenticeship began earlier. Their sister Harriet, unlike the other girls on the plantation, was not sent to learn to weave until she was fourteen.

Hemings also said that he and his siblings were generally happy growing up because they knew they were not going to be slaves forever and because they were always able to be with their mother. They do not seem to have done very much hard work, as Edmund Bacon noted when he described Harriet

Hemings.[67] So, it seems that up until the age of twelve in Beverley's case, and fourteen for the other children, Madison Hemings and his siblings spent most of their time running errands, doing other childhood activities, and being with their mother. The boys, at least, seem to have gone straight from the relatively easy life of a child to the most prestigious apprenticeship on the plantation.

Other interesting facets of the lives of Sally Hemings's children suggest that they were different than the other young people at Monticello. Isaac Jefferson recalled that after he moved to the city of Petersburg, Madison Hemings was there twice. Petersburg, a few miles south of Richmond, for many years had the largest free black population in the South. Isaac Jefferson said that Hemings "was here when the balloon went up, the balloon that Beverley sent off."[68]

Isaac did not say it, but the most reasonable inference is that he was speaking of Madison's brother Beverley Hemings. The reference was made during his discussion of Sally Hemings and her children, and the phrasing suggests that Madison had come to Petersburg to watch the event. Isaac evidently associated the balloonist with Madison's visit. The odds that Madison Hemings would come to Petersburg at the time some other Beverley should happen to launch a balloon and that Isaac would remember and say the name "Beverley" during his description of the Hemings family seem slim. Moreover, when Isaac referred to white people in his memoirs, he always used a title and did not refer to them just by their first names. In any event, Isaac's recollections suggest that, on some date, Beverley Hemings ascended a hot air balloon.

Isaac gave no date for when this event occurred. There is evidence that a balloon ascension did take place in Petersburg during the period after Jefferson died and before Madison Hemings left Virignia in 1836. On July 4, 1834, a balloon ascension was scheduled to take place in Petersburg. Someone anonymously placed a notice in the advertisement section of the city's major paper announcing the event. Not part of the town's official Independence Day celebration, it was to occur an hour after those ceremonies concluded. The balloon was to ascend from Poplar Lawn, the city park that was the site of the town's annual Fourth of July festivities. Poplar Lawn had a huge field bounded on one side by Jefferson Avenue.[69]

There is no way to tie this particular ascension to Beverley Hemings. However, the anonymous nature of the notice is itself suggestive. Balloon ascensions were occasions of great interest, and the persons who accomplished them were proud of their achievements; most announcements and descriptions of such exciting events gave the name of the agent or agents responsible.

If Beverley Hemings, the runaway slave passing for white, came back to Virginia to set off this balloon, he may have been hesitant about drawing too much advance attention to himself.

Even before Jefferson witnessed the famous Robert-Hullin ascension in Paris, he was greatly interested in balloon flight, suggesting to a professor at his alma mater, the College of William and Mary, that the school form a Balloon Club. Over the years Jefferson and the college's president, his old school friend Bishop James Madison, corresponded about the successes and failures of the students' efforts. In the month before he sailed for France, Jefferson went to watch Dr. John Fuolke, a physician from Philadelphia, fly several large paper balloons. During his time as minister to France, Jefferson not only went to view balloon ascensions, he wrote to his friends about the technology, giving them advice about constructing balloons. Jefferson's enthusiasm continued after he returned to the United States. He corresponded with scientists and friends about the subject until a few years before his death and kept a multivolume set about the mechanics of balloon ascensions in his library. After attending Blanchard's ascension in 1793, he wrote to his daughter Martha saying that he "wished for one sincerely" to cut travel time between Philadelphia and Monticello.[70] By today's standards ballooning may seem a trivial activity, a thing of sport. During Jefferson's era it was considered a scientific venture with travel and even military implications. It would be intriguing if he passed his interest in aerial transportation on to Beverley and Madison Hemings, all the more so if Beverley undertook to become a ballonist.

The Historians and the Slave Children

Dumas Malone did express concern about the idea that Jefferson could have treated his children as slaves, but only in an interview.[71] He never cited this concern in his biography of Jefferson. There he chose to frame his defense of Jefferson's character by referring to what the truth of this story would have meant to Jefferson's white family. Perhaps Malone was not so sure that Jefferson could not have treated his own flesh as slaves as he was that Jefferson would not have hurt his white family by fathering a black one. Malone's seeming hesitancy on this aspect of the character question actually answers my own personal dilemma about this story.

Of all historians, John C. Miller wrote the most extensively about this aspect of the Hemings story. He asserted that it would have been impossible for Thomas Jefferson to have treated his own children—even if they were black—in the manner that Madison Hemings described. Miller, however, mischaracterized Madison's description. He transformed Hemings's statement that Jefferson was "not in the habit" of showing him and his siblings any fatherly affection into a claim that Jefferson "never" showed them any affection.[72]

After noting Jefferson's almost obsessive concern with his daughters Martha and Maria and his anguish upon the deaths of his other four children, Miller cited as evidence of Jefferson's indifference to the Hemings children that "he failed to record the birth of several of Sally's children especially those who died in infancy." This is incorrect. Jefferson's Farm Book has the name and date of birth of every one of Sally Hemings's children except the one who was most recently discovered. Her birth date is not in the Farm Book, but Jefferson announced this child's birth in a letter to his son-in-law. Some years after Miller wrote his biography, researchers looking more closely at that letter were prompted to recheck the Farm Book, whereupon they found that Thenia, a young girl the age of the child minders at Monticello, had moved into Hemings's household at this time.[73]

Miller also compared Jefferson's displays of grief at the deaths of his children with Martha Jefferson to the lack of any evidence of grief at the death of Hemings's first daughter.[74] But we do not know how Thomas Jefferson reacted to the deaths of Sally Hemings's children. Perhaps he did grieve. Obviously he could not have written to anyone about his grief even if he felt it strongly. If he could not restrain any open displays of sadness, family members would have been careful not to notice. Jefferson, and his family, would have had to keep any special feelings about Sally Hemings, or any children he may have had or lost with her, as secret as possible.

How would Miller expect Jefferson to have acted? As in his statement that Madison Hemings was trying to curry favor with whites when he claimed to be the son of Thomas Jefferson, Miller seems naive about the reality of racism and the position that Jefferson, if he was carrying on this relationship, would have been in. He could not have freed the family and let them stay at Monticello. Such an action would have drawn great attention and opprobrium. Could he have freed them, set them up in a household nearby, and gone to visit periodically? If they stayed legally anywhere in Virginia, he would have to get the formal permission of the state legislature, an exceedingly public act.

Miller also assumed that Jefferson would have seen the children that he had with his black mistress in the same light as he saw children that he had with his lawfully wedded white wife. Yet throughout history men have treated their illegitimate children differently than the children from their lawful unions. Even men with two sets of children from two legal marriages sometimes will favor one set over the other. Adding the racial component to

Jefferson's alleged situation makes it even more likely that there would be disparate treatment.

This does not mean that Jefferson may not have felt some degree of affection for these children. The circumstances of his household would have required him not to treat them in an openly affectionate manner, as Madison Hemings thought he should have done more often. How could Jefferson have explained to his young grandchildren why slave children were being treated exactly as they were? How could the Hemings children's expectations from Jefferson not grow in direct proportion to his expressions of attachment to them? Couldn't Jefferson have seen the costs of such a balancing? Under the social circumstances of the day, whatever he gave to the Hemings children would necessarily have come out of what he had to give to his white family, thus limiting what he could do for them.

Perhaps Jefferson did start out giving favorable attention to Beverley Hemings, who, according to Madison Hemings, would have been his oldest son. Beverley's balloon-ascending activities suggest that he may have had a scientific bent and an intelligence that were nurtured in his early life. Beverley Hemings was born in 1798, the year before a newspaper first hinted at the rumor about Jefferson's involvement with a slave woman. Thomas Turner's letter in the *Boston Repertory* in 1805, the year of Madison Hemings's birth, mentioned Beverley by name and referred to him as being well known by many people in the area. Why would a seven-year-old slave boy have been known or noticed by Turner or any other white person in the vicinity of Monticello? Why would Turner, who knew that Hemings had more than one child, single out Beverley and not mention Harriet or even the infant Madison?

Madison Hemings was born at exactly the wrong time to expect that Jefferson would have either wanted or been free to treat him openly as a son. By 1805 Jefferson had been considerably battered in the press for his alleged relationship with Sally Hemings and other matters. His character became an issue in heavily publicized political crises in Massachusetts in 1805 and in Connecticut in 1806. On the home front Madison Hemings would have had only a few years at Monticello before Martha Randolph and her children became permanent fixtures on the mountain. When he reached the age of five, whatever status Hemings may have had would have disappeared overnight with the arrival of a group of white children, with one whom he shared a name and almost a birth date.[75]

What kind of conflict would Jefferson's equal treatment of his grandchildren and alleged slave children have created between Jefferson and his daughter Martha? Martha Randolph's letters to her father, and his to her, reveal an almost unceasing effort to assure one another that the two loved each other above everyone else. That this sentiment had to be expressed continually cannot simply be attributed to the letter-writing style of the eighteenth and early nineteenth centuries. Other families from that period who loved each other did not carry on in this way in their family letters. The correspondence between father and daughter suggests a degree of insecurity on the parts of both. To have shown normal fatherly affection toward the Hemings children would have exacerbated that insecurity to a point beyond all control. To do what Miller suggested Jefferson would have done had he been the father of Beverley, Harriet, Madison, and Eston would have destroyed the carefully balanced emotional equilibrium that he attempted to maintain among those who lived at Monticello.

If one accepts the notion that Jefferson did nothing to advance the intellectual lives of the Hemings children, one could argue that his plan for them was the result of his practical calculations about their likely paths in life. If his white son had lived, Thomas Jefferson would have expected that son to follow in his footsteps and would have trained him to do so. A black son, even one whom Jefferson loved in some way, would have had a different path in life. It is interesting to compare Madison Hemings's statements about his education with those of the man who was, perhaps, the closest thing to a son that Jefferson had—his grandson T. J. Randolph. Writing in his memoirs, not long after Madison Hemings's statement to the *Pike County (Ohio) Republican,* Randolph pointedly mentioned that he had "been sent to inferior schools all of his life and not even to college." He went on to say, just as Hemings had said, that whatever education he received was obtained after he became an adult.[76] Both men, from opposite ends of the social spectrum, who grew up in the same place and in the shadow of Jefferson, spoke with bitterness about being prevented from reaching their full intellectual potential because of decisions made during their childhood.

Although Randolph's comments were clearly directed toward his father, Thomas Mann Randolph, with whom he had great difficulties, the situation was more complex. Jefferson was consulted about his grandson's education and helped to direct the course of it. Why didn't he do better by Randolph? Malone indicated that Jefferson was aware of the limits of T. J. Randolph's intellect.[77] Evidently Jefferson so adhered to the notion of an aristocracy of talent that he was willing to accept his grandson's consignment to a lower tier of educational training. This attitude could have influenced what Jefferson might have been willing to do for the Hemings children even if he was their father.

In fact, the Hemings children were treated in exact accordance with Jefferson's plans for the proper education of young blacks in preparation for their emancipation and eventual separation from white society. He suggested that young blacks be educated "to tillage, arts, or sciences" until they reached twenty-one if they were male and eighteen if they were female.[78] If Jefferson was their father, he may have thought that training Beverley, Madison, and Eston Hemings to become carpenters and musicians and Harriet to become a wife and either freeing them or allowing them to pass into white society were about the best he could do considering where they had started in life. In that regard they fared much better than Martha Randolph. If what Madison Hemings said was true, Jefferson left the Hemings siblings to the care of their mother when they were young children, turned the boys over to their uncle (his best and most trusted slave artisan) when they were adolescents, and let them all go when they became adults.

Malone's Final Word on the Character Issue

Near the end of his life, Dumas Malone admitted in an interview in the *New York Times* that he might be able to accept that Jefferson had sex with Hemings "once or twice" but he could not accept that there was a thirty-eight-year liaison.[79] This might seem a baffling statement in light of the defense of Jefferson that he had long mounted. Having sex with Hemings "once or twice" could have produced one or two children. Why would Jefferson's character not permit a long-term relationship with Sally Hemings but instead allow him to sleep with her a couple of times, in essence to use her? Casual sex would be all right; commitment would be something else. Why would that use of a person under one's authority not amount to a more serious character flaw? What problem did the length of the liaison create?

More than likely Malone could accept the "one or two times" scenario because it keeps Thomas Jefferson well within what could be considered the normal range of behavior that some white men have traditionally exhibited toward black women. That a white man might, on a few occasions, satisfy his temporary carnal urges by the use of a black woman is one thing. The Hemings allegation would be something else again: a man cannot be true to his white heritage and engage in a thirty-eight-year liaison with a black woman.

Even if one does not use thirty-eight years as a yardstick, Madison Hemings's account indicates that Thomas Jefferson and Sally Hemings had sex with one another over a twenty-year period, from their time together in France to the year her last child was born. Lust can last from twenty seconds to twenty months; it probably cannot last twenty years. For what could only be called a relationship to exist over that span of time, there would have to be more involved than just lust or even mere convenience. People tire of one another too quickly, particularly if there are other choices easily available.

Malone probably understood, given his view of Jefferson's personality and of human nature in general, that an almost four-decade relationship would have put these two people in something that resembled a form of marriage. It would mean that a slave woman, whom historians have spent generations either ignoring or explaining away, would have lived in this state with Thomas Jefferson four times as long as he lived with Martha Wayles Jefferson. If she was his mistress for that many years, Sally Hemings most likely would have known the real Thomas Jefferson better than anyone, and the one whom she knew would be unrecognizable to the historians who had devoted their lives to knowing him. That just could never be.

5

Sally Hemings

The person who distrusts himself has no touchstone for reality—for this touchstone can only be oneself. Such a person interposes between himself and reality nothing less than a labyrinth of attitudes. And these attitudes, furthermore, though the person is usually unaware of them (is unaware of so much!), are historical and public attitudes. They do not relate to the present any more than they relate to the person. Therefore, whatever white people do not know about Negroes reveals, precisely and inexorably, what they do not know about themselves.

—James Baldwin, *The Fire Next Time*

SALLY HEMINGS has been described as an enigma.[1] Very little is known about the woman whose identity has become linked to that of one of the most famous men in history. The interest in Hemings and the idea that she might have been Thomas Jefferson's lover have lasted, with varying degrees of intensity, for almost two centuries. Before I decided to write about this subject, I mentioned to some friends on separate occasions that I had spent part of my vacation rereading biographies of Jefferson. Not one of them launched into a discussion of the Kentucky Resolutions or the Louisiana Purchase. Almost instantly each of my friends asked, "What's the story with Sally Hemings?" or "Wasn't there something about him and a slave woman?" or "Didn't he have a mistress named Sally Hemings?"

This is, of course, exactly the kind of anecdote that must drive some Jefferson scholars to distraction. The fact that Hemings's name comes so automatically to the lips of ordinary citizens discussing Jefferson must be the realization of their greatest nightmare. Why not talk about the Declaration of Independence, his battles with Hamilton and Burr, . . . the Kentucky Resolutions? There is a legitimate fear that the American obsession with the personal lives of great figures will exceed their awareness of the contributions of those figures. In Jefferson's case there is little chance this will happen. There is no reason to believe that the question of Sally Hemings could ever overshadow Jefferson's legacy to this country.

That Sally Hemings is in anyone's thoughts in this era is a testament to her singularity. Americans generally have not taken an interest in the lives of individual slaves unless they escaped slavery to become famous, as did Harriet Tubman or Frederick Douglass. For the most part it has been slaves as a group—and individuals who served as a metaphor for the group or as a type within the group—who have been the primary focus of any attention directed toward slaves. This focus has made it difficult to see a given slave as an individual who might possess the entire range of sensibilities, strengths, and weaknesses of other members of the human race. The person becomes totally lost within the system.

Over the past two decades there have been two major attempts to rescue Sally Hemings from this fate, the first in a historical work and the other in a work of fiction. Both efforts brought on the proverbial firestorm of controversy and strangely enough, particularly with respect to the work of fiction, altered the nature of the commentary on Thomas Jefferson.

The historical work was Fawn Brodie's biography of Jefferson. In her book Brodie devoted an entire chapter to Sally Hemings, telling the world more about her than had been known up to then.[2] Before Brodie, Hemings was just the bit player in the Jefferson-Callender debacle. "Dusky Sally," "Monticellian Sally," and the other names used to describe her over the years revealed nothing at all about who she was. James Callender's malicious renderings gave no serious person a clue. Historians, primarily interested in proving Callender's charges false, had no interest in attempting to discover who this woman was, because writing about her would draw more attention to the underlying allegation. The project of defeating the notion of a relationship between Jefferson and Hemings demanded that Hemings herself be kept invisible.

Fawn Brodie attempted to bring Hemings into focus by detailing everything she could find about her, noting references in Jefferson's records from France and Monticello. Because Brodie believed that the real story of Hemings's life began when she was in Paris, she found the details relating to that time of particular importance. When one adds what is known about Sally Hemings's life before Paris to Brodie's recounting of the known information about her life in that city, it is possible to get a sense of what the young Sally Hemings might have been like. The crucial turn in Brodie's approach was to treat Sally Hemings, as she had Madison Hemings, as a human being and to make full use of her humanity. That approach had not been taken by white historians up to that point and generally has not been taken by their successors.

Brodie offered some of the details of Hemings's experiences in Paris as evidence to support her thesis that the Jefferson-Hemings relationship began there. She based her conclusion on Madison Hemings's statement, documents showing Jefferson's actions toward Hemings that she believed supported that statement, and Jefferson's actions and statements to others. Brodie's interpretation of these items has been the subject of intense criticism. Examining her arguments allows us to focus our attention on Sally Hemings. We can thereby reference our own knowledge of human thoughts and emotions in trying to gauge what effect the events in her life would have had upon her—to see her as a being who could be shaped, as we all are, by our experiences.

Who Was Sally Hemings?

As the daughter of a woman who was half white and a white man, Sally Hemings was, according to the racial classifications of the day, a quadroon. She was described as being nearly white in appearance with "straight hair down her back." According to the accounts of slaves who lived on the plantation and Jefferson's grandson, she was considered to be very beautiful, so much so that she was known as "Dashing Sally."[3] As a Hemings who worked in the big house, she was at the top of the slave hierarchy of Monticello and spent her early years running errands for Martha Jefferson.

The fourteen-year-old Sally accompanied nine-year-old Mary Jefferson, later called Maria, to Paris in 1787. After the death of his youngest daughter, Lucy, Thomas Jefferson sent for Mary, who had been living with her aunt and uncle Elizabeth and Francis Eppes. The decision to send Sally with Mary countermanded Jefferson's instructions; he had specifically requested that an older woman travel with her, suggesting that a woman named Isabel be sent if she had already had smallpox. But Isabel was about to give birth, so the Eppeses sent Sally instead. Jefferson's specifications were not trivial. He wanted to ensure that his nine-year-old daughter would be properly supervised and that the person who came with her would not catch, and possibly spread, a potentially fatal disease. Sally fit neither of these requirements. She was not an adult, and she had not had smallpox; Jefferson paid to have her vaccinated after she arrived in Paris.[4]

John and Abigail Adams met Sally Hemings and Mary Jefferson in London, where Jefferson was to come to pick them up. Abigail Adams, who had been expecting an older servant as Mary's traveling companion, thought Sally was fifteen or sixteen and described her as "quite a child" and "as wanting more care" than Jefferson's daughter. Ramsey, the captain of their ship, offered his opinion that Hemings would not be particularly helpful and suggested that he take her back to the United States. These observations have been used to paint a picture of Hemings as extremely immature. Douglass Adair and John C. Miller, in particular, used these statements to buttress the argument that it would have been impossible for Jefferson to have been attracted to Hemings because he would have seen her as little more than a child.[5]

Abigail Adams was expecting a middle-aged woman to accompany Mary Jefferson; instead a girl, who was not sixteen but only fourteen, arrived. Think of the fate of the child physically advanced for his or her age, acting that age and meeting the disapproval of those who innocently, though wrongly, expect more. The gap between what Adams expected and what she saw may have been so great that Sally Hemings seemed even more immature than she actually was. There is no wonder that Adams felt impatient and annoyed that the reality fell so short of her expectations. No matter how responsible Sally Hemings may have been, she could not have been as mature as the middle-aged woman Abigail Adams thought she should be.

Captain Ramsey's remedy, that he just take Sally Hemings back to Virginia, suggests that he either was not very thoughtful or was not thinking in a totally disinterested manner about the situation. One wonders at his effrontery, thinking it proper that he decide who would be of no use in Jefferson's household and that, without consulting Jefferson, he would take Hemings back to Virginia. Jefferson knew that Hemings would be arriving with his daughter. The Eppeses had written to inform him while the two were in transit. He knew Hemings's age, and although her youth may have concerned him, he did not write to suggest that Hemings be sent back home. In truth, as the die had already been cast, he may have wanted Hemings to stay, both for his daughter's sake and for the benefit of James Hemings.

As Fawn Brodie pointed out, it does not take much imagination to determine why Captain Ramsey might have been desirous of having the beautiful young girl make the voyage back to the United States with him. Think of "Dashing Sally" on a six-week ocean voyage with Captain Ramsey and his crew. During the trip to Europe Mary Jefferson, despite her youth, as a white person and the daughter of an eminent man served as a form of protection for Sally Hemings. On the way back Hemings would have been on her own.

The facts suggest an exactly opposite conclusion about Sally Hemings than the one put forth by Jefferson scholars. Instead of accepting at face value a judgment made by a person who did not know Hemings, one should consider that she was chosen to make the trip under circumstances that required an exercise of careful consideration. Jefferson's four-year-old daughter Lucy had died of whooping cough while in the care of the Eppeses, a fact that mortified them and led Jefferson to request that Mary be sent to him. The Eppeses' own daughter, also named Lucy, had died of the same disease a week before Lucy Jefferson.[6] It would be highly unlikely that the Eppeses would send Jefferson's other daughter across the Atlantic Ocean with a person who was "wanting more care" than she. Nor would they have ignored Jefferson's specifications about the type of person he wanted sent with Mary, if they did not think that Sally Hemings could handle the job. Jefferson had other female slaves, and the Eppeses had their own. That Sally Hemings was chosen over the rest for what was, after all, a remarkable assignment suggests that the people in the best position to judge her considered her worthy of it. We must remember that everything we know about the Hemings family suggests that they were intelligent, creative, and capable individuals. When one considers this, along with the serious nature of the assignment and the circumstances that led to Mary Jefferson's going to Paris, it is more probable than not that Adams's and Captain Ramsey's assessments of Sally Hemings were incorrect.

It is not enough simply to make arguments. One must consider the implications of one's arguments. Adair and Miller, in asserting that Sally Hemings was an abnormally immature child, were, in effect, charging Francis and Elizabeth Eppes with both extreme negligence and callous defiance of Jefferson's wishes with regard to his daughter. Even had they not had the unfortunate circumstance of having her sister die while in their care, the couple loved Mary and considered her almost a daughter.[7] Implying that they would have been so careless as to pick an abnormally immature girl as her traveling companion—one who could have hurt Mary more than helped her—was unfair to them. These historians' characterizations of Hemings were based upon one person's reaction—most likely spurred by surprise—and the statement of another who may have had his own personal reasons for disparaging Sally Hemings's capabilities. The reputations of Francis and Elizabeth Eppes, like those of the Carr brothers, have been sacrificed to counteract the idea that Thomas Jefferson and Sally Hemings could have been involved in a relationship.

The formulation of Adair and Miller is familiar in another troubling regard: it provides one more example of the practice of molding the identity of a slave to fit the requirements of a historian's argument, whether the mold fits or not. Neither man exhibited any sense of a need to be careful when writing into history a particular view of Sally Hemings as an individual, because it was not the truth of her life that mattered. Miller and Adair, in their determination to present reasons why the story of a Jefferson-Hemings liaison would be impossible, accepted the words of Adams and Ramsey uncritically, even though the context in which they were spoken suggests that extreme skepticism is warranted.

To Abigail Adams's further distress, Jefferson did not come personally to retrieve his daughter and Hemings but sent an assistant. After the pair reached the Hôtel de Langeac, Jefferson's residence in Paris, Mary joined her sister Martha at the Abbaye Royale de Panthémont, an exclusive convent school.[8]

Brodie stated that soon after Hemings came to Paris, a French teacher named Monsieur Perrault was engaged. It was apparently James Hemings who hired the tutor. There is no indication from documents from France that Sally Hemings was included in the lessons, although in later years one political enemy of Jefferson referred to Hemings as having had the "benefits of a French education." Though the presence of a tutor does not support Fawn Brodie's claim about Jefferson's feelings toward Hemings, it does illustrate the extraordinary things she was exposed to as a young woman.[9]

Sally Hemings, who had been entrusted with an assignment and had succeeded in carrying out that assignment, was now living in an opulent residence, learning a new language (either formally or informally) and a new set of customs. Her brother James, who had been in the city long enough to know his way around, was being trained as a chef. There is no indication that Jefferson discouraged free movement on James's part while in France. When the two men arrived in the country along with Jefferson's daughter, Martha, Jefferson sent James, who spoke no French at that time, ahead to make hotel reservations for the party.[10] It is likely that James would show Paris to his sister and talk to her about the life he had led up until that point. In other words, they would do all the things that a brother and sister would do.

Residence in France most certainly affected Thomas, Martha, and Mary Jefferson's views of life; would it not also have affected the views of James and Sally Hemings? Edmund Bacon commented that he had "often" heard Sally Hemings refer to her voyage to France. Bacon came to Monticello seventeen years after Hemings returned from France. If the trip over the ocean meant so much to her so many years later, riding through the streets of London and living in and going about Paris also would have made an indelible impression upon her. What might those times have meant to a young woman who left them behind to return to the United States to live the rest of her life on a mountain in Albemarle County, Virginia?

There probably was not much work for Sally Hemings to do during her stay in France. Martha and Mary were boarding at school. Jefferson had been in Paris for three years, and the residence already had a staff of servants. When Jefferson wrote to Francis Eppes telling him to send Mary along with a female servant, he had proposed that he meet her at a designated port and send the servant immediately back to Virginia.[11] The servant's job was to escort Mary to France. Jefferson had not contemplated bringing a slave from Monticello to be a servant at the Hôtel de Langeac.

Sally Hemings was also beautiful in a city where beauty was of extreme importance. If she was thought of as dashing at Monticello, there is no doubt that she would be made even more aware of her attributes in a city and a country whose inhabitants are notorious for expressing their appreciation for attractive women. Paris was fashion mad even then. It was important for the Jeffersons and the Hemingses to be dressed appropriately, for being ill attired or having servants who were poorly outfitted would reflect badly upon the minister and the country that he represented. As a result, Jefferson spent lavishly on all of the members of his household.

A young woman in this situation could begin to think of herself differently. Or, in Sally Hemings's case, since she had led such a privileged existence up until that point, her new way of life probably confirmed what she may have thought of herself all along: that she was special. In either case, we cannot accept the view that her experiences in Paris would not change the way Hemings thought about the world and would not have had an influence upon her. Seeing herself differently may have changed the way others, including Thomas Jefferson, saw her.

Most commentary on this subject proceeds from the assumption that any relationship between Jefferson and Hemings would have involved a degree of force. Again, this is implied largely to make the situation look as bad as possible, so that no one will believe, or want to believe, that the story could be true.[12] At this point we have to confront the unpleasant notion for many, both black and white, that Sally Hemings may have welcomed any advances that Thomas Jefferson might have made.

Consider her origins. She was a young woman whose grandmother had been the mistress of a white man. Her mother had been the mistress of another white man, a plantation owner, Sally's father. Historians attribute her family's special position at Monticello to her mother's relationship with John Wayles. Although her mother had not derived the ultimate benefit from that relationship—Wayles did not free the family—it had allowed Elizabeth Hemings and her children to live better and have more opportunities than the rest of Jefferson's slaves. It was, in fact, most likely the reason that James and Sally Hemings got to go to France.

Might not Sally Hemings have thought being the mistress of a slave master a suitable role? Social hierarchies existed even within the slave system. Just as individual members of each class tend to look for mates from among their own or from a higher class, Hemings might have acted in a similar fashion. The males of her family were treated more like white servants than black slaves. When Jefferson found he was to go to France and wanted to take James Hemings along, he had to send word to Hemings, who was in Richmond serving as a tour guide for English visitors, to meet him at Monticello.[13] The Hemings women were not given as much freedom, but even white women did not have as much freedom as white men. Hemings, as a young person who had not been subjected personally to the most brutal realities of slavery, could easily have seen herself as closer to Jefferson and his family than to the slaves who worked in his fields. In one important sense, she was. She was Jefferson's wife's half sister and his daughter's aunt.

That a black woman in slavery would seek out a relationship with a slave master, or if not seek it out, not run away from it, is not a particularly attractive idea. Some view such a person as a traitor, giving the ultimate aid and comfort to the enemy. Our notions about women and sexuality probably play a major role in our discomfort about these situations. Sex between a slave master and a woman who was a slave has always been seen differently than sex between a slave mistress and a man who was a slave, both by whites and blacks. Whites tolerated the former because it posed no real threat to the established order. They claimed it did, but they did not react against it with the same vehemence that they did to relationships between slave males and white women, which were seen as threatening the social order and could never be tolerated.

Blacks by and large have accepted this formulation because they along with most whites see the male as the prime mover in both situations. A master's taking a slave woman was in keeping with the process of subjugation. A male slave taking a white mistress (and it would be seen that way rather than the other way around) puts a black man in the position of prime mover, which represented a threat to the power of white males. Most blacks probably would consider a slave woman who voluntarily joined a relationship with her master as a collaborator. On the other hand, they might see a black man who had a relationship with a slave mistress as a rebel who was striking at the heart of the slave system. These ideas, rooted in our visions of sex roles, may have some validity as far as generalizations go. They do not take into account the differing circumstances and contexts in which such relationships could arise. Therefore, we should not allow them to control any serious consideration of an individual case.

We must consider all of the known circumstances in Sally Hemings's life that might be relevant to this issue, rather than coming to a conclusion based upon general ideas of what would have or should have happened. Hemings's father and both of her grandfathers were white men. Why assume that this young girl would not see a white man as her most likely mate? Her father died the year she was born. As a small child she was in contact with Thomas Jefferson, who was the male authority figure at Monticello and who by all accounts exercised that authority benignly when it came to the Hemingses. She came to France in time to see Jefferson during a period when he was always at the height of fashion and seems to have recovered his spirits after his depression over his wife's death. Why couldn't this fatherless daughter of two generations of white men not fixate on a white man who was old enough to have been her father? Then after fixating on him, why would it be impossible for her to have loved him? One could, of course, cite chapter and verse as to why she should not have. However, that would be completely beside the point.

Mammy Love versus Romantic Love

Some commentators have deemed the possibility that Sally Hemings could have loved Thomas Jefferson and that he could have loved her as fanciful. This sentiment apparently stems from the view that love between a master and a slave could not take place.[14] It is interesting to compare that notion with some common ideas put forth about other aspects of the slave system. For example, consider the image of Mammy that has comforted southern whites for so many years.[15] Mammy is a caricature. "Lawdy, Massa Joe, you betta git in here 'fo' you ketch yo' death!"—as if she cared. Whites seem willing, almost anxious, to believe that Mammy really did care, when Mammy may well have been thinking to herself, "Joe, I hope you slip on that ice and break your God-damned neck."

Of course, not all slave women in that position would think that way. We are talking about human beings. There must have been women who raised children from infancy to adulthood who did feel affection for those children, for all the reasons that women feel affection for children whom they raise. This would be so even though they knew these children would grow up to be their masters and their children's masters. We could not exist as a species if we were not, to some extent, programmed to respond to infants and to develop attachments to them. Of course a major tragedy of slavery was that it ran counter to human nature and demanded that people try to suppress and deny the existence of feelings that are completely natural to human beings. Still, no man-made system can stamp out all constitutive aspects of the human personality.

If a woman who was a slave could love a child who was her future master for all the reasons that women love children, why could not a woman who was a slave love a man who was her present master for all the reasons that women love men? In every era women have loved men who they thought were intelligent, attractive, kind, and, most important of all, had some prospect of helping them make a good life for their children. This has been a fact of life driven by the relative positions of women and men with respect to child-bearing and family life. Hemings could have seen all these things in Jefferson. If Brodie was correct, Hemings was right in this regard. Jefferson did end up making life better for her children. He let all of them go free, and she was freed as well. In the end Hemings's family line got a forty-year head start on emancipation, with her grandchildren making the most of it, some of them by becoming public-spirited individuals and millionaires.[16]

Why do some whites accept the notion that love could exist in a maternal relationship between a black slave woman and a white child, while they view the possibility of romantic and sexual love between a black slave woman and a white man during that same era as absurd and perhaps slightly alarming? It is, I believe, because of the possibility of reciprocation. Just as some slave women could have felt affection for children in their charge, there must have been instances when the objects of their affection reciprocated to the extent that circumstances would allow. It is okay for Mammy to love a child and for the child to love Mammy in return. This type of bonding could exist openly and be celebrated in song and literature without threat to the idea that blacks and whites must exist separately and that this separation could be maintained through the imposition of rigid social structures or beliefs. No matter how much a white person loved Mammy and how much Mammy loved the white person, Mammy never became part of the white person's family by blood.

Love between a man and a woman is different because the union of men and women of different races creates a mingled bloodline that conflicts with the notion that blacks and whites must be kept separate to some degree. The American vision, even today, is of blacks and whites living together in har-mony, so long as we do not live in too much harmony. That some version of romantic love could exist even in a system where whites militantly asserted their superiority and treated most blacks with open contempt leaves whites living in a system that is not wholly rigid, vulnerable to the possibility that they (or their children) in certain circumstances might feel compelled to re-ciprocate. It suggests that some critical aspects of human existence are beyond our control.

One can always question the nature or extent of reciprocation that could be possible under conditions of slavery. Yet there is no reason to believe that there could not be situations where it extended to complete emotional

involvement. There were men and women who existed under the legal relationship of master and slave but did not act toward one another according to
the dictates of the laws and customs associated with that relationship.[17] This
should not be surprising, for personal actions do not always accord with the
dominant ideas expressed in either law or culture. People often make the most
of whatever crippling situation they may find themselves in.

Remember Thomas Bell and Mary Hemings, the white man and black
woman who lived together as husband and wife but had the legal relationship
of master and slave. Why would anyone doubt that Mary Hemings and
Thomas Bell felt something for one another that one could call love? Had it
just been a matter of exploitation, Hemings probably would not have asked
Jefferson to sell her to Bell. Who would ask to be sold to his or her rapist?
Moreover, there is no reason to suppose that Hemings would not have been
able to gauge the depth of Bell's feelings toward her and to make a decision
based upon her knowledge.

The situation of Thomas Bell and Mary Hemings lays bare the dilemma.
Those two people wanted to have a relationship, but the law of their state
made that relationship criminal. The only way they could be together and
remain near their families and things familiar was to exist in the one legal
relationship that gave them an excuse to live together—that of master and
slave. Bell could have sold his business, and he and Mary could have left the
state. To go where? Where would such a couple have been welcomed? Where
and when in America would it have been easier for a white man to keep a
black woman in his home than in the antebellum South?

We might say that if a master really loved a slave, he would free that
person so that there was no master-slave relationship. We may think this because we have a romantic idea that love makes people unselfish, strong, and
brave enough to stand openly against all convention. Sometimes it does, and
sometimes it does not. Many white men have acted (and do act) selfishly
and cowardly in their relationships with black women. This does not mean
that none of these men had (or have) feelings that we would not recognize as
a form of love.

That individuals who lived during slavery made the same distinction between Mammy love and romantic love does not settle the matter. One cannot
take the pronounced beliefs, customs, and values of any era at face value.
This is particularly true if doing so requires us to ignore human nature. Two
unassailable truths of that nature are that the vast majority of men and
women are prone to becoming attracted to one another and that the concept
of love is often used as an excuse for communion between the two. Writing
history in a way that seeks control over the circumstances under which love

could exist—allowing for it among some acceptable categories of people and denying the possibility among others—has no basis in any reality other than desires and wishes that can never be considered as truth.

Garry Wills on Jefferson and Hemings

Historian Garry Wills has written that it was "psychologically implausible" for Jefferson to have had "a love affair with one of his slaves," in part because Jefferson was dedicated "to beauty and refinement" and had the desire to "hover above the squalor and horror of the slavery that existed below him on the mountain top." Wills's statements attribute the characteristics of the slave system to the people who were held as slaves, and should be considered along with other of his comments about Jefferson and Hemings. In his review of Fawn Brodie's biography of Jefferson, Garry Wills expressed extreme contempt for Brodie's supposition that the Jefferson-Hemings liaison was based upon affection, arguing that there was no evidence that this was the case. Rather than denying that the relationship existed, Wills offered his own alternative characterization of its nature. He wrote of Sally Hemings: "She was like a healthy and obliging prostitute, who could be suitably rewarded, but would make no importunate demands. Her lot was improved, not harmed, by the liaison." [18] In Wills's view Hemings slept with Jefferson, and her payment was the freedom of her children and eventually herself.

Wills's statement is problematic on many levels, but one aspect must be highlighted. Being "like . . . a prostitute" sounds very much like being a little bit pregnant. One who has sex for the sole purpose of getting some kind of payment is not like a prostitute; that person is a prostitute. Because Wills was saying that Hemings had done just that, he was calling her a prostitute. This is an astoundingly cruel statement to make about a woman who was a slave, particularly when there is no evidence to support the claim.

Just as Fawn Brodie had to make an inference about the probable states of mind of Thomas Jefferson and Sally Hemings when she reached her conclusion that they had affection for one another, Garry Wills's opinion on the nature of the relationship required that he do the same. In order to state that two people are in a client-prostitute relationship, one must know what the two people were thinking about themselves and one another. Did Wills know Jefferson's and Hemings's states of mind about one another and their alleged relationship? Wills knew his particular take on Jefferson's overall personality, and he offered that. That is not enough. Few people, if any, always act in character or according to what others take to be their personality. Human beings do surprise one another, and we often think that we know someone when we do not. This is particularly likely to be true if the person in question died well over a century before we were born.

Wills did not offer any specific evidence to bolster the notion that Jefferson thought Sally Hemings was like a prostitute. The glimpse that Brodie offered into Jefferson's state of mind with respect to Hemings was his decision to free her children and the possibility that he asked his daughter Martha to free Hemings after his death. These acts do not, on their face, suggest that Jefferson thought Hemings was a prostitute. What observers make of Jefferson's actions along these lines says more about the observers than about Jefferson. There are, in fact, levels of male-female attachment that exist between being a trick and her John and being the equivalent of Tristan and Iseult. One should ask whether the evidence suggests that Jefferson and Hemings could be placed somewhere in that middle ground closer to where Brodie chose to place them or whether they must be where Wills chose to place them.

Apparently Wills felt that Jefferson's act of freeing Hemings's children was her "suitabl[e]" reward for services rendered and could not have been in response to an "importunate demand" on her part. One might ask if it is common for a client to tender part of his reputation as payment to a prostitute for services rendered? This is, in effect, what Jefferson did when he freed the Hemings children in the manner that he chose to do so. It would have been much simpler (and more rational) for Jefferson to have left their emancipation to his daughter or grandson, perhaps with as many other Hemingses as his creditors would allow thrown in to provide some cover. Had Jefferson chosen this expedient, this story would not have continued to be so tantalizing. Callender's exposé brought the story into the public arena. Jefferson's emancipation of Sally Hemings's children, the strange ways that he did this, and the equally strange story of her emancipation are the reasons it has endured.

Moreover, if Hemings had extracted a promise that Jefferson would free her children at twenty-one, the Thomas Jefferson that Garry Wills described would have come to see that promise as an "importunate demand" after the Callender episode. That Jefferson went through with it after all the negative attention that had been drawn to Monticello and while his finances were collapsing does not support Wills's assertion that Jefferson saw Hemings just as a prostitute.

Even more importantly than what Thomas Jefferson thought about the matter, in considering whether Hemings was a prostitute one must know something about her state of mind. What evidence of Sally Hemings's state of mind did Wills have that would allow him to draw the conclusion that she was a prostitute, or even like a prostitute? What did Wills, or Brodie, know of Hemings's thoughts about Jefferson and the nature of their alleged relationship?

Brodie considered one matter and concluded that Hemings seems not to have been having sex with anyone while Jefferson was away for long periods at a time. The era in which Hemings lived was a time of poor birth control and crude abortion techniques. If Hemings were having sex during Jefferson's absences, she would have been at a high risk for getting pregnant, but she did not. Perhaps she was afraid that Jefferson would punish her if she became involved with another man. But if Jefferson thought of her as a prostitute, why would he not expect that she would take up with another man, or men? Why would he care if she did?

One wonders when reading this part of Wills's review how Sally Hemings's situation was different from that of any other slave woman who had a relationship with her master and benefited from it. The answer, of course, is that there was no difference, other than the prominence of the man with whom Hemings was reputedly involved. If there was no difference, then all slave women who had liaisons and children with slave masters and derived some benefit from the relationship (which would include a good number of the female forebears of black Americans) would fall into Wills's category of prostitutes or women who were like prostitutes.

Wills's assertions about Sally Hemings are particularly troubling because he filled the gaping hole in his analysis—the lack of evidence to support his claim—with the most common stereotype of black women: that they are all prone to being whores. Brodie had to offer specific evidence that the Jefferson-Hemings relationship was based upon affection, even though a thirty-eight-year relationship between a man and a woman should be presumed to suggest feelings beyond mere hedonism. On the other hand, no specific evidence was required to prove that Sally Hemings was like a prostitute.

Garry Wills was not the first to adopt this view of Sally Hemings's alleged situation. In 1802, in response to a query from Jonathan Dayton, a Federalist operative looking into James Callender's allegations, Thomas Gibbons described Hemings as "the most abandoned prostitute of her color—pampered into a lascivious course of life, with the benefits of a French education, she is more lecherous than the other beasts of the Monticellian Mountain."[19] Hemings could not just be a slave woman living on a plantation involved in a long-term affair with her master, like her sister down the road in Charlottesville, Mary Hemings. She could not even be a simple prostitute; she had to be "the most abandoned" one "of her color." In addition, Hemings, the "pampered" slave woman with the "French education," had moved so far beyond what Gibbons evidently thought was her rightful station that she became literally monstrous in his eyes.

To Gibbons, the alleged relationship that put Hemings in this position could not have sprung from any remotely decent human emotion. His narrow frame of reference allowed only one possible way to portray it: Sally Hemings was a prostitute. She was that simply by virtue of being involved with Thomas Jefferson. Gibbons took this view despite the fact that he believed that all of Hemings's children were fathered by Jefferson and cited no examples of her involvement with anyone else. An explanation that took into account the complexities and contradictions in southern slaveholding society, such as the situation of Mary Hemings and Thomas Bell, was most likely beyond Gibbons's comprehension.

Ironically, since one cannot include Garry Wills with Malone, Adair, and Miller as a Jefferson defender on this topic, Wills's assertions about the Sally Hemings story are of a piece with the arguments that those three men adopted in order to defeat the idea that Jefferson and Hemings had a relationship. Although he gets there from the opposite direction, Wills's depiction of events allows him to arrive at the same destination as Jefferson defenders: he ends up assuring the American public that it is ridiculous even to consider the notion that Thomas Jefferson could ever have been under the positive influence of an insignificant black slave woman.

All of these men would say that Jefferson did not free Hemings's children because of the influence of her, or their, love. Malone, Adair, et al. would say that Jefferson did so because he loved his white wife, their aunt. Wills would say that he did so because he was just rewarding his prostitute, a cipher. With each of these conclusions, Thomas Jefferson remains a true white man impervious to the influence of blacks, in perpetual and total control of every aspect of his relationships with them. If one wonders why this story has any meaning for today, one has only to consider the convergence of these men at the point of their ultimate message to their readers.

When It Began, according to Fawn Brodie

Fawn Brodie believed that Jefferson's intimate relationship with Hemings began in 1788 and intensified in 1789. She listed behavior on Jefferson's part that she thought showed he was paying extraordinary attention to Sally Hemings. In 1788 Jefferson began to pay James and Sally monthly wages, about half of what French servants were paid, when he had not paid James regular wages before.[20] This may show that Jefferson was solicitous of Sally Hemings's feelings in some way. It is also likely that this circumstance, rather than suggesting a budding romance, fixes the time that James and Sally Hemings realized— or made it known to Jefferson that they realized—that on French soil they were considered free. Jefferson may have responded by deciding to treat them almost as French servants. Jefferson paid wages to slaves after his sojourn in Paris whenever they worked away from Monticello in the company of other paid employees. That the Hemingses were paid while they were in Paris suggests that their status as free people in France became a concern to him at some point.

James Bear versus Madison Hemings

Jefferson's payment of wages to Sally and James Hemings should be considered in conjunction with Madison Hemings's statement that his mother and uncle decided that they were going to stay in France. Receiving wages would have drawn the Hemings siblings' attention to the differences between their lives in France and what their lives would be like should they return to the United States. Why couldn't they have come to think that being free and getting paid to work presented an attractive alternative to being a slave? Most people have thought so. The transition from being slaves to paid employees held out the hope that they could make their way in France. Under the circumstances, Madison Hemings's statement about his mother's and his uncle's threat to stay in France does not seem improbable.

Yet one commentator on the subject disputed this claim. James Bear, who wrote a series of biographical sketches of the Hemings family, said: "According to French law, James and his sister Sally, who joined the Jefferson party in France in 1787, could have claimed their freedom had they so desired or if a third party had notified the authorities of their servitude. Jefferson was aware of the French law and probably James was too, yet the issue was never raised. If he [James] were aware of the law, he did not choose to claim its protection and returned with Jefferson from France."[21] Bear did not broach the subject in his discussion of Sally Hemings, nor did he mention Madison Hemings's statement on this issue even though he referred to Hemings's memoirs in the introduction to his work.

Why did Bear not point out Madison Hemings's assertion that his mother and his uncle had threatened to stay in France? The intelligent and volatile James Hemings had been trained as a chef and may have thought—and convinced his sister—that he had a skill that would serve him well, allowing him to make a life for them in France. The hiring of a tutor may have been in furtherance of his plan to remain in France. Even if one argued that James and Sally Hemings would have been unrealistic had they thought this, this is not an unknown state for people in their early twenties and their teens. The issue of claiming freedom could have been separated from the issue of the alleged promise to Madison's mother. Why could not Bear have explained that Madison Hemings said that James and his mother claimed their freedom in France; Hemings alleged that Jefferson made certain promises to Sally Hemings if they returned to the United States with him, but there is no evidence that such a promise was made. Why was it important to state that the issue was never raised and no claim of freedom was made?

The probable answer is that a discussion of Madison Hemings's contention would have required Bear to demonstrate why his assertion, as opposed to Hemings's, was correct. This would present the risk that at least some readers might choose to believe Madison Hemings's version of events over Bear's. If Hemings's version was not even mentioned, then no choice could be made. Scholars have commented upon the great degree to which items in Madison Hemings's memoirs can be substantiated. Even if one disbelieves him on the question of Jefferson being his father, not every word in Hemings's statement is a lie. As a person who had talked to one of the principals in this story, Madison Hemings was in a much better position to know what his mother and her brother had done in this situation. In a contest between Bear and Hemings on the narrow point of whether a claim of freedom was made, it would not be unreasonable to believe Madison Hemings.

A question remains. What about James Hemings? The alleged agreement between Thomas Jefferson and Sally Hemings would not have affected him. If James Hemings ever balked at coming home, why did he change his mind and return to the United States? A possible answer is suggested by the fact that Jefferson continued to pay James Hemings wages after they returned to America.[22] Perhaps James Hemings, whom Jefferson had always given a great amount of personal freedom, thought that being near his family, working, and receiving wages presented a better prospect than living in France all alone.

Bear's positive assertion that James Hemings did not attempt to claim his freedom in France, his silence on Sally Hemings's having done so, and his silence on Madison Hemings's statement on this subject work together to negate the idea that there had been a struggle between Sally Hemings and Thomas Jefferson over Hemings's return to America. It turns aside the notion of any deal to free Hemings's children if she came back to the United States and strikes a blow at the notion that Jefferson was the father of her children. As often happens in the scholarly writings on this matter, an answer to a problem is given without making the reader aware that the problem even exists.

Sally Hemings at Madame Dupré's

After discussing the Hemings siblings' wages, Brodie went on to note that a woman named Dupré was paid for boarding Sally for five weeks. Brodie surmised that Hemings was sent to live at Madame Dupré's while Jefferson took his second tour through Europe. This suggested to her that Jefferson was extremely protective of Hemings and would not leave her at the Hôtel de Langeac when he was gone for a long period, even though she could have been under the care of her brother.[23]

Because Jefferson's notation does not indicate the dates that Sally Hemings boarded at Madame Dupré's, there is no way to tie the period of boarding to the dates of Jefferson's trip. James Bear suggested that Sally went to live with Madame Dupré, the Jefferson family laundress, to learn how to be a lady's maid. This may be a more plausible explanation than Brodie's because Jefferson's trip lasted for seven weeks, while Madam Dupré's services apparently lasted only five. The date the bill was paid provides no answer because Jefferson, as Brodie said, did not always pay bills immediately. He noted payment of the bill on April 29, 1789, one year after Jefferson's second trip through Europe. It was also almost two years after Hemings had arrived in France. As this seems a little late in the day to think of training Hemings to be a lady's maid, it is likely that Jefferson did pay this bill long after Hemings's residence at the boardinghouse. In sum, it remains unclear why Jefferson paid to have Hemings boarded at Madame Dupré's. There is no way at present to tie this circumstance to any romantic relationship.[24]

Jefferson's Correspondence

After speculating about whether Jefferson wrote to Hemings while he was away on his tour through northern Europe or wrote letters to others that may have mentioned her, Brodie noted that "the letter index volume recording Jefferson's incoming and outgoing letters for this critical year of 1788, has disappeared. It is the only volume missing in the whole forty-three-year epistolary record. Julian Boyd tells us that the 'entries once existed but cannot now be found.'"[25] Brodie then raised the possibility that someone, in order to protect Jefferson, removed evidence of letters that he may have written to Hemings during the time he was away.

Brodie noted further that when Jefferson went away on his first trip through the European countryside, he took one of his polygraphs with him and wrote five letters to his daughter Martha. He also carried the polygraph with him on the second trip taken after Sally and Mary's arrival. Either Jefferson wrote no letters to his daughters during a trip that lasted seven weeks, which would have been uncharacteristic, or he wrote letters and both the originals and copies have been lost.[26] If he wrote letters to Martha and Mary that are now gone, he may have mentioned or inquired, even in an innocuous way, after James and Sally. One would not expect declarations of his love for Sally Hemings in his letters to his daughters, but there might be statements in them that could illuminate aspects of her personality or her relationships with Jefferson and his daughters.

Virginius Dabney, addressing Brodie's charge that some of Jefferson's records may have been destroyed, ridiculed the notion that Jefferson would have written to Hemings and asked why it would have been necessary to destroy letters Jefferson wrote to his daughters during his trip.[27] To be concerned about the suggestion that someone would have destroyed some of the Jefferson family correspondence is justified. That letters were destroyed is, of course, pure speculation. But Dabney's consideration of why someone might have wanted to destroy them was not insightful. If one wanted to protect Jefferson from the charge that he had been involved with Hemings, what would one want the written record to look like? Most likely, as though Sally Hemings never crossed Thomas Jefferson's mind in any serious way.

Making notations about Sally Hemings in records of clothing bought and doctor's bills paid would be different from references to her in letters to his family. Jefferson made quotidian listings about slaves all the time. Mentioning a slave in a letter is a more important indication of Jefferson's level of involvement with that person. For example, the references to James Hemings and John Hemings in his letters tell us about Jefferson's closeness to them. If Jefferson wrote letters to his daughters during his second trip through Europe and made even the most mundane references to Sally Hemings, it would show that she was on his mind to some degree.

If one does not believe that any of Jefferson's documents have been tampered with, one might say that the lack of references to Sally Hemings, during his stay in France and later, shows that she was of no particular significance to him. Modern-day commentators have taken this tack, citing Hemings's absence from Jefferson's correspondence as a strong indication that the two were not intimately involved.[28] Yet it should not be surprising that a man's alleged mistress does not figure prominently—or at all—in his letters to and from his family and friends. The relationship might have been a source of tension or unease. There might have been a sense that the liaison should be kept secret, and the best method of doing so would have been to refrain from drawing any attention to the alleged mistress. The need for circumspection about such a relationship would only have grown if the alleged liaison between the man and the mistress had become the subject of intense public scrutiny, scorn, and ridicule.

Thomas Jefferson and his family knew that by virtue of his accomplishments, they would have a place in history. Accordingly, they knew that their letters might be read. Jefferson had a polygraph to make sure that all of his letters that he wanted preserved would be preserved. When he did not want letters to be left for posterity, he destroyed his copies and asked others to destroy theirs. It seems strange to assume that the Jefferson family letters contain the complete record of the family's existence. Historians often write as though Jefferson and the Randolphs had no life outside of what appears in their letters. If a thought, feeling, or description of an action does not appear in a letter, the thought never occurred, the feeling was not felt, and the action was not taken, despite evidence to the contrary outside of their correspondence.

If one considers Jefferson and his family's pattern of writing letters and the relationship that Sally Hemings bore to the Jeffersons, particularly in France, there is something strange about the scarcity of references to her in their correspondence. It is not as though the Jeffersons did not mention their slaves in letters. Such references, while not a matter of course, were not infrequent. Jefferson wrote to those of his slaves who could read, and when the slaves could not read, he wrote to them through individuals who could. For example, he sent word through his gardener to Elizabeth Hemings that her son James was doing well in France.[29] One might expect that once during the twenty-six months that Sally Hemings was in France, he would have let Elizabeth know about her youngest daughter.

The dispute about the meaning of the few references to Sally Hemings in Jefferson's correspondence boils down to what one thinks is more important. Do actions and circumstances speak louder than words or the lack of words? The known circumstances of Hemings's life and the Jeffersons' actions toward her and her family are such that one would assume that, absent some reason not to, she would have been mentioned more frequently.

Sally Hemings was Maria Jefferson's personal companion of many years from their childhood. Hemings had shared pivotal moments in the lives of Maria, Martha, and Thomas Jefferson. Even Martha and Maria's friends in France made mention of Hemings in their correspondence, with one person directing Martha to give his regards "to Mademoiselle Sally" for him. When

Maria Jefferson wrote to Kitty Church, daughter of Jefferson's friend Angelica Church, she noted that Sally sent her regards, as well.[30] There is evidence that Hemings was Jefferson's chambermaid. All of Hemings's children were freed by Thomas Jefferson, and she herself was freed.

Hemings's name comes up in the most important nonfamily personal memoirs of Monticello, by black people and white. She and her children figure prominently in the memoirs of Isaac Jefferson recorded in 1842.[31] Isaac Jefferson's statement, admittedly a somewhat rambling affair, focuses on Sally Hemings as the daughter of Elizabeth Hemings and, almost apropos of nothing, mentions or describes her children. Why did Isaac remember so much about Sally Hemings's nuclear family? Did Charles Campbell, the man who took Isaac's statement, ask about her? It is hard to believe that Campbell sat through this discourse on the Hemings family (which starts almost at the beginning of the memoirs) and did not attempt, directly or indirectly, to feel Isaac Jefferson out on the subject of Thomas Jefferson and Sally Hemings. Had Isaac Jefferson said something exculpatory of Jefferson on this question, Campbell would have printed it. Instead, the very candid Isaac Jefferson—who offered that "Old Master" was never "in this world" as handsome as one of his portraits portrayed him—could well have said something that Campbell thought it better not to repeat.

In 1862 Edmund Bacon recalled Sally Hemings, by name, telling stories about her trip to France. That she would be one of the few female slaves besides her daughter, Harriet, and in Bacon's case the only one, singled out for a special description in these memoirs gives an indication of the degree of her importance at Monticello. When people who were not members of the Jefferson family thought back on and spoke freely about Monticello, Sally Hemings, out of Jefferson's many slaves and her many female relatives, came to mind. Her prominence in their memoirs belies the argument that Sally Hemings must have been an insignificant figure in the lives of Jefferson and his daughters because she does not appear regularly in Jefferson family letters.

Thomas Jefferson's only direct reference to Sally Hemings was in a letter that he wrote in 1799 to his son-in-law John Wayles Eppes in which he mentioned that she had given birth. He wrote two other letters that mention her indirectly when an epidemic of measles broke out among some of the slave children at Monticello in 1802. Jefferson's grandson Francis Eppes was very fragile as a child, given to having fits that incapacitated him. His family feared for his life. Although Martha Randolph wanted her children to contract the disease and be done with it, Maria was greatly concerned about Francis visiting Monticello during the epidemic. Jefferson sought to reassure her by changing the living arrangements of children on the mountain. He wrote to

Martha Randolph, stating that if "Bet or Sally's children" came down with the measles, they should be sent to live in the home of their grandmother Elizabeth Hemings, somewhat removed from the main house at Monticello. Any other children who came down with the disease were to be sent off the mountain. The second letter, written on the same date, informed Maria of his planned precautions to prevent Francis from catching the measles.[32]

The question whether Thomas Jefferson, while in Europe, went seven weeks without writing a letter to his daughters remains. The notion that some of Jefferson's records from this period or from later periods were deliberately "lost" to hide possible references to Sally Hemings is speculation that incites curiosity but sheds little light on matters. One could understand why it might have been done, but there is no way to know that it was done.

The End of the Time in France

Brodie listed other events in 1788 and 1789 that suggested to her that something serious had happened at the Hôtel de Langeac. Jefferson began to extricate himself from his dalliance with Maria Cosway. He also began to write letters highly critical of the type of women he had met in France, characterizing them as Amazons who had forgotten "what they left behind them in their nurseries" and contrasting them with American women, who were the "Angels" who could provide "the tender and tranquil amusements of domestic life."[33]

Jefferson also began to spend what Brodie thought was a good amount of money on Hemings's clothes—not as much as he spent on his daughters but more than he had spent when she first arrived. Brodie noted that in the early part of April 1789, Jefferson spent two hundred francs "on clothes for Sally" and later that same month his daughter Martha announced that she was going to become a nun, an idea which Jefferson rejected. Brodie speculated that Martha may have been prompted to take this action because of her suspicions that something was going on between Jefferson and Hemings.[34]

In the final weeks before the party was to leave for Virginia, Jefferson was afflicted with one of his recurring migraines and was ill for six days. Brodie placed this at the point of James and Sally's threat to stay in France. After Jefferson made a baggage list, he waited a long time before he wrote to his representative in London, James Maurice, to make arrangements for the trip home. This suggested to Brodie that it was unclear at a very late date just who would be returning to America. She also stated that Sally Hemings was carrying the child that Madison Hemings said was born shortly after her return to Monticello. Sometime during that period of delay, Brodie surmised, Jefferson promised to free Sally Hemings's children when they reached the age of twenty-one.[35]

Jefferson instructed Maurice to arrange for master berths for himself and his two daughters and berths for the two Hemingses. He made no specifications about the placement of James's berth. But Jefferson stated that Sally's berth should be "convenient to that of my daughters" and that he wanted "a cabbin in common with the others, and not exclusive of them which serves only to render me odious to those excluded." Brodie cited this as an example of Jefferson's unwillingness to be separated from either his daughters or Hemings.[36] But one does not have to take the language as far as Brodie. At a minimum this note indicates that Jefferson counted Sally Hemings among those who would have been offended if they were excluded from his company on the voyage home and that this concerned him to some degree. Thomas Jefferson and Sally Hemings had spent over two years together in a foreign country. They may have grown fond of one another at some level less than a grand passion. Jefferson simply may not have wanted to offend Hemings, especially given her relationship to his daughters.

The discussion of the Jeffersons and Hemingses' return to the United States from France has produced some of the most offensive phraseology in all the writings on this subject. Jonathan Daniels, whose consideration of the Jefferson-Hemings controversy was generally balanced, reproduced Malone's ill-considered description of the party's return to America and made his own unfortunate contribution to the historical literature.

> His daughters, seventeen-year-old Martha called Patsy and eleven-year-old Mary called Polly, were with him. With them were two slaves: Sally Hemings, pretty sixteen-year-old octoroon, who had come to France with Polly as her only attendant two years before; and Sally's brother Jim, whom Jefferson had had taught the art of French cooking. So in the fairest weather, as the great Virginian's biographer Dumas Malone wrote, the diplomat and his daughters came home with "slaves, bitch and baggage." Also tenaciously held slave tradition said that, like the dog, young bright-skinned Sally was pregnant too.[37]

The "tenaciously held slave tradition" was, of course, publicly recounted in Madison Hemings's memoirs. Hemings said that his mother conceived a child that was born "soon after" her return from France. That phrase has been taken to suggest that Sally Hemings must have been far along in her pregnancy when they took the voyage home. Both Douglass Adair and Virginius Dabney scoffed at the picture of Jefferson taking his pregnant mistress on an ocean voyage with his two daughters.[38]

The problem is that we do not know what Madison Hemings meant by "soon after." A few hours? A day? One week? Two or three months? When one says Sally Hemings was pregnant when she left France, the image that immediately comes to mind is of Hemings waddling around the deck of the *Clermont* with her palms supporting her aching back. Yet some women, especially during their first pregnancies (while their abdominal muscles still function), can get to their third trimesters before they even look pregnant. This is particularly true if the woman has well-developed breasts. Because she was to have her own berth, there is no reason to suppose that either Martha or Maria would have seen Hemings in any state of undress.

To deem the story of Sally's pregnancy false because she crossed the Atlantic with Jefferson, Martha, and Maria on the same ship assumes too much. We do not know what Madison Hemings meant by "soon after," so we do not know how pregnant Sally Hemings may have been upon her departure from France or how pregnant she may have looked. Those considerations aside, one must ask, If Sally Hemings was pregnant, what would one expect Thomas Jefferson to have done—leave behind a sixteen-year-old girl who was carrying his child to avoid a potentially embarrassing ocean voyage?

Sally Hemings : The Novel

Despite Brodie's use of her description of Sally Hemings's life in Paris to prove the assertion that Jefferson had become infatuated with her, the focus of the criticism of her work has remained on Jefferson and whether he would or would not have become involved with Hemings. There had been little attention to the question of what effect the events in Hemings's life in Paris may have had upon her until Barbara Chase-Riboud decided to explore the question in a novel entitled *Sally Hemings.*

The novel, which sold over a million and a half copies worldwide during the early 1980s and was re-released in 1994, probably has had a more profound effect upon the popular view of this story than Fawn Brodie's biography. The debate between Brodie and her critics was conducted scholar to scholar. Chase-Riboud's work presented a particular problem for Jefferson defenders. Telling the Sally Hemings story as a historical novel blunted the edge of any criticism that a historian could level at the book in terms of factual accuracy. As long as Chase-Riboud stayed within certain parameters—not casting Thomas Jefferson as the king of Spain, for example—she had the freedom to do what had not been done before: to present, without hesitation or qualification, a version of how the story could have been true. Some Jefferson scholars and commentators reacted with great alarm and attacked the book ferociously even as others extolled its literary merits.[39]

The problem, of course, was the matter of perceptions. Before Brodie and Chase-Riboud, Jefferson biographers had pretty much succeeded in keeping Sally Hemings as an abstraction, giving the barest details of her life and leaving the blanks to be filled in with most Americans' stereotypical notions of what slave women were like, images that alternate between the characters of Prissy and Mammy in *Gone with the Wind.* By doing so they were able to assert with authority unchallenged that the whole story was too preposterous to be believed: no construction of events could make it possible. For this prohibition to succeed, it was necessary to short-circuit the instinctive reaction that it is almost always possible for a heterosexual man to be interested in forming a relationship with a woman known for her beauty, particularly one with whom he was in close and frequent contact. Instead of considering ways that the story could be true, most writing on the subject encouraged readers to think only of the reasons that it could not be.

Chase-Riboud, with the help of information from Fawn Brodie's biography as well as her own research, took Sally Hemings and made her into a person whom one could believe that Jefferson could have loved. The real importance of this feat lay not in how closely the work followed historical details and events. It was the book's presentation of Hemings's humanity, by telling the story from her point of view and giving her an inner monologue based on common emotions, that caused the biggest problem for Jefferson defenders. Hemings was portrayed as a person with actual thoughts and conflicts, giving her a depth of character seldom attributed to American slaves or to black people in general. She became real—and the possibility of the relationship became real—once she was taken seriously and presented as a full human being.

Chase-Riboud's achievement was so alarming that Virginius Dabney, in a book written primarily to attack Fawn Brodie's thesis, detoured and devoted an entire chapter to Chase-Riboud's work. Dabney referred to the novel as "faction," a new species of literature that he distinguished from the well-recognized genre of the historical novel. Dabney was also angered by another historical novel that he felt dealt unfairly with Thomas Jefferson, Gore Vidal's *Burr,* which drew a brilliant and amusing fictionalized portrait of Thomas Jefferson that was, at points, both believable and devastating. Although Dabney was upset about *Burr,* in which Sally Hemings makes a brief appearance, he decided to focus his attention upon Brodie and Chase-Riboud.[40]

As bothered as Dabney and other Jefferson defenders were by the novel *Sally Hemings,* they were more disturbed at the thought that the bestseller would be brought to the screen. As with any successful novel that tells a good story, there was talk of making *Sally Hemings* into a miniseries for television.

Dabney was kept informed on the progress of the project by a network executive named Frank McCarthy. Dabney informed Malone, and the two launched what can only be called a campaign, which included contacting the president of CBS, William Paley, to make sure that the plans were scrapped.[41]

One cannot imagine that Malone and others would have tried to stop a book publisher from publishing *Sally Hemings* or would have succeeded. Aside from questioning the networks' response to being pressured in this situation, one must ask why a television production or a movie of this novel would be so terrifying. The whole event could have stirred a public discussion, with scholars debating the question and citizens giving their opinions, the kind of thing that is supposed to happen in this country. Instead, a small group of individuals—in the United States of America, where "the marketplace of ideas" and "the marketplace" supposedly rule—decided that the American people would not see a television serialization of a book that they had bought in droves.

The reason is, of course, that a picture is worth a thousand words. Although Jefferson scholars claimed to be worried about historical accuracy, I think they were concerned about something more subtle. If a beautiful woman appears on screen as a capable and trustworthy person, as Francis and Elizabeth Eppes must have considered Sally Hemings to be, "good naturd," as Abigail Adams described her, and "industrious and orderly," as one newspaper editor described her, all talk about impossibility would be rendered meaningless.[42] Jefferson defenders could never occupy that territory again.

How would a film adaptation of the novel add its own special power to the process of making the story believable? Film, unlike literature, allows for the simultaneous absorption of actions and reactions. We are able to see a character close up and, at the same time, to see the effect that the character has upon others. We also register and compare our own reactions based upon our experiences of being human and of watching others. That is one reason that movies, at some level, seem more real to us than either books or even plays.

Seeing a movie of *Sally Hemings* would remind us that unless he has fallen over into the abyss of pathological race hatred, it is always possible for a man who is attracted to women to respond to an attractive woman. If someone made a movie that purported to show Thomas Jefferson's long-term relationship with his slave Jupiter, historians might be on firmer ground in speaking of impossibility, as no evidence exists to support the notion that Jefferson had a sexual interest in men. However, although Jefferson assured his daughters that physical beauty is not the most important thing about a woman, all the women he has been linked to romantically had a reputation for great beauty.[43]

It is precisely because the story of his attraction to Sally Hemings is believable at this threshold level that the defenses mounted to challenge this notion have been so unwavering and, in some cases, reckless. If the story were preposterous, no one would be worried.

Because Jefferson defenders have not been able to remove him from the list of possible fathers of Sally Hemings's children and because they have not presented a convincing case for another man's paternity, they must rely on particular characterizations of Jefferson and Sally Hemings that render him incapable of such a response. The characterization of Jefferson relies upon people seeing him as something more than a human being. The characterization of Hemings relies upon the difficulty that many Americans might have in visualizing her as a human being. A film adaptation, with real people playing these two roles, would tend to bring Jefferson down from the status of god to mortal, and if it was true to the novel, would lift Sally Hemings from the status of mere chattel to that of a human being. Viewers would then be able to recognize themselves and others in these two people and would be able to make up their own minds about the likelihood that they could have formed a human bond. The public's perception of the likely truth of this story would have escaped from the hands of the Jefferson defenders forever.

Maria Cosway

The figure of Sally Hemings has lurked behind some of the writing upon another aspect of Thomas Jefferson's life in Paris, his relationship with Maria Cosway, the woman to whom he wrote his love letter "My Head and My Heart." Jefferson met Maria Cosway in 1786 and seems to have fallen instantly in love. She was an artist who was married to another artist. Despite the publication of his love letter to her in 1828 and, in 1945, of additional correspondence between the two, many Jefferson scholars have played down Maria Cosway's effect upon Jefferson. While acknowledging Jefferson's infatuation, most scholars flatly dismiss the notion of any sexual intimacy between the two.[44]

Some historians and commentators have been hostile to Cosway, viewing her as having toyed cruelly with Jefferson's affection. Their attitudes can best be summed up by one historian's description of Cosway as a "spoiled, egocentric young woman with a very limited emotional capacity," not the sort of person that Jefferson would have taken seriously.[45]

John Dos Passos, who wrote extensively on the affair, portrayed Cosway as having seen Jefferson as something of the flavor of the month. "Maria Cosway was a young lady very much taken up with her own affairs. She and her husband had their careers to make. Americans were the vogue of the season.

Nothing could have been more in the fashion of the moment than a few weeks' flirtation with the longlimbed minister plenipotentiary from the wilds of Virginia; but all the really important customers were in England." Dumas Malone was more sympathetic to Cosway and noted that to Jefferson, "she was art and music and the embodiment of loveliness." Cosway, he wrote, "loved the sound of church bells, believed in prayer, and in her immature and unsystematic but endearing way was philosophical. Her mind had no such strength as that of Abigail Adams, but it was bright and sensitive and she must have had exquisite taste."[46]

For the most part, whether the particular historian felt the affair was serious or not, Cosway has occupied center stage as Jefferson's romantic interest during his days in Paris. This is understandable given the first-party documentation that the two were involved. It is possible that Dumas Malone early on understood the link between the Hemings and Cosway stories. After describing the nature of the Jefferson-Cosway relationship and discussing whether the two had resumed their affair after a long separation, Malone decided that Jefferson "did not embark upon another adventure with her, but he embarked on no romantic adventure with anybody else. She had to share his friendship with other women, but her position in his life and memory was unique, and in the more restrained and mature sense he loved her all the rest of his life."[47]

There is no indication that Malone made this statement as a defense against the Sally Hemings story. His words predate the publication of Madison Hemings's memoirs by a few years and Brodie's biography by over two decades. Still, James Callender had mentioned that Sally Hemings was in Paris with Jefferson, so that someone might think that Jefferson could have been involved with her there. Perhaps the image of Thomas Jefferson secretly carrying a torch for Maria Cosway to the end of his life could be used to explain why he never fell in love again. For some reason Malone felt it necessary to go beyond the Paris years and state emphatically that Jefferson had no romantic adventures with anyone else and loved Maria Cosway for the rest of his life, for which there is no evidence. With what other woman, besides his wife and Mrs. John Walker, has Jefferson's name been so famously linked?

Douglass Adair and Maria Cosway versus Sally Hemings

Historian Douglass Adair took his turn with the Hemings story in an essay written in 1960. Entitled "The Jefferson Scandals," it was not published immediately, but Adair shared it with some of his colleagues.[48] Several months after

the appearance of Fawn Brodie's biography of Jefferson, it was published posthumously in *Fame and the Founding Fathers*, a collection of Adair's writings.

In Adair's essay we can see the origins of what can be called Clio's version
of the "prevent defense." That is to say, Douglass Adair showed historians and
commentators how to give up a few yards on the subject of Maria Cosway in
order to keep the Sally Hemings story from reaching the end zone. Indeed,
subsequent commentary has taken up Adair's themes and assigned to Cosway
an additional role as foil to Sally Hemings. This theme has been employed to
counter the notion that Jefferson would have had any reason to give Hemings
a second thought romantically. The technique involves contrasting Maria
Cosway's exalted state with Sally Hemings's degraded one.

Adair's piece was the first and most extensive defense of Jefferson by
means of an attack on Sally Hemings. Before Madison Hemings's memoirs
were rediscovered, responses to the allegations were directed at James Callender as the first publisher of the story. Because no Hemings was known to
have spoken on the matter, no Hemings could be attacked. After studying the
memoirs, Adair believed that Madison Hemings thought he was telling the
truth. The liar was not Madison Hemings, then, but his mother, Sally Hemings.[49] She had deliberately misled her son. Why would Sally Hemings do such
a thing? Adair suggested, first, vanity, but admitted that this cliché was too
easy. He then declared that the real reason Sally Hemings lied was because
she was angry at Peter Carr, her lover, for getting married.

According to Adair, "Sally, however, asks us to believe that the author of
the 'Dialogue between his Head and his Heart,' one of the most sensitive and
revealing love letters in the English language, would turn his back on the delectable Cosway, to whom it was addressed, to seduce a markedly immature,
semi-educated, teen-age virgin, who stood in a peculiarly dependent personal
relationship to him, both as slave, and as half-sister to his dead wife, and as
the companion and almost sister to his young daughters."[50]

Much stranger things in the world have happened, and happen every day
of the week. Moreover, Adair's list of adjectives for Sally Hemings stack the
deck. One could alternatively describe her as being nubile and beautiful,
standing in relation to Jefferson as Galatea stood to Pygmalion, a reminder of
the young wife whom he dearly loved and lost, and a person who liked and
was liked by his daughters. She was all of these things, and with this rendering
of her the whole conception of the relationship and its possibility is transformed.

Adair exhibited a dogged determination to make Sally Hemings seem as
low as possible and Maria Cosway as high. Yet Cosway was a woman who

may well have been committing adultery with Thomas Jefferson. At the very least she was acting inappropriately and in a way that Jefferson would not have tolerated from his own wife. While it is true that Cosway was unhappy in her marriage, this has never generally been thought a valid excuse for this type of behavior. This same woman, a year after Jefferson left France, abandoned her three-month-old daughter to run off with an Italian opera singer, prompting the writer Horace Walpole to remark, "Surely it is odd to drop a child and her husband and country all in a breath."[51] Delectable? That depends upon one's tastes.

Adair also presented his idea of what Thomas Jefferson thought to be the perfect type of woman, of which Martha Wayles and Maria Cosway were exemplars and which Sally Hemings could never have been. "Obviously, the women who attracted him most powerfully were those with some artistic, musical or literary sophistication who offered intellectual as well as physical communion."[52]

Maria Cosway, a painter of miniatures, and Jefferson's wife Martha, who was musical, were both women with some degree of talent. While there is no evidence that Sally Hemings was similarly inclined, there is some irony in the implicit assumption of her deficiency in the one area that blacks are stereotypically portrayed—even by Thomas Jefferson—as naturally proficient: music.

Moreover, in contrast to Adair's description of Hemings's extreme immaturity, he failed to note that Malone's description of Cosway and some of her actions—one woman who knew her said Cosway showed friends the love letters Jefferson wrote to her—demonstrate no great maturity on Cosway's part. In fact, Malone wrote that Jefferson saw her as a "lovely, talented, capricious creature—half woman and half child" and this was part of her appeal.[53]

We do not know the level of Martha Jefferson's "literary sophistication," for Jefferson destroyed all of her letters. When she prepared a list of household supplies, Jefferson checked and corrected her spelling. Maria Cosway's letters show that she was literate, but Malone described her as more domestic and "not bookish." Jefferson made literary allusions in his letters to her that went over her head, as her replies demonstrate.[54]

We probably will never know the state of Sally Hemings's literacy. On one hand, Madison Hemings claimed that he learned to read by inducing white children to teach him. If Sally Hemings was literate, one might expect that she would have taught her son. However, Madison Hemings's bitterness about the circumstances of his life may have led him to emphasize the extent to which his education had been neglected by his alleged father, rather than mention any of the positive things—beyond his freedom—that had happened to him. On the other hand, at least two of Sally Hemings's brothers were literate, and some of the documents written by James Hemings are solidly proficient.[55] A tradition among black American families, which can be found in some African societies as well, is that when one family member possesses something valuable, that individual is expected to share it with others in the family. Slaves thought the ability to read of extreme value. James Hemings would have been in a position to help his sister and encourage her along these lines, particularly when they were living together in France. We just do not know whether he did. Nor can we say with certainty that the haphazard nature of Sally Hemings's schooling would have precluded Jefferson's interest in her, for she may have had other attributes besides her beauty—femininity, natural intelligence, good humor, submissiveness, kindness—that were of greater importance to him.

Some scholars have expressed skepticism at the notion that an uneducated woman could have held any real attraction for Thomas Jefferson. Garry Wills expressed doubt that Jefferson would have considered his "unlettered mistress" a true companion and suggested that he could have been interested in her only for sex.[56]

This view equates a lack of education with a lack of intelligence or insight and, as with Wills's argument about Hemings being like a prostitute, ends up as a commentary on the capacities and characteristics of slaves in general. It also implies that men have judged the women whom they seek as mates on the basis of their intellectual capabilities rather than their other attributes. Arguments about Jefferson's unique nature can hardly disassociate him from what has been the more common preference of males when having to choose between beauty or educational attainment in a woman. The evidence indicates that on this issue Jefferson was a typical man of his era. He neither wanted women to be, nor believed that they could be, the intellectual equals of men.

In answer to a query, Jefferson explained: "A plan of female education has never been a subject of systematic contemplation with me. It has occupied my attention so far only as the education of my own daughters occasionally required." Jefferson's daughters were highly educated compared to their contemporaries. Probably because Jefferson was appointed a minister to France, they were certainly better educated than their mother. Yet there is no reason to assume that because Jefferson wanted his daughters "more qualified than common," he would have required a similar level of education in a wife or a mistress. Fathers have many expectations for daughters that they do not have for wives and mistresses. Jefferson saw the educations of his daughters as being for the limited purpose of being able to fulfill their maternal duties, ensuring that they could "teach their daughters and even to direct the course for sons should the fathers be lost, or incapable or inattentive." Nothing in that comment suggests Thomas Jefferson believed a woman should be educated so that she could have serious political or philosophical discussions or debates with her husband.[57]

What did Jefferson expect in the way of education for those women who were not his daughters? He often advised individuals who asked him (and probably some who did not) on the proper course of study. While he told young men to study the classics, hard sciences, history, and the law, he did not suggest these subjects for young women. Jefferson thought that women's educations should be geared to making them amiable companions for men. Accordingly, Jefferson believed that women should be instructed in "dancing, drawing, [and] music," although he did not think that women should dance after they were married. He thought the study of French important, as it enhanced cultural refinement. While he considered the reading of "moral literature" appropriate, he did not approve of women reading too much fiction or poetry, for it might make them bored at the routine of day-to-day life.[58]

This does not sound like a man who would have required (or even been able to tolerate) a Madame de Staël as a life's companion. Of course, there was a great distance between that great French writer and Sally Hemings— and probably between any other white women Jefferson would have encountered in Virginia—but it is not clear that there would have been so vast a distance between the daughter of a typical southern planter and Sally Hemings. Scholars often write about black slaves without taking account of their individual lives, choosing to portray them as a people of uniformly limited experience and abilities. Conversely, the lives of the aristocratic whites of that era tend to be romanticized, and their accomplishments exaggerated. The truth is that Sally Hemings, who is written of as though she spent her entire life walking behind a plow, had experiences that few, if any, female members of the Virginia gentry of her day enjoyed.

While members of that set were being given an education that consisted of reading minor novels considered suitable for young women, doing needlepoint, and learning to dance and to paint, Hemings was traveling over the Atlantic, first to the London home of John and Abigail Adams and then to Paris. She was perhaps being tutored in French, probably learning a great deal from the people who surrounded her and attaining a good level of proficiency in the language. She was going out on social occasions with Jefferson's daughters and observing the dress and manner of people of great sophistication, who also came to the home in which Hemings lived.[59] These experiences would have been her education. Significantly, Hemings was in a position to observe Jefferson in these same contexts and to learn the things about women that were of importance to him.

If Sally Hemings was a woman of even normal intelligence, and there is no reason to assume that she was not, these experiences could have helped her develop into a young woman of great attraction to a man, particularly to one with whom she shared common memories of some quite extraordinary people, places, and times. Jefferson loved France and things French until he died. Malone believed that Jefferson's years in Paris were among the happiest of his life because he could be himself without worrying about politics or what others felt about his actions. When musing late in life about where he would live if he left Virginia, Jefferson without equivocation said France.[60] Not only was Hemings linked to that city and his memories of it, Jefferson could turn to her and speak in French, and she would understand him. She could do the same to him. Who is to say these aspects of Hemings—when added to her appearance and reported good nature—would not have been enough to overcome the fact that she did not share the polite education of most women in Virginia.

His hysterical rantings about Hemings aside, it is significant that Thomas Gibbons referred to Hemings as having "had the benefits of a French educa-tion." Gibbons was writing in 1802, twelve years after Hemings had returned to the United States. Her facility with the language and knowledge of French customs must have been the subject of some talk during those years, lead-ing to Gibbons's comment. It appears, then, that Sally Hemings could easily have been more attractive—in the ways that counted to Jefferson—than a white Virginia female.

After labeling Hemings a "teen-age virgin," Adair tried to show that Jefferson would not have been attracted to such a female because he had a penchant for women who had been or were still married, that is, women who were sexually experienced. Adair cited Jefferson's marriage to the widow Martha Wayles Skelton, his attempted seduction of Mrs. John Walker, and his relationship with Mrs. Richard Cosway. But Jefferson's actions with respect to each of these women can be distinguished from one another. Several biogra-phers have noted that when the lawyer Jefferson filled out his marriage license, he first referred to his wife as being a "spinster," then crossed this out and wrote "widow." One does not have to delve too far into psychoanalysis to see that Jefferson might actually have preferred that his new wife have been a spinster, since he knew well that she had been married and had a son.[61] That Mrs. John Walker, whom Jefferson tried to seduce when her husband was away, was a convenient neighbor was probably more important to him than her married state. In any event, she was an insignificant figure in his life, other than through the later scandal. By the time Jefferson got around to Maria Cosway, his reason for dallying with married women was plain: he had no intention of marrying again. Jefferson was attracted to married women because they were safe. He would not let himself get seriously involved with a woman whom he might have to marry. This would not have been a concern in a relationship with Sally Hemings because he could never have married her.

Whether the fact that Sally Hemings was Martha Jefferson's sister would have made her more or less attractive to Jefferson is unclear. Jefferson, who counseled his daughters to marry within their family, may well have felt more comfortable with someone who was, in truth, in his family. Moreover, the two had shared experiences before her arrival in France that may have made it easier for a bond to form between them. Sally Hemings, along with the other female members of the household at Monticello, helped in the care of Martha Jefferson during her last months. Sally Hemings was among those present when Martha asked Jefferson not to marry again and when he acceded to her request.[62] Hemings was there when Jefferson, riven with pain, was led away from the room just before his wife died. She would have known that Jefferson became unconscious for a long period in the moments after Martha's death. One must at least consider what these shared experiences might have made these two people think of one another.

Except for his oldest daughter, Martha, Sally Hemings was the only individual in Thomas Jefferson's life who shared with him intimate memories of two defining periods in his personal life: his years with his wife, especially the months leading up to and after her death, and his experiences in France. His younger daughter Maria had been in France, but she was only four when her mother died, and her memories of her mother and of that period most likely would have been very faint. There were other female relatives and slaves at Monticello who remembered Martha Wayles Jefferson and were involved in her care at the end of her life, but they had not lived in France with Jefferson. Only Thomas Jefferson, Martha Randolph, and Sally Hemings had known both the last days of Martha Wayles Jefferson and the time in Paris.

Finally, there may also have been things about Sally Hemings that were reminiscent of Martha Jefferson. The southern slave system was strong but not strong enough to obliterate the laws of biology. Sisters often resemble each other in many ways—physical appearance, mannerisms, and timbre and tone of voice. Jefferson, despite his affair with Maria Cosway, may not have let go of his dead wife and could have been moved by similarities between the two women to take an action that he might not otherwise have taken.

Martha Wayles, Sally Hemings, and Jefferson's Type

It is important to remember that Jefferson knew that he was not going to stay in France forever. He would return to his home and the way of life that he cherished above all else. With which woman, Maria Cosway or Sally Hemings, could Jefferson resume that way of life and be true to his renunciation of a second marriage? To help answer this question it is worth examining the side of Martha Jefferson that would make her more similar to Sally Hemings than to Maria Cosway.

Both Martha Jefferson and Sally Hemings were women who had lived their entire lives on plantations. Although they occupied different positions, they both knew what that way of life meant for women. Martha Jefferson knew how to brew beer. She, along with slaves, made soap. She made candles and butter. She would have been expected to tend sick relatives and sick slaves.[63] We can assume that Jefferson appreciated these skills as well as the fact that she could play the harpsichord and sing.

Jefferson saw a distinction between the type of woman who could please the man he was at Monticello and the one who could enchant him in France. We can see this by looking at notes that Jefferson seems to have written for his daughter Martha upon her wedding. He counseled: "Sweetness of temper, affection to a husband and attention to his interests, constitute the duties of a wife and form the basis of domestic felicity. The charms of beauty, and the brilliancy of wit, though they captivate in the mistress will not long delight in the wife; they will shorten even their own transitory reign if as I have often seen they shine more for the attraction of everybody else than their husbands."[64]

Jefferson valued the domestic woman whose purpose in life was to serve her husband. He referred to childbearing (Malone claimed that he was joking) as a woman's "trade." Although he was generally pleased with his daughters' education in France, he told his sister-in-law that Martha would need her help to "render her useful in her own country. Of domestic economy she can learn nothing here, yet she must learn it somewhere, as being of more solid value than anything else." Later, when they had returned to America, Jefferson wrote to inquire of the teenager Maria, "How many hours do you sew? whether you have had the opportunity of continuing your music? whether you know how to make a pudding yet, to cut out a beefsteak, to sow spinach, or to set a hen?" Except for the reference to music, it is difficult to conceive of Maria Cosway fitting into this picture of a woman married to a farmer.[65]

What seems insupportable, then, is the claim that Jefferson took his relationship with Maria Cosway so seriously that he could not have turned his interests to a relationship that could survive his stay in France. He most likely never seriously contemplated bringing Cosway back to Virginia to reign as mistress of Monticello. The rational man that was Jefferson knew that he was not going to stay in France forever, and he also knew that he was not going to take Maria Cosway home with him. If he married her, he would be presenting himself to his constituents and his governmental associates with a new wife who was a divorced woman, whom he took from her husband while he was representing the people of the United States as minister to France. It was the continuance of his relationship with Maria Cosway that could rightfully be called impossible. Using Cosway as an antidote to the Sally Hemings story is, to say the least, ineffective.

Money to Sally Hemings

After Sally Hemings returned to the United States, there are fewer references to her in any records Jefferson kept. Brodie's evidence of a continuing relationship focused on cryptic notions in Jefferson's records, the circumstances surrounding the births of Hemings's children, and the ultimate destinies of Sally Hemings and her children.

Brodie said that while there are no direct references to Jefferson giving Hemings money, there are unexplained notations in Jefferson's account book that could represent gifts to her. Brodie noted that he left what often came to fairly substantial amounts of money in the "small drawers" of his room, and she speculated that these sums were for Sally Hemings, who as Jefferson's chambermaid would have been one of the few people who had access to his rooms. In addition, the account books contain references to his having given sums of money as "charity" upon his returns to Monticello, apparently a way of noting that he had given money to people whose names he wanted to conceal. But neither the unexplained references to money nor those to charity support Brodie's speculation, for such references appear in Jefferson's account books well before he could have been involved with Hemings.[66]

Brodie's conjectures about Sally Hemings receiving money from Jefferson illustrate the difficult nature of her investigation. Uncovering circumstances in a person's life that the person would want to keep hidden is a very different and more difficult project than gathering up open facts. One would not expect to be able to look at Jefferson's records and find direct evidence that he was involved in a relationship with Sally Hemings. When direct approaches do not work, collateral approaches may yield, if not a definite answer, at least a probable one.

Consider the following. Jefferson's slaves sold produce, chickens, and eggs to the Jefferson household. One of his granddaughters kept detailed records of those financial transactions for the years 1805–8. Those records show that all the adult slaves at Monticello, save for three, made sales to the household. The three who did not were Jefferson's two cooks and Sally Hemings.[67] Why didn't these three individuals participate in a practice that was otherwise universal at Monticello? Why were these slaves apparently uninterested in getting money in this fashion?

That two of the three people had the same job suggests that there was something about that job that made it difficult and/or unnecessary for them to enter the market with Jefferson and his family. Some reasonable explanations come to mind. Being a cook at Monticello was a serious and time-consuming activity. The cooks produced meals for Jefferson, his family, and guests. This had to be done precisely according to Jefferson's detailed preferences. The cooks may not have had the time to devote to gardening or raising and selling chickens. They also may not have had any need to. As cooks they had ready access to food. They could have entered the market at Monticello at another phase, as sellers of leftovers or unused supplies to those individuals who got money from Jefferson and the Randolphs. Alternatively, from visitors' accounts of meals at Monticello, Jefferson's cooks deserve to be called chefs. They may well have seen themselves as above the ordinary run of slaves and may not have wanted to be involved with the menial tasks of raising and selling chickens and produce.

What of Sally Hemings? Hers was the only other slave household at Monticello that did not seek to obtain money by selling items to Jefferson and the Randolphs. She was a woman with four children and no husband. Why would she have been uninterested in getting money either to save or to buy things for herself and her children? She knew from her experience in France what it was like to get money for one's work. Her children's lives as adults do not support the idea that they were raised by a person who was just lazy or did not care about improving her family's position.

One could argue that it is useless to speculate about why Sally Hemings never sold anything to Jefferson and the Randolphs. However, it is important to consider this because people who had no idea about the record of these sales to Jefferson offered information about Hemings's status at Monticello that may well explain why her household was not involved. The kind of relationship they said that Hemings had with Jefferson would have made it unnecessary for her to sell anything to him and awkward to sell to him through his surrogates, namely, his daughter and his granddaughter. We may sell to our children to teach them the value of money or to parents, siblings, and friends to maintain the integrity of those relationships. We do not usually sell to our spouses or to those who are the equivalent of spouses, because that is like selling to oneself.

The Births of Sally Hemings's Children

The pattern of Sally Hemings's conceptions of children and Jefferson's presence at Monticello is perhaps the most compelling evidence of the existence of a relationship between the two. Jefferson and Hemings returned to the United States just before Christmas 1789. There is, of course, a controversy about what happened to her in 1790. Hemings either had a child who died, or she had a child who lived, or she had no child at all that year. Her first child conceived and born at Monticello arrived in 1795, which raises an interesting question. Is there anything to account for the five-year period in which Hemings, supposedly having an affair with Jefferson, conceived no children?

If Hemings was pregnant when she returned from France and gave birth to a child who died or lived, nursing this child—or abstaining from sexual activity—might explain why there were no conceptions in 1790 and even 1791. Another possible explanation is that Jefferson, who was serving as secretary of state, was away from Monticello for almost nine months in 1790, eleven months in 1791, nine months in 1792, and eleven months in 1793.[68]

The first child that Sally Hemings conceived and gave birth to at Monticello was a daughter named Harriet, born on October 5, 1795. Jefferson, who had retired from his cabinet post, was in residence at Monticello from January 1794 until February 1797. Brodie wrote that Hemings had another daughter named Edy in 1796, but this was actually a young girl who moved in with Hemings to look after Hemings's daughter, Harriet. At some point Edy moved back in with her own parents, and her younger sister Aggey moved in with Hemings until Harriet died. Jack McLaughlin cited the "private baby-sitter" arrangement for Hemings's children as "one of the few examples of Jefferson's giving her preferential treatment."[69]

Jefferson was elected vice president of the United States in late 1796 and left for Philadelphia in February 1797 to begin his term. He returned to Monticello on July 11 and stayed there until December 4, 1797. Hemings next had a son named Beverley, born on April 1, 1798. On March 8, 1799, Jefferson returned to Monticello and stayed until December 21, when he left for Philadelphia. At the beginning of December 1799, Sally Hemings gave birth to a daughter, the child whose existence was only recently discovered. That child was also tended by a young slave girl, but it died in infancy. Jefferson arrived at Monticello at the end of May in 1800 and stayed there until November 24. In February 1801 he was elected president on the thirty-sixth ballot in the House of Representatives. In May 1801 Hemings had another daughter whom she named Harriet, after the child who had died. After his usual summer and fall breaks at Monticello the next three years, Jefferson returned there on April 4, 1804, because his daughter

Maria was gravely ill. Maria died at age twenty-five on April 17. Jefferson left Monticello on May 11. Madison Hemings was born on January 19, 1805.[70]

Brodie's assertion that Jefferson and Hemings conceived Madison Hemings when Jefferson came home to attend his dying daughter has caused particular consternation. Some view the idea that Jefferson would have sex during the time that his daughter was ill as particularly insulting.[71] Once again, we have moved over into the realm of value judgments coupled with the determination to make this story seem as sordid as possible. If Jefferson had been married and his wife had conceived a child during this period, there would be no hint that their sexuality amounted to a vile, degraded activity. Someone might even have alluded to the symbolism of new life in the midst of death.

Human beings have sex for many reasons other than depraved lust. Humans have sex when they are happy and carefree. They also have sex when they are depressed and do not know how to express their feelings, or when they are frightened and need to be distracted. People have sex to be nurtured and comforted. Those who expressed horror at the thought that Jefferson might have turned to Hemings during this crisis seem to have had no sense that a woman who was a slave could provide this type of refuge to a decent man; if it happened, it can only be seen as an example of Thomas Jefferson's depravity. This attitude is suitably in keeping with the notion that all aspects of an alleged Jefferson-Hemings relationship must be portrayed as foul.

Eston Hemings, Sally Hemings's last child, was born on May 21, 1808. Jefferson had been at Monticello from the beginning of August to October 3, 1807. He returned the next spring, making Eston the only son of Sally Hemings's born when Jefferson was at Monticello. Brodie referred to the entry in Jefferson's account books for the day after Eston's birth: "May 22, Gave the children 1 D[ollar]." Later that week he wrote, "Pd. for whisky @ 2/6 15.83." Jefferson preferred wine to whiskey, but he bought whiskey for celebrations. Brodie surmised that these entries suggested that Jefferson was in a particularly good mood on the day after Eston Hemings's birth and that there had been some sort of celebration during that week. It is also possible that Jefferson was noting an early purchase of the whiskey he sometimes provided to the slaves who participated in the harvest at Monticello, which usually took place at the end of June.[72]

The Children's Names

Do the names of Sally Hemings's children give any indication of the likely identity of their father? Names often signal family ties. Fawn Brodie addressed this question in her last written piece on the Hemings story, focusing mainly on the names of Beverley and Eston Hemings. Brodie considered it possible that Jefferson provided the name Beverley for Sally Hemings's first-known son, taking it from a play that he liked, Richard Sheridan's *School for Scandal*, in which "the hero, a young man named Beverly, the son of an aristocrat, conceals his identity."[73] This explanation reveals one of the most problematic aspects of Brodie's work on this subject. Although she must be commended for the seriousness with which she approached this topic, at times her zeal to solve this riddle led her to think that things were much more mysterious and complicated than they actually were.

Beverley is a name from the Jefferson-Randolph family tree. William Randolph, one of Jefferson's maternal ancestors, married Elizabeth Beverley. Throughout the Randolph family genealogy, Beverley appears quite frequently, sometimes with "-ley" and sometimes as "-ly." For example, in the Jefferson family letters T. J. Randolph's cousin and friend Beverley Randolph is referred to in both fashions. In some references to Beverley Hemings, Jefferson clearly spelled the name as "-ley," and in other of his references the *e* is not apparent, although slurred writing may have merged the letter with the final *y*.

It has been ascertained through the oral history of the Hemings family that Madison, who was called "Jim-Mad" by his family, had given the names of his nuclear family at Monticello to his children. Hemings's memoirs also suggest this. He did not mention the name of his first son who died while his family still lived in Virginia. His first daughter was named Sarah. A common nickname for Sarah is Sally, which indicates that Sally Hemings's given name was probably Sarah. Madison named his next daughter Harriet after his older sister. When he and his wife began to have boys, they named them William Beverley, James Madison, and Thomas Eston. These were also the full names of Sally Hemings's sons.[74]

The question, of course, is who among the four individuals with some possible parental connection to Sally Hemings's children would most likely have suggested these names? Because others in the Jefferson-Randolph circle had the same names as the Hemings children, it is useful to consider the putative parents' connections to those people, bearing in mind that the records are far fuller for Thomas Jefferson than for Sally Hemings or the Carr brothers.

William Beverley was the name of one of the men who participated with Peter Jefferson, Thomas's father, on an expedition through Virginia in 1746 to mark the Fairfax Line, the section of Lord Fairfax's property in Virginia for which there was no natural boundary. William Beverley was connected to

Jefferson's mother's family, the Randolphs, by blood and by marriage. He was one of the commissioners chosen to represent Lord Fairfax's interests and with the commissioners representing the Crown supervised the work of Peter Jefferson and the other surveyors on the trip. This was Peter Jefferson's first major expedition and proved to be a good start to his career. Malone noted that during the course of this expedition, Peter Jefferson carved his initials "on a beech near the Fairfax Stone." This ritual was actually performed along with William Beverley and the other members of the party. As described by a biographer of Lord Fairfax:

> On October 23rd, the party carved King George's "GR" on one side of the beech and the proprietor's "FX" on the opposite side.
> On other beeches they cut 1746, "GFX" (for George Fairfax), "W. BEVERLEY," "FRY," "LUN. LOMAX," "P. HEDGEMAN," "P.J." (for Peter Jefferson), "T. LEWIS," "R. BROOKE" . . . and thus, by name or initial, nearly all of the members of the party were memorialized.[75]

A year later William Beverley and the other participants met at Peter Jefferson's temporary residence, Tuckahoe, to draw a map of the final boundaries of the Fairfax properties. Thomas Jefferson was only four years old when the men gathered to complete their task, but his father told him stories about the exceptionally grueling journey that Malone indicates made a great impression upon him. Although Jefferson did not list the Fairfax commissioners by name he wrote with evident knowledge about all of the various Fairfax Line expeditions in an 1816 letter to then-governor Wilson C. Nicholas.[76]

Jefferson knew other men named Beverley, though none to whom he would have had any sentimental attachment. He knew well and corresponded with his relative Beverley Randolph, a governor of Virginia during the late 1780s and early 1790s. That Beverley Randolph died in 1797, the year before Beverley Hemings's birth. Jefferson would have known his grandson's cousin and friend Thomas Beverley Randolph, the son of William Randolph, a Jefferson relative. Jefferson secured an appointment for that Beverley Randolph to the United States Military Academy. David Meade and Mary Randolph, the two Jefferson cousins who came to despise him near the end of the 1790s, also had a son named William Beverley, who was born in 1789, eleven years before William Beverley Hemings.[77]

Harriet was the name given to Sally Hemings's first daughter, who lived only two years, and to her only daughter who survived to adulthood. Harriet is a common name, although there were no other Jefferson slaves with that name at the time of her birth. There were, however, Harriets in the Randolph family. It was the name of both a sister and a niece of Thomas Mann Randolph, Jefferson's son-in-law. The sister is frequently mentioned in family letters as visiting Monticello. In fact, she came to Monticello one year for the expressed purpose of giving birth. When the two Harriet Hemings were born, she was only one of many family members who occasionally visited. However, she did become a part of Jefferson's life as president when he departed from his policy against hiring relatives and appointed her husband, Richard Hackley, to be a United States consul to Sanlúcar. Harriet Randolph Hackley named her only son, born in 1808, William Beverley.[78]

Madison Hemings was given his name at the request of Dolley Madison, which may give an indication of Sally Hemings's special status at Monticello. Even if Dolley Madison had not made the request, Jefferson's relationship to the man who bore that name is well known. James Madison was one of his closest friends.

On the question of Eston Hemings's name, Brodie consulted Wilson Randolph Gathings, "collateral kin to Jefferson," who suggested that "Jefferson chose [Eston] because it was the name of the birthplace of William Randolph, his maternal ancestor in Yorkshire, England." She also pointed out, without giving any source, that Jefferson's favorite cousin was Thomas Eston Randolph, the son of Jefferson's maternal uncle, William. In later life he was described as Jefferson's "intimate friend." Jefferson mediated a family dispute over ownership of Dungeness—Jefferson's mother's girlhood home—which afterwards became T. E. Randolph's estate. T. E. Randolph leased Jefferson's flour mill for many years. In 1817 Jefferson attempted, without success, to have Randolph appointed postmaster at Richmond. In a letter to James Madison, Jefferson described his and Thomas Eston Randolph's families as being "almost as one." Thomas Eston Randolph had a daughter named Harriet, born in the year after the second Harriet Hemings. In keeping with the practice of marrying within the family, Jefferson's grandson Francis Eppes married another of Thomas Eston Randolph's daughters. These individuals, Thomas Eston Randolph and his wife Jane and Francis Eppes and his wife, along with Jane's sister Harriet Randolph Hackley and her family, all removed to Florida in the years immediately following Jefferson's death.[79]

Sally Hemings also would have had some associations with those who had the same names as her children. William Beverley Randolph's mother, Mary, was a frequent visitor to Monticello. She would also have known Mary's sister Harriet Randolph Hackley for the same reason. Their sister Jane, wife of Thomas Eston Randolph, was close to Maria Jefferson, and, of course, Hemings had been Maria's personal companion. The nature of Hemings's association with Maria Jefferson after their return from France is not known. Maria was married in 1797 and moved away from Monticello, but she visited whenever Jefferson came home, so she and Hemings may have remained close. Hemings would have known Maria's friend Jane and her husband Thomas Eston Randolph.

Hemings also would have known Thomas Eston Randolph through his friendship with Thomas Jefferson. There is one reason to think that the Jefferson connection may have been more important. Thomas Eston Hemings was born in 1808, which suggests that Hemings's association with the T. E. Randolph wing of the family survived Maria Jefferson's death in 1804. As to James Madison, Dolley Madison asked Hemings to give her son that name, a request not to be refused.

One wonders whether Sally Hemings on her own accord would have so consistently favored Randolph family names over names from her own family, the Wayleses. The Wayles connection was of importance to Hemings's nuclear family, for the name Wayles reappeared among her grandchildren, their progeny, and beyond.[80] It appears that it was not Sally Hemings who was naming her children. The names were more likely chosen by the men who have been cited as their possible fathers; three of the names came directly from people within their family and one from a man who was close to at least two of the possible fathers.

Peter and Samuel Carr also would have known of the name Beverley and its connection to their family. In addition, James Madison was a pivotal figure in the life of Peter Carr. At the request of Jefferson, Madison had been Peter's mentor, giving him advice on education and later helping him during his career in government.[81] Madison's connection to Samuel Carr was not so great, but Samuel knew him as well. Of course, Jefferson's maternal ancestor in England was also the Carr brothers' ancestor, just as Thomas Eston Randolph was their kinsman as he was Jefferson's. Either of the Carrs could have drawn inspiration from those sources.

There is no record or indication of any action, word, or deed from the Carr brothers toward Sally Hemings's children. Why would men who left no evidence (that has come to light) of even knowing these children existed have allowed or suggested names for them from within their prominent family or that of a longtime mentor. Both Carr brothers had several sons with their white wives, and those sons were not named for people from within that illustrious family tree.[82] That either one or both of these men would save the names of particular members of the Randolph family and of another important Virginian to whom they were close for the sons they were having with their black slave mistress and give their white sons names that do not identify them as being part of a first family of Virginia would seem quite strange. In a society where one's social status was largely determined by family relation-

ships, such a choice on the part of the Carrs would have been a not insignificant slight to their white progeny. This sounds far more like the act of a white
man who has no white sons to name.

Consider Thomas Jefferson's penchant with regard to names. His children
with Martha Jefferson were given the names of his sisters and mother. Jefferson was given the privilege of naming his grandchildren. All of the boys, save
the first grandson who was named after him at his mother's insistence, were
given the full names of people who were in some way important to him:
Meriwether Lewis, James Madison, Benjamin Franklin, and George Wythe.[83]

If Jefferson did suggest the Randolph names for Hemings's children and
if he was their father, it might offer a degree of insight into the nature of his
relationship with her. It would suggest that he did not view Sally Hemings
as a prostitute. Would a man who had children with a prostitute name those
children for an illustrious relative, two close cousins, and his closest friend?
It seems particularly unlikely that he would do this when the latter three
people were frequent visitors to his home and would have learned of his
choice. Giving the names of these valued individuals to children from such a
union would be an insult to them.

Why Sally Hemings's Children Went Free: Douglass Adair

Along with the timing of Hemings's conceptions of children, the strongest
item of evidence cited to support the idea that Jefferson fathered those children is the fact that he freed them all. This fact is made more suggestive by
Madison Hemings's claim that the plan to do so was set near the beginning
of his parents' relationship. Douglass Adair attempted to deal with Jefferson's
actions toward the Hemings children by saying that their grant of freedom
was not as extraordinary as one might think.

Adair said that Sally Hemings could tell Madison that Jefferson promised
to free all of her children at age twenty-one because she knew that this was
Jefferson's plan for all the Hemings males, not just her sons. According to
Adair, Jefferson decided as early as 1774 "that the Hemings boys when they
were grown and after they had learned a trade and could support themselves,
would be given their freedom if they wished it." He said that Robert and James
Hemings "chose freedom in the 1790's, as is proven by two documents still
preserved in the Jefferson papers," the two legal indentures that Jefferson drew
up freeing the two men.[84]

To Adair these indentures were significant for three reasons. First, he said,
they reveal Jefferson's policy of freeing Hemings males if they chose it. Second,
the indenture freeing James Hemings was "probably the basis of the twisted

story Sally told her children about the supposed contract Jefferson made with her in Paris . . . [and it] explains why Sally could be so sure that her children would be free when they were grown"; "her fictitious account invited her sons to give her the credit for arranging a policy that Jefferson had already decided on." Third, because the freed James Hemings was established in Philadelphia, Jefferson felt comfortable violating his rule against freeing women and sent Harriet Hemings when she was of age to join him.[85]

Jefferson's Policy of Freeing All Hemings Males

In describing Jefferson as having had a policy of freeing all Hemings males who wanted to be free when they had come of age and had a skill, Adair was attempting to save himself from the implications of what turns out to be his somewhat tortured logic. Why did Adair have to qualify the statement by specifying that the Hemings males were freed if they chose to be free? To account for the facts that some skilled Hemings males were not freed and that others who were freed were substantially older than twenty-one-year-old Madison and Eston Hemings and twenty-three-year-old Beverley Hemings. Thus, Adair could assert that Jefferson had a policy and explain why it had been applied only to two people besides Sally Hemings's children before Jefferson was on his deathbed. But there is no document stating that Jefferson had such a policy, and there is only Adair's assertion that some of the skilled Hemings males did not want to be free.[86]

If Jefferson had this policy, why did he make one of the Hemings men he freed, Robert Hemings, age thirty-two, pay him for his freedom? Why did he complain that Robert Hemings's new employer had "debauched" Hemings from him, referring to the fact that Hemings had fallen in love with a woman who was owned by his new employer?[87] These do not sound like the words of a man who intended all along to let the slave go free. If Jefferson intended to free James Hemings all along, why not do it in France when James originally asked or have him begin to train his replacement as chef as soon as they got back to the United States? Neither the freeing of Robert Hemings nor that of James Hemings comes close to proving that Jefferson had planned to free every skilled Hemings male who requested freedom.

Sally Hemings's Contract

Adair's second point, that Sally Hemings looked to the indenture that freed James Hemings as a prototype for her own story of a contract with Jefferson to free her children at twenty-one, is even harder to understand. Why would an indenture drawn up when James Hemings was twenty-eight, the terms of which were not fulfilled until he was thirty-one, lead Sally Hemings to make up a story about Jefferson promising to free her children at age twenty-one? Why would Jefferson's emancipation of James Hemings make Sally Hemings believe that Jefferson intended to free all Hemings males who had a skill when they reached that age? Why would Hemings have been so sure of this "fact" that she would have planted this poignant hope in her offspring while they were young children, knowing the bone-crushing disappointment that would follow if the promise was not fulfilled?

What made Adair believe that Sally Hemings would have been so careless in her treatment of her children? An indenture that said nothing about any policy of freeing Hemings males would not have been enough to make a slave mother tell her small children that they would all be given their freedom when they turned twenty-one. A mother would hold out such a hope only if the circumstances warranted her complete confidence that this eventuality would take place.

Finally, what of Harriet Hemings's freedom? How did this fit in with the indenture and a policy of freeing skilled Hemings males? Would Sally Hemings have reason to think that Harriet would go free at twenty-one as well and then tell her little girl this? Or was it mere coincidence that the time in Harriet's life when Jefferson became greatly concerned with her virtue just happened to coincide with the age that Sally Hemings could state that Jefferson intended to free all Hemings males?

Adair tried to sidestep this inconsistency in his theory by stating firmly, with no evidence, that Jefferson freed Harriet Hemings because he was determined to break the cycle of miscegenation that had operated in her family for three generations. He then attempted to provide cover for the weakness of this claim by following it with a short, informative (though utterly beside the point) discourse on the fates of mulatto women who lived in New Orleans, as though his knowledge of this matter could shore up his supposition about the circumstances of Harriet Hemings's life.[88]

Harriet Hemings and James Hemings

About Adair's claim that Harriet Hemings was sent to meet James Hemings in Philadelphia, we must be charitable. James Hemings was twenty-one years dead when Jefferson arranged to have Harriet take the stagecoach from Virginia to Philadelphia. Anyone can make a mistake, and the story does involve a rather large cast of characters with the same last name. Still, it must be pointed out that this was not likely a mere typographical error or a good-faith misreading of an ambiguous document. This assertion was part of what purported to be a coherent theory. Adair had to have thought about this.

Douglass Adair, Sally Hemings, and Peter Carr

Adair more than any other scholar did attempt to deal with Sally Hemings as a person. He recognized that she was an exceptional individual because of her beauty and because she had had experiences that most Americans, then and now, do not have. She had traveled abroad, become acquainted with a foreign language, lived in grand style, and seen France at a pivotal point in history.

In Adair's view Sally Hemings the woman, scorned and twisted with jealousy, found out about James Callender's charge, subtracted "President Tom," and made the newspaper articles the basis of her life story. She betrayed the man who had treated her family so kindly. Adair was dismayed at Sally Hemings's betrayal of Thomas Jefferson after all he had done for her family. Adair wrote: "No Hemings ever felt the whip. The control, while they were little things, was exercised by Jefferson himself, helping them by instruction and example to grow up, along with his own children, as decent God-fearing individuals, prepared at maturity to manage their lives." [89]

No one can accuse Adair of squeamishness about miscegenation. He threw himself into his rendition of the Hemings-Carr relationship with gusto, describing it as a real "love match exhibiting deep and lasting emotional involvements for both partners." He wrote that their affair began "in hot youth and continu[ed] until middle age." He noted that Sally Hemings was not promiscuous, having accepted the "middle-class standards of monogamy" and passed them on to her children. Peter Carr was faithful to her, too—in his fashion, of course. He married another, but "he could not divorce himself from Sally." [90]

Carr's marriage, according to Adair, affected Sally deeply.

> It was this situation productive of fierce jealousy—of feeling of betrayal even—on Sally's part, that must be remembered in judging her repudiation of Carr's paternity of her children. In as much as Sally loved Carr, so much more must she have hated his wife, and on occasion hated him, too, for taking a wife. Her revenge was neither to refuse him her body nor to punish him by accepting other lovers but, more subtly, to deny to her children— the children who were the continuing mark of their mutual affection—that Carr was their father. Pride and revenge were equally compounded in the fictitious story she told her children about being Jefferson's mistress.
>
> Love and rejection were strands in the twisted emotional knot that tied Sally to Peter Carr; love and guilt were strands twisted into the knot binding

Peter to Sally during most of their adult lives. We have the record of an eyewitness report on Carr's confessed shame over the sorrow his attachment had caused Jefferson and the rest of the Monticello family after the newspapers began to mock the president for his supposed amours, but the guilt must have been present earlier. Peter Carr must have been conscious, long before Callender made Sally's name notorious, that his affair was only the most obvious and sensational way in which he had disappointed Jefferson's hopes and plans for his career.[91]

All of this may be true. There is one problem. There are no citations to sources for any of this, and Adair gave no indication that he was speculating about these matters. Perhaps Adair had a basis for the certainty and detail with which he recounted the story of Peter Carr and Sally Hemings. If there was a basis, Adair should have revealed it or else made it clear that he was speculating. Fawn Brodie always pointed to particular events that suggested to her that the Jefferson-Hemings relationship was real. She may have been completely wrong in her interpretation of the events, but at least the events could be documented. All Adair thought he needed was T. J. Randolph's claim that Peter Carr was Sally Hemings's lover and Bacon's statement that ".... " was Heming's lover. Adair said that we could presume that Bacon's ellipsis referred to Peter Carr in light of T. J. Randolph's statement. We might have had enough confidence in Adair to take him up on his suggestion had he not been so careless with several of his other presumptions at key points in his essay.

My objection to all of this is not that Douglass Adair did not believe that Thomas Jefferson was Sally Hemings's lover. That is, for many, still an open question. It is, however, his poor standard for assessing evidence that grates, his assumption of the reader's ignorance of the facts and inability to reason that offends. That historians and commentators would ride to the kill over Fawn Brodie's methods and conclusions and accept those of Adair in "The Jefferson Scandals" says a great deal about the way history is constructed in the United States.

The editor of the volume in which "The Jefferson Scandals" appeared wrote in the prologue to the piece that Adair had worked hard on this essay, rewriting it many times. Even after these efforts, Adair pronounced the piece "a horror story that I hope to rewrite and publish," and he described it as "crude."[92] On this score Adair's judgment was sound. Malone and Hochman referred to Adair's piece in their article "A Note on Evidence." By the time Malone's *Sage of Monticello* appeared in 1981, he must have realized the extreme weakness of Adair's effort. At the end of the book, in Malone's second appendix on the Hemings affair, he suggested readers consult several other sources that "shed new light on the politics and personalities involved in the scurrilous attacks on Jefferson at the beginning of his presidency." Malone cited his "Note on Evidence," as well as several other works; he did not mention Adair's article.[93] Having published Ellen Randolph Coolidge's letter naming Samuel Carr as the father of Hemings's children, Malone felt that Coolidge was more likely to have been accurate and that Samuel, not Peter, Carr was the true father. Under the circumstances Adair's too assured and unsubstantiated creation of an entire story line for the Sally Hemings–Peter Carr romance might have seemed too problematic.

Some might think it unfair to criticize so strenuously a piece that the author did not think a finished product, particularly one published by others after his death. However, the piece clearly has influenced writing about Thomas Jefferson and Sally Hemings. Malone's mistake about Harriet Hemings going to meet James Hemings in Philadelphia may have come from his reading of Adair's piece, which was shared among scholars in the early 1960s. Adair's version of a love affair between Peter Carr and Sally Hemings has appeared in at least one young adult biography of Jefferson, with no language indicating that it was based upon his speculation. One can see echoes of Adair's conclusions in some of the current commentary on Maria Cosway versus Sally Hemings. In addition, other historians either have used Adair as a source for their own critiques or, when they do not want to deal specifically with the issue of Sally Hemings, have referred readers to Adair's work.[94] For these reasons, "The Jefferson Scandals," even in its unfinished state, must be evaluated. It is an interesting piece of work, but it is not up to the task the author assigned to it.

Would Thomas Jefferson Have Failed to Free Sally Hemings If She Had Been His Mistress?

What Madison Hemings's memoirs do not say is that Jefferson made any sort of promise to free Sally Hemings. He spoke of her departure from Monticello as if it was a natural occurrence. Brodie suggested that Martha Randolph freed Sally Hemings at her father's request, noting that Israel Jefferson included Sally Hemings among the list of slaves for whom freedom was arranged by Jefferson before he died.[95] While this may have been Israel Jefferson's understanding of what happened, Sally Hemings's name does not appear in Thomas Jefferson's will.

Sally Hemings's absence from the will has been cited as proof that she was not his mistress. This is another example of the failure to think seriously about the context in which these events were unfolding. It is by no means obvious that Jefferson, if he had wanted Sally Hemings to be free, would have sought to accomplish this by putting her in his will with her two sons. Whatever impression his freeing of Madison and Eston might have created, formally freeing Sally Hemings upon his death would have been taken as an even more certain admission of their relationship. People in Jefferson's home territory would have thought that they (along with the two children who had left earlier) comprised a family. That some modern-day historians see Jefferson's failure to put Hemings in his will as a litmus test supports this. Leaving aside what mentioning Sally Hemings in his will might have done to Jefferson's reputation, it would have drawn unfavorable attention to three vulnerable ex-slaves and also would have created more heartache for Martha and his grandchildren.

John C. Miller made much of the fact that Sally Hemings was not freed in Jefferson's will and cracked wise about Hemings's predicament after his death. "In his will, Jefferson freed five slaves all Hemingses and he petitioned the state legislature, as the law required, for permission for those freed slaves to remain in Virginia. But Sally Hemings was not among those manumitted: her name appeared on the slave inventory of his estate and her value was set at fifty dollars, although she might have been regarded as a collector's item by anyone who believed Callender's story." Miller went on to ask: "Who would believe that he failed to free a slave woman with whom, according to Fawn Brodie, he had enjoyed decades of idyllic bliss and for whose love he had risked the presidency and the good opinion of posterity; and how could it be explained that he had not stipulated that she be buried in the family plot at Monticello rather than an obscure Negro cemetery?"[96]

We can assume that Miller was being sarcastic when he wrote the last clause of this sentence. As to Miller's first point, there is a possible answer. In a letter to his grandson, as he attempted to explain the correct approach to dealing with politics and politicians, Thomas Jefferson made an analogy to a man coming upon an angry bull in the middle of the road. There was no point in getting into a dispute with an irrational beast over ownership of the road. The most sensible thing to do is to give the beast the right of way and then proceed to one's original destination unharmed.[97] When facing a situation where reason cannot possibly prevail and one has no chance of winning by brute force, the best thing to do is to go around the problem. This is not cowardice; it is just good sense. If there was a route to Sally Hemings's freedom other than by confronting and attempting to best the angry bull of publicity and scandal that would have arisen had he placed Sally Hemings's name in his will, why would Jefferson not take it?

Madison and Eston Hemings were different. Jefferson may have made a specific and—for Sally Hemings—a life-defining promise that he would free them. Jefferson's financial situation meant that with no legal emancipation these young men were at enormous risk of missing the opportunity to go free. As young and highly skilled men, they would have been in great demand. Jefferson had to take specific legal action to make sure that they were out of reach of his creditors, or he would have gone back on his word on a matter of extreme importance. Moreover, Madison and Eston could not have remained in Virginia without a formal declaration of their freedom. In the system that defined the worth of her existence, Sally Hemings was old enough to be almost without value. It was much easier for her to be freed by extralegal, that is, more private, means—which is exactly what happened.

People are forgiven many things in this life for being discreet. If Sally Hemings was his mistress, Thomas Jefferson's freeing of her in a document that would become a public record and petitioning the legislature to allow her to remain in the state would have been the very opposite of discretion. He would have been rubbing his violation of the ultimate taboo in the faces of white society. One cannot discount the possibility that the legislature would have turned down Jefferson's request that Hemings and her children be allowed to stay in Virginia. It was all that Jefferson could do to persuade the legislature to help him stabilize his financial position by allowing him to sell his land by lottery.[98] The legislators' attitude would not have inspired confidence that they would have granted the extraordinary request to allow Sally Hemings to remain in the state, as she seems to have wanted.

The handling of Jefferson's lottery indicates that his family could appeal to the legislature through their connections instead of through normal channels. Jefferson made no formal application to hold the lottery, as was required by law. Instead, his grandson and he contacted friends in the assembly and asked them to help matters proceed.[99] If an application to hold a lottery for the sale of an estate could be handled in this informal fashion, the freedom of one aged female slave and permission for her to remain in the state could be handled quietly, and with no paperwork, as well. Members of the legislature might have even appreciated the fact that Jefferson did not embarrass them by making a formal, written request.

If Jefferson had named Sally Hemings in his will, it is very likely that her life and those of her sons would not have been particularly pleasant after Jefferson died. Miller, Dabney, and Adair assumed that Sally Hemings knew of the publicity surrounding her alleged relationship with Thomas Jefferson. If she was familiar with this literature, she would have known that she was one of the most vilified women in American history. Some of the newspaper articles and ballads that referred to Hemings and Jefferson were extremely hostile, even violent in their images. Think of what the reaction might have been if Jefferson had freed Sally Hemings and her two children in his will and asked the legislature to let what everyone would have assumed to have been his slave family remain in the state.

With this in mind, why would Sally Hemings even have wanted Jefferson to free her in his will, if she had assurances that she would be freed by Martha Randolph and allowed to leave Monticello under the protection of her two youngest sons when they became free men? Jefferson's freeing of Hemings himself would have caused problems far greater than any psychic reward she could have gotten from such an action after thirty-eight years. The more intelligent thing for her to do was, not to insist upon some symbolic and potentially dangerous gesture on Jefferson's part, but instead to wait until both of her sons became free men and then settle quietly in the vicinity. After this, Hemings could, as she apparently did, live out the rest of her life in obscurity and peace.

The End

Brodie calculated that Sally Hemings was freed within two years after Jefferson's death, evidently believing that the directions in Jefferson's will about when the nineteen-year-old Eston Hemings would be free were followed. However, Eston Hemings was not required to remain at Monticello until he was twenty-one but was freed shortly after Jefferson's death. Madison Hemings became free upon Jefferson's death. The three Hemingses went to live in a house that they rented in Charlottesville. No record of Sally Hemings's life during that period survives. Both of her sons married and became property owners in the town, and their relationship to Monticello was not severed. Madison Hemings worked as a paid employee for Thomas Jefferson Randolph. In the year before Madison Hemings moved to Chillicothe, T. J. Randolph and Eston Hemings served as co-guarantors on an application for a loan that Madison Hemings sought and apparently received. In what Brodie called the "final irony" of Sally Hemings's life, she and her sons were listed as white by a census taker in 1830. The three former slaves had become free white people in their own community. She lived for nine years after Jefferson's death and died in 1835 at age sixty-two.[100]

6

Summary of the Evidence

WHEN ALL the items of evidence offered to support Thomas Jefferson's involvement with Sally Hemings have been examined, it appears that the standard for judging them has been manipulated. As a result, the quantum of evidence that exists to support the notion has been seriously underestimated. At the same time an alternative theory—that the Carr brothers were responsible—has been offered to counter the claim that Jefferson fathered Hemings's children, and the worth of the evidence cited to support that claim has been overestimated. By comparing historians' treatment of the two theories, one can assess the wisdom of trusting their pronouncements that Thomas Jefferson and Sally Hemings were not involved in a long-term relationship. The extent to which individual prejudices and preferences influence the writing of history also becomes evident.

Proponents of the Carr brothers theory and opponents of the notion that Jefferson fathered Sally Hemings's children have had their say to the fullest extent. The opposing viewpoint, for fairness' sake, needs to be summarized. This is done not to prove or disprove the allegation definitively, because I do not believe that can be accomplished through this medium. Nor do I believe that definitive proof is required, for it is plainly not the case that all things taken as historical truths are based upon what could be called definitive proof. The purpose of this summary is to try to present the strongest case to be made that the story might be true. Doing this serves to demonstrate the lack of seriousness and care with which Jefferson scholars approached the task of considering this issue. As a result of their efforts over the past thirty-odd years, members of the public who know anything at all about this matter probably believe that the sum total of the evidence that supports the story is:

1. The statement of a disgruntled office seeker who invented the story that Thomas Jefferson had a slave mistress.

2. The memoirs of a simpleminded black man induced by a northern carpetbagger to say that he was the son of Thomas Jefferson.

3. Fawn Brodie's assertion that she thought that Thomas Jefferson and Sally Hemings had a long-term liaison because Thomas Jefferson used the

word *mulatto* an inordinate number of times in the travel diary he kept on a trip through Europe after Sally Hemings joined him in Paris in 1787.

But that is not all there is.

Items Supporting the Assertion That Thomas Jefferson Fathered Sally Hemings's Children

Madison Hemings's Claim to Be the Son of Thomas Jefferson

As we approach the beginning of a new century, it is time to lay to rest the allegation that an individual who had been involved with the abolitionist movement either invented the notion that Madison Hemings was the son of Thomas Jefferson or put Madison Hemings up to saying that he was. That myth, dubious to begin with, can now be established as having no historical validity.

A newspaper report shows that as early as the 1840s, three decades before S. F. Wetmore interviewed Madison Hemings, the alleged parentage of Eston Hemings and Madison Hemings was spoken of in the area of Ohio where the two men lived. There are reports of conversations that members of the community had with Eston Hemings about the matter during that same period. Eston Hemings was a celebrity there as the leader of a small band, before he left Ohio for Wisconsin in 1852. The talk of his parentage arose, not as part of an abolitionist strategy, but for the same reason that people gossip about celebrities today: curiosity about the private lives of entertainers.

Not only did Madison Hemings claim to be Jefferson's son; his brother Eston did as well. The evidence indicates that the claim was made long before S. F. Wetmore made contact with Madison Hemings. Eston Hemings had left Ohio and been dead for almost twenty years before Wetmore arrived in Pike County. Moreover, oral history from both men's families, individuals who had lost touch with one another after one side vaulted over the color line, establishes that this story was a part of Hemings family history and did not originate with S. F. Wetmore.

That Madison Hemings actually believed, before S. F. Wetmore could have put the idea in his head, that he was the son of Thomas Jefferson should have been clear to any historian who read Hemings's statement and saw the names of his children—names they shared with people connected by blood and/or intimate relationship to Thomas Jefferson. Jane was the name of Thomas Jefferson's mother and favorite sister and Thomas Eston Randolph's wife; Ellen Wayles was the name of Jefferson's granddaughter, who was also Sally Hemings's niece; Harriet, William Beverley, Thomas Eston, and James

Madison were not only the names of Madison and his Hemings siblings but of Jefferson's Randolph relatives and one of his closest friends.

Three years before S. F. Wetmore's piece in the *Pike County (Ohio) Republican* and before Wetmore decided to interview black residents in the area, census taker William Weaver made a notation in his report that Madison Hemings was Jefferson's son. The notation doesn't prove the proposition, but it shows that others had been informed of the rumor, perhaps by Hemings himself or because of Eston Hemings's fame, at least three years before Wetmore began his interviews of the black residents in the area. In addition, I have demonstrated that S. F. Wetmore was a census taker himself and may have come upon the claim that Hemings was Jefferson's son because of that activity, rather than from a search for material to demonstrate the evils of slave owning.

In addition, some information in Hemings's statement could not have been known or guessed by S. F. Wetmore. In fact, many of the statements seem irrelevant to what was allegedly Wetmore's purpose in inventing the story, that is, furthering the Republican cause in that part of Ohio. For example, it is difficult to see how Jefferson's preference for working with his mechanics over agricultural pursuits would have produced more Republican voters.

It is clear that S. F. Wetmore, the "fanatical abolitionist," did not invent this story, and historians should stop stating or implying that he did. The level of seriousness of a historian's consideration of this controversy should now be measured in inverse proportion to the extent to which he or she relies on the idea of Madison Hemings as puppet of S. F. Wetmore.

Madison Hemings's memoirs must stand or fall on the basis of his credibility alone. To that end, it must be said that these memoirs are properly described as an item of direct evidence that Thomas Jefferson and Sally Hemings were involved in a relationship. It is considered direct evidence because if we believe the proposition that Hemings put forth, then the issue is settled. No other inferences must be made, no other arguments advanced. Just because one does not believe Hemings does not justify pretending that this statement was never made or that its substance does not have to be analyzed, although historians and other commentators seem to think these responses are proper. As it is most assuredly evidence, the only question is whether it is credible. Hemings's detractors can:

1. Destroy Hemings's credibility by taking apart his statement and showing him to have been such a liar about material aspects of the story that he cannot be believed on the main idea advanced in the statement.

2. Argue that Hemings's claim that Jefferson was his father does not meet his burden of proof.

3. Argue that Hemings's claim and the circumstantial evidence to support it fail to convince.

As to the first point, it would be difficult to make the case that Madison Hemings lied about material aspects of his story. Even his detractors have acknowledged that the vast majority of Hemings's remarks can be verified by outside sources. His few mistakes can be attributed to the passage of time and, in one case, a possible misunderstanding about the operation of legal documents, in this case Jefferson's will. Hemings said that Jefferson made provision for the freedom of all four Hemings siblings in his will, when the will only referred to Madison and Eston. Beverley and Harriet Hemings had gone free four years before Jefferson's death at his leave and, in the case of Harriet, under his direction and with his aid. Madison Hemings's statement may show him to have been confused about how Jefferson carried out his intent, but he was not wrong about the substance of that intent, which was to let all four of the Hemings children leave when they became adults.

On the second point, it is rational and right to say that Hemings's statement that Thomas Jefferson was his father does not meet his burden of proof on that issue. However, the matter cannot end there. That a person accused of something doesn't have to mount a defense does not mean that a case can never be proved. If the accused or supporters sit back and say nothing, or do not provide credible explanations as the evidence mounts, the accusation can still be proved. Hemings's detractors could more easily rest upon the notion of a failed burden of proof if Madison Hemings's flat statement that Jefferson was his father was the only evidence to support that proposition. It is not. Sometimes even without his realizing it, a number of details offered in Hemings's statement give rise to circumstantial evidence that supports his basic claim. For example, the notion that there was a promise of freedom for Sally Hemings's children when they reached the age of twenty-one is supported by the circumstances and timing of her children's departures from Monticello.

What is the reason, if not the one given by Madison Hemings, for Jefferson's decision to free these young people according to a timetable measured by their reaching adulthood? Jefferson did this for no other person, no other set of siblings, in his entire life as a slave master. He took a course of action with respect to Madison Hemings and his three siblings that was against his normal course of conduct and, in the case of Harriet Hemings, unprecedented because he did not free women. Although freeing children of their slave paramours was not common, enough slave masters did this for the idea of the likely parenthood of such children to become a cliché. It happened often enough to be considered circumstantial evidence of a parental connection.

Strong circumstantial evidence from sources other than Hemings also tends to support his contention, and it must be aggregated with the direct evidence. Two major items of direct evidence to support the proposition—the statements of Madison Hemings and Israel Jefferson—have been mischaracterized and misunderstood by Jefferson scholars. In addition, a number of items of circumstantial evidence to support the proposition were either unknown to, overlooked by, or distorted by some of these same individuals. Therefore, we cannot rely upon the contention that the weight of the direct and circumstantial evidence has been measured by the experts and found too slight. That determination can be made only after a full and fair consideration of the total amount of evidence.

Israel Jefferson's Corroboration of Madison Hemings's Statement

Israel Jefferson's statement is also direct evidence of a liaison between Thomas Jefferson and Sally Hemings. He corroborated Hemings's statement and even gave a basis for his alleged knowledge about the nature of the relationship between Thomas Jefferson and Sally Hemings. Israel Jefferson did not simply say, "I lived at Monticello and I heard all the talk about the 'Master' and Sally." He said that in his boyhood he ran errands and did other small tasks for Jefferson that gave him access to Jefferson's living quarters, of which Hemings was chambermaid. Israel Jefferson would have been in the position, on some occasions, to have observed the interactions between the two parties.

There are inaccuracies in Israel Jefferson's account, but they are of the sort that can be attributed to the passage of time and understandable confusion about the way in which Sally Hemings and her family achieved their freedom. Although he did not use the term *will* specifically, Israel Jefferson said that Thomas Jefferson had "provided for" the freedom of Sally Hemings and her children. He may have thought that provision had been made in Jefferson's will. We know that this is not true: Jefferson's will did not mention Sally Hemings or her children Beverley and Harriet Hemings who had left Monticello four years before Jefferson's death. Israel Jefferson's apparent confusion on this point is understandable, and his description of the uncertainty among the slaves upon Jefferson's death rings true. The issue of how many of Jefferson's slaves were disposed of at auction and who bought them remains unclear even today.

Israel Jefferson, along with other of Jefferson's slaves, went on the auction block. From his perspective there had to have been some reason why Sally Hemings and her children escaped this fate. He would have known that several years earlier Beverley and Harriet had left Monticello with Jefferson's blessing. Because Sally Hemings and her remaining children left Monticello shortly after Jefferson's death, it was logical for Israel to conclude that Jefferson had left orders for their future. Other important items in his account can be verified, and Israel Jefferson also has been used as a source for information about Monticello and Thomas Jefferson.

John Hartwell Cocke's Statement That Jefferson Had a Slave Mistress

John Hartwell Cocke, one of the founders and first board members of the University of Virginia, wrote in his diary in 1853 and 1859 that Jefferson had a slave mistress. Cocke was not an enemy of Jefferson. He was a visitor to Monticello and worked with him on the project of building the university. He helped Jefferson personally by aiding his effort to have some of his lands sold by lottery to avoid loss of his estates. His references to Jefferson's having a slave mistress were matter-of-fact statements made almost as asides to the larger points he was discussing. They were not diatribes against Jefferson.

James Callender's Assertion Corroborating Madison Hemings's Statement

James Callender's statement in 1802 that Sally Hemings had five children is extrinsic evidence that corroborates Madison Hemings's claim that Sally Hemings had a child upon her return to the United States from France.

Despite his tone of bitter fury, it is important to read and consider James Callender's articles on the subject of Sally Hemings and Thomas Jefferson. In one article Callender said that Sally Hemings had five children and thirty lovers. Thirty lovers would further his description of her as a "slut as common as the pavement." But why five children? Why not eight or ten? The statement that Sally Hemings had five children made her look neither good nor bad and seems simply a statement of what Callender took to be a fact.

Although Hemings had only two children living at the time of Callender's writing, if all the children she has been reported to have borne had lived, there would indeed have been five children. Callender's sources evidently did not know that any of Hemings's children had died. The number is important because it suggests that Madison Hemings was right when he said that his mother had given birth to a child during the months after her return from France. When one adds that alleged child to the other children that we know of from Jefferson's records about Sally Hemings's childbearing, the number adds up to five. It seems highly improbable that James Callender could have picked the same number out of thin air.

Hemings's Conceptions and Jefferson's Proximity

Hemings's pattern of conceiving children (and not conceiving them) can be tied to Jefferson's presence at and absences from Monticello. Jefferson can be placed at Monticello during the time periods when Sally Hemings conceived each of her children. This is an item of circumstantial evidence that should be weighed along with the items of direct evidence. It is only circumstantial because even if we know that this true, there are additional steps of reasoning or items of information that must be advanced before those circumstances can be said to prove the proposition.

There is no evidence placing the other putative lovers of Hemings—the Carr brothers—at Monticello during the relevant time periods when the children would most likely have been conceived, although the Carr brothers did live in the vicinity of the plantation. Hemings never conceived a child when Jefferson was not in residence at Monticello. During the years that she was having children, Jefferson was often away from Monticello for many consecutive months, usually between six to eight months at a time. This raises the questions of why over a fifteen-year-period the Carr brothers were unable to father children during those months, and why they regained the capacity to do so only upon Jefferson's return to Monticello, even for short visits. The improbability of that scenario advances the circumstantial evidence about the relationship between Jefferson's presence at Monticello and Hemings's conceptions of children toward proof of Madison Hemings's proposition.

The Resemblance of Sally Hemings's Children to Thomas Jefferson

The fact that Hemings only conceived when Jefferson was at Monticello is made more suggestive because all of the children Hemings conceived looked very much like him. Proponents of the Carr brothers theory are suggesting, not only that the Carr brothers, despite many opportunities, could conceive children only when Thomas Jefferson was at home, but that all the children that both men conceived in this fashion would look just like Thomas Jefferson.

The evidence of the children's resemblance to Jefferson was provided by Thomas Jefferson Randolph. He is a prime example of why lawyers do not allow their clients to volunteer information that they think will be helpful. Randolph, who thought that he was aiding his grandfather, made what was in truth a very serious declaration against his own interest. He said, in very forceful terms, that all of Sally Hemings's children resembled Thomas Jefferson and that one of the boys looked almost exactly like him. He also indicated that his mother thought so, as well. Various visitors to Monticello mentioned seeing slave children who were white running around the premises.

A declaration from a close Jefferson relative saying that it was obvious that Jefferson's "blood ran in [the] veins" of Sally Hemings's children and that one child could be mistaken for Jefferson must be regarded as strong evidence indeed. Declarations against interest are regarded as having a high degree of credibility because of the presumption that people do not make up lies in order to hurt themselves; they lie to help themselves. We are more likely to trust Randolph's assertion that the children looked like Jefferson because he was more familiar with the way Thomas Jefferson looked and because it was undoubtedly something that he wished was not true. Randolph also tied at least some of the white slave children to Sally Hemings, which the visitors to Monticello did not. Randolph probably felt that he could be so free in describing how much the children resembled Jefferson because he had an explanation as to why they did. But his explanation does not negate the value of the evidence for the other side. The supporters of Madison Hemings and Fawn Brodie can still cite the resemblance as evidence to support their claim.

Even further, Randolph's statements on the resemblance effectively narrowed the universe of white men who could have fathered Hemings's children from that of any white man who visited Monticello during the years that Sally Hemings was giving birth. Had Randolph never said that the children looked so much like Jefferson, those who wanted to absolve Jefferson of responsibility could say, as did Meriwether Jones of the *Richmond Examiner,* that the father could have been any one of hundreds of visitors to Monticello. Randolph's assertions brought the possible fathers down to three men: Thomas Jefferson, Peter Carr, and Samuel Carr.

John C. Miller argued that the children's resemblance to Thomas Jefferson was unimportant, noting that one other person unrelated to Jefferson was said to resemble him and that there were Alexander Hamilton look-a-likes as well. He pointed out that it was possible for Sally Hemings's children to resemble Thomas Jefferson but not be his children or even related to him. Yet Miller's argument is not quite on point. Everyone in the world may have a double somewhere, but what are the odds of four doubles winding up in an unrelated person's household?

It is important to keep in mind the relationship between the two competing theories as to who fathered Sally Hemings's children. Members of the

Jefferson family offered the Carr brothers as the likely fathers to explain why Sally Hemings's four children looked so much like Thomas Jefferson. Eliminating the Carr brothers does not erase the children's close resemblance to Jefferson. Some other as yet undesignated Jefferson relative must be substituted, or Thomas Jefferson remains the most likely father. In the absence of any contemporary source suggesting that another relative might have been the father or any present-day indication that it might have been someone else, such speculation seems a desperate attempt to absolve Jefferson at the cost of all reason.

The Treatment of Sally Hemings's Children

One of the first things anyone would want to know is whether Jefferson treated the children of Sally Hemings any differently. When one says differently, one means to ask if they were treated any better. The answer appears to be yes. With Sally Hemings's children, Jefferson seems to have strayed from his work plan for young slaves. Madison Hemings stated that until they were put to a trade, he and his siblings spent their time running errands or with their mother. There is no evidence that Beverley Hemings, the son who would have been eligible to work in Jefferson's nail factory when he turned ten, did so before he was listed as a tradesman at age twelve. Jamey Hemings, son of Sally Hemings's sister Critta and grandson of Elizabeth Hemings, did work in the nail factory, one of the most debilitating tasks on the plantation. Instead, Beverley, Madison, and Eston went to early apprenticeships with the best slave artisan at Monticello, carpenter John Hemings.

Beverley was seven years older than Madison and ten years older than Eston, and at the appropriate time Jefferson made the same decision for each one, despite the passage of years. It seems as though Jefferson had a definite plan for these young people that did not vary. Harriet Hemings did not begin to work as a weaver until age fourteen, four years after other girls on the plantation. Even though these four people were individuals, they were also part of a single unit, a group of siblings.

The timing of the freeing of Sally Hemings's children tracks strongly with the alleged promise that Madison Hemings said Jefferson made to Hemings about when her children would be freed. The strongest evidence for a relationship between Jefferson and Hemings is what happened to Hemings's children. They all left Monticello at age twenty-one or, in the case of Beverley, two years after his twenty-first birthday, the same year that Harriet Hemings turned twenty-one. Beverley's delay may provide an answer to the concern about whether the extremely paternalistic Jefferson would have sent a twenty-one-year-old woman who had lived on a farm all of her life off alone to a big city. Jefferson's records indicate that Beverley left in 1822 before Harriet; she may have been sent to meet her older brother.

That these four siblings' freedom was tied to their coming of age is significant because Jefferson freed no other slave in this fashion. The other people he freed were older men who had rendered valuable services to him over the years. Jefferson's freeing of Harriet Hemings, the lone female among the group, was carried out under circumstances that suggest a high degree of involvement on his part. The only female slave that Jefferson ever freed was the daughter of Sally Hemings.

Another factor in the treatment of Sally Hemings's children is the assignment of what seem to have been private baby-sitters. Jefferson constructed the slave cabins to allow for communal care of babies by young children while their mothers worked. But when Sally Hemings gave birth to her daughter Harriet in 1795, a young girl named Edy was sent to live with Hemings apparently to serve as a private baby-sitter. After some time Edy's younger sister Aggey replaced her, and when Harriet died, Aggey moved back in with her parents. This arrangement was repeated in 1799 when Hemings gave birth to a daughter who seems to have died before being named. A girl named Thenia went to live with Hemings to care for the child, and when that baby died, Thenia moved back in with her parents.

It has been suggested that this arrangement allowed Hemings to continue to work in the big house. However, it was not followed when any other of Hemings's children were born. Several possible reasons come to mind. The two Hemings children who were cared for by Edy, Aggey, and Thenia may have been sickly from birth and required more constant monitoring than could be provided in the communal care setting. There is no indication that the arrangement was Jefferson's idea, but Hemings must have consulted him about it, so that this could be cited as an example of what Thomas Gibbons meant when he said Sally Hemings had been pampered. The other things setting these two children apart is that both were born when Jefferson was at home and when Hemings had no older children to help care for them. The first Harriet Hemings was born when Jefferson had retired from George Washington's cabinet. The unnamed child was born at the end of Jefferson's term as vice president. Jefferson was also at home when Eston Hemings was born, but by that time Beverley was ten and the second Harriet was eight, suitable ages to be child minders. Hemings's three other children were born when Jefferson was away and had no special attendants. This suggests that whatever Sally Hemings's role at Monticello was, it could not be neglected when Jefferson was at home, or likely to be at home, for any extended period.

The items concerning the treatment of Sally Hemings's children come to us from records or declarative statements from witnesses that tie Thomas Jefferson to some action or circumstance. There are also some items that are suggestive but less concrete.

All of Sally Hemings's children but one were given the names of people in the Jefferson-Randolph family tree who can be connected to Thomas Jefferson. The first son had the same name as a Jefferson kinsman associated with one of Jefferson's father's notable achievements. The only daughter had the name of a cousin who was a frequent visitor to Monticello and whose husband was given a job in the Jefferson administration. The third son was given the name of Jefferson's first cousin, his neighbor and close friend. The only Hemings child who was not named for a Randolph bore the name of another of Jefferson's closest friends.

It is important to note that Hemings's last two sons were given the names of people closely associated with Thomas Jefferson even after Jefferson had been publicly charged with having an affair with Hemings. If the charge was not true, it seems especially likely that Jefferson, for the sake of his white family if not for himself, would have prevented Sally Hemings from taking these actions on her own. It seems needlessly reckless and cruel for the Carr brothers to have given these children the names of individuals so closely linked to their uncle when they understood the delicate nature of the problem Jefferson faced with respect to the Hemings story.

All of the children Jefferson had with Martha Jefferson were given the names of people from within his family, though it is not known who chose the names. Jefferson did name his grandchildren and chose either Randolph names or the names of other people who were important in his life. The Carr brothers did not name any of their many white sons for people in the Randolph family but instead gave them combined names from the Carr family and from their wives' families. That they would bestow more socially prominent names on their black sons seems implausible, particularly in a society obsessed by family relationships.

The records show that all three of Hemings's sons played the same instrument associated with Thomas Jefferson, the violin. They played well enough for her oldest son to be asked to play at dances at Monticello, for someone to comment upon her middle son's facility with the instrument, and for her youngest son to make a good living as a professional musician. This raises the possibility that Jefferson may have stimulated their interest in the violin, given them their instruments, and provided lessons or taught them himself.

Of course, neither Jefferson's encouragement nor his genes were necessary for Hemings's sons to have been naturally gifted musicians. The Hemings family was quite creative in other areas. Still, this circumstance should be considered along with the other information that we know about Hemings's children in weighing whether Madison Hemings and Israel Jefferson were telling the truth. All three brothers were conceived when Jefferson was home from one of his many absences from Monticello, all three looked like Jefferson, all three were trained by Jefferson's best slave artisan, all three played the violin, all three went free in their early twenties with Jefferson's approval. There is a lockstep quality to the progression of Hemings's sons through childhood that suggests that Jefferson singled them out for a particular reason.

Isaac Jefferson's cryptic comment that Beverley set off a balloon in Petersburg, Virginia, and that Madison Hemings was there when it happened is one of the more exasperating references in this whole story. One wonders what Charles Campbell, who took down Isaac's memories, could have been thinking as Isaac spoke. Why didn't he ask, "Balloon, Isaac? What balloon?" It evidently happened because Isaac remembered it and Madison even went down to see it. Were Beverley Hemings's interests along these lines spurred by Jefferson, who expressed a long-term interest in ballooning?

Beverley and Harriet, Hemings's two oldest children, passed for white and married white people. The youngest married a black woman who was white enough to pass for white and, at a later point in life, changed his racial designation. Madison Hemings described the families that his two older siblings married into as being "in good standing" and "in good circumstances." Hemings was not necessarily saying that these families were rich or prominent, but clearly he meant that they were respectable people. The Hemings children's ability to deal with white spouses and in-laws suggests that they may have been prepared as young people to take on this role.

Ascending a balloon is no small achievement. In addition to a knowledge of science, it requires money and leisure time. Marrying into a family "in good circumstances" could have provided Beverley Hemings with both. That a runaway slave from Monticello could end up in this position suggests that his childhood was privileged, even by Hemings family standards.

Consider the suppositions now required to support the Carr brothers theory. The Carr brothers, who lived close to Monticello, could only conceive children during the few months of each year when Thomas Jefferson was at Monticello. The Carr children produced under these circumstances all looked like Thomas Jefferson, and they were given the names of people who were connected to Thomas Jefferson, two of them his closest friends. The Carr sons were trained in their youth to play the instrument that Thomas Jefferson was noted for playing. Then one of the Carr sons grew up to engage in ascending balloons, an activity that fascinated Thomas Jefferson, that he bought books about, and that he wrote and spoke of on numerous occasions. That son of one of the Carr brothers returned to Virginia from his flight from slavery to ascend a balloon, perhaps on the Fourth of July, along an avenue named in honor of Thomas Jefferson.

The Freeing of Sally Hemings

It is unclear how Sally Hemings obtained her freedom. Madison Hemings did not mention any promise on the part of Jefferson to free her, simply saying that shortly after Jefferson's death, he and his brother took their mother to live with them. Perhaps her freedom was never an issue. In any event, it is not difficult to understand why it would make more sense for Sally Hemings's freedom to be achieved through informal means. Why reopen a scandal in so spectacular a fashion as putting Sally Hemings's name in Jefferson's will, when the desired result could be achieved by other means? The most important thing that Jefferson did in his will with respect to the Hemingses was to ensure that Madison and Eston would have the legal right to remain in Virginia. They could work and move about without fear of exile. Their freedom and status gave protection to their mother, who by the standards of the day was an old woman and therefore much less likely to be bothered.

Other Considerations

That people gossiped in the 1790s and 1800s about Jefferson's relationship with Hemings does not prove that the relationship existed. The gossip is still relevant because it provides an explanation for Jefferson's actions toward the four Hemings siblings. Significantly, that possible explanation arose before he took those actions. Unlike Ellen Coolidge's explanation that "they were sufficiently white to pass for white," still offered by some historians today, the gossip about Jefferson's parental connection to the children was not an after-the-fact rationale. The people who were doing the talking had no interest in explaining anything; they were merely gossiping. They had no way of knowing that Jefferson at a later date would take actions that seemed to confirm the substance of their gossip. Ellen Coolidge, on the other hand, had a vested interest in trying to explain a circumstance in the life of her family that looked suspicious. She made her statement long after all of the major participants in the story were dead.

On the other hand, there are no documents or statements indicating that at the time the children were being born anyone thought the Carr brothers were involved with Sally Hemings. Although T. J. Randolph and Ellen Coolidge claimed that the Carr brothers' activities were notorious, no contemporary reports of rumors or statements about their relationships with Sally Hemings or other black women at Monticello have ever been offered to support Randolph's and Coolidge's assertions. During the years of the Callender crisis, Jefferson supporters and detractors looked for information to help their respective causes, but there is no indication that the brothers' names ever came up. Even if Jefferson did not want the Carrs mentioned, others who wanted Jefferson to stay in power most likely would have put them forward as candidates, even if they did not use the brothers' names. The biographer James Parton did just that when he absolved Jefferson and referred to "a near relation" of Jefferson's as the father of Hemings's children.

Contemporary talk about the Carrs and Sally Hemings would not prove that they were the fathers of her children. It would be some evidence that could be weighed along with T. J. Randolph and Ellen Coolidge's statements, particularly if it dated to the time before those two individuals came of age. There are not even any records indicating that the Carrs and Hemings had dealings of any kind with one another. The only information we have is based upon the statements of T. J. Randolph as recounted by his sister and by a biographer of Jefferson. Edmund Bacon's elliptical reference may have been to one of the Carrs, but there is no extrinsic evidence to support the proposition. Bacon's interest in protecting his former employer's reputation and the two grandchildren's interest in protecting the reputation of their grandfather should be given equal weight in considering the value of their statements.

In contrast, Madison Hemings's statement and that of Israel Jefferson can be supported by known aspects of the lives of Sally Hemings's children. There is evidence besides these men's statements to indicate that Jefferson treated Sally Hemings and her children with special favor. Her offspring fared better than any other group of siblings at Monticello. This circumstance was the direct result of actions that Thomas Jefferson took with respect to them, actions that were contrary to Jefferson's own interests and the interests of his white family. The only question is why he took them.

7

Conclusion

The Corrosive Nature of the Enterprise of Defense

I HAVE TRIED to approach the writings of scholars and commentators on the subject of Thomas Jefferson and Sally Hemings as though their considerations represented serious attempts to get at the truth of the story. I wanted to consider how those upon whom we have relied to provide assessments of this issue approached the question. To what standard should they have been held? What kind of questions should they have asked of themselves and of their sources? What did these historians actually ask? And, to measure their commitment to ferreting out the truth, how did they respond to information that tended to favor the side to which they may have been personally opposed?

It is my belief that those who are considered Jefferson scholars have never made a serious and objective attempt to get at the truth of this matter. This is not a criticism of their work on any other aspect of Thomas Jefferson's life or any other subject about which they have written. Indeed, it is because of the impressive work produced by some of these scholars that journalists and other members of the public have given them the presumption of expertise and believability on this matter. That presumption can no longer be sustained.

The failure to look more closely into the identities of the parties involved, the too ready acceptance and active promotion of the Carr brothers story, the reliance upon stereotypes in the place of investigation and analysis, all indicate that most Jefferson scholars decided from the outset that this story was not true and that if they had anything to do with it, no one would come to think otherwise. In the most fundamental sense, the enterprise of defense has had little to do with expanding people's knowledge of Thomas Jefferson or the other participants in the story. The goal has been quite the opposite: to restrict knowledge as a way of controlling the allowable discourse on this subject.

This attitude betrays a basic disrespect for readers of history. One of the most disheartening things about going through this material was to see the extent to which some of the authors seem to have relied on their expectation that most readers would never check, or even be able to check, assertions they made. Historians' prejudices and individual desires to keep inviolate their particular image of Jefferson prevented a fair, hardheaded, and thorough presentation and consideration of all the facts.

The other example of disrespect for readers is the way in which Jefferson defenders dealt with "the opposition," which for all intents and purposes was one woman, Fawn Brodie. Critics of Brodie have picked the weakest of her arguments to criticize—such as the significance of Jefferson's "mulatto" landscape references—thus concealing the far stronger evidence that Brodie presented. That commentators often chose to make this one case of overspeculation a metaphor for the story as a whole reveals their lack of confidence in their own positions and probably, in some cases, their lack of familiarity with the material on this subject. Fawn Brodie is seen today as a hysteric in the grips of a romantic fantasy, deliberately distorting information in order to promote her point of view. On the other hand, the men whom I have discussed are seen as the levelheaded, clear-eyed experts on Thomas Jefferson, interested in the facts and nothing but the facts, influenced by no agenda or romantic fantasy of their own. I think we can see that view is not entirely correct. If any of the historians whom I have discussed had approached this issue with a commitment to finding the truth, instead of seeing their role as protecting their image of Thomas Jefferson, they most likely would have seen, and been willing to acknowledge, that there is more to the story than they have let on. There may not be as much as Fawn Brodie thought, but there is a great deal more than Jefferson defenders have been willing to admit.

There are many legitimate reasons to criticize Fawn Brodie. She was less than careful in her reading of documents and sometimes ran ahead of her evidence without making it clear that she was speculating. However, she made no errors more egregious than those of some of the Jefferson scholars discussed here. For all of her faults, Brodie at least tried to meet the opposition head-on. In her writings about Jefferson and Hemings, Brodie raised arguments against her position and attempted to provide answers to them. Sometimes she answered well, other times she failed miserably. An important point in her favor, however, is that she did not hide the ball.

Jefferson defenders, having staked their arguments on the notion of the impossibility or improbability of this story, could not afford to set before the readers all the known information about the lives of Sally Hemings and her children. They probably could not let themselves know them, either. The safer course was to rely on what they believed they knew about Thomas Jefferson— and on others' acceptance of their expertise on that general topic—and avoid any substantive investigation, analysis, or presentation of the facts in their writings. Had they done otherwise, they would never have been able to present, with any real degree of comfort, their expert judgment that the story was utterly without foundation. Even if they had made a strong argument in support of their view, there is enough evidence on the other side for reasonable people to believe that Madison Hemings was telling the truth.

At the outset I stated that my interest in writing about this subject was largely stimulated by reading the arguments advanced to prove Thomas Jefferson's innocence of the charge of miscegenation. Those efforts, I felt (and feel) led scholars into presenting both a warped view of black people and of the history of the South as well. If the historians whose works have been discussed here had stated, "I don't believe that Thomas Jefferson and Sally Hemings had a relationship. But there is no proof one way or the other," that would have been acceptable. The problem has arisen because they could not leave things at that. By taking the extra step and saying, "Now let me tell you why the story cannot be true," and by presenting truncated and in some cases downright misleading versions of the facts of this matter, they have done damage.

When one sets out to prove that something that is manifestly possible is impossible, one is on the road to recklessness. The personal attacks on Madison Hemings that seem rooted in his status as a former slave and, by extension, his race, rather than in any knowledge about him personally, are examples of this. Expressions of certainty as to the content of documents that one has not seen is another example. The willingness to overlook obvious flaws and contradictions in the statements of those upon whom one relies as sources is another. The creation of a story line for a romance between two people without any sure evidence that the two even knew each other is yet another example. I could go on.

Trying to prove the possible to be impossible also requires that one either distort or ignore reality. With their treatment of Madison and Sally Hemings, historians have pursued both courses. For almost forty years Madison Hemings's memoirs have been portrayed as something other than what they really were. In the process Hemings himself has been made a type of man that historians had no evidence he was. With a little effort they could have known that his story was not the product of a third party's imagination, sparing the world another insulting treatment of the testimony of a former slave.

Sally Hemings's life story has been distorted as well. Historians have failed to pull together and consider information about her that could give readers a sense of who she was and what sort of person she might have been. Although we do not know as much about Hemings as, say, Maria Cosway, enough things are known about her to make it clear that Sally Hemings could not have been the stereotype of a slave woman that historians seem to have wanted the public to assume she was.

Some might argue that the process of drawing a picture of Sally Hemings would involve too much speculation on the part of historians, who must rely only on facts. But the notion that Jefferson scholars or other historians deal only with hard facts, proven by documents, is false. The writing of history often involves speculation (sometimes called "interpretation"), and Jefferson specialists, as well as other historians, engage in it. Were history just a matter of hard facts and documents, we would need just one biography of Thomas Jefferson containing all the facts supported by authenticated documents, which could be updated any time a new document comes to light. It has not worked that way.

Think of the treatment of Martha Jefferson and Peter Jefferson. Relatively little is known about these two individuals, but historians have been willing to render opinions about their natures and personalities. Malone acknowledged the deficiencies in the records about Peter Jefferson. Yet he pulled together the little that was known and extrapolated from what he knew about Peter's son Thomas to arrive at what he thought to be the likely character of the father.

Why could not the same process have been followed for Sally Hemings? We know of her position as a young person at Monticello. We know that she had what was probably a life-defining experience of living in France. We can look to the successes of her children to get an idea of what she might have been like. All of these are the things that historians look to when they want to know someone. Of course, it is likely that the more one knows about Sally Hemings and presents to the public, the harder it is to make the claim that a Jefferson liaison with her would have been impossible.

Something valuable was lost with the determination to ignore the lives of the Hemingses in favor of protecting the image of Thomas Jefferson. The voices of blacks from that era are so few and so faint, information about the circumstances of their lives so sketchy, that any echo or glimpse should be presumed important and treated accordingly. We do not have to believe everything those voices tell us. But they should be carefully considered, and not dismissed in favor of mere stereotype.

Just because there are no family documents or letters saying that Thomas Jefferson was the father of Sally Hemings's children, why should this matter be thought off-limits for consideration? One can look to other sources of information. That there may be no definitive answer to the question from such an inquiry does not mean that the investigation is without value. Being realistic about the possibilities in life is also important, and historians have a responsibility to be candid about the possibilities. The end conclusion may be that Thomas Jefferson did not have a relationship with Sally Hemings, but to have generations of people believing that it would have been impossible for him to have done so and that there is no good evidence that he did does no one any good, because those ideas have no basis in reality.

Jefferson and Hemings: The Public View

At various times since James Callender first published the allegation that Sally Hemings was Thomas Jefferson's mistress, historians and commentators have noted with dismay that Americans appeared to be on the verge of accepting the story as a part of history. Henry Randall, in his three-volume biography of Jefferson published in 1858, voiced the concern that the story was "beginning to pass into pseudo 'history.'" During the 1950s and 1960s, as blacks began to question the available version of United States history, they looked to the testimony of blacks as a way of creating a more balanced view of that history. Madison Hemings's statement, along with those of various other descendants of the Hemings family, provided that kind of evidence. With the appearance of these statements, the story of Thomas Jefferson and Sally Hemings gained currency among some blacks and other supporters of the idea that history should include the perspectives of blacks and other minorities. Douglas Wilson has noted that college professors of today are surprised to find that their students accept the story of the Jefferson-Hemings relationship as fact.[1]

Indeed, it appears that there have been, probably from 1802 until today, a number of Americans who want to believe the story is true. Randall's statement, the reemergence of the story in the 1960s, and the speed with which Fawn Brodie's biography of Jefferson and Barbara Chase-Riboud's novel about Sally Hemings flew off the bookshelves support this. For whatever reason, the desire to believe this story persists.

While writing this book, I had a conversation with a journalist who had written a critical review of the movie *Jefferson in Paris*, which accepted the truth of the Jefferson-Hemings liaison. After he had, without realizing it, confirmed all of my suspicions about the way members of the public have been misled about this story, he asked me why I thought that the story has survived, despite all efforts by Jefferson scholars to kill it. I could only reply that I didn't know why members of the public seem so attached to the story. I said something about metaphors and Jefferson as representative of the American psyche at given periods in history, basically a quick version of Merrill Peterson's *Jefferson Image in the American Mind.*

After more thought on the matter, I have come to the conclusion that one answer to this question, with different components, stands out to me. It seems that some people may believe in the Jefferson-Hemings liaison because they have a particular view of human beings, and they seem determined to see Thomas Jefferson as a part of the species both as a slaveholder and as a man. It is possible that most people do not accept the romantic vision of the southern slaveholding gentleman that some modern historians claim to discount but rely upon much more than they may realize. The image of a set of gentlemen with particularly heightened sensibilities and characters is hard to reconcile with the reality of those men's involvement with a degrading and cruel social and economic system. This does not mean that there was no such thing as a southern gentleman. It means that even those who fit that term were human beings in whom the capacity for good and for bad was always present and those capacities must be considered in light of the society in which they lived.

That many members of the public accept Thomas Jefferson's greatness and his membership in the group called "gentlemen," but insist on keeping him within the human sphere can be seen in an incident that occurred when I took a trip to Monticello in connection with writing this book. Visitors to Monticello are offered several types of tours of the plantation. I decided to see Mulberry Row, the site of the dwellings of slaves at Monticello, and the interior of the main house. The guide for the tour of Mulberry Row was truly a teacher. Instead of just pointing at things and telling us what they were, he asked questions that made us reason our way to the likely answer, forcing us to consider the true nature of the system of which we were speaking.

I began to wonder if anyone would ask about Sally Hemings (it was hardly appropriate for me to do so); at the end of the tour, a black man, obviously of mixed ancestry, raised the issue. Our guide, in a matter-of-fact fashion, explained that some historians thought the story was true but a substantial majority of historians discounted it. This brought a "humph" and a slight shake of the head from the inquisitor. A woman raised her hand and asked why the historians did not believe the story. Our guide went through the list of reasons, with the major one being that historians felt that engaging in such a relationship would have been out of character for Thomas Jefferson. The woman responded that it did not seem out of character to her after what she had heard about Mulberry Row, and a few others in the group murmured their assent. She then said that she could not understand how anyone could think that a man who used others' labor for his pleasure in so many other

ways could not use a woman for such a universally recognized form of pleasure, especially if the woman may have liked him. By this time it was clear
that there was no way out of this, and the tour guide ended by saying that
because there was no definitive proof either way, they (meaning the Thomas
Jefferson Memorial Foundation) could not say the story was definitely true
or false. The only reasonable thing to be done is to present both sides of
the story.

In drawing the relationship between what she had learned about Mulberry Row and the Sally Hemings story, the woman hit upon the central problem with the defense that has been mounted to counter the miscegenation
charge: the story is believable to many precisely because of their knowledge
of Jefferson's actions in other regards. No doubt, for many, as an item of mal-
feasance on Jefferson's part, his having an affair with a woman who may have
felt about him the way visitors to Monticello are encouraged to feel would
seem trivial when compared to his making ten-year-old boys work in a nail
factory twelve hours a day. Jefferson scholars, on the other hand, having forgiven him for the mountain of depravity that was his involvement in slavery
despite his knowledge of the evils of the system, view what would be the relative molehill of his intimate involvement with a possibly willing slave woman
as the prime threat to his legacy.

While some historians try to lift Thomas Jefferson above the slave system
by invoking the notion of a southern gentleman's unbreakable code of honor,
ordinary citizens, upon viewing and considering the system those gentlemen
created, seem to have moved beyond the belief that such a code existed, other
than as a weak rationalization for otherwise barbarous activities. Even those
who believe there was a strong honor code seem to have far less faith in its
power to regulate human behavior than do some historians. In this view the
section of the code that forbade sexual or emotional intimacy with an individual slave could not have been so rigid that under certain circumstances, with
a particular person, that item in the code was never broken.

Just as people's ideas about the true nature of slaveholders make them
tend to believe the story about Jefferson and Hemings, people's ideas about
the nature of men may also point them in this direction. It may be hard for
some to believe that a man who had lived the life of a heterosexual male for
forty-three years, interested in women and having a loving marriage with one
woman, would cease such activity for the remaining forty years of his life,
without some physical or emotional ailment or some affirmed commitment
to a new higher purpose.

Most Americans probably do not want anything to have been wrong with

Thomas Jefferson. As there is no evidence that he experienced anything like a call to the priesthood after his dalliance with Maria Cosway, the only alternative is to face the unpalatable thought that there may have, indeed, been something wrong with him. An affair with Sally Hemings provides a believable answer to this dilemma. While Jefferson biographers are content with the picture of Jefferson alone, sitting in his room, fingering a lock of his deceased wife's hair for four decades, others contemplating this scene find this image disturbing. For them the thought that there may have been a Sally Hemings in his life brings more of a sense of relief than of horror. While his involvement in such a relationship might, for some, seem a troubling lapse on Jefferson's part, it would be a normal human lapse.

When nonhistorians consider Thomas Jefferson outside of the context of philosophy or politics, they focus on their own knowledge of human beings as they come to a conclusion about the possible nature of his personal life. They also do not seem ready to accept Jefferson historians' claim to know Thomas Jefferson and what he was capable of. Ordinary citizens may feel that they do not need an expert to tell them what a heterosexual man would or would not be likely to do when living in a household with an attractive woman. In truth, when all that is known about Thomas Jefferson, Sally Hemings, and her children is fairly set out, one does not have to be a Jefferson scholar or a trained historian to come to a reasonable conclusion about the likely nature of their relationship.

Moreover, each historian has his or her own version of Thomas Jefferson that is both influenced and limited by that historian's experiences and values. The version can be of enormous value, depending upon the talents, industry, and insight of the historian. But it has to be seen for what it is: a version of Thomas Jefferson that, most likely, will not encompass all he was and everything he was capable of being.

One of the most colorful episodes of Jefferson's second term was the visit of the ambassador from Tunis, Sidi Suliman Mellimelli. Mellimelli arrived in Washington wearing his traditional dress of "rich scarlet and gold silks topped by a twenty-yard turban of white muslin." Presenting his credentials to James Madison, he assured the secretary of state that he was happy with his accommodations and then requested that he and his entourage be provided with concubines. Madison acceded to his request and provided at State Department expense the services of, among others, "Georgia a Greek." Madison charged the expense to "appropriations to foreign intercourse."[2]

It is unlikely that James Madison acquiesced to Mellimelli's request without consulting Jefferson, for the president would have borne the brunt of any scandal that arose if anything went wrong. Others in Washington knew of this situation. William Plumer noted in his diary that "our government has, on his application, provided him with one or more women, with whom he spends a portion of the night." If Jefferson had said no, that particular accommodation would not have been made, so the president must have agreed to it. A few months after Mellimelli's departure, Madison joked about the State Department's payment for the concubines in a letter to Jefferson on another matter. Madison wrote, underlining the useful phrase, "It is not amiss to avoid narrowing too much the scope of the *appropriations to foreign intercourse,* which are terms of great latitude, and may be drawn on by any urgent and unforeseen occurrences."[3]

Nothing of this episode appears in Malone's six-volume biography of Thomas Jefferson or in other major biographies of Jefferson. Malone covered Mellimelli's visit in a short passage that noted his arrival and departure.[4] More important things happened in Jefferson's administrations, but few were more interesting or more humorous, with the possible exception of the gift to Jefferson of a mammoth cheese that he spent a long time trying to be rid of. This meeting of the Occident and the Orient gives a side of Jefferson and Madison that would surprise many Americans. But it does not fit the version of Thomas Jefferson that Dumas Malone and other biographers wanted to present to the world.

It is possible that had Jefferson angrily turned aside Mellimelli's request, this anecdote may have become an integral part of Jefferson lore, as that response would have fit the image of the straitlaced man who blushed when others told dirty jokes. Madison's biographer Irving Brant felt no problem in telling this story in the 1950s because he had no image to protect: his subject had never been accused of keeping a concubine. The predominate image of James Madison is that of a brilliant but somewhat drab and plain man very luckily married to a much younger beautiful and vivacious woman. The implications of the Mellimelli episode are more problematic for Jefferson defenders. To show Thomas Jefferson allowing government funds to be used to provide concubines for other men—and for his best friend to appear so comfortable with the matter that he would joke with him about it—would pose a problem for historians who had expended a great amount of energy quelling the story that Jefferson had a concubine of his own.

In an interview conducted in 1981, Dumas Malone was asked if he had ever "left out something that might discredit Jefferson in the eyes of others, or that has affected your view of him?" Malone replied:

The short answer is no; but I have to qualify this somewhat. The biographer can't put everything in his book; he has to select. He selects the things which he regards as characteristic of the person he is writing about. You come to have a pretty good knowledge of a person, and you find some things that are in character and some things that are not. There might be one action that would be very much out of character. For example, Jefferson is said to have never been profane. But suppose I found an instance when he was very profane, should I put it in or not? Is it worth doing? You have to answer questions like that from time to time, and you include things that are in accord with what you think the man was. The quotation which is in the Jefferson Memorial in Washington—"I have sworn upon the altar of God eternal hostility against every form of tyranny over the mind of man"—is recognized by all students of Jefferson as a supremely characteristic remark. Of course you put that one in. But you find something else which is not in character or is neutral, so you have to be selective. You can't put in everything. But consciously, no, I haven't dodged any difficult questions. Somebody may say I have.[5]

There is no question that we owe a tremendous debt to Dumas Malone for the energy and devotion he brought to the study of the life of Thomas Jefferson. Everyone who writes about Jefferson builds upon the foundation that he laid. Still, Malone's answer is deeply troubling. Malone's readers may not know that he was selective in the manner that he described, that he had made the choice to include or exclude particular information according to whether it fit his vision of Thomas Jefferson's character. I imagine that most readers have a somewhat different expectation from biographies, believing that they should contain, at a minimum, the record of the important things that a person did or said in life.

Of course one cannot put in everything, but why shouldn't the record of a person's life include that person's characteristic and uncharacteristic actions; all individuals are the sum total of both. Indeed, it is especially appropriate for the biographer to point out and reasonably discuss a subject's uncharacteristic actions, because they help to define the outer limits of that person's capabilities. Why shouldn't people know how far Thomas Jefferson would go in a given context? Isn't the lack of such knowledge what makes us underestimate or overestimate people? When we do not know of incidents in a person's life that show that he was capable of doing some things exactly like, or similar to, things we thought him incapable of doing, we really do not have the full picture of that person.

Ironically, twentieth-century scholars who voice alarm at the growing acceptance of the truth of the Hemings story do not understand how their defenses of Jefferson have contributed to people's belief in the story. The argument that it would be impossible or even highly unlikely for a man to perform some action because he had written letters highly critical of that action has little or no resonance with anyone living in the modern world. It is not that we have become more cynical or less credulous; we have come to know better, and are willing to say so. Our experiences have taught us. We know more about the personal lives and contradictions of our leaders and our fellow citizens than any other generation that has ever existed. We know about them faster, too. Things it might have taken several generations of historians to discover and communicate are revealed almost instantly. In addition, we know far more about the private lives of leaders, present and past, than people have ever known before.

Contradictions are always on display. We have seen people present themselves as belonging to one kind of family only to find that family was the opposite of its projected image. We have seen people thunder against homosexuals and homosexuality only to learn that they themselves were homosexual. We have seen people claim to be friends of certain racial groups when they in fact harbored great racial resentments against those groups.

It is not good enough to say with regard to this question, "Well, we live in the twentieth century and Thomas Jefferson lived in the eighteenth and nineteenth centuries." People had internal conflicts during those periods as well as today, probably more regarding the question of race and sex. Whites and blacks in the South often lived and interacted with one another under a system that made them, at once, enemies and intimates. How could such a system fail to promote internal conflicts?

To claim, even after reading all that has been written by or about a man, to know what that individual would or would not do in life—particularly with regard to sex—is to invite disbelief. Moreover, if there is any evidence to support the idea that the man performed the disputed act, the expert will be perceived as extremely naive or just devious, for no serious or honest person could suggest that an individual's beliefs and actions are always in complete accordance. Therefore, in the absence of a change in strategy on the part of Jefferson defenders or the discovery of conclusive proof that Thomas Jefferson was not the father of Sally Hemings's children, it is likely that the public's acceptance of the story will continue to grow.

Madison Hemings as Metaphor

One last word about Madison Hemings. For some, his mother, Sally Hemings, has come to be seen as a metaphor for the condition of blacks in American society. I would suggest that in some ways Madison Hemings may be an even better one. He was a black man who watched this three siblings voluntarily disappear into the white world. He chose to remain black and to speak for himself. When he spoke and presented a view of the world that many did not want to accept, he was vilified and ridiculed in a vicious manner. Then he was forgotten. Since his statement was rediscovered, he has been vilified and ridiculed again, as though nothing had happened in America between 1873 and the 1990s. Whether we think he was telling the truth or not, he, black people, and all Americans deserve better.

Blacks of today can reward those who suffered and endured for our bene-fit only through our present and future acts. The hope is that we, and those of any race who recognize their contributions and appreciate their struggle, will never leave their stories to be told by people whose primary interests lie elsewhere. We should understand the importance of defending the former slaves when we feel that they have been unfairly attacked. This does not mean that we travel down the road of defense at all cost—to claim what was not true was true. It means that we should let no negative charge, no offensive theory or supposition, no unsubstantiated claim about the nature of those who were forced to "labor" for the "happiness" of others, go unchallenged.[6] We can do no less.

Appendixes

Notes

Bibliography

Index

Appendix A

Key to Important Names

This is a list and brief description of the important people whom one interested in this subject should know. The first section is divided into family groups and miscellaneous individuals. The second section lists the historians who have dealt with this issue and when they wrote.

Historical Figures

The Hemings Family

Beverley Hemings—Full name William Beverley Hemings. Born in 1798. Son of Sally Hemings. Alleged son of Thomas Jefferson or Peter or Samuel Carr. Ran away from Monticello in 1822. Lived in Washington as a white man, marrying into a white family. Isaac Jefferson remembered him as being responsible for a balloon ascension in Petersburg, Virginia.

Critta Hemings—Sister of Sally Hemings. Daughter of Elizabeth Hemings and John Wayles. Mother of Jamey Hemings.

Elizabeth ("Betty") Hemings—Mother of Critta Hemings, James Hemings, John Hemings, Peter Hemings, Robert Hemings, and Sally Hemings. Grandmother of Jamey Hemings. Her other children do not figure into this story. Mistress of John Wayles.

Eston Hemings—Full name Thomas Eston Hemings. Born in 1808, died in 185–. Son of Sally Hemings. Alleged son of Thomas Jefferson or Peter or Samuel Carr. Freed by the terms of Thomas Jefferson's will executed in 1826. Resident of Chillicothe, Ohio, from the mid-1830s until the early 1850s. Violinist who led a popular society musical trio during his time in Ohio. Moved to Wisconsin and continued to make his living as musician until his death.

Harriet Hemings—Daughter of Sally Hemings. Alleged daughter of Thomas Jefferson or Peter or Samuel Carr. Born in 1801. Left Monticello for Philadelphia in 1822 with the aid of Jefferson and his overseer Edmund Bacon. Resided in Washington, passing for a white woman and marrying into a white family.

James Hemings—Son of Elizabeth Hemings and John Wayles. Born in 1765, died in 1801. Brother of Sally Hemings; uncle to Beverley, Harriet, Madison, and Eston Hemings. Accompanied Jefferson to Paris. Chef. Freed by Jefferson in 1796.

Jamey Hemings—Son of Sally Hemings's sister Critta. Cousin of Beverley, Harriet, Madison, and Eston Hemings. Born in 1787. Ran away from Monticello after brutal treatment at the hands of overseer Gabriel Lilly. Not to be confused with James Hemings.

John Hemings—Half brother of Sally Hemings. Son of Elizabeth Hemings and Joseph Neilson. Uncle to Beverley, Harriet, Madison, and Eston Hemings. Carpenter. Jefferson's most accomplished and valued slave artisan. Freed by Jefferson's will in 1826.

Madison Hemings—Full name James Madison Hemings. Born in 1805, died in 1877. Son of Sally Hemings. Alleged son of Thomas Jefferson or Peter or Samuel Carr. Interview printed in *Pike County (Ohio) Republican* in 1873, in which he said that he was the son of Thomas Jefferson. Freed by the terms of Thomas Jefferson's will executed in 1826. After his mother's death left Virginia and moved to Ohio, making his living as a carpenter and farmer until his death.

Peter Hemings—Son of Elizabeth Hemings and John Wayles. Born in 1770. A cook trained by his older brother James Hemings.

Robert Hemings—Son of Elizabeth Hemings and John Wayles. Brother of Sally Hemings. Born in 1762. One of two slaves formally emancipated by Thomas Jefferson in the 1790s. Died in 1794.

Sally Hemings—Probable given name Sarah. Alleged mistress of Thomas Jefferson. Born in 1773, died in 1835. Daughter of Elizabeth Hemings and John Wayles. Mother of Beverley, Harriet, Madison, and Eston Hemings, her children who lived to adulthood, and another Harriet and an unnamed daughter who both died in infancy. Alleged mother of Tom Hemings who may have become Tom Woodson.

Tom Hemings or Tom Woodson.—The child allegedly born to Sally Hemings shortly after her return from France with Thomas Jefferson.

The Jeffersons, Randolphs, and Carrs

Peter Carr—Nephew of Thomas Jefferson. Alleged lover of Sally Hemings and alleged father of her children. Born in 1770, died in 1815.

Samuel Carr—Nephew of Thomas Jefferson. Brother of Peter. Alleged lover of Sally Hemings and alleged father of her children. Born in 1771, died in 1855.

Ellen Randolph Coolidge—Granddaughter of Thomas Jefferson. Born in 1796, died in 1876. Daughter of Martha Jefferson Randolph and Thomas Mann Randolph, Jr. Wrote a letter to her husband saying that Samuel Carr was the father of Sally Hemings's children.

Mary Jefferson Eppes—Youngest surviving daughter of Thomas Jefferson and Martha Wayles Jefferson. Also called Maria and Polly. Born in 1778, died in 1804. Sally Hemings accompanied her to France in 1787. Married John Eppes.

Harriet Randolph Hackley—Sister of Thomas Mann Randolph, Thomas Jefferson's son-in-law. Frequent visitor to Monticello.

Martha Wayles Jefferson—Wife of ten years of Thomas Jefferson. Born in 1748, died in 1782. Daughter of John Wayles. Mother of two children who survived to adulthood, Martha and Mary ("Maria").

Thomas Jefferson—Author of the Declaration of Independence. Third president of the United States of America. Born in 1743, died in 1826. Alleged lover of Sally Hemings and father of her children.

David Meade Randolph—Cousin and enemy of Thomas Jefferson. Federal marshal who arrested and jailed James Callender. Credited by some historians with giving information about Sally Hemings to James Callender. Married to Mary Randolph, sister of Thomas Mann Randolph, Jr.

George Wythe Randolph—Youngest grandson of Thomas Jefferson. Born in 1818, died in 1867. Son of Martha Jefferson Randolph and Thomas Mann Randolph, Jr. His mother attempted to prove to him and his older brother that Jefferson could not have been the father of Sally Hemings's children.

Martha Jefferson Randolph—Oldest daughter of Thomas Jefferson. Also called Patsy. Born in 1772, died in 1836. Married to Thomas Mann Randolph, Jr. Mother of twelve children, including Thomas Jefferson Randolph, Ellen Randolph Coolidge, and George Wythe Randolph.

Thomas Eston Randolph—Thomas Jefferson's first cousin. Son of his mother's brother William Randolph. Jefferson's close friend and lessee of Jefferson's flour mill. Married to Jane Randolph, sister of Thomas Mann Randolph, Jr.

Thomas Jefferson Randolph—Oldest grandson of Thomas Jefferson. Born in 1792, died in 1875. Son of Martha Jefferson Randolph and Thomas Mann Randolph Jr. Told his grandfather's biographer that Peter Carr had confessed to being the father of Sally Hemings's children. Told his sister Ellen Randolph Coolidge that he had overheard Peter Carr saying that he and his brother were the fathers of Sally Hemings's children.

John Wayles—Father of Thomas Jefferson's wife, Martha Wayles Jefferson. Died in 1773. Father of Robert, James, Critta, Thenia, Peter, and Sally Hemings.

Miscellaneous Figures

Edmund Bacon—Thomas Jefferson's overseer at Monticello from 1806 to 1823.

James Callender—Journalist. First published allegation that Thomas Jefferson had fathered the children of Sally Hemings. A Jefferson supporter who turned against him after he was denied a job and after he heard stories about Jefferson's alleged relationship with Hemings.

Maria Cosway—English-Italian artist. Recipient of Thomas Jefferson's love letter "Dialogue between My Head and My Heart." It is generally thought that the relationship between the two was intense but platonic.

Isaac Jefferson—Former slave from Monticello. Memoirs taken down in 1842 in Petersburg, Virginia, by historian Charles Campbell. Born in 1781. Son of George and Ursula, house slaves at Monticello.

Israel Jefferson—Former slave from Monticello. Gave a statement to the *Pike County (Ohio) Republican* affirming Madison Hemings's assertion that Thomas Jefferson and Sally Hemings had children together. Born in 1800. Son of Edward and Jane Gillett, slaves at Monticello.

John A. Jones—Editor of the *Waverly Watchman*, rival newspaper to the *Pike County (Ohio) Republican*. Wrote an editorial ridiculing Madison Hemings's statement.

Meriwether Jones—Publisher of the *Richmond Examiner*. Led the response to James Callender's charges about Jefferson and Sally Hemings. (Not to be confused with Meriwether Lewis, who led the expedition to the West with William Clark.)

Thomas Turner—Virginian. In 1805 wrote a letter to a Boston newspaper in which he claimed that the Sally Hemings–Thomas Jefferson story was true. He also stated that John Wayles was reputedly the father of Sally Hemings, as well as Martha Jefferson. He identified Beverley Hemings as Sally Hemings's oldest child.

William Weaver—Federal marshal. Wrote in the margins near Madison Hemings's census data in 1870 that Hemings was the son of Thomas Jefferson.

S. F. Wetmore—Editor of the *Pike Country (Ohio) Republican*. District marshal who took the census for Pike County in 1870. Wrote down and published Madison Hemings's memoirs in 1873.

The Historians and the Novelist

Douglass Adair.—Author of "The Jefferson Scandals," essay published in a collection of his works entitled *Fame and the Founding Fathers*. The piece was written in the early 1960s but was not published until 1974, after Adair's death.

Fawn Brodie.—Wrote controversial biography on Jefferson entitled *Thomas Jefferson: An Intimate History* published in 1974. Accepted Madison Hemings's statement that he and his siblings were the sons of Sally Hemings and Thomas Jefferson.

Virginius Dabney.—Wrote *The Jefferson Scandals*, published in 1981, a rebuttal to Brodie's biography of Thomas Jefferson and Chase-Riboud's novel *Sally Hemings*. A direct descendant of Thomas Jefferson's sister Martha Carr.

Dumas Malone.—Author of the six-volume biography of Jefferson, *Jefferson and His Time*, published between 1948 and 1981. Considered the foremost authority on Thomas Jefferson.

John C. Miller.—Wrote *The Wolf by the Ears: Thomas Jefferson and Slavery*, published in 1977.

James Parton.—Early biographer of Jefferson. Published *The Life of Thomas Jefferson* in 1874. Recipient of a letter from Henry Stephens Randall alleging that one of Jefferson's nephews fathered Sally Hemings's children.

Merrill Peterson.—Author of *The Jefferson Image in the Mind of America*, published in 1960, in which he dealt explicitly and extensively with Madison Hemings's statement to the *Pike Country (Ohio) Republican*.

Hamilton Pierson.—Author of *Jefferson at Monticello*, published in 1862, which records the recollections of Edmund Bacon, Jefferson's overseer at Monticello.

Henry Stephens Randall.—Published a three-volume biography of Jefferson in 1858. Wrote a letter to James Parton stating that Jefferson's grandson T. J. Randolph said that one of the Carr brothers, not Jefferson, was the father of Sally Hemings's children.

Willard Sterne Randall.—Author of *Thomas Jefferson: A Life*, published in 1993.

Barbara Chase-Riboud.—Author of *Sally Hemings*, a historical novel based upon the Thomas Jefferson–Sally Hemings story, published 1978. Also wrote *The President's Daughter*, a historical novel about Harriet Hemings's departure from Monticello and her life afterward, published in 1994.

Appendix B

The Memoirs of Madison Hemings

I never knew of but one white man who bore the name of Hemings; he was an Englishman and my great grandfather. He was captain of an English tracking vessel which sailed between England and Williamsburg, Va., then quite a port. My great-grandmother was a fullblooded African, and possibly a native of that country. She was the property of John Wales, a Welchman. Capt. Hemings happened to be in the port of Williamsburg at the time my grandmother was born, and acknowledging her fatherhood he tried to purchase her of Mr. Wales, who would not part with the child, though he was offered an extraordinarily large price for her. She was named Elizabeth Hemings. Being thwarted in the purchase, and determined to own his own flesh and blood he resolved to take the child by force or stealth, but the knowledge of his intention coming to John Wales' ears, through leaky fellow servants of the mother, she and the child were taken into the "great house" under their master's immediate care. I have been informed that it was not the extra value of that child over other slave children that induced Mr. Wales to refuse to sell it, for slave masters then, as in later days, had no compunctions of conscience which restrained them from parting mother and child of however tender age, but he was restrained by the fact that just about that time amalgamation began, and the child was so great a curiosity that its owner desired to raise it himself that he might see its outcome. Capt. Hemings soon afterwards sailed from Williamsburg, never to return. Such is the story that comes down to me.

Elizabeth Hemings grew to womanhood in the family of John Wales, whose wife dying she (Elizabeth) was taken by the widower Wales as his concubine, by whom she had six children—three sons and three daughters, viz: Robert, James, Peter, Critty, Sally and Thena. These children went by the name of Hemings.

Williamsburg was the capital of Virginia, and of course it was an aristocratic place, where the "bloods" of the Colony and the new State most did congregate. Thomas Jefferson, the author of the Declaration of Independence, was educated at William and Mary College, which had its seat at Williamsburg. He afterwards studied law with Geo. Wythe, and practiced law at the bar of the general court of the Colony. He was afterwards elected a member of the provincial legislature from Albemarle county. Thos. Jefferson was a visitor at the "great house" of John Wales, who had children about his own age. He formed the acquaintance of his daughter Martha (I believe that was her name, though I am not positively sure,) and intimacy sprang up between them which ripened into love, and they were married. They afterwards went to live at his country seat Monticello, and in course of time had born to them a daughter whom they named Martha. About the time she was born my mother, the second daughter of John Wales and Elizabeth Hemings was born. On the death of John Wales, my grandmother, his concubine, and her children by him fell to Martha, Thomas Jefferson's wife, and consequently became the property of Thomas Jefferson, who in the course of time became famous, and was appointed minister to France during our revolutionary troubles, or soon after independence was gained. About the time of the appointment and before he was ready to leave the country his wife died, and as soon after her interment as he could attend to and arrange his domestic affairs in accordance with the changed circumstances of his family in consequence of this misfortune (I think not more than three weeks thereafter) he left for France, taking his eldest daughter with him. He had sons born to him, but they died in early infancy, so he then had but two children—Martha and Maria. The latter was left home, but afterwards was ordered to follow him to France. She was three years or so younger than Martha. My mother accompanied her as a body servant. When Mr. Jefferson went to France Martha was just budding into womanhood. Their stay (my mother's and Maria's) was about eighteen months. But during that time my mother became Mr. Jefferson's concubine, and when he was called back home she was *enciente* by him. He desired to bring my mother back to Virginia with him but she demurred. She was just beginning to understand the French language well, and in France she was free, while if she returned to Virginia she would be re-enslaved. So she refused to return with him. To induce her to do so he promised her extraordinary privileges, and made a solemn pledge that her children should be freed at the age of twenty-one years. In consequence of his promise, on which she implicitly relied, she returned with him to Virginia. Soon after their arrival, she gave birth to a child, of whom Thomas Jefferson was the father. It lived but a short time. She gave birth to four others, and Jefferson was the father of all of them. Their names were Beverly, Harriet, Madison (myself), and Eston—three sons and one daughter. We all became free agreeably to the treaty entered into by our parents before we were born. We all married and have raised families.

Beverly left Monticello and went to Washington as a white man. He married a white woman in Maryland, and their only child, a daughter, was not known by the white folks to have any colored blood coursing in her veins. Beverly's wife's family were people in good circumstances.

Harriet married a white man in good standing in Washington City, whose name I could give, but will not, for prudential reasons. She raised a family of children, and so far as I know they were never suspected of being tainted with African blood in the community where she lived or lives. I have not heard from her for ten years, and do not know whether she is dead or alive. She thought it to her interest, on going to Washington, to assume the role of a white woman, and by her dress and conduct as such I am not aware that her identity as Harriet Hemings of Monticello has ever been discovered.

Eston married a colored woman in Virginia, and moved from there to Ohio, and lived in Chillicothe several years. In the fall of 1852 he removed to Wisconsin, where he died a year or two afterwards. He left three children.

As to myself, I was named Madison by the wife of James Madison, who was afterwards President of the United States. Mrs. Madison happened to be at Monticello at the time of my birth, and begged the privilege of naming me, promising my mother a fine present for the honor. She consented, and Mrs. Madison dubbed me by the name I now acknowledge, but like many promises of white folks to the slaves she never gave my mother anything. I was born at my father's seat of Monticello, in Albemarle county, Va., near Charlottesville, on the 19th day of January, 1805. My very earliest recollections are of my grandmother Elizabeth Hemings. That was when I was about three years old. She was sick and upon her death bed. I was eating a piece of bread and asked if she would have some. She replied: "No, granny don't want bread any more." She shortly afterwards breathed her last. I have only a faint recollection of her.

Of my father, Thomas Jefferson, I knew more of his domestic than his public life during his life time. It is only since his death that I have learned much of the latter, except that he was considered as a foremost man in the land, and held many important trusts, including that of President. I learned to read by inducing the white children to teach me the letters and something more; what else I know of books I have picked up here and there till now I can read and write. I was almost 21½ years of age when my father died on the 4th of July, 1826.

About his own home he was the quietest of men. He was hardly ever known to get angry, though sometimes he was irritated when matters went wrong, but even then he hardly ever allowed himself to be made unhappy any great length of time. Unlike Washington he had but little taste or care for agricultural pursuits. He left matters pertaining to his plantations mostly with his stewards and overseers. He always had mechanics at work for him, such as carpenters, blacksmiths, shoemakers, coopers, &c. It was his mechanics he seemed mostly to direct, and in their operations he took great interest. Almost every day of his later years he might have been seen among them. He occupied much of the time in his office engaged in correspondence and reading and writing. His general temperament was smooth and even; he was very undemonstrative. He was uniformly kind to all about him. He was not in the habit of showing partiality or fatherly affection to us children. We were the only children of his by a slave woman. He was affectionate toward his white grandchildren, of whom he had fourteen, twelve of whom lived to manhood and womanhood. His daughter Martha married Thomas Mann Randolph by whom she had thirteen children. Two died in infancy. The names of the living were Ann, Thomas Jefferson, Ellen, Cornelia, Virginia, Mary, James, Benj. Franklin, Lewis Madison, Septemia and Geo. Wythe. Thos. Jefferson Randolph was Chairman of the Democratic National Convention in Baltimore last spring which nominated Horace Greeley for the Presidency, and Geo. Wythe Randolph was Jeff. Davis' first Secretary of War in the late "unpleasantness."

Maria married John Epps, and raised one son—Francis.

My father generally enjoyed excellent health. I never knew him to have but one spell of sickness, and that was caused by a visit to the Warm Springs in 1818.

Till within three weeks of his death he was hale and hearty, and at the age of 83 years walked erect and with a stately tread. I am now 68, and I well remember that he was a much smarter man physically, even at that age, than I am.

When I was fourteen years old I was put to the carpenter trade under the charge of John Hemings, the youngest son of my grandmother. His father's name was Nelson, who was an Englishman. She had seven children by white men and seven by colored men—fourteen in all. My brothers, sister Harriet and myself, were used alike. We were permitted to stay about the "great house," and only required to do such light work as going on errands. Harriet learned to spin and to weave in a little factory on the home plantation. We were free from the dread of having to be slaves all our lives long, and were measurably happy. We were always permitted to be with our mother, who was well used. It was her duty, all her life which I can remember, up to the time of father's death, to take care of his chamber and wardrobe, look after us children and do such light work as sewing, &c. Provision was made in the will of our father that we should be free when we arrived at the age of 21 years. We had all passed that period when he died but Eston, and he was given the remainder of his time shortly after. He and I rented a house and took mother to live with us, till her death, which event occurred in 1835.

In 1834 I married Mary McCoy. Her grandmother was a slave, and lived with her master, Stephen Hughes, near Charlottesville, as his wife. She was manumitted by him, which made their children free born. Mary McCoy's mother was his daughter. I was about 28 and she 22 years of age when we married. We lived and labored together in Virginia till 1836, when we voluntarily left and came to Ohio. We settled in Pebble township, Pike County. We lived there four or five years and during my stay in the county I worked at my trade on and off for about four years. Joseph Sewell was my first employer. I built for him what is now known as Rizzleport No. 2 in Waverly. I afterwards worked for George Wolf Senior. and I did the carpenter work for the brick building now owned by John J. Kellison in which the Pike County Republican is printed. I worked for and with Micajab Hinson. I found him to be a very clever man. I also reconstructed the building on the corner of Market and Water Streets from a store to a hotel for the late Judge Jacob Row.

When we came from Virginia we brought one daughter (Sarah) with us, leaving the dust of a son in the soil near Monticello. We have born to us in this State nine children. Two are dead. The names of the living, besides Sarah, are Harriet, Mary Ann, Catharine, Jane, William Beverly, James Madison, Ellen Wales. Thomas Eston died in the Andersonville prison pen, and Julia died at home. William, James and Ellen are unmarried and live at home in Huntington township, Ross County. All the others are married and raising families. My post office address is Pee Pee, Pike County Ohio.

"Life among the Lowly, No. 1," *Pike County (Ohio) Republican*, March 13, 1873.

Appendix C

The Memoirs of Israel Jefferson

I was born at Monticello, the seat of Thos. Jefferson, third President of the United States, December 25—Christmas day in the morning. The year, I suppose was 1797. My earliest recollections are the exciting events attending the preparations of Mr. Jefferson and other members of his family on their removal to Washington, D.C., where he was to take upon himself the responsibilities of the Executive of the United States for four years.

My mother's name was Jane. She was a slave of Thomas Jefferson's and was born and always resided at Monticello till about five years after the death of Mr. Jefferson. She was sold, after his death, by the administrator, to a Mr. Joel Brown, and was taken to Charlottesville, where she died in 1837. She was the mother of thirteen children, all by one father, whose name was Edward Gillet. The children's names were Barnaby, Edward, Priscilla, Agnes, Richard, James, Fanny, Lucy, Gilly, Israel, Moses, Susan, and Jane—seven sons and six daughters. All these children, except myself, bore the surname of Gillett. The reason for my name being called Jefferson will appear in the proper place.

After Mr. Jefferson had left his home to assume the duties of the office of President, all became quiet again in Monticello. But as he was esteemed by both whites and blacks as a very great man, his return home, for a brief period, was a great event. His visits were frequent, and attended with considerable ceremony. It was a time looked forward to with great interest by his servants, for when he came home many of them, especially the leading ones, were sure to receive presents from his hands. He was re-elected President in 1804, and took his seat for the second term in 1805. Of course, his final term closed in March 1809, when he was succeeded by James Madison. At that time I was upwards of twelve years of age.

About the time Mr. Jefferson took his seat as President for the second term, I began the labors of life as a waiter at the family table, and till Mr. J. died was retained in Monticello and very near his person. When about ten years of age, I was employed as postillion. Mr. Jefferson rode in a splendid carriage drawn by four horses. He called the carriage the landau. It was sort of a double chaise. When the weather was pleasant the occupants could enjoy the open air; when it was rainy, they were protected from it by the closing of the covering, which fell back from the middle. It was splendidly ornamented with silver trimmings, and, taken altogether, was the nicest affair in those aristocratic regions. The harness was made in Paris, France, silver mounted, and quite in keeping with the elegant carriage. The horses were well matched, and of a bay color. I am now speaking of the years of my boyhood and early manhood. My brother Gilly, being older than

249

I was, rode the near wheel horse, while I was mounted on the near leader. In course of time, Mr. Jefferson rode less ostentatiously, and the leaders were left off. Then but one rider was needed. Sometimes brother Gilly acted as postillion; at other times I was employed. We were both retained about the person of our master as long as he lived. Mr. Jefferson died on the 4th day of July, 1826, when I was upwards of 29 years of age. His death was an affair of great moment and uncertainty to us slaves, for Mr. Jefferson provided for the freedom of 7 servants only: Sally, his chambermaid, who took the name of Hemings, her four children— Beverly, Harriet, Madison and Eston—John Hemmings, brother to Sally, and Burrell Colburn [Burwell Colbert], an old and faithful body servant. Madison Hemmings is now a resident of Ross county, Ohio, whose history you gave in the Republican of March 13, 1873. All the rest of us were sold from the auction block, by order of Jefferson Randolph, his grandson and administrator. The sale took place in 1829, three years after Mr. Jefferson's death.

I was purchased by Thomas Walker Gilmer, I married Mary Ann Colter, a slave, by whom I had four children—Taliola (a daughter), Banobo (a son), Susan and John. As they were born slaves they took the usual course of most others in the same condition of life. I do not know where they now are, if living; but the last I heard of them they were in Florida and Virginia. My wife died, and while a servant of Mr. Gilmer, I married my present wife, widow Elizabeth Randolph, who was then mother to ten children. Her maiden name was Elizabeth Farrow. Her mother was a white woman named Martha Thackey. Consequently, Elizabeth, (my present wife) was free-born. She supposes that she was born about 1793–1794. Of her ten children, only two are living—Julia, her first born, and wife of Charles Barnett, who live on an adjoining farm, and Elizabeth, wife of Henry Lewis, who resides within one mile of us.

My wife and I have lived together about thirty-five years. We came to Cincinnati, Ohio, where we were again married in conformity to the laws of this State. At the time we were first married I was in bondage; my wife free. When my first wife died I made up my mind I would never live with another slave woman. When Governor Gilmer was elected a representative to Congress, he desired to have me go on to Washington with him. But I demurred, I did not refuse, of course, but I laid before him my objections with such earnestness that he looked me in the face with his piercing eye, as if balancing in his mind whether to be soft or severe, and said,

"Israel, you have served me well; you are a faithful servant; now what will you give me for your freedom?"

"I reckon I will give you what you paid years ago—$500," I replied.

"How much will you give to bind the bargain?" he asked.

"Three hundred dollars," was my ready answer.

"When will you pay the remainder?"

"In one and two years."

And on these terms the bargain was concluded, and I was, for the first time, my own man, and almost free, but not quite, for it was against the laws of Virginia for a freed slave to remain in the State beyond a year and a day. Nor were the colored people not in slavery free; they were nominally so. When I came to Ohio I considered myself wholly free, and not till then.

And here let me say, that my good master, Governor Gilmer, was killed by the explosion of the gun Peacemaker, on board the Princeton, in 1842 or 1843, and had I gone to Washington with him it would have been my duty to keep very close to his person, and probably I would have been killed also, as others were.

I was bought in the name of my wife. We remained in Virginia several years on sufferance. At last we made up our minds to leave the confines of slavery and emigrate to a free State. We went to Charlottesville Court House, in Albemarle county, for my free papers. When there, the clerk, Mr. Garret, asked me what surname I would take, I hesitated, and he suggested that it should be Jefferson, because I was born at Monticello and had been a good and faithful servant to Thomas Jefferson. Besides, he said, it would give me more dignity to be called after so eminent a man. So I consented to adopt the surname Jefferson, and have been known by it ever since.

When I came to Cincinnati, I was employed as a waiter in a private house, at ten dollars a month for the first month. From that time on I received $20, till I went on board a steamboat, where I got higher wages still. In time, I found myself in receipt of $50 per month, regularly, and sometimes even more. I resided in Cincinnati about fourteen years, and from thence came on to the farm I am now on, in Pebble township, on Brushy Fork of Pee Pee creek. Have been here about sixteen years.

Since my residence in Ohio I have several times visited Monticello. My last visit was in the fall of 1866. Near there I found the same Jefferson Randolph, whose service as administrator I left more than forty years ago, at Monticello. He had grown old, and was outwardly surrounded by the evidence of former ease and opulence gone to decay. He was in poverty. He had lost, he told me, $80,000 in money by joining the South in rebellion against the government. Except his real estate, the rebellion stripped him of everything, save one old blind mule. He said that had he taken the advice of his sister, Mrs. Cooleridge [Ellen Coolidge], gone to New York, and remained there during the war, he could have saved the bulk of his property. But he was a rebel at heart, and chose to go with his people. Consequently, he was served as others had been—he had lost all his servants and nearly all his personal property of every kind. I went back to Virginia to find the proud and haughty Randolph in poverty at Edge Hill, within four miles of Monticello, where he was bred and born. Indeed, I then realized more than ever before, the great changes which time brings about in the affairs and circumstances of life.

Since I have been in Ohio I have learned to read and write, but my duties as a laborer would not permit me to acquire much of an education. But such as I possess I am truly thankful, and consider what education I have as a legitimate fruit of freedom.

The private life of Thomas Jefferson, from my earliest remembrances, in 1804, till the day of his death, was very familiar to me. For fourteen years I made the fire in his bedroom and private chamber, cleaned his office, dusted his books, run of errands and attended him about home. He used to ride out to his plantations almost every fair day, when at home, but unlike most other Southern gentlemen in similar circumstances, unaccompanied by any servant. Frequently gentlemen would call upon him on business of great importance, whom I used to usher into his presence, and sometimes I would be employed in burnishing or doing some other work in the room where they were. On such occasions I used to remain; otherwise I retired and left the gentlemen to confer together alone. In those times I minded but little concerning the conversations which took place between Mr. Jefferson and his visitors. But I well recollect a conversation he had with the great and good Lafayette, when he visited this country in 1824 and 1825, as it was of personal interest to me and mine. General Lafayette and his son George Washington, remained with Mr. Jefferson six weeks, and almost every day I took them out to a drive.

On the occasion I am now about to speak of, Gen. Lafayette and George were seated in the carriage with him. The conversation turned upon the condition of colored people—the slaves. Lafayette spoke indifferently; sometimes I could scarcely understand him. But on this occasion my ears were eagerly taking in every sound that proceeded from the venerable patriot's mouth.

Lafayette remarked that he thought that the slaves ought to be free; that no man could rightly hold ownership in his brother man; that he gave his best services to and spent his money in behalf of the Americans freely because he felt that they were fighting for a great and noble principle—the freedom of mankind; that instead of all being free a portion were held in bondage (which seemed to grieve his noble heart); that it would be mutually beneficial to masters and slaves if the latter were educated, and so on. Mr. Jefferson replied that he thought the time would come when the slaves would be free, but did not indicate when or in what manner they would get their freedom. He seemed to think that the time had not then arrived. To the latter proposition of Gen. Lafayette, Mr. Jefferson in part assented. He was in favor of teaching the slaves to learn to read print; that to teach them to write would enable them to forge papers, when they could no longer be kept in subjugation.

This conversation was very gratifying to me, and I treasured it up in my heart.

I know that it was a general statement among the older servants at Monticello, that Mr. Jefferson promised his wife, on her death bed, that he would not again marry. I also know that his servant, Sally Hemmings, (mother to my old friend and former companion at Monticello, Madison Hemmings,) was employed as his chamber-maid, and that Mr. Jefferson was on the most intimate terms with her; that, in fact, she was his concubine. This I know from my intimacy with both parties, and when Madison Hemmings declares that he is a natural son of Thomas Jefferson, the author of the Declaration of Independence, and that his brothers Beverly and Eston and sister Harriet are of the same parentage, I can as conscientiously confirm his statement as any other fact which I believe from circumstances but do not positively know.

I think that Mr. Jefferson was 84 years of age when he died. He was hardly ever sick, and till within two weeks of his death he walked erect without a staff or cane. He moved with the seeming alertness and sprightliness of youth.

"Life among the Lowly, No. 3," *Pike County (Ohio) Republican*, December 25, 1873.

Appendix D

Henry S. Randall to James Parton

Courtland Village, N.Y.
June 1, 1868

Dear Sir—

The "Dusky Sally Story"—the story that Mr. Jefferson kept one of his slaves, (Sally Hemings) as his mistress and had children by her, was once extensively believed by respectable men, and I believe both John Quincy Adams and our Bryant sounded poetical lyres on this very poetical subject!

Walking about mouldering Monticello one day with Col. T. J. Randolph (Mr. Jefferson's oldest grandson) he showed me a smoke blackened and sooty room in one of the collonades, and informed me it was Sally Henings' room. He asked me if I knew how the story of Mr. Jefferson's connexion with her originated. I told him I did not. "There was a better excuse for it, said he, than you might think: she had children which resembled Mr. Jefferson so closely that it was plain that they had his blood in their veins." He said in one case that the resemblance was so close, that at some distance or in the dusk the slave, dressed in the same way, might be mistaken for Mr. Jefferson.—He said in one instance, a gentleman dining with Mr. Jefferson, looked so startled as he raised his eyes from the latter to the servant behind him, that his discovery of the resemblance was perfectly obvious to all. Sally Henings was a house servant and her children were brought up house servants—so that the likeness between master and slave was blazoned to all the multitudes who visited this political Mecca.

Mr. Jefferson had two nephews, Peter Carr and Samuel Carr whom he brought up in his house. There were the sons of Mr. Jefferson's sister and her husband Dabney Carr that young and brilliant orator, described by Wirt, who shone so conspicuously in the dawn of the Revolution, but died in 17—. Peter was peculiarly gifted and amiable. Of Samuel I know less. But he became a man of repute and sat in the State Senate of Virginia. Col. Randolph informed me that Sally Henings was the mistress of Peter, and her sister Betsey the mistress of Samuel—and from these connections sprang the progeny which resembled Mr. Jefferson. Both the Henings girls were light colored and decidedly goodlooking. The Colonel said their connexion with the Carrs was perfectly notorious at Monticello, and scarcely disguised by the latter—never disavowed by them. Samuel's proceedings were particularly open.

Col. Randolph informed me that there was not the shadow of suspicion that Mr. Jefferson in this or any other instance ever had commerce with his female slaves. At the periods when these Carr children were born, he, Col. Randolph, had charge of Monticello. He gave all the general directions, gave out their clothes to the slaves, etc., etc. He said Sally Henings was treated, dressed, etc., exactly like the rest. He said Mr. Jefferson never locked the door of his room by day: and that he (Col. R.) slept within sound of his breathing at night. He said he had never seen a motion, or a look, or a circumstance which led him to suspect for an instant that there was a particle more of familiarity between Mr. Jefferson and Sally Henings than between him and the most repulsive servant in the establishment—and that no person ever living at Monticello dreamed of such a thing. With Betsy Henings, whose children also resembled him, his habitual meeting, was less frequent, and the chance for suspicion still less, and his conexion with her was never indeed alleged by any of our northern politicians, or *poets.*

Col. Randolph said that he had spent a good share of his life closely about Mr. Jefferson—at home and on journeys—in all sorts of circumstances and he fully believed him chaste and pure—as "immaculate a man as God ever created."

Mr. Jefferson's oldest daughter, Mrs. Gov. Randolph, took the Dusky Sally stories much to heart. But she never spoke to her sons but once on the subject. Not long before her death she called two of them—the Colonel and George Wythe Randolph—to her. She asked the Colonel if he remembered when "——— Henings (the slave who most resembled Mr. Jefferson) was born." He said he could answer by referring to the book containing the list of slaves. He turned to the book and found that the slave was born at the time supposed by Mrs. Randolph. She then directed her sons attention to the fact that Mr. Jefferson and Sally Henings could not have met—were far distant from each other—for fifteen months prior to such birth. She bade her sons remember this fact, and always to defend the character of their grandfather. It so happened when I was afterwards examining an old account book of the Jeffersons I came *pop* on the original entry of this slaves birth: and I was then able from well known circumstances to prove the fifteen months separation—but those circumstances had faded from my memory. I have no doubt I could recover them however did Mr. Jefferson's vindication in the least depend upon them.

Colonel Randolph said that a visitor at Monticello dropped a newspaper from his pocket or accidentally left it. After he was gone, he (Colonel R.) opened the paper and found some very insulting remarks about Mr. Jefferson's Mulatto Children. The Col. said he felt provoked. Peter and Sam Carr were lying not far off under a shade tree. He took the paper and put it in Peters hands, pointing out the article. Peter read it, tears coursing down his cheeks, and then handed it to Sam. Sam also shed tears. Peter exclaimed, "arnt you and I a couple of —— pretty fellows to bring this disgrace on poor old uncle who has always fed us! We ought to be —— by ——!"

I could give fifty more facts were there time, and were there any need of it, to show Mr. Jefferson's innocence of this and all similar offenses against propriety.

I asked Col. R. why on earth Mr. Jefferson did put these slaves who looked

like him out of the public sight by sending them to his Bedford estate or elsewhere—He said Mr. Jefferson never betrayed the least consciousness of the resemblance—and although he (Col. R.) had no doubt his mother, would have
been very glad to have them removed, that both and all venerated Mr. Jefferson
too deeply to broach such a topic to him. What suited him, satisfied them. Mr.
Jefferson was deeply attached to the Carrs—especially to Peter. He was extremely
indulgent to them and the idea of watching them for faults or vices probably
never occurred to him.

Do you ask why I did not state, or at least hint the above facts in my Life of
Jefferson? I wanted to do so, but Colonel Randolph, in this solitary case alone,
prohibited me from using at my discretion the information he had furnished me
with. When I rather pressed him on the point he said, pointing to the family
graveyard, "You are not bound to prove a negation. If I should allow you to take
Peter Carr's corpse into Court and plead guilty over it to shelter Mr. Jefferson, I
should not dare again to walk by his grave; he would rise and spurn me." I am
exceedingly glad Col. Randolph *did* overrule me in this particular. I should have
made a *shameful* mistake. If I had *unnecessarily* defended him (and it was purely
unnecessary to offer any defense) at the expense of a dear nephew—and a noble
man—hating a single folly.—

I write this currente calamo, and you will not understand that in telling what
Col. R. and others said, I claim to give the precise language. I give it as I *now*
recall it. I believe I hit at least the essential purport and spirit of it in every case.

Do you wonder that the above explanations were not made by Mr. Jeffersons
friends when the old Federal Party were hurling their missiles at him for keeping
a Congo Harem! Nobody could have furnished a hint of explanation outside of
the family. The secrets of an old Virginia manor house were like the secrets of an
Old Norman Castle. Dr. Dungleson, and Professor Tucker had lived years near
Mr. Jefferson, in the University, and were often at Monticello. They saw what
others saw. But Dr. D told me that neither he nor Professor T. ever heard the
subject *named* in Virginia. An awe and veneration was felt for Mr. Jefferson
among his neighbors which in their view rendered it shameful to even talk about
his name in such a connexion. Dr. D. told me that he never heard of Col. Randolph talking with anyone on the subject but me. But he said in his own secret
mind he had always believed the matter stood just as Col. Randolph explained
it to me.

You ask if I will not write a cheap Life of Jefferson of 600 pages, to go into
families who will not purchase a larger work. I some years ago commenced such
a condensed biography. I suspended the work when the storm of Civil War burst
over the land. I have not again resumed it. I may yet do so hereafter—I have been
strongly urged to the work by a prominent publishing house, and if I find time I
may again mount my old hobby.

I must again express my regret that I cannot send you a fine autograph letter
of Mr. Jefferson on some interesting topic—but I am stripped down to those his

family expected me to keep. But I send you some characteristic leaves—one from his draft of his Parliamentary Law.

Very truly yours,
Henry S. Randall

James Parton, Esq.

Appendix E

Ellen Randolph Coolidge to Joseph Coolidge

Edgehill
24 October 1858
I am just from church, a church originally planned by Grandpapa, where I heard a good sermon from an Episcopalian Clergyman, a young man, the Revd. Mr. Butler.

I have been talking freely with my brother Jefferson on the subject of the "yellow children" and will give you the substance of our conversation, with my subsequent reflections.

It is difficult to prove a negative. It is impossible to prove that Mr. Jefferson never had a coloured mistress or coloured children and that these children were never sold as slaves. The latter part of the charge however is disproved by its atrocity, and its utter disagreement with the general character and conduct of Mr. Jefferson, acknowledged to be a humane man and eminently a kind master. Would he who was always most considerate of the feelings and the well-being of his slaves, treat them barbarously only when they happened to be his own children, and leave them to be sold in a distant market when he might have left them free—as you know he did several of his slaves, directing his executor to petition the Legislature of Virginia for leave for them to remain in the State after they were free. Some of them are here to this day.

It was his principle (I know that of my own knowledge) to allow such of his slaves as were sufficiently white to pass for white men, to withdraw quietly from the plantation; it was called running away, but they were never reclaimed, I remember four instances of this, three young men and one girl, who walked away and staid away. Their whereabouts was perfectly known but they were left to themselves—for they were white enough to pass for white. Some of the children currently reported to be Mr. Jefferson's were about the age of his own grandchildren. Of course he must have been carrying on his intrigues in the midst of his daughters family and insulting the sanctity of the home by his profligacy. But he had a large family of grandchildren of all ages, older & younger. Young men and young girls. He lived, whenever he was at Monticello, and entirely for the last seventeen years of his life, in the midst of these young people, surrounded by them, his intercourse with them of the freest and most affectionate kind. How comes it that his immoralities were never suspected by his own family—that his daughter and her children rejected with horror and contempt the charges brought against him. That my brother, then a young man certain to know all that was going on behind the scenes, positively declares his indignant belief in the imputa-

258

tions and solemnly affirms that he never saw or heard the smallest thing which could lead him to suspect that his grandfather's life was other than perfectly pure. His apartments had no private entrance not perfectly accessible and visible to all the household. No female domestic ever entered his chambers except at hours when he was known not to be in the public gaze. But again I put it to any fair mind to decide if a man so admirable to his domestic character as Mr Jefferson, so devoted to his daughters and their children, so fond of their society, so tender, considerate, refined in his intercourse with them, so watchful over them in all respects, would be likely to rear a race of half-breeds under their eyes and carry on his low amours in the circle of his family.

Now many causes existed which might have given rise to suspicions, setting aside the inveterate rage and malice of Mr. Jefferson's traducers.

The house at Monticello was a long time in building and was principally built by Irish workmen. These men where known to have had children of whom the mothers were black women. But these women were much better pleased to have it supposed that such children were their master's. "Le Czar m'a fait l'honneur de me faire cet enfant." There were dissipated young men in the neighborhood who sought the society of the mulatresses and they in like manner were not anxious to establish any claim of paternity in the results of such associations.

One woman known to Mr. J. Q. Adams and others as "dusky Sally" was pretty notoriously the mistress of a married man, a near relation of Mr. Jefferson's, and there can be small question that her children were his. They were all fair and all set free at my grandfather's death, or had been suffered to absent themselves permanently before he died. The mother, Sally Hemmings, had accompanied Mr. Jefferson's younger daughter to Paris and was lady's maid to both sisters. Again I ask is it likely that so fond, so anxious a father, whose letters to his daughters are replete with tenderness and with good counsels for their conduct, should (when there were so many other objects upon whom to fix his illicit attentions) have selected the female attendant of his own pure children to become his paramour? The thing will not bear telling. There are such things, after, as moral impossibilities.

The habit that the Southern slaves have of adopting their master's names is another cause of misrepresentation and misapprehension. There is no doubt that such of Mr. Jefferson's slaves as were sold after his death would call themselves by his name. One very notorious villain who never had been the property of Mr. Jefferson, took his name and proclaimed himself his son. He was as black as a crow, and born either during Mr. Jefferson's absence abroad, or under some other circumstances which rendered the truth of his assertion simply impossible.

I have written thus far thinking you might chuse to communicate my letter to Mr. Bulfinch. Now I will tell you in confidence what Jefferson told me under the like condition. Mr. Southall and himself young men together, heard Mr. Peter Carr say with a laugh, that "the old gentleman had to bear the blame of his and Sam's (Col. Carr) misdeeds."

There is a general impression that the four children of Sally Hemmings were *all* the children of Col. Carr, the most notorious good-natured Turk that ever was master of a black seraglio kept at other men's expense. His deeds are as well known as his name.—I have written in great haste for I have very little time to write. We sat down sixteen at my brother's table today, and are never less than twelve—Children, grandchildren, visitors, friends—I am in a perfect whirl. Yet this is the way in which I lived during all my girlish days, and then it seemed the easiest and most natural thing imaginable. Now I wonder how any head can bear it long. But Jefferson and Jane are the most affectionate parents and the kindest neighbors that I know.

Coolidge Family Papers, acc. no. 9090, Special Collections Department, University of Virginia Library.

Notes

Madison Hemings

1. Peterson, *Jefferson Image in the American Mind*, 181–87; Malone, *Jefferson and His Time* 4:494–95; Malone and Hochman, "Note on Evidence," 523.

2. Malone and Hochman, "Note on Evidence," 525.

3. Julian Boyd to James Bear, June 28, 1974, Virginius Dabney Papers, box 2, acc. no. 7690-AG, Special Collections Department, University of Virginia Library, Charlottesville.

4. Malone and Hochman, "Note on Evidence," 524.

5. Ibid., 525.

6. *Waverly Watchman*, April 1, 1873.

7. Record of Ohio Census of 1870, Pike Country, microfilm, Library of Virginia, Richmond.

8. Ibid., Ross County.

9. Ibid.

10. Malone and Hochman, "Note on Evidence," 528; Dabney, *Jefferson Scandals*, 48.

11. Malone and Hochman, "Note on Evidence," 524.

12. Ibid., 525.

13. Ibid., 526.

14. John A. Jones, editor, *Waverly Watchman*, March 18, 1873, ibid., 527–28.

15. Ibid., 526.

16. Ibid.

17. Dabney, *Jefferson Scandals*, 49. See also Chandler, *Jefferson Conspiracies*, 146, declaring that "Madison's story was ridiculed by those who knew him best" and then reprinting part of the same passage by Jones to show that Hemings was most likely lying.

18. See, e.g., *Waverly Watchman*, March 7, April 25, 1872.

19. "A Sprig of Jefferson Was Eston Hemings—The Gazette's Delver into the Past Brings Up a Romantic Story . . . Was Natural Son of the Sage of Monticello . . . Had the Traits of Good Training," *Daily Scioto Gazette*, Aug. 1, 1902. I give special thanks to Beverly Gray, consultant to the Thomas Jefferson Memorial Foundation, for providing me with a copy of this article.

20. Ibid. The statue of Jefferson that is in the U.S. Capitol today was on display on the lawn of the White House in the 1840s (Goode, *Outdoor Statuary of Washington*, 521).

21. Brodie, *Thomas Jefferson*, 476.

22. *Daily Scioto Gazette*, Aug. 1, 1902.

23. Miller, *Wolf by the Ears*, 174.

24. Burstein, *Inner Jefferson*, 230–31.

25. *Daily Scioto Gazette*, Aug. 1, 1902.

26. Miller, *Wolf by the Ears*, 173–74; Dabney, *Jefferson Scandals*, 52.

27. Dabney, *Jefferson Scandals*, 46.

28. Miller, *Wolf by the Ears*, 173–74; Daniels, *Ordeal of Ambition*, 265.

29. Pierson, *Jefferson at Monticello*, 107–8.

30. Dabney, *Jefferson Scandals*, 46.

31. Ibid.

32. See Appendix B; Jack McLaughlin, *Jefferson and Monticello*, 110; Dabney, *Mr. Jefferson's University*; Malone, *Jefferson and His Time* 6:250–82.

33. McLaughlin, *Jefferson and Monticello*, 373.

34. Betts, *Farm Book*, 130.

35. George Wythe to TJ, Dec. 21, 1781, Boyd, 6:144.

36. Betts, *Farm Book*, 60; McLaughlin, *Jefferson and Monticello*, 113–15.

37. McLaughlin, *Jefferson and Monticello*, 114.

38. Betts, *Farm Book*, 130.

39. Pierson, *Jefferson at Monticello*, 110.

40. Betts, *Farm Book*, 149.

41. Malone, *Jefferson and His Time* 4:496–97; Adair, *Fame and the Founding Fathers*, 160–91; Dabney, *Jefferson Scandals*, 79–80; W. S. Randall, *Thomas Jefferson*, 477.

42. Betts, *Farm Book*, 149, 130; Malone, *Jefferson and His Time* 4:496 n. 7; Dabney, *Jefferson Scandals*, 80–81.

43. Excerpt of TJ to John Eppes, June 30, 1820, in Betts, *Farm Book*, 45–46.

44. Malone, *Jefferson and His Time* 6:308–15, 511.

45. Adams, "Wage Rates in the Early National Period."

46. Miller, *Wolf by the Ears*, 165–68.

47. Ibid., 252.

48. Malone, *Jefferson and His Time* 4:496.

49. Ibid.; Adair, *Fame and the Founding Fathers*, 185–86.

50. TJ to Thomas Mann Randolph, Jr., Dec. 4, 1801, Jefferson Collection, no. 20356, Library of Congress. See also McLaughlin, *Jefferson and Monticello*, 222. McLaughlin wrote that Jefferson asked a friend to investigate the circumstances of Heming's death.

51. Malone, *Jefferson and His Time* 3:208–9; Adair, *Fame and the Founding Fathers*, 185.

52. Baron, *Garden and Farm Books*, 471, 479.

53. Pierson, *Jefferson at Monticello*, 110.

54. Ibid., 130–31.

55. Ibid., 111, 36.

56. Ibid., 110.

57. Ibid., 80.

58. Ibid., 109–10.

59. Peterson, *Jefferson Image in the American Mind*, 181–87.

60. Dabney, *Jefferson Scandals*, 80.

61. Malone, *Jefferson and His Time* 6:488.

62. Pierson, *Jefferson at Monticello*, 106.

63. Malone, *Jefferson and His Time* 6:488; TJ's will, Ford, *Writings* 10:392–96.

64. Ford, *Writings* 10:395–96.

65. Malone, *Jefferson and His Time* 6:488–89.

66. McLaughlin, *Jefferson and Monticello,* 222.

67. Malone, *Jefferson and His Time* 6:496.

68. Ford, *Writings* 10:395–96.

69. Pierson, *Jefferson at Monticello,* 129.

70. Adair, *Fame and the Founding Fathers,* 165.

71. Ford, *Writings* 10:396.

72. Malone, *Jefferson and His Time* 6:488.

73. W. S. Randall, *Thomas Jefferson,* 591.

74. Appendix B.

75. *Intelligencer and Petersburg Commercial Advertiser,* July 26, 1826.

76. Malone and Hochman, "Note on Evidence," 527.

77. Miller, *Wolf by the Ears,* 174.

78. Brodie, "Thomas Jefferson's Unknown Grandchildren," 96–97.

79. Malone, *Jefferson and His Time* 4:495–97.

80. Ibid., 496.

81. See, e.g., Burstein, *Inner Jefferson* 230; Miller, *Wolf by the Ears,* 165–69; Malone, *Jefferson and His Time* 4:496.

82. W. S. Randall, *Thomas Jefferson,* 477.

83. Adair, *Fame and the Founding Fathers,* 173; Dabney, *Jefferson Scandals,* 107; McLaughlin, *Jefferson and Monticello,* 110.

84. Malone, *Jefferson and His Time* 4:498 n. 11; Dabney, *Jefferson Scandals,* 46; Peterson, *Jefferson Image in the American Mind,* 186.

85. W. S. Randall, *Thomas Jefferson,* 181; Peterson, *Jefferson Image in the American Mind,* 184; Malone, *Jefferson and His Time* 4:497; Jordan, *White over Black,* 467; Adair, *Fame and the Founding Fathers,* 173; Brodie, *Thomas Jefferson,* 82; Miller, *Wolf by the Ears,* 162; Bear, "Hemings Family at Monticello," 79; Dabney, *Jefferson Scandals,* 27; McLaughlin, *Jefferson and Monticello,* 199.

86. McLaughlin, *Jefferson and Monticello,* 122; Malone, *Jefferson and His Time* 4:496 n. 5; Bear, "Hemings Family at Monticello," 79.

87. W. S. Randall, *Thomas Jefferson,* 591, 691, 688, 477.

88. Ibid., 477.

89. Bear, *Jefferson at Monticello,* 4; W. S. Randall, *Thomas Jefferson,* 96, 101, 144, 180. Isaac Jefferson was the son of George and Ursula, two slaves who came to Monticello before the Hemingses arrived at the plantation (McLaughlin, *Jefferson and Monticello,* 103–4, 186).

90. TJ to Francis Grey, March 4, 1815, Lipscomb and Bergh, *Writings* 14:267–71, cited in Lucia Stanton, "Those Who Labor for My Happiness: Thomas Jefferson and His Slaves," in Onuf, *Jeffersonian Legacies,* 156.

91. Malone, *Jefferson and His Time* 1:42, 160–61.

92. Malone, "Mr. Jefferson's Private Life."

93. Brodie, *Thomas Jefferson,* 287.

94. *Daily Scioto Gazette,* Aug. 1, 1902.

95. See Appendix E and Malone, "Private Life of Mr. Jefferson," 68.

96. The Code of Virginia, Legislation to the Year 1860, title 30, chap. 103, sec. 16, p. 511: "Any person may emancipate any of his slaves by last will in writing or by deed, recorded in the court of his county or corporation."

97. Malone, *Jefferson and His Time* 6:447.

2. James Callender

1. See Dabney, *Jefferson Scandals*, 33, noting with a rueful tone, "Had it not been for James T. Callender's excursions into the realm of fiction, we should probably have never heard of any of them [the Hemingses]."

2. Malone, *Jefferson and His Time* 3:331–34; Brodie, *Thomas Jefferson*, 315; Durey, *With the Hammer of Truth*, 173–74.

3. Malone, *Jefferson and His Time* 3:333; Brodie, *Thomas Jefferson*, 319.

4. Brodie, *Thomas Jefferson*, 323.

5. Brodie, *Thomas Jefferson*, 344–45, 346; Durey, *With the Hammer of Truth*, 144–45; Malone, *Jefferson and His Time* 4:208; TJ to Monroe, May 26, 1801, Ford, *Thomas Jefferson and James Callender*, 38; Brant, *James Madison* 4:51.

6. TJ to James Monroe, May 29, 1801, Ford, *Thomas Jefferson and James Callender*, 38–39. See also Malone, *Jefferson and His Time* 4:210–11; Brodie, *Thomas Jefferson*, 345.

7. Brodie, *Thomas Jefferson*, 323, 537 n. 37; Durey, *With the Hammer of Truth*, 156–57. Brodie cited correspondence between Henry S. Randall and his fellow historian Hugh Blair Grigsby in which Randall wrote that Callendar was helped by "some of Mr. Jefferson's neighbors" (*Correspondence between Randall and Grigsby*, 29–30).

8. Durey, *With the Hammer of Truth*, 116, 152–155.

9. Malone, *Jefferson and His Time*, 3:469.

10. *Richmond Recorder*, Sept. 1, 22, 1802.

11. Ibid., Sept. 22, 29, Nov. 5, Dec. 1, 1802.

12. Durey, *With the Hammer of Truth*, 160.

13. *Richmond Recorder*, Sept. 22, 1802.

14. Brodie, *Thomas Jefferson*, 323; Durey, *With the Hammer of Truth*, 160; *Richmond Recorder*, Nov. 3, Dec. 8, 1802; *Gazette of the United States*, reprinted in the *Richmond Recorder*, Sept. 8, 1802; Peterson, *Jefferson Image in the American Mind*, 182. Callender made reference to the hints about Sally Hemings in Rind's *Virginia Federalist* in the years before his own article.

15. Brodie, *Thomas Jefferson*, 537 n. 37.

16. Ibid., 352–55.

17. *Frederick-Town Herald*, reprinted in the *Richmond Recorder*, Dec. 8, 1802.

18. Brodie, "Thomas Jefferson's Unknown Grandchildren," 28.

19. *Richmond Recorder*, Sept. 8, 1802.

20. Malone, *Jefferson and His Time* 4:213; Adair, *Fame and the Founding Fathers*, 174–75; Miller, *Wolf by the Ears*, 164; Dabney, *Jefferson Scandals*, 47.

21. Malone, *Jefferson and His Time* 4:214.

22. Adair, *Fame and the Founding Fathers*, 174–75.

23. Brodie, *Thomas Jefferson*, 359, 531–32 n. 20.

24. Ibid., 297–98.

25. Ibid., 298.

26. Ibid., 292.

27. "The District's Woodson Family: A History of Pride, Patriotism and Determination," *Washington Post*, Dec. 1, 1977, District Weekly, DC3.

28. Ibid.

29. Brodie, "Thomas Jefferson's Unknown Grandchildren," 98–99; Woodson, *Historical*

Genealogy of the Woodsons and Their Connections, 44–46; Railey, *The Railley's and Kindred Families,* 17–18.

30. *Richmond Examiner,* Sept. 25, 1802.

31. Brodie, *Thomas Jefferson,* 292; Adair, *Fame and the Founding Fathers,* 176.

32. *Boston Repertory,* May 31, 1805.

33. *Richmond Recorder,* Sept, 15, 1802.

34. Stanton, "Those Who Labor for My Happiness," in Onuf, *Jeffersonian Legacies,* 174 n. 20.

35. Peterson, *Thomas Jefferson and the New Nation,* 706; Brodie, *Thomas Jefferson,* 345; Betts and Bear, *Family Letters,* 318 n. 1; Daniels, *Randolphs of Virginia,* 196–97, 130; Malone, *Jefferson and His Time* 4:208.

36. See Hobson, *Papers of John Marshall* 5:117–60, on *Executors of Wayles v. Randolph et al.*

37. Durey, *With the Hammer of Truth,* 143.

38. Blennerhassett, *Breaking with Burr,* 134. Blennerhassett said that he had heard from Mary Randolph "more pungent strictures upon Jefferson's head and heart" and he believed them because they were "better founded than he had heard before." He used the phrase "Jefferson's head and heart" in 1807, a full twenty-one years before the publication of Jefferson's famous love letter, "Dialogue between My Head and My Heart."

39. *Boston Repertory,* May 31, 1805.

3. The Randolphs and the Carrs

1. See, e.g., Meltzer, *Thomas Jefferson,* 209–10; Chandler, *Jefferson Conspiracies,* 146; Wilson, "Thomas Jefferson and the Character Issue"; Walter Clemons, "A Monument to Jefferson," *Newsweek,* July 27, 1981, 66.

2. Malone, *Jefferson and His Time* 4:497.

3. Malone, "Mr. Jefferson's Private Life," 72.

4. Malone, *Jefferson and His Time* 4:498 n. 11.

5. Brodie, *Thomas Jefferson,* 493; Miller, *Wolf by the Ears,* 170.

6. Malone, *Jefferson and His Time* 4:497; Adair, *Fame and the Founding Fathers,* 181; Miller, *Wolf by the Ears,* 171; Dabney, *Jefferson Scandals,* 74–79. Malone at least acknowledged that Randall's memory may not have been perfect.

7. Peterson, *Jefferson Image in the American Mind,* 150.

8. Ibid., 187.

9. Ibid.

10. Ibid., 185.

11. Malone, *Jefferson and His Time* 6: app. 1 (chart of the Descendants of Thomas Jefferson).

12. H. S. Randall, *Life of Jefferson* 3:334.

13. Pierson, *Jefferson at Monticello,* 48; Malone, *Jefferson and His Time* 6:9.

14. Burstein, *Inner Jefferson,* 230.

15. Ibid.

16. Malone, "Mr. Jefferson's Private Life," 71, 72 n. 14.

17. Ibid., 72 n. 14.

18. Ibid., 67–68, 71 n. 13.

19. Dabney, *Jefferson Scandals*, 78–79.

20. Adair, *Fame and the Founding Fathers*, 180, 187–91; Malone, "Mr. Jefferson's Private Life," 68.

21. Pierson, *Jefferson at Monticello*, 86, 127–28, 129.

22. Peterson, *Jefferson Image in the American Mind*, 185.

23. Parton, *Life of Jefferson*, 569.

24. Henry Randall to James Parton, June 1, 1868, bMS Am 1248.1 (240), Houghton Library, Harvard University (Appendix D below).

25. Malone, *Jefferson and His Time* 4:498.

26. Burstein, *Inner Jefferson*, 230, 319 n. 67.

27. TJ to Mary Jefferson Eppes, April 13, 1799, Bear, *Family Letters*, 177.

28. Stanton, "Those Who Labor for My Happiness," in Onuf, *Jeffersonian Legacies*, 174 n. 20.

29. Brodie, *Thomas Jefferson*, 298, 381, 344, 539 n. 17, 392.

30. Adair, *Fame and the Founding Fathers*, 181.

31. Betts, *Farm Book*, 130; Malone, *Jefferson and His Time* 4:5, xxviii, 3:xxix-xxx.

32. Dabney, *Jefferson Scandals*, 81.

33. Betts, *Farm Book*, 130; Malone, *Jefferson and His Time* 4:xxviii-xxix.

4. Thomas Jefferson

1. Malone, *Jefferson and His Time* 4:214.

2. Peterson, *Thomas Jefferson and the New Nation*, 707.; W. S. Randall, *Thomas Jefferson*, 477.

3. Jordan, *White over Black*, 136–78; Genovese, *Roll Jordan Roll*, 413–31.

4. Malone, *Jefferson and His Time* 1:265, 3:208, 4:496; McLaughlin, *Jefferson and Monticello*, 102–4, 106, 121–23; Miller, *Wolf by the Ears*, 207. See also Binder, *Color Problem in Early National America*, 48, noting that "the phenomenon of having exponents of all sides of a question claim Jefferson's support is a tribute to the great man's prestige, but, to say the least, it causes considerable confusion among the uncommitted and those seeking the truth. The color problem is an example of this. Racists and integrationist, abolitionists, and states righters have claimed Jefferson as their own."

5. Peterson, *Thomas Jefferson and the New Nation*, 707; Miller, *Wolf by the Ears*, 164.

6. Adair, *Fame and the Founding Fathers*, 176; Hogan, "How Not to Write a Biography."

7. Mapp, *Thomas Jefferson*, 264.

8. W. S. Randall, *Thomas Jefferson: A Life*, 476; *New York Times*, Sept. 6, 1993, Herbert Mitgang, "For Jefferson, the Presidency Held Second Place"; *San Diego Union*, Aug. 22, 1993, Peter Rowe, "Books Help the Undecided Judge Jefferson"; *Star Tribune*, Nov. 14, 1993, Dennis Watley, "New Book on Jefferson Hardly Overcritical."

9. Morris and Weene, *Thomas Jefferson's European Travel Diaries*, 40, 106; Malone, *Jefferson and His Time* 2:xxvi, xxvi; Brodie, *Thomas Jefferson*, 228–30.

10. See, e.g., Adair, *Fame and the Founding Fathers*, 182; Dabney, *Jefferson Scandals*, 48; Miller, *Wolf by the Ears*, 164; *Virginian-Pilot* (Norfolk), April 17, 1995.

11. Smith, *Republic of Letters*, 228–29, 242, 264; Brant, *James Madison* 2:283.

12. Wilson, "Thomas Jefferson and the Character Issue," 58.

13. Ibid., 62.

14. Bear and Stanton, *Jefferson's Memorandum Books*, 1393–94, Monticello Research Library.

15. Malone, *Jefferson and His Time* 1:153, 434.

16. Adair, *Fame and the Founding Fathers*, 182.

17. Excerpts from the journal of John Hartwell Cocke, Jan. 26, 1853, April 23, 1859, Monticello Research Library.

18. Bear, *Jefferson at Monticello*, 61; Malone, *Jefferson and His Time* 6:142, 477.

19. *Frederick-Town Herald,* reprinted in the *Richmond Recorder,* Sept. 29, 1802.

20. Boyd, *Papers* 10:453; Schachner, *Thomas Jefferson,* 323; Wills, "Uncle Thomas's Cabin."

21. Malone, *Jefferson and His Time* 3:452.

22. Wilson, *Jefferson's Literary Commonplace Book,* 16.

23. McLaughlin, *Jefferson and Monticello,* 148; TJ. to William Fleming, March 10, 1764, Boyd, *Papers,* 1:16.

24. Smith, *Forty Years of Washington Society,* 55–59; Eliza House Trist to TJ, April 13, 1784, Boyd, *Papers* 7:97.

25. Boyd, *Papers* 10:453; Jordan, *White over Black,* 461–62.

26. Burstein, *Inner Jefferson,* 231.

27. Malone, *Jefferson and His Time* 4:214.

28. Jordan, *White over Black,* 136–78; Genovese, *Roll Jordan Roll,* 413–31.

29. Brodie, *Thomas Jefferson,* 83; Robert Wernick, "At Monticello, A Big Birthday Bash for the Former Owner, Thomas Jefferson," *Smithsonian* 14:2 (May 1993): 81.

30. Jordan, *White over Black,* 467; Dabney, *Jefferson Scandals,* 27.

31. Pierson, *Jefferson at Monticello,* 107.

32. Johnston, *Race Relations in Virginia and Miscegenation in the South;* Jordan, *White over Black,* 136–78; Genovese, *Roll Jordan Roll,* 413–31.

33. Malone, *Jefferson and His Time* 6:301–15; McLaughlin, *Jefferson and Monticello,* 375–85. See also Drew R. McCoy, *Last of the Founding Fathers,* chaps. 5 and 6, for the extent of Virginia's economic woes.

34. Miller, *Wolf by the Ears,* 252; Brodie, *Thomas Jefferson,* 456; Dabney, *Jefferson Scandals,* 110–11; McLaughlin, *Jefferson and Monticello,* 379, 377; Pierson, *Jefferson at Monticello,* 124–26.

35. Malone, *Jefferson and His Time* 6:290–92.

36. Brodie, *Thomas Jefferson,* 429–30.

37. McLaughlin, *Jefferson and Monticello,* 380; *Intelligencer and Petersburg Commercial Advertiser,* May 18, 1827.

38. *Richmond Enquirer,* May 1, 1827; McCoy, *Last of the Founding Fathers,* 214.

39. Miller, *Wolf by the Ears,* 207; Dabney, *Jefferson Scandals,* 123–24; Miller, "Slavery," in Peterson, *Thomas Jefferson: A Reference Biography,* 428–29.

40. Jefferson, *Notes on the State of Virginia,* 191–93.

41. Stanton, "Those Who Labor for My Happiness," in Onuf, *Jeffersonian Legacies,* 158.

42. Miller, *Wolf by the Ears,* 207.

43. Brodie, *Thomas Jefferson,* 92, 390, 391; Miller, *Wolf by the Ears,* 43. Wythe biographer Joyce Blackburn expressed skepticism about the charge that Wythe had engaged in miscegenation. She noted, however, that there had been talk about Wythe's relationship and quoted from a "memorandum" from Dr. John Dove stating that Wythe had lived with "a yellow woman by the name of Lydia . . . as a wife or mistress as was common in the city. . . . By this woman he had a son named Mike" (Blackburn, *George Wythe of Williamsburg,* 132–33).

44. Stanton, "Those Who Labor for My Happiness," in Onuf, *Jeffersonian Legacies*, 151, 170, 173 n. 15.

45. Miller, *Wolf by the Ears*, 207, 277–79; Malone, *Jefferson and His Time*, 6:343–44; Dabney, *Jefferson Scandals*, 111.

46. Stanton, "Those Who Labor for My Happiness," in Onuf, *Jeffersonian Legacies*, 170.

47. Benjamin Banneker to TJ, Aug. 19, 1791, TJ to Banneker, Aug. 30, 1791, TJ to Joel Barlow, Oct. 8, 1809, Ford, *Works* 6:309–10, 10:261.

48. Jordan, *White over Black*, 452.

49. Memoirs of Thomas Jefferson Randolph (1874), 8, typescript in James A. Bear, Jr., Papers, acc. no. 5454-C, Special Collections Department, University of Virginia Library.

50. Brodie, *Thomas Jefferson*, 159: Binder, *Color Problem in Early National America*, 72.

51. TJ to Francis Grey, March 4, 1815, Lipscomb and Bergh, *Writings* 14:267–68, cited in Stanton, "Those Who Labor for My Happiness," in Onuf, *Jeffersonian Legacies*, 152.

52. Malone, *Jefferson and His Time* 4:215, 216, 498 n. 11, 6:513.

53. Ibid., 1:448.

54. Ibid.; Brodie, *Thomas Jefferson*, 375.

55. Malone, *Jefferson and His Time* 1:448; Brodie, *Thomas Jefferson*, 374.

56. *Boston Repertory*, May 31, 1805.

57. Brodie, *Thomas Jefferson*, 543.

58. Ibid., 375; Malone, *Jefferson and His Time* 1:448.

59. Brodie, *Thomas Jefferson*, 543 n. 60.

60. Miller, *Wolf by the Ears*, 196–97.

61. Ibid., 292, n. 3 to chap. 22.

62. TJ to John Walker, April 13, 1803, Virginia Historical Society, Richmond. It is unclear exactly how Chief Justice Marshall and Bishop Madison came to certify this copy of Jefferson's letter. Malone suggested that some of the correspondence between Jefferson and Walker was destroyed by mutual consent. It is possible that Walker may have used this copy of the letter as a form of insurance. A notation on the letter says that the original had been shown to Marshall and Bishop Madison in 1803, during the period when it was received. Walker evidently made a copy of the letter before he returned it to Jefferson. When the controversy arose again in 1806, he probably called upon the two men to certify the copy of the letter they had seen in 1803.

63. Brant, *James Madison* 4:354; Malone, *Jefferson and His Time* 1:448.

64. Henry Mitchell, "The Jefferson Romance Debate," *Washington Post*, July 19, 1981; Malone, *Jefferson and His Time* 4:498 n. 11.

65. Betts, *Farm Book*, 77.

66. Ibid., 128.

67. Pierson, *Jefferson at Monticello*, 110.

68. Bear, *Jefferson at Monticello*, 4.

69. *American Constellation* (Petersburg), July 1, 1834; Wyatt, *Along Petersburg's Streets*, 52–53; Scott and Wyatt, *Petersburg's Story*, 130–32.

70. Crouch, *Eagle Aloft*, 39–41, 43–45, 99, 126; Sowerby, *Catalogue of the Library of Jefferson* 1:551; TJ to Martha Randolph, Jan. 14, 1793, Randolph, *Domestic Life of Jefferson*, 220; Rutland, *James Madison*, 118–19. See also Smith, *Republic of Letters*, 332, 351, 369.

71. *New York Times*, Oct. 14, 1975.

72. Miller, *Wolf by the Ears*, 165.

73. See Bear, *Farm Book*, 130.

74. Miller, *Wolf by the Ears*, 165–67.

75. James Madison Hemings was born on Jan. 19, 1805; James Madison Randolph, named by his grandfather, was born Jan. 17, 1806 (Brodie, *Thomas Jefferson*, 473; Malone, *Jefferson and His Time*, app. 1, "The Descendants of Thomas Jefferson").

76. Memoirs of Thomas Jefferson Randolph, 4, University of Virginia Library.

77. Malone, *Jefferson and His Time* 6:11.

78. Jefferson, *Notes on the State of Virginia*, 190.

79. *New York Times*, July 4, 1984, sec. C, p. 9.

5. Sally Hemings

1. Chase-Riboud, *Sally Hemings*.

2. Brodie, *Thomas Jefferson*, 228–45.

3. Bear, *Jefferson at Monticello*, 4; Brodie, *Thomas Jefferson*, 216.

4. Brodie, *Thomas Jefferson*, 216–17, 233; Bear, "Hemings Family at Monticello," 85.

5. Abigail Adams to TJ, June 27, July 6, 1787, Cappon, *Adams-Jefferson Letters*, 179, 183; Adair, *Fame and the Founding Fathers*, 182; Miller, *Wolf by the Ears*, 163–64.

6. Brodie, *Thomas Jefferson*, 190–91.

7. Malone, *Jefferson and His Time* 2:134.

8. Ibid., 136.

9. Brodie, *Thomas Jefferson*, 233.

10. Ibid., 186–87.

11. Ibid., 216.

12. Miller, *Wolf by the Ears*, 162–76; Adair, *Fame and the Founding Fathers*, 182; W. S. Randall, *Thomas Jefferson*, 477; Wilson, "Thomas Jefferson and the Character Question," 57.

13. Bear, "Hemings Family at Monticello," 81.

14. *St. Petersburg Times*, March 14, 1995, 1A; Adair, *Fame and the Founding Fathers*, 182–83; Genovese, *Roll Jordan Roll*, 418.

15. W. E. B. Du Bois listed "I Love My Black Mammy" as number six on his list of the "Ten Phrases" that "white students in Southern colleges [could find] quite sufficient for all possible discussions of the race problem" ("Ten Phrases," *Crisis*, July 1922, reprinted in Huggins, *Writings*).

16. Brodie, "Thomas Jefferson's Unknown Grandchildren," 94; *Daily Scioto Gazette*, Aug. 1, 1902; *Collections of the State Historical Society of Wisconsin* 6 (1908): 63, listing Beverly Jefferson, son of Eston Hemings, for the donation of books to the society.

17. Genovese, *Roll Jordan Roll*, 417–19.

18. Wills, "The Aesthete"; Wills, "Uncle Thomas's Cabin."

19. Thomas Gibbons to Jonathan Dayton, Dec. 20, 1802, William L. Clements Library, University of Michigan, Ann Arbor, copy at Monticello Research Library.

20. Brodie, *Thomas Jefferson*, 233.

21. Bear, "Hemings Family at Monticello," 82.

22. Bear and Stanton, *Jefferson's Memorandum Books*.

23. Brodie, *Thomas Jefferson*, 233.

24. Bear, "Hemings Family at Monticello," 85.

25. Brodie, *Thomas Jefferson*, 233–34.

26. Ibid., 234.

27. Dabney, *Jefferson Scandals*, 58.

28. See, e.g., Alan Brinkley, "When Thomas Met Sally," *Newsweek,* April 3, 1995, 70; "History's Mystery: Did Jefferson Have an Affair with a Slave. He'll Never Tell," *People,* May 15, 1995, 66, quoting Willard Sterne Randall as saying that Jefferson was "a real Type A. If something was bothering him he would spill his guts."

29. Brodie, *Thomas Jefferson,* 220.

30. Thomas Jefferson Memorial Foundation Curator's Annual Report, 1979, 20; Boyd, *Papers* 16:xxxi.

31. Bear, *Jefferson at Monticello,* 4.

32. TJ to Martha Randolph, July 2, 1802, to Maria Eppes, July 1, 1802, Betts and Bear, *Family Letters,* 231, 232.

33. Brodie, *Thomas Jefferson,* 227, 238. Malone also noted that Jefferson's relationship with Maria Cosway cooled after the arrival of Maria; Maria's arrival made Jefferson's domestic situation more complete, and he fell more intensely into the role of father (*Jefferson and His Time* 2:81).

34. Brodie, *Thomas Jefferson,* 239–40. See also Malone, *Jefferson and His Time* 2:207; Randolph, *Domestic Life,* 146.

35. Brodie, *Thomas Jefferson,* 243.

36. Ibid.

37. Daniels, *Ordeal of Ambition,* 19.

38. Adair, *Fame and the Founding Fathers,* 182; Dabney, *Jefferson Scandals,* 48.

39. Dabney, *Jefferson Scandals,* 65–73; Scot A. French and Edward L. Ayers, Jr., "The Strange Career of Thomas Jefferson," in Onuf, *Jeffersonian Legacies,* 437. Barbara Chase-Riboud's book won an award for best first novel of the year in 1979.

40. Dabney, *Jefferson Scandals,* 1–5.

41. Frank McCarthy to Dumas Malone, March 19, 1980, Virginius Dabney to Robert A. Daly, Jan 24, 1979, Virginius Dabney Papers, box 2, University of Virginia Library.

42. Brodie, *Thomas Jefferson,* 217; *Frederick-Town Herald,* reprinted in the *Richmond Recorder,* Sept. 8, 1802.

43. McLaughlin, *Jefferson and Monticello,* 192.

44. See, e.g., Jordan, *White over Black,* 462; Peterson, *Thomas Jefferson and the New Nation,* 348.

45. Kimball, *Jefferson and the Scene of Europe,* 168, 172.

46. Dos Passos, *Head and Heart of Jefferson,* 299; Malone, *Jefferson and His Time* 2:80.

47. Malone, *Jefferson and His Time* 2:80–81. Cf. Dabney, *Jefferson Scandals,* 44.

48. Malone and Hochman, "Note on Evidence," 524.

49. Adair, *Fame and the Founding Fathers,* 175.

50. Ibid., 182.

51. Horace Walpole to Mary Berry, June 1791, cited in Brodie, *Thomas Jefferson,* 253. Walpole's statement may also have been prompted by his hostility to a woman's attempt to be taken seriously as an artist.

52. Adair, *Fame and the Founding Fathers,* 181–82.

53. Malone, *Jefferson and His Time* 2:72.

54. McLaughlin, *Jefferson and Monticello,* 181, 218; Malone, *Jefferson and His Time* 2:72; Brodie, *Thomas Jefferson,* 231.

55. McLaughlin, *Jefferson and Monticello,* 121.

56. Wills, "Uncle Thomas's Cabin," 27.

57. Sanford, *Thomas Jefferson and His Library,* 32; Boyd, *Papers* 11:251.

58. TJ to Nathanial Burwell, March 14, 1818, Lipscomb and Bergh, *Writings* 15:165–67; Sanford, *Thomas Jefferson and His Library,* 32.

59. Thomas Jefferson Memorial Foundation Curator's Annual Report, 1979, p. 19.

60. *Malone and Jefferson,* 16; Malone, *Jefferson and His Time* 6:131.

61. Adair, *Fame and the Founding Fathers,* 182 n. 26; Brodie, *Thomas Jefferson,* 81; McLaughlin, *Jefferson and Monticello,* 147–48.

62. Pierson, *Jefferson at Monticello,* 106.

63. McLaughlin, *Jefferson and Monticello,* 177–82.

64. Malone, *Jefferson and His Time* 2:251–52.

65. Malone, *Jefferson and His Time* 4:160, 411; McLaughlin, *Jefferson and Monticello,* 191.

66. Brodie, *Thomas Jefferson,* 393; Bear and Stanton, Jefferson's Memorandum Books.

67. Stanton, "Those Who Labor for My Happiness," in Onuf, *Jefferson Legacies,* 167 n. 68.

68. Malone, *Jefferson and His Time* 2:xxvii–xxix, 3:xxi–xxii.

69. Betts, *Farm Book,* 31; Malone, *Jefferson and His Time* 3:xxii–xxv; Brodie, *Thomas Jefferson,* 291; McLaughlin, *Jefferson and Monticello,* 406.

70. Betts, *Farm Book,* 128, 56; Malone, *Jefferson and His Time* 3:xxvi–xxx, 4:xxviii–xix; Stanton, "Those Who Labor for My Happiness," in Onuf, *Jefferson Legacies,* 174 n. 20.

71. Miller, *Wolf by the Ears,* 166; Muzlish, "Review of *Thomas Jefferson: An Intimate History.*"

72. Betts, *Farm Book,* 128; Malone, *Jefferson and His Time* 5:xxviii; Brodie, *Thomas Jefferson,* 392; McLaughlin, *Jefferson and Monticello,* 235.

73. Brodie, "Thomas Jefferson's Unknown Grandchildren," 94 n. 23.

74. McGill, *Beverley Family of Virginia,* 117–18; Betts and Bear, *Family Letters,* 220, 381; Betts, *Farm Book,* 128, 130; Monticello Research Library.

75. McGill, *Beverley Family of Virginia,* 5; Lewis, *Fairfax Line,* 4, 7, 8, 41; Malone, *Jefferson and His Time* 2:24; Brown, *Virginia Baron,* 107.

76. Morton, *Colonial Virginia,* 547; Malone, *Jefferson and His Time* 2:22–23; TJ to Wilson C. Nicholas, April 19, 1816, Lipscomb and Vaughn, *Writings* 14:471–81.

77. Betts and Bear, *Family Letters,* 220, 329; "The Randolphs," *William and Mary Quarterly,* 1st ser., 9 (April 1901): 250.

78. Gaines, *Thomas Mann Randolph,* 7; "Library of Dabney Carr, 1773," 221; Betts and Bear, *Family Letters,* 398; Whitfield and Chipman, "The Florida Randolphs, 1829–1978," University of Virginia Library.

79. Brodie, "Thomas Jefferson's Unknown Grandchildren," 33 n. 17; Daniels, *Randolphs of Virginia,* xiv; Betts, *Farm Book,* 218, 410; Smith, *Republic of Letters,* 3:1786; Randolph, *Randolphs of Virginia,* 107; Betts and Bear, *Family Letters,* 448 n. 1.

80. Brodie, "Thomas Jefferson's Unknown Grandchildren," 96–97.

81. Coleman, "Peter Carr of Carr's-Brook," 5–6, 12.

82. Peter Carr's sons were Dabney Smith Carr and John Hollins Carr; his daughters were Ellen Carr and Jane Margaret Carr (Coleman, "Peter Carr of Carr's-Brook," 15). Samuel Carr's sons, by two wives, were named John, Dabney Overton, James Lawrence, and

George Watson; his daughters were Martha, Maria Jefferson, and Sally. Sally was also the name of his mother-in-law ("Library of Dabney Carr, 1773," 223–24).

83. Malone, *Jefferson and His Time* 1:430, 434; Betts and Bear, *Family Letters,* 8, 11; Gaines, *Thomas Mann Randolph,* 78.

84. Adair, *Fame and the Founding Fathers,* 185.

85. Ibid.

86. Betts, *Farm Book,* 15–16.

87. Brodie, *Thomas Jefferson,* 289.

88. Adair, *Fame and the Founding Fathers,* 186.

89. Ibid., 184–85.

90. Ibid., 188.

91. Ibid.

92. Ibid., 160.

93. Malone and Hochman, "Note on Evidence," 524; Malone, *Jefferson and His Time* 6:514.

94. Bober, *Thomas Jefferson,* 225; Mapp, *Thomas Jefferson,* 263–64; Cunningham, *In Pursuit of Reason,* 366 n. 9; *Newsweek,* July 21, 1981, 65, describing Adair's essay as a "dazzling piece of detective work."

95. Brodie, *Thomas Jefferson,* 466.

96. Miller, *Wolf by the Ears,* 168.

97. TJ to T. J. Randolph, Nov. 24, 1808, Ford, *Writings* 5:391.

98. Malone, *Jefferson and His Time* 6:473–78.

99. Ibid., 473–74.

100. Madison Hemings to T. J. Randolph, Jan 15, 1833, requesting payment for wages owed, Justus, *Down from the Mountain,* 86; June 22, 1836, Albemarle County Deed Book 33:338–39; Brodie, *Thomas Jefferson,* 362–63, 469.

Conclusion

1. H. S. Randall, *Life of Jefferson* 3:18 n. 2; Bennett, "Thomas Jefferson's Negro Grandchildren"; Wilson, "Thomas Jefferson and the Character Problem," 58.

2. Brant, *James Madison* 4:306.

3. Plumer, *Memorandum of the Proceedings in the United States Senate,* 359; Madison to TJ, Sept. 27, 1806, Smith, *Republic of Letters,* 1446.

4. Malone, *Jefferson and His Time* 5:43–44.

5. *Malone and Jefferson,* 24–25.

6. This is a nod to Lucia Stanton and her article entitled "Those Who Labor for My Happiness," in Onuf, *Jefferson Legacies,* 171; that title in turn was a nod to Thomas Jefferson who wrote, "I have my house to build, my fields to farm, and to watch for the happiness of those who labor for mine."

Bibliography

Writings by Thomas Jefferson and the Jefferson-Randolph Family

The Adams-Jefferson Letters: The Complete Correspondence between Thomas Jefferson and Abigail Adams. Ed. Lester J. Cappon. 2 vols. Chapel Hill, N.C., 1959.

Autobiography of Thomas Jefferson. With an Introductory Essay by Dumas Malone, Boston, 1948.

Carr and Cary Papers, 1785–39. Special Collections Department, University of Virginia Library.

Catalogue of the Library of Thomas Jefferson. Comp. E. Millicent Sowerby. 5 vols. Washington, D.C., 1952–59.

Coolidge, Thomas Jefferson. *An Autobiography.* Boston, 1923.

The Family Letters of Thomas Jefferson. Ed. Edwin M. Betts and James A. Bear, Jr. Columbia, Mo., 1966.

The Garden and Farm Books of Thomas Jefferson. Ed. Robert C. Baron. Golden, Colo., 1987.

Jefferson's Memorandum Books: Accounts with Legal Record and Miscellany, 1767–1826. Ed. James A. Bear, Jr., and Lucia C. Stanton. Monticello Research Library.

Notes on the State of Virginia. 1784; rept. Boston, 1802.

Randolph, Sarah N., *The Domestic Life of Thomas Jefferson.* 1871; rept. Charlottesville, Va., 1978.

Randolph, Thomas Jefferson. Memoirs, 1974. Typescript in James A. Bear, Jr., Papers, acc. no. 5454-C, Special Collections Department, University of Virginia Library.

The Republic of Letters: The Correspondence between Thomas Jefferson and James Madison, 1776–1826. Ed. James Morton Smith. New York, 1995.

Thomas Jefferson and James Thomson Callender. Ed. Worthington C. Ford. Brooklyn, 1897.

Thomas Jefferson's Farm Book, with Commentary and Relevant Extracts from Other Writings. Ed. Edwin Morris Betts. Princeton, N.J., 1953.

Thomas Jefferson's Garden Book, 1766–1824, with Relevant Extracts from His Other Writings. Ed. Edwin Morris Betts. Philadelphia, 1944.

The Papers of Thomas Jefferson. Ed. Julian Boyd et al. 25 vols. to date. Princeton, N.J., 1950—.

The Papers of Thomas Jefferson: Jefferson's Literary Commonplace Book. Ed. Douglas Wilson. Princeton, N.J., 1989.
The Works of Thomas Jefferson. Ed. Paul Leicester Ford. 12 vols. New York and London, 1904–5.
The Writings of Thomas Jefferson. Ed. Andrew A. Lipscomb and Albert E. Bergh. 20 vols. Washington, D.C., 1903.

Newspapers

American Constellation (Petersburg, Va., 1834–36)
Boston Repertory (1805)
Daily Scioto Gazette (1902)
Frederick-Town Herald (1802)
Gazette of the United States (New York, 1802)
Globe (Washington, D.C., 1830–45)
Intelligencer and Petersburg Commercial Advertiser (1824–36)
New York Times
Petersburg Republican (1843–44)
Pike County (Ohio) Republican (1835)
Richmond Examiner (1802)*Richmond Enquirer* (1824–36)
Richmond Recorder (1802–3)
Virginia Free Press (Charleston, 1830–36)
Virginia Gazette (Richmond,)
Virginian-Pilot (Norfolk)
Waverly Watchman (1835)
Washington Post

Books, Articles, and Other Secondary Sources

Adair, Douglass. *Fame and the Founding Fathers.* Ed. Trevor Colbourn. New York, 1974.
Adams, Donald, Jr., "Wage Rates in the Early National Period: Philadelphia, 1875–1830," in Bureau of the Census. *Historical Statistics of the United States: Colonial Times to 1970.* Washington, D. C., 1975.
Anderson, Jefferson Randolph. "Tuckahoe and the Tuckahoe Randolphs," *Register of the the Kentucky State Historical Society* 35 (1937): 39–59.
Bailyn, Bernard. *Faces of the Revolution: Personalities and Themes in the Struggle for American Independence.* New York, 1990.
Banner, Lois W. Review of *Thomas Jefferson: An Intimate History,* by Fawn Brodie, in *American Historical Review* 80 (1975): 1390.
Banning, Lance. *Jefferson and Madison: Three Conversations from the Founding.* Madison, Wis., 1995.
Bear, James A., Jr. "The Hemings Family at Monticello," *Virginia Cavalcade* 29 (Autumn 1979): 78–87.

———. *Jefferson at Monticello:* Memoirs of a Monticello Slave *as Dictated to Charles Campbell by Isaac and* Jefferson at Monticello: The Private Life of Thomas Jefferson *by Rev. Hamilton Wilcox Pierson.* Charlottesville, Va., 1967.

Bennett, Lerone, Jr. "Thomas Jefferson's Negro Grandchildren," *Ebony* 10 (Nov. 1954): 78–80.

Beveridge, Albert J. *Life of John Marshall.* 4 vols. Boston, 1919.

Binder, Frederick M. *The Color Problem in Early National America as Viewed by John Adams, Jefferson, and Jackson.* Paris, 1968.

Binger, Carl. *Thomas Jefferson: A Well-Tempered Mind.* New York, 1970.

Biographical Review of Dane County, Wisconsin, Containing Biographical Sketches of Pioneers and Leading Citizens. Chicago, 1893.

Blackburn, Joyce. *George Wythe of Williamsburg.* New York, 1975.

Blasingame, John. *Slave Testimony.* Baton Rouge, La., 1997.

Blennerhassett, Harman. *Breaking with Burr: Harman Blennerhassett's Journal, 1807.* Ed. Raymond E. Fitch. Athens, Ohio, 1988.

Bober, Natalie S. *Thomas Jefferson, Man on a Mountaintop.* New York, 1988.

Boller, Paul F. Review of *Thomas Jefferson: An Intimate History,* by Fawn Brodie, in *Southwest Review* 59 (1974): 321.

Bontemps, Arna. *Great Slave Narratives.* Boston, 1969.

Boyd, Julian. "The Murder of George Wythe," *William and Mary Quarterly,* 3d ser. 12 (1955): 513.

Brant, Irving. *James Madison.* 6 vols. Indianapolis, 1941–53.

Brodie, Fawn. "The Great Jefferson Taboo," *American Heritage* 22 (June 1972): 49–57, 97–100.

———. "Jefferson Biographers and the Psychology of Canonization," *Journal of Interdisciplinary History* 2 (1971): 155–71.

———. *Thomas Jefferson: An Intimate History.* New York, 1974.

———. "Thomas Jefferson's Unknown Grandchildren: A Study in Historical Silences," *American Heritage* 27 (Oct. 1976): 28–33, 94–99.

Brown, Stuart, Jr. *Virginia Baron: The Story of Thomas, 6th Lord Fairfax.* Berryville, Va., 1965.

Burstein, Andrew. *The Inner Jefferson: Portrait of a Grieving Optimist.* Charlottesville, Va., 1995.

Burwell, William. "Vindication of Mr. Jefferson," *Richmond Enquirer,* Aug. and Sept. 1805.

Chandler, David Leon. *The Jefferson Conspiracies: A President's Role in the Assassination of Meriwether Lewis.* New York, 1994.

Chase-Riboud, Barbara. *Sally Hemings.* New York, 1979.

Cocke, John Hartwell. Journal. University of Virginia Library.

Coleman, Elizabeth Dabney. "The Carrs of Albemarle." M. A. thesis, University of Virginia, 1944.

———. "Peter Carr of Carr's-Brook (1770–1815)," *Papers of the Albemarle County Historical Society* (1943–44): 4–23.

Collections of the State Historical Society of Wisconsin. Ed. Lyman Copeland Draper. Vol. 6. Madison, Wis., 1808.

Cresson, William P. *James Monroe.* Chapel Hill, N.C., 1946.

Crouch, Tom D. *The Eagle Aloft: Two Centuries of the Balloon in America.* Washington, D.C., 1983.

Cunningham, Noble Jr., *In Pursuit of Reason: The Life of Thomas Jefferson.* Baton Rouge, La., 1987.

Dabney, Virginius. *Across the Years: Memories of a Virginian.* New York, 1978.

———. *The Jefferson Scandals: A Rebuttal.* New York, 1981.

———. *Mr. Jefferson's University: A History.* Charlottesville, Va., 1981.

Daniels, Jonathan. *Ordeal of Ambition: Jefferson, Hamilton, and Burr.* New York, 1970.

———. *The Randolphs of Virginia.* Garden City, N.Y., 1972.

Davis, Arthur Kyle. *Three Centuries of an Old Virginia Town: The History and Memorials and Charm of Petersburg and the Appomattox.* Petersburg, Va., 1912.

Davis, David Brion. *Was Thomas Jefferson an Enemy of Slavery?* New York and London, 1970.

Dos Passos, John. *The Head and Heart of Thomas Jefferson.* Garden City, N.Y., 1954.

Du Bellet, Louise Pecquet. *Some Prominent Virginia Families.* 4 vols. Baltimore, 1976.

Du Bois, W. E. B. *Writings.* Ed. Nathan Higgins. New York, 1986.

Durey, Michael. *With the Hammer of Truth: The Autobiography of James Callender.* Charlottesville, Va., 1990.

Eckenrode, Hamilton J. *The Randolphs.* New York, 1946.

Farrison, William E. "Origin of Brown's *Clotel,*" *Phylon* 15 (1954): 347–54.

Felzenberg, Alvin Stephen. Review of *Thomas Jefferson: An Intimate History,* by Fawn Brodie, in *American Political Science Review* 71 (1977): 339.

Fithian, Philip Vickers. *Journals and Letters: A Plantation Tutor of the Old Dominion.* Ed. Hugh Dickinson Farish. Richmond, 1943.

Fleming, Thomas. *The Man from Monticello: An Intimate Life of Thomas Jefferson.* New York, 1969.

Flower, Milton E. *James Parton: The Father of Modern Biography.* Durham, N.C., 1951.

Ford, Worthington Chauncey. *Thomas Jefferson and James Thomson Callender, 1798–1802.* Brooklyn, N.Y., 1897.

Gaines, William H. *Thomas Mann Randolph, Jefferson's Son-In-Law.* Baton Rouge, La., 1966.

Genovese, Eugene. *Roll Jordan Roll: The World the Slaves Made.* New York, 1972.

Gibbs. C. H. *Ballooning.* London, 1948.

Golladay, Dennis. "Jefferson's 'Malignant Neighbor,' John Nicolas, Jr.," *Virginia Magazine of History and Biography* 86 (1978): 306–19.

Goode, James M. *The Outdoor Statuary of Washington, D.C.: A Comprehensive Guide.* Washington, D.C., 1974.

Graham, Pearl N. "Thomas Jefferson and Sally Hemings," *Journal of Negro History* 44 (1961): 89–103.

Hamilton, Halmon. Review of *Thomas Jefferson: An Intimate History,* by Fawn Brodie, in *Journal of Southern History* 41 (1975): 107–9.

Hazleton, Jean Hanvey. "The Hemings Family of Monticello." Manuscript in University of Virginia Library.

A History of Dade County, Wisconsin. Chicago, 1880.

History of Ross and Highland Counties, Ohio, with Illustrations and Biographical Sketches. Cleveland, 1880.

Hobson, Charles F., ed. *The Papers of John Marshall,* Vol. 5. Chapel Hill, N.C., 1987.

Hogan, Clifford. "How Not to Write a Biography: A Critical Look at Fawn Brodie's *Thomas Jefferson,*" *Social Science Journal* 14:2 (1977): 132–33.

Jellison, Charles A. "James Thomson Callender: 'Human Nature in a Hideous Form,'" *Virginia Cavalcade* 29 (Autumn 1978): 62–69.

——. "That Scoundrel Callender," *Virginia Magazine of History and Biography* 67 (1959): 295–306.

Johnston, Hugo James. *Race Relations in Virginia and Miscegenation in the South, 1776–1860.* Amherst, Mass., 1970.

Jordan, Winthrop. *White over Black: American Attitudes toward the Negro, 1550–1812.* Chapel Hill, N.C., 1968.

——. Review of *Thomas Jefferson: An Intimate History,* by Fawn Brodie, in *William and Mary Quarterly,* 3d ser., 32 (1975): 510.

Justus, Judith. *Down from the Mountain.* Perrysburg, Ohio, 1990.

Katz, Gertrude, ed. "Old Letters, Old Biographies, and Old Family Trees of Bourne, Carr, Darden, and Allied Families. . . ." Tampa, Fla., 1976, copy in New York Public Library.

Kennedy, John P. *The Life of William Wirt.* 2 vols. Philadelphia 1850.

Ketcham, Ralph. *James Madison: A Biography.* New York, 1971.

Koch, Adrienne. *Jefferson and Madison: The Great Collaboration.* New York, 1950.

Langhorne, Elizabeth. *Monticello: A Family Story.* Chapel Hill, N.C., 1989.

Levy, Leonard. *Jefferson and Civil Liberties: The Darker Side.* Cambridge, Mass., 1963.

Lewis, Thomas. *The Fairfax Line: Thomas Lewis's Journal of 1746.* J. W. Wayland. New Market, Va., 1925.

"Library of Dabney Carr, 1773, with a Notice of the Carr Family," *Virginia Magazine of History and Biography* 2(1894): 221–28.

McCoy, Drew. *The Last of the Founding Fathers: James Madison and the Republican Legacy.* Cambridge, Mass.: 1989.

McDonald, Forrest. *The Presidency of Thomas Jefferson.* Lawrence, Kans. 1976.

McGill, John. *The Beverley Family of Virginia: Descendants of Major Robert Beverley (1641–1687) and Allied Families.* Columbia, S.C., 1956.

McKittrick, Eric. "The View from Jefferson's Camp," *New York Review of Books,* Dec. 17, 1970.

McLaughlin, Jack. *Jefferson and Monticello: Biography of a Builder.* New York, 1988.

Malone, Dumas. *Jefferson and His Time*. 6 vols. Boston, 1948–81.

——. Mr. Jefferson's Private Life," *Proceedings of the American Antiquarian Society* 84 (1974): 65–72.

Malone, Dumas, and Stephen H. Hochman. "A Note on Evidence: The Personal History of Madison Hemings," *Journal of Southern History* 41 (1975): 523–28.

Malone and Jefferson. Conversation with Anne Freudenberg. Charlottesville, Va., 1981.

Mapp, Alf, Jr. *Thomas Jefferson: A Strange Case of Mistaken Identity*. New York, 1987.

——. *Thomas Jefferson, Passionate Pilgrim: The Presidency, the Founding of the University, and the Private Battle*. Lanham, Md., 1991.

Mayo, Bernard. *Myths and Men: Patrick Henry, George Washington, Thomas Jefferson*. Athens, Ga., 1959.

——. *Thomas Jefferson and His Unknown Brother Randolph*. Charlottesville, Va., 1942.

Meltzer, Milton. *Thomas Jefferson: Revolutionary Aristocrat*. New York, 1991.

Miller, John Chester. *The Wolf by the Ears: Thomas Jefferson and Slavery*. New York, 1977.

Morton, Richard L. *Colonial Virginia*. 2 vols. Chapel Hill, N.C., 1960.

Muzlish, Bruce. Review of *Thomas Jefferson: An Intimate History*, by Fawn Brodie, in *Journal of American History* 61 (1975): 1090–91.

Nock, Albert J. *Jefferson*. New York, 1926.

Onuf, Peter S. "The Scholars' Jefferson," *William and Mary Quarterly*, 3d ser., 50 (1993): 671.

——. ed. *Jeffersonian Legacies*. Charlottesville, Va., 1993.

Parton, James. *The Life of Thomas Jefferson*. Boston, 1874.

Peterson, Merrill. *The Jefferson Image in the American Mind*. New York, 1960.

——. *Thomas Jefferson and the New Nation*. New York, 1970.

——. *Thomas Jefferson: A Reference Biography*. New York, 1986.

Pierson, Hamilton. *Jefferson at Monticello: The Private Life of Thomas Jefferson*. 1862; rept. Freeport, N.Y., 1971.

Pleasants, Edward Valentine. *The Edward Valentine Pleasants Papers*. Richmond, 1927.

Plumer, William. *Memorandum of Proceedings in the United States Senate, 1803–1807*. Ed. Everett S. Brown. New York, 1923.

Railey, William Edward. *The Railey's and Kindred Families: The Woodsons, the Keiths, the Pleasants, and the Mayos*. Frankfort, Ky., 1911.

Randall, Henry S. *The Life of Thomas Jefferson*. 3 vols. 1858; rept. New York, 1972.

——. *Correspondence between Henry Randall and Hugh Blair Grigsby, 1851–61*. Ed. Frank J. Klingberg. Berkeley, Calif., 1952.

Randall, Willard Sterne. *Thomas Jefferson: A Life*. New York, 1993.

Randolph, Robert Isham. *The Randolphs of Virginia: A Compilation of the Descendants of William Randolph of Turkey Island and His Wife, Mary Isham of Bermuda Hundred*. Chicago (?), 1936.

Risjord, Norman K. *Thomas Jefferson*. Madison, Wis., 1994.

Roseboom, Eugene Holloway, and Francis Phelps Weisenburger. *A History of Ohio.* New York, 1934.

Rutland, Robert Allen. *James Madison: The Founding Father.* New York and London, 1987.

Sanford, Charles B. *Thomas Jefferson and His Library: A Study of His Literary Interests and of the Religious Attitudes Revealed by Relevant Titles in His Library.* Hamden, Conn., 1977.

Schachner, Nathan. *Thomas Jefferson: A Biography.* 2 vols. New York, 1951.

Scott, James G., and Edward A. Wyatt. *Petersburg's Story: A History.* Petersburg, Va., 1960.

Sloan, Herbert E. *Principle and Interest: Thomas Jefferson and the Problem of Debt.* New York, 1995.

Smith, Margaret Bayard Smith. *The First Forty Years of Washington Society.* New York, 1906.

Smith, Page. *Thomas Jefferson: A Revealing Biography.* New York, 1976.

———. *John Adams.* 2 vols. New York, 1962.

Smith, William Loughton. *The Pretensions of Thomas Jefferson to the Presidency Examined.* Philadelphia, 1796.

———. "The Family of William Randolph of Bristol, England, Second Son of Isham Randolph of Dungeness, Virginia." *Virginia Magazine of History and Biography* 49 (Jan. 1941): 78.

Thomas Jefferson Memorial Foundation Curator's Annual Report, 1979, Acc. no. 7690-AG, box 2, University of Virginia Library.

Thompson, Jesse Ball. *Tuckahoe Plantation.* Richmond, 1975.

Trollope, Frances. *Domestic Manners of the Americans.* Ed. Michael Sadleir. London, 1927.

Tucker, George. *The Life of Thomas Jefferson.* 2 vols. Philadelphia, 1837.

Wills, Garry. "The Aesthete," review of *The Worlds of Thomas Jefferson,* by Susan R. Stein, in New York *Review of Books,* 40 (Aug. 12, 1993) 6–10.

———. *Inventing America: Jefferson's Declaration of Independence.* New York, 1978.

———. "Uncle Thomas's Cabin," review of *Thomas Jefferson: An Intimate History,* by Fawn Brodie, in *New York Review of Books* 21 (April 18, 1974): 26.

Wilson, Douglas, "Thomas Jefferson and the Character Issue," *Atlantic Monthly* 270 (Nov. 1992): 57–74.

Woodson, Henry Morton. *A Historical Genealogy of the Woodsons and Their Connections.* Columbia, S.C., 1915.

Wright, Benjamin F. Review of *Thomas Jefferson: An Intimate History,* by Fawn Brodie, in *Social Science Quarterly* 56 (1975): 157.

Wyatt, Edward A. *Along Petersburg's Streets: Historic Sites and Buildings of Petersburg, Virginia.* Richmond, 1943.

Index

Abolitionists, role in disseminating the Hemings story, 3, 8, 66, 82–83, 94–95, 211–12

Adair, Douglass, 3, 67, 180, 243; on Harriet Hemings's departure from Monticello, 33, 203–4; on Sally Hemings, 86, 201, 204; on paternity of the Hemings children, 92, 101, 102, 205; theory about why the Hemings children went free, 201–4, 208, 243; shares "The Jefferson Scandals" with scholars before publication, 185, 206; reconstructs Peter Carr–Sally Hemings relationship, 204–5, 206; dissatisfied with "The Jefferson Scandals," 205

Adams, Abigail, 160–63, 183, 189

Adams, John, 160, 189

Aggey, baby-sitter for the first Harriet Hemings, 195, 219

Association of the Bar of the City of New York, sponsors mock trial of TJ, 105

Ayers, Edward L., Jr., 4

Bacon, Edmund, 20, 163, 187, 242; on Sally Hemings, 20, 163, 178; on Harriet Hemings's departure from Monticello, 27–30, 33–34; fails to mention TJ's emancipation of Madison and Eston Hemings, 36; historians accept his statements about the paternity of the Hemings children, 47, 92–93; denies TJ's paternity of the Hemings children, 92–93

Banneker, Benjamin, 139–40

Bear, James A., 173–74

Bell, Thomas, 136, 168, 172

Beverley, Elizabeth, 197

Beverley, William, 197–98

Blanchard, Jean Pierre, 152

Boyd, Julian, 8

Brant, Irving, 118, 144

Brodie, Fawn, 3–4; use of Freudian analysis, 4, 14, 48, 111, 125; on resemblance of Hemings children to TJ, 50; on Tom Hemings, 68, 72; arguments mischaracterized, 111–12; on beginnings of TJ-Hemings relationship, 112, 172–73; differs with Callender on TJ and Hemings, 113–14, 119; accused of engaging in presentism, 114–16; on the Walker affair, 142–44, 146, 154; on Sally Hemings, 159–60, 163, 181, 209; historians attitude toward, 169, 225, on nature of relationship between TJ and Hemings, 169, 171, 175, 180; on Capt. Ramsey and Sally Hemings, 171; hints at destruction of TJ's correspondence to hide liaison, 175–76; on the conception of Madison Hemings, 196; suggests that TJ celebrated Eston Hemings's birth, 196; on choice of the name "Beverley" for Sally Hemings's son, 197; on Thomas Eston Randolph, 199; says that Martha Randolph freed Sally Hemings, 206; popularity of her biography of TJ, 228

Burwell, Rebecca, 121–22

Burr, Aaron, 158

Burnstein, Andrew, 18–19, 81, 86, 98–99, 107, 124–25

Callender, James, 242; first publisher of Hemings allegation, 1, 59, 186; on "President Tom," 24, 25, 61–62, 67, 70, 77; historians' strategy regarding, 59, 65, 66, 75–76, 77, 78; character of, 59, 60–61, 70; relationship with TJ, 59–61, 76; revolted by miscegenation, 61, 113; on

Callender, James (*cont.*)
Sally Hemings, 61–62; method of operation, 62, 76; on Alexander Hamilton, 62; motivations of, 62; likely informants, 63, 72, 74; feuds with Federalist editor over the Hemings allegation, 64–65; on the number of Sally Hemings's children, 73, 215–16; relations with David Meade Randolph, 74–75; compared to Fawn Brodie, 114; set the tone for scholars' characterizations of the Hemings allegation, 119; southern and northern responses to Callender, 123–24; effect of attacks on life at Monticello, 124; influence on Sally Hemings, 204
Campbell, Charles, 178, 221
Carr, Dabney, 4, 53
Carr, Martha, 4, 53
Carr, Peter, 2; named as father of Sally Hemings's children, 23–24, 79, 92, 94, 99; cited by T. J. Randolph as lover of Sally Hemings, 70; said to have confessed paternity of the Hemings children, 79, 87; and the conception of the Hemings children, 86, 100, 101; death of, 93; treatment by historians, 98; lack of extrinsic evidence to support claim of paternity, 103; and James Madison, 200; names of his children, 200–201; relationship with Hemings reconstructed by Adair, 204–5
Carr, Samuel: named as father of the Hemings children, 23–24, 78, 79, 89, 94, 102, 106; T. J. Randolph cites as lover of Betsey Hemings, 79; reputation of, 79, 90–91; and the conceptions of Hemings children, 86, 100, 101; death of, 93; treatment by historians, 98; lack of extrinsic evidence to support claim of paternity, 103; children's names, 200–201
Chase-Riboud, Barbara, 4, 14, 181–82, 244
Cocke, John Hartwell, 119, 215
Colbert, Burwell, 36, 38, 39
Coolidge, Ellen Randolph: tells husband that Samuel Carr was father of the Hemings children, 2, 79, 83, 89; on TJ's

"principle" of allowing slaves who were white enough to pass for white to go free, 53–54, 222; discusses Hemings allegation with T. J. Randolph, 55, 79; disdain for Samuel Carr, 79, 91; on how T. J. Randolph came to know that Samuel Carr was the father of the Hemings children, 87–88; makes no mention of confession by Peter Carr, 88–89; vague nature of statements about the Hemings controversy, 89–90, 92, 94; T. J. Randolph as source for information about the Hemings story, 89–90; Virginius Dabney on, 90; relationship with TJ, 94; status confers presumption of believability, 94–96, 97–98, 103, 222–23, 241, 247
Coolidge, Joseph, 258; correspondence from Ellen Coolidge about the Hemings story, 87–88
Cosway, Maria, 118, 123, 179, 184–87, 191–93

Dabney, Virginius: as relative of the Jeffersons, the Carrs, and the Hemingses, 4; writes *The Jefferson Scandals* to debunk the Hemings story, 4, 14; response to Madison Hemings, 14, 20–22; on Edmund Bacon, 37; supports Ellen Coolidge, 90; cites Samuel Carr as likely father of the Hemings children, 102; accepts Malone's "character defense" of TJ, 107; on possible destruction of TJ's correspondence, 176; on Hemings's pregnancy upon leaving France, 180, 243
Daily Scioto Gazette, article about Eston Hemings, 15, 16, 18, 149
Daniels, Jonathan, 20–21, 180
Days, Drew, 105
Dayton, Jonathan, 171
Dos Passos, John, 184–85
Douglass, Frederick, 159
Dupré, Madame, 175, 189
Durey, Michael, 175
"Dusky Sally," 24

Eppes, Elizabeth, 160, 162, 183
Eppes, Francis, 160, 162, 163–64
Eppes, Francis (grandson of TJ), 178–79

Eppes, John Eppes, 29, 178
Eppes, Mary Jefferson (Polly, Maria), 1, 23, 130; and trip to Paris with Sally Hemings, 160–64, 177–78, 181, 192, 199, 241

Fairfax, Lord, 197–78
Fairfax Line, 197
Faulkner, William, 140
Federalists, role in disseminating the Hemings story, 2, 3, 63–66, 74, 82, 143, 144, 256
Floyd, Catherine (Kitty), 112
Fossett, Joe, 36, 38, 39
French, Scot A., 4

Garrett, Alexander, 132
George III, 106
Gibbons, Thomas, 171–72, 219
Goliah, 68

Hackley, Harriet Randolph, 199
Hackley, Richard, 199
Hackley, William Beverley, 199
Hamilton, Alexander, 62, 76, 158, 217
Hemings, Betsey, 91–92, 254, 255
Hemings, Beverley, 2, 239; departure from Monticello, 25–26, 33, 36, 58; Madison Hemings on, 25, 45; chooses to live as a white man, 27, 149; training at Monticello, 40, 149, 154, 218; violinist, 51; legal whiteness of, 53–57; TJ does not formally emancipate, 56–57; described as well known in Charlottesville, 73, 75; as possible "President Tom," 76–77; ascends balloon, 151–52; conception and birth of, 195; significance of his full name, 196–198
Hemings, Critta, 25, 218, 239, 245
Hemings, Elizabeth (Betty): mistress of John Wayles, 1, 23, 128, 164; mother of Sally Hemings, 1, 23; mother of John Hemings, 23, 50; seen as reason for TJ's treatment of Sally Hemings's children, 46–47; and Martha Wayles Jefferson, 128–30; TJ sends word to about James Hemings, 177, 239, 245
Hemings, Eston: freed by TJ's will, 2, 38, 39–43, 202, 213; residents of Chilli-

cothe talk about connection to TJ, 14, 211; as professional violinist, 15, 51; resemblance to TJ noted, 15; comments on Hemings story, 15; statue of Jefferson said to resemble, 15; popularity of in Chillicothe, 16; descriptions of, 16, 54; chooses to live as a white man, 18–19, 57; training at Monticello, 40, 218; leaves Monticello soon after TJ's death, 42, 57–58; legal whiteness of, 53–57; TJ petitions legislature to allow to remain in Virginia, 57–58, 222; conception and birth of, 196; full name of, 197, 239; significance of name, 199–201, 211; relationship with Thomas Jefferson Randolph after TJ's death, 209; shared experiences with siblings, 218–21
Hemings, Harriet (first daughter of Sally Hemings), 68, 73; shared name with members of the Randolph family, 75, 199; conception, birth, and death of, 195; attended by Aggey and Edy, 195, 219
Hemings, Harriet (third daughter of Sally Hemings), 2; Madison Hemings on departure from Monticello, 24, 26–27; chooses to live as a white woman, 27, 45, 148, 149; Edmund Bacon on, 27–29; TJ involved in her departure from Monticello, 27–31, 219; historians explain TJ's emancipation of, 31–33; conflicting accounts of destination after Monticello, 33; training at Monticello, 33, 150; gossip about, 34, 72; Madison Hemings on, 45–46; legal whiteness of, 53–57; shares name with members of Randolph family, 75, 199; Douglass Adair on, 203–4, 239, 246
Hemings, James: in Paris with TJ, 1, 164; trained as a chef in France, 1, 39; declines to return to the United States, 24, 173–75; historians suggest was likely contact for Harriet Hemings in Philadelphia, 32, 203–4; suicide of, 32, 39; trained younger brother Peter, 39; literacy of, 149; hires French tutor, 163; unrestricted movement of, 163, 165; TJ sends word to Elizabeth He-

Hemings, James (*cont.*)
    mings about, 177; returns to the
    United States, 180; Adair on TJ's
    emancipation of, 202, 240
Hemings, Jamey, 25–26, 36, 240
Hemings, John: Sally Hemings's sons ap-
    prenticed to, 22, 40, 218; freed by TJ's
    will, 36, 38–39; master carpenter and
    joiner at Monticello, 38; TJ's bequest
    of the services of Madison and Eston
    Hemings to, 39, 41–43; son of Joseph
    Neilson and Elizabeth Hemings, 50;
    literacy of, 149, 240, 248
Hemings, Madison: recounts family his-
    tory, 2, 7, 12, 23–27, 33, 43–46, 58, 150–
    51, 154, 173–74, 206; historians'
    characterizations of and responses to,
    7–22, 34–37, 46–51, 78–79, 82–83, 84,
    87, 93, 94–98, 211–12, 213; life in Ohio,
    9, 11–12, 14–15, 248; described by S. F.
    Wetmore, 13, 16; apprenticed to John
    Hemings, 22, 39–43, 150, 156; descrip-
    tion of and attitude toward TJ, 43–45,
    147–50; description of and relation-
    ship with siblings, 45–46, 221; as vio-
    lin player, 50; conception and birth
    of, 195–96, 240, 247; named "James
    Madison" by Dolley Madison, 197,
    247; relationship with the Randolphs
    after TJ's death, 209; children of, 248
Hemings, Mary, 136, 168, 171
Hemings, Peter, 39, 47, 240, 245
Hemings, Robert, 47, 201–2, 240, 245
Hemings, Sally, 240, 245; accompanies
    Mary Jefferson to Paris, 1, 23, 160–62;
    daughter of John Wayles, 1, 49, 73,
    128, 164; rumors about affair with TJ,
    1, 40–41, 42–43, 60–61, 222; Callender
    publishes allegation of affair with TJ,
    1, 59; children of, 2, 23, 26, 30, 38, 73,
    75, 76–77, 85; TJ's chambermaid, 10,
    214, 219; novel about, 14, 181–84; histo-
    rians suggest fabricated story of liai-
    son with TJ, 18, 201–4; likely effect of
    experiences in France, 20–21; age at ar-
    rival in France, 23, 160; alleged origins
    of relationship with TJ, 23; concep-
    tion of child in France, 23, 24, 67; al-
    leged relationship with Carr brothers,
    24, 55, 78–79, 88–89; declines to re-

turn to the United States, 24, 173–75;
    Madison Hemings on TJ's promise to
    free her children at age twenty-one,
    24; Edmund Bacon on children's pa-
    ternity, 28–29, 35, 92–93; and Harriet
    Hemings's departure from Monti-
    cello, 31–33; historians deny special sta-
    tus of, 46–48, 86; possible
    resemblance to Martha Jefferson, 49,
    191; evidence of special status, 51–53,
    193–94, 195, 219; Callender's hostility
    toward, 61–62, 63; character of, 64,
    183; informally freed after TJ's death,
    66; seen as protecting Tom Hemings,
    71; bears children after Callender cri-
    sis, 72; TJ at Monticello for concep-
    tion of children, 80, 84, 99–101;
    conceived no children in TJ's absence,
    101–2, 115–16; concern about her age
    at alleged seduction, 111–13, 190; char-
    acterizations of, 113–14; possible an-
    swer to TJ's predicament, 118; and
    Martha Jefferson, 129, 160, 187, 190,
    191–92; TJ's racism and, 133–35, 135–
    37, 140–41; appearance of, 134–35, 160;
    possible formal instruction in France,
    149; implications of relationship with
    TJ, 157; historians' reactions to,
    158–60; racial classification of, 160;
    life in Paris, 163–64; possible identifi-
    cation with TJ's family, 164–65; and
    TJ in Paris, 166; nature of feelings for
    TJ, 170, 171; receives wages from TJ,
    172–73; boards at Madame Dupré's,
    175; few references to in Jefferson fam-
    ily letters, 177–79; relationship with
    friends of TJ's daughters, 177; men-
    tioned in memoirs of Monticello, 178;
    TJ's expenditures on clothing for, 179;
    return trip to America, 180–81; linked
    to Maria Cosway, 184–85, 185–87, 190,
    191, 192–93; attributes that were attrac-
    tive to TJ, 186, 189–90; pattern of con-
    ceptions, 195–96; probable given
    name of, 196, 239; children's names
    and, 196–97, 199–200; TJ's failure to
    free, 206–9, 222; life after Monticello
    and death of, 209
Historians: ignore details of lives of slaves
    and former slaves, 4, 14, 19, 20–22, 32,

Historians (*cont.*)
  182, 224, 226–28; use of blatantly racist source material, 13–14; double standards for assessing statements in
  Hemings controversy, 29, 34–38, 78–
  79, 84–98, 103, 223; strategy for dealing with Hemings allegation, 52, 59,
  65, 66, 75–76, 77; character defense of
  TJ driven by personal values, 107, 119,
  120–21, 127, 131, 147, 157; rely too heavily on Jefferson family documents,
  126–27, 177
Hochman, Stephen A., 8–17

Isabel, 160

Jackson, Andrew, 132
Jefferson, Isaac, 50–51, 242
Jefferson, Israel (Gillett), 10, 12, 103, 206,
  214–15, 242
Jefferson, Jane (TJ's mother), 95
Jefferson, Lucy, 1, 162
Jefferson, Martha Wayles Skelton, 120, 121,
  126, 225, 241; daughter of John
  Wayles, 23; sister of Sally Hemings, 23,
  73, 191; wife of TJ, 23, 125, 190, 245–46;
  childbearing of, 118, 125; request that
  Jefferson not remarry, 118, 129; Sally
  Hemings and, 128–29, 191, 192–93;
  state of knowledge about miscegenation, 128–30; and Elizabeth Hemings,
  130
Jefferson, Peter (TJ's father), 75, 197–98,
  227
Jefferson, Thomas, 241; goes to Paris, 1; fa-
  vors members of the Hemings family,
  1, 26, 46–47, 164–65; rumors about
  affair with Hemings, 1, 65; James
  Callender publishes stories about, 1;
  surrogates respond to Callender, 1–2,
  70–71; response to allegation, 1,
  141–47; frees Sally Hemings's children,
  2, 38–41, 51–53, 66; Madison Hemings
  claims as father, 2, 7, 9; historians defend against charge of miscegenation,
  2–3, 4–5; Sally Hemings as chambermaid, 10, 214, 219; statue in Washington said to resemble Eston Hemings,
  15; prefers mechanics and building
  over agriculture, 21–22; origins of rela-

tionship with Sally Hemings, 23;
  promise to free Hemings's children,
  24–27, 213–14; notes departure of Beverley and Harriet Hemings, 25, 26; on
  departure of Jamey Hemings, 25–26;
  helps Harriet Hemings leave Monticello, 27–28, 29, 29–34; on relative importance of female slaves, 29, 31;
  image used by Pierson, 34–35, 37;
  strange construction of will, 41–43;
  treatment of Hemings children, 44,
  147–48, 150, 152–56, 218–22; special
  treatment of Sally Hemings, 47–48;
  Isaac Jefferson's memories of, 49;
  grandson on resemblance between
  Hemings children and, 50, 70, 216–18;
  on racial classifications in Virginia,
  53; possible concern for Hemings children's status as legally white, 53–58;
  James Callender and, 59–60, 76; politically motivated attacks upon, 63, 82;
  connections to the Woodson family,
  69; attempted seduction of John Walker's wife, 72; Jefferson's records of
  births to Sally Hemings, 73, 76; and
  David Meade Randolph, 74; favorite
  grandchildren of, 79, 94; at Monticello when Hemings conceived children, 80, 99–102, 195–96; chronology
  of his life, 81; other slave children said
  to resemble, 91; mock trial of, 105–6;
  public's fondness for and identification with, 106–7; historians cite character and personality as answers to
  love affair with Hemings, 107–8, 118–
  19, 155–57, 169–70; Jefferson as gentleman, 108–11; attitude toward teenaged
  girls, 112, 161; feelings toward Hemings, 115; attitude toward slavery,
  116–17; as benign despot, 117–18;
  Cocke's statements that TJ had a slave
  mistress, 119, 215; said to lack sexual
  passion, 120–22; use of "Head and
  Heart" as guide to psyche, 122–27; conflict between role as lover of Hemings
  and as father and grandfather, 127–31;
  financial collapse and its effect upon
  family, 131–33; racism of, 133–41; interest in balloon ascensions, 152; linked
  to Hemings, 158; instructions regard-

Jefferson, Thomas (*cont.*)
  ing Polly Jefferson's trip to France,
  161–62; resides at the Hôtel de
  Langeac, 163; as possible object of Hemings's affection, 164–66; as a symbol
  of whiteness, 172; concern about status of James and Sally Hemings, 173;
  continues to pay James Hemings
  wages upon return to America, 174;
  disappearance of index of letters written in 1788, 175; scarcity of references
  to Hemings in family letters, 177,
  178–79; expenditure on clothing for
  Hemings, 179; return to the United
  States, 180–81; control of public image, 183–84; and Maria Cosway,
  184–85; use of Cosway to rebut the Hemings story, 185–87; attitude toward
  women, 188–89, 190–91, 192; shared
  memories with Sally Hemings and
  Martha Jefferson Randolph, 191; record of sales to household, 194; relationship to people for whom the
  Hemings children were named,
  196–99; pattern of naming, 201; emancipation of Hemings's brothers,
  201–4; fails to formally emancipate
  Sally Hemings, 206–9, 222; Hemings
  children named for relatives and
  friends of, 211–12; defended at great
  cost, 224–28; public's desire to human-
  ize, 228–31; varying "versions" of,
  231–34
Johnson, Samuel, 50
Jones, John A., 12–14, 242
Jordan, Winthrop, 3
Jupiter, 183

Lee, Henry, 141, 143
Lewis, Meriwether, 60, 71, 217
Lilly, Gabriel, 26, 135
Lincoln, Abraham, 106
Lincoln, Levi, 141–42, 144–46

McCarthy, Frank, 183
McLaughlin, Jack, 122, 195
Madison, Dolley, 112, 199
Madison, James, 135
Malone, Dumas, 3, 61, 152, 172, 205–6, 243;
  on publication of Madison Hemings's
  memoirs, 7–17; on TJ's freeing of Harriet Hemings, 31–32; on TJ's emancipation of slaves in his will, 38–39;
  considers the substance of the Hemings story, 46–48; on standard for
  considering the Hemings memoirs,
  80; explains Randolph siblings' contradictory accounts, 89; sets the parameters for the character defense of
  TJ, 107–8, 156–57; on the Walker
  affair, 141–46; describes the return of
  the Jeffersons and Hemingses to
  America, 180; efforts to derail miniseries based on the novel *Sally Hemings*,
  183; on Peter Jefferson's storytelling,
  198
Mapp, Alf E., 112
Marshall, John, 74, 144
Maurice, James, 179–80
Miller, John Chester, 4, 243; devotes chapter to debunking the Hemings story,
  4; on Madison Hemings, 17–18, 19, 45;
  skeptical of Madison Hemings's language, 20–21; on TJ's attitude toward
  the Hemings children, 30–31, 152–55;
  treatment of TJ's purported denial of
  Hemings allegation, 143–45; on TJ's
  failure to formally free Sally Hemings,
  207; on the Hemings children's resemblance to TJ, 217
Miscegenation: frequency in antebellum
  South, 60–61, 113, 130–31, 136–37,
  164–66; historians' seeming discomfort with, 166–69
Mitchell, Margaret, 19
Monroe, James, 60, 132

Neilson, Joseph (father of John Hemings),
  49–50
Nicholas, Wilson Cary, 30, 198

Ogletree, Charles, 105

Paley, William, 183
Parton, James, 3, 243; writes to Henry Randall about Madison Hemings, 79, 81;
  responds to Madison Hemings's memoirs, 83, 96–97
Perrault, Monsieur, French tutor, 163

Peterson, Merrill, 3; emphasizes role of abolitionists in promoting the Hemings story, 37; notes gossip about TJ and Sally Hemings, 63; cites Federalists' role in spreading the Hemings story, 63; on Henry Randall, 81–82, 83–84; describes blacks' motivations for believing the Hemings story, 82–83; on TJ's character, 82

Pierson, Hamilton W.: use of Bacon memoirs to promote antisecessionist cause, 34–35; possible motive to dispute Hemings allegation, 35, 37–38, 243

"President Tom," 1, 24, 25, 61–62, 67, 70, 77, 204

Ramsey, Capt. Andrew, 161, 162

Randall, Henry Stephens, 2, 80–82, 243

Randall, Willard Sterne: on Madison Hemings, 48–51; responds to Fawn Brodie, 111–12, 244

Randolph, Beverley (governor of Virginia), 198

Randolph, David Meade: refuses to remit Callender's fine, 60; as source for Hemings story, 74–75

Randolph, George Wythe, 80, 241, 247

Randolph, Harriet, 199

Randolph, James Madison, 156, 247

Randolph, Jane, 199–200

Randolph, Martha Jefferson, 44, 148, 176, 178–79, 192, 241; daughter of TJ, 1; attempts to disprove TJ's paternity of a Hemings child, 80–81, 84, 85, 86, 98; tells sons to defend TJ, 80, 93; gave out supplies to slaves, 85; status confers believability, 86; family's involvement with miscegenation, 130–31; difficulties in marriage, 131; financial extremis after TJ's death, 132; relationship with TJ, 153, 154–55, 156; at French convent school, 163; possible desire to become a nun, 179; TJ on education of, 188–89; shared experiences with Sally Hemings and TJ, 191; and freedom of Sally Hemings, 206, 207, 209

Randolph, Mary, 75

Randolph, Thomas Beverley, 198

Randolph, Thomas Eston, 199–200, 241

Randolph, Thomas Jefferson: denies TJ's paternity of the Hemings children, 28; comments upon Hemings children's resemblance to TJ, 50, 91, 217–18; closeness to TJ, 54–55, 79; as source for Carr brothers story, 79, 83, 85, 86, 87; contradictory statements about the Hemings story, 87–89, 94; conversation with sister about the Hemings story, 88; drafts letter to respond to Israel Jefferson, 88; anecdote about TJ, 139; complains about quality of his education, 155; relationship with Madison and Eston Hemings, 204

Randolph, Thomas Mann, Jr., 42, 131, 155

Randolph, William, 197

Randolph, William (TJ's uncle), 199

Randolph, William Beverley, 198

Rehnquist, William, 105

Sally Hemings (the novel), 4, 14, 181–84

The Scotts (family of black musicians), 138

Selznick, David O., 19

Shackelford, Tom, 68

Sloan, Herbert, 132

Smith, Robert: and TJ's letter on the Walker affair, 141–44

Stereotypes, role of in assessment of Hemings controversy, 10–22, 94–95, 108, 165–66, 171, 182, 188

Staël, Mme de, 189

Thomas Jefferson Memorial Foundation, 69, 230

Trist, Nicholas, 132

Tristan and Iseult, 170

Tubman, Harriet, 159

Turner, Thomas: on Sally Hemings's oldest child, 72; on connection between Martha Wayles and Sally Hemings 73, 129; and the Walker affair, 142

Unnamed daughter of Sally Hemings: recent discovery of, 73; young girls help Hemings with, 153; TJ on birth of, 153; conception of, 195

Vidal, Gore, 182

Walker, Elizabeth Moore (Mrs. John): and TJ, 141–46, 190–91
Walker, John: TJ's attempted seduction of his wife, 72, 76; confrontation with TJ, 141–46
Walpole, Horace, 187
Washington, George, 106
Wayles, John: father of Sally Hemings, 1, 23, 49–50, 73, 242; father of Martha Jefferson, 23, 73, 164, 242; failed joint venture with father of David Meade Randolph, 74; relationship with Elizabeth Hemings, 128–30, 164, 239, 242
Weaver, William (census taker): makes note about Madison Hemings's parentage, 9, 212, 242
Wetmore, S. F.: editor of *Pike County (Ohio) Republican,* 8, 243; sympathy for former slaves, 8, 13, 16; and Madison Hemings's interview, 8, 12, 13–14, 15, 24, 43–44, 45–46, 59; historians'

characterizations of and responses to, 8–10, 17, 21, 34, 45, 84, 211–12; work on behalf of Republican party, 9; takes 1870 census in Pike County, 9–10; interviews Israel Jefferson, 10; attacks TJ for treatment of Madison Hemings, 13; describes Madison Hemings, 13, 16
Wills, Garry: skepticism toward a TJ and Hemings love affair, 169–72; on Hemings's lack of education, 188
Wilson, Douglas: on "presentism" in modern-day depictions of TJ and Hemings, 114–15; on implications of a TJ and Hemings relationship, 116, 121
Woodson, Dorothea (Dorothy), 69
Woodson, John (father), 69
Woodson, John (son), 69
Woodson, Josiah, 69
Woodson, Tarleton, 69
Woodson, Thomas (Tom Hemings), 1; Woodson oral history regarding, 69, 240